THREE WORLDS OF LABOR ECONOMICS

THREE
WORLDS
OF LABOR
ECONOMICS

Edited by

Garth Mangum

and

Peter Philips

M.E. Sharpe, Inc.
Armonk, New York
London, England

Copyright © 1988 by M. E. Sharpe, Inc.
80 Business Park Drive, Armonk, New York 10504

Library of Congress Cataloging-in-Publication Data

Three worlds of labor economics.

Papers from an Oct. 1985 meeting.
    1. Labor economics—Congresses.   2. Neoclassical school of
economics—Congresses.   3. Income distribution—Congresses.
4. Pay equity—Congresses.
I. Mangum, Garth L.   II. Philips, Peter, 1947–
HD 4813.T48   1988   331   87-26423
ISBN 0-87332-455-2
ISBN 0-87332-456-0 (pbk.)

Printed in the United States of America

TABLE OF CONTENTS

PART I • INCOME DISTRIBUTION

PAPERS:

COMMENTS:

PART II • RACIAL WAGE GAP

PAPERS:

PART III • COMPARABLE WORTH

PAPERS:

COMMENTS:

PART IV • INTERNATIONAL DIVISION OF LABOR

PAPERS:

COMMENTS:

LIST OF FIGURES

LIST OF TABLES

THREE WORLDS OF
LABOR ECONOMICS

1

INTRODUCTION

Garth Mangum and Peter Philips

If all of the world's economists were laid end to end, they wouldn't reach a conclusion (or perhaps would be more comfortable). That old diatribe obviously has some basis in fact. Differences in assumptions, projects, and policy recommendations are inevitable in a complex world and an inexact science. But economics as a discipline also lacks a common ideology and a uniform set of analytical tools.

The "dismal science" of economics is increasingly divided among three schools of thought, each approaching its analysis of issues from differing world views and separate sets of assumptions. In the development of economic thought neoclassicism emerged from the classical school as the mainstream. Both approaches were challenged by Karl Marx and his followers, but their impact was in the political rather than the academic realm—Marx had few adherents within the economics profession.

As economics focused on the practical day-to-day problems of an industrial society, a school of thought emerged that considered familiarity with the institutions of the economy more important than the vagaries of economic theory. Institutionalism became the favored approach in dealing with labor markets and policy issues.

As economics increased its use of quantitative measures, neoclassicism, which lent itself to rigorous mathematical analysis, began to replace institutionalism as the predominant approach in labor economics as well as in other branches of the discipline. At the same time radical neo-Marxism gained far more adherents among professional economists than the original Marxian school could ever boast. Although neoclassicism was once again in the forefront, the institutionalist and radical paradigms had sizable numbers of adherents.

If sensible and well-trained people predominate in a school of thought, that approach will be a useful guide to economists. However if those same people are sharply divided on the merits of their preferred approaches to economic analysis, there will be substantial differences in assumptions, approaches and results.

The economics department at the University of Utah is divided somewhat equally among advocates and practitioners of the three alternative paradigms, who therefore thought it worthwhile to probe the differences and test the effectiveness of these paradigms by addressing four current policy issues from each of the three vantage points. Labor economics is the best arena for such an experiment because its adherents are more active than those in any other subdiscipline of economics. This book is the record of the October 1985 conference that comprised that experiment.

The conference proved useful for investigating the analytical as well as the emotional differences between the paradigms and their adherents. At the analytical level the paradigms act as supplements and complements rather than competitors. The issue here is not the rightness or wrongness of a theory but its usefulness. Given the inherent complexity of all economic problems in the real world, can an analytical approach sift through the chaff, isolate the rich kernels that are explanatory determinants, and expose the cause and effect interactions between independent and dependent variables? A theory that can do so, thereby providing a basis for description, prediction, or prescription, is useful.

By these criteria, the neoclassical paradigm is a prime analytical tool. It provides powerful analyses with minimum information, simply by assuming that most economic actors at most times would prefer more rather than less income, whether pursued as wages, interest, rents, or profits. With no more information than, say, the direction of movement of prices, costs, or incomes, it is possible to (a) describe at a highly generalized level how the economic mechanisms works, (b) predict with a high degree of probability the decisions the various economic actors will make, or (c) prescribe policies to cause movement in the desired direction. Neoclassicism might even be described as the economics of nonothingism. The analyst using its tools can function with a minimum of information and yet make useful generalizations about what is going on in the economy and useful recommendations as to how to make the economy function better.

However, if a few simple assumptions about human motivation can provide useful economic insights, how much clearer would be the insights, how much sharper the predictions, and how much more practical the prescriptions with more detailed knowledge of the intimate workings of the institutions through which economic interactions take place. However, it is not possible for one person to attain such detailed knowledge of more than a narrow range of economic institutions, and the economist who would add the richness of institutional knowledge to his or her analysis must therefore sacrifice breadth for depth—but should be able to offer more dependable description, prediction, and prescription within that area of specialization.

Although man is an economic animal he is not only that. And often the invisible guiding hand of competition is all thumbs. Economic self-interest may combine along lines of class, race, or sex in ways that result in exploitation, unexplained by analysis that concentrates on individual interaction within economic institutions. In this respect, radical analysis may add to the insights attainable through neoclassical and institutional approaches.

If complimentarity of paradigms exists, why is antipathy often evident among the various schools of economic thought? As one moves from the antiseptic level of analysis to the value-laden realms of welfare assessment and policy determination, inherent conflicts emerge. Preconceptions of what the world is like and preferences about what it should be like intrude. There is an inherent conservatism to the neoclassical model. Its assumed world of perfect competition is benign, and policy intervention in that world could only make it worse. Although no one believes that world exists, if the real world is more like than unlike that theoretical world, waiting patiently for things to work themselves out may be preferable to hasty intervention. "If it ain't broke, don't fix it."

The institutionalist is an interventionist. A mechanic with a nuts-and-bolts knowledge is likely to believe that with some tinkering and tuning up the machine can be made to work better, and if it malfunctions, a major overhaul may be necessary. The institutionalist, as not only an observer of institutions but an involved practitioner or friend of practitioners, may identify with and lose objective distance from the institutions observed, with consequent bias in policy recommendations. But, at least the recommendations will be based on knowledge. Too impatient for static analysis, the institutionalist indeed concludes that "in the long run, we are all dead."

The radical also brings a load of intellectual baggage to policy prescriptions and perceives injustices that are beyond the reach of tinkering. Institutions must be rejected, perhaps even destroyed, and replaced rather than repaired. There can be useful debate but little consensus among the economic paradigms at the policy level.

At the ideological level even debate is impossible. Certainty of the righteousness of a cause is what identifies an ideologue. Conversion or condemnation are the only bases for discussion. The neoclassicist and the radical have each found a grand design that explains the economic world and the motives, reactions, and status of the actors within it.

To the neoclassical ideologue, man is economic man. If people are not rational, they should be. Everything can be explained by marginal analysis. The invisible hand is visible and pervasive and will, if given time, solve all solvable economic problems. Those that are left are not solvable. Government and public policy are the enemy. Public policy interventions can only make matters worse, and even intervention to preserve competition is misguided. The only monopolies that can survive this untrammeled drive of self-interest are those of the government. Intervention in such a system is sacrilege and its advocacy is blasphemy.

The radical's grand design involves the pervasiveness of exploitation and the inevitability of the class struggle. Any division along the lines of race, sex, education, or national origin as well as economic class can serve as the vehicle for exploitation. Whereas to the conservative all persons are conceived in economic sin and are inherently selfish, to the radical only the ruling class—however defined—is intrinsically evil, exploitative, and domineering. All others are potentially good. The abolition of private property and of the profit motive will remove the incentive of greed, at which point all people will either be converted or destroyed. To achieve that end is the messianic call.

The institutionalist emphasizes a close descriptive understanding of the operation of particular institutions and believes that these institutions can be continually reformed and adapted to emerging needs. To neoclassical economists, the institutionalist's method is unscientific, and the subject matter is just not economics. To the radical, the institutionalist's focus on the trees of particular institutions hides the importance of the forest of the overall economy. Both the neoclassical and the radical economist suspect that the institutionalist comes to love the institutions in question and tinkers with them in an effort to uncritically defend the status quo from both those who would make the market more competitive and those who would seek to fundamentally transform the market.

These may be stereotypes, but they are valid guideposts for evaluating the papers of this conference. While authors may tend to borrow from other approaches as they see fit, on the whole we think that they present three distinct viewpoints on the issues of income distribution, the racial wage gap, comparable worth, and the international division of labor. In the main section of this book, critical comments from other economists follow the three papers of each panel. The selection of commentators was based on their methodological orientations so as to maximize the interactions and debate from the three paradigmatic worlds of labor economics.

A Comparative Summary of the Panels

Income Distribution

The question of wage and income differentials is the analytical linchpin around which all other issues of labor economics are wrapped. While all three paradigmatic perspectives admit the importance of both labor demand and labor supply factors in determining wage differentials, in practice neoclassical economics tends to emphasize labor supply issues while both the institutional and radical approaches tend to emphasize labor demand. Although they go about it differently, all three approaches also believe that it is important to explain individual behavior. The neoclassical analyst tends to set up the problem of individual behavior in a static way. Given the constraints an individual faces and the set of options within those constraints, the neoclassical economist asks why individuals choose one particular option over all the others. Of course, constraints vary, and the neoclassical theorists will frequently analyze the causes of changes in relative prices or incomes. When other constraints change, however, neoclassical economists typically introduce those changes without further explanation. This view of the labor market presumes that individuals face a wide array of meaningfully different options and that consequently the choices one makes are important.

Institutional and radical economists tend to believe that the customs and institutions of the labor market or conflictual forces rooted in social inequality significantly limit the choices an individual faces within the labor market. Thus individuals must choose between a rock and a hard place, and it is not the choice among limited options, but the origin of those options and whether they are likely to change over time that is of interest. The first set of papers covering the neoclassical, institutional, and radical approaches to income distribution clearly reveal these theoretical differences.

Neoclassical

George Borjas begins his review of neoclassical approaches to earnings determination with the observation that since the mid–1950s this question has been reformulated into a purely neoclassical framework. The essence of that framework is the notion that people have well-defined objectives and that a market equilibrium exists which balances the conflicting goals of all the individuals making choices within the market. Thus, the analysis begins with the questions of how people choose among their options and how the market mediates those choices.

Borjas arranges his survey of human capital theory into three questions: (1) how do individuals accumulate human capital? (2) how are earnings a function of human capital? and (3) why would individuals differ in the amounts of human capital they choose to accumulate? Borjas replies that human capital is accumulated through formal schooling and on-the-job experience, which lower an individual's early career earnings since schooling takes time away from the labor market and on-the-job training is acquired at a wage discount. At a later stage in the trained individual's career that person's earnings overtake the initially higher earnings of the untrained worker and from then on, the person who has accumulated human capital will receive higher earnings.

Individuals differ in the amounts of human capital they accumulate according to their age, family background, and abilities. Since there is a life cycle in human capital investments (the older one gets, the lower will be the lifetime payoff), the young generally accumulate human capital. Furthermore, where capital markets are imperfect, individuals with greater family resources or favorable access to education or training will accumulate more human capital. Finally, people with greater natural abilities are likely to accumulate more human capital. Individuals are paid the value of their marginal product and the more able trainee will translate training into greater productivity and consequently higher earnings. It is important to note that neoclassical theorists are reluctant to attribute differences in human capital accumulation to differences in individual tastes—which they avoid for fear of allowing ad hoc explanations into the analysis.

Although human capital theory is not the only economic theory with political implications, it is useful to point out those implications at this point. Earnings inequality can exist within the market. However, if the market is perfectly competitive, these differences are either fair or preordained and due to unequal accumulations of human capital or differences in innate ability which translate that human capital into productivity. If capital markets are perfect, everyone has equal access to funds for training. If labor markets are perfect, everyone has equal access to positions that provide on-the-job training. If there are any inequities stemming from the market, they are due to imperfect competition. Thus, the only market reform should be toward encouraging competition and avoiding regulation.

It may be necessary to amend these policy prescriptions stemming from human capital theory when one considers what Borjas identifies as the key theoretical weakness of this theory. Neoclassical economics understands markets as the interplay of supply and demand forces. However, human capital theory has traditionally ignored demand factors in the determination of wage and income differentials. Borjas' solution is to focus on the microeconomic aspects of labor demand by modeling firm behavior. The institutionalists and radicals believe that aggregate demand and unemployment at the level of the economy as a whole are crucial factors in determining the distribution of earnings.

In conclusion, Borjas emphasizes that neoclassical economics is willing to incorporate institutional factors into the analysis of labor markets. Institutions should be viewed as constraints on market operations, and the effects of key institutions, such as unions and the government, should be and can be analyzed within the context of neoclassical theory.

Institutional

The institutionalist, Clair Brown, objects to this neoclassical treatment of institutions as exogenous parameters which constrain market behavior, thereby relegating them to a secondary and static role in the analysis. Brown wishes to move institutions to center stage in the analysis and begins with what Borjas downplays—unemployment.

Behind Borjas' assumption of the existence of a market equilibrium which balances the conflicting goals of various individuals, there lies the presumption that this is a full employment equilibrium. Brown presumes the opposite. She asserts that unemployment and underemployment are endemic to labor markets. The source of unemployment is the periodic insufficiency of aggregate demand. With unemployment comes the need to ration scarce jobs among the existing labor supply. This job rationing must be done in a way that associates a wage structure with the existing job structure and labor force. Borjas thinks that dickering over wages in the labor market achieves this end while Brown suspects that wages are not as flexible or variable as neoclassical economists suppose.

For Brown, social rule and custom describe a set of labor market institutions that allocate groups of workers to the various segments that make up the overall labor market and, at the same time, set wages for those jobs. Thus, at the outset of the analysis, institutionalists present a major reorientation to the problem of labor markets. Labor demand, not so much at the firm level as in the aggregate, is the starting point of a causal chain. Unemployment circumscribes the opportunities faced by individuals. It is this process of institutional circumscription within the labor market that attracts the institutionalist, who studies why various segments of the labor market are so different, why certain groups are confined to certain labor market segments, and why there is such restricted mobility between segments. Neoclassical economists, Brown asserts, focus too narrowly on the available choices within labor market segments rather than on the severely constrained choices that channel individuals into one segment and exclude them from another. Institutionalized rules and customs within the family, in the schools, and in the labor market sort out people and channel them into different market segments. This perspective leads one to believe that in the determination of earnings the important overall causal phenomena are institutions and not markets.

Thus, to explain earnings distribution Brown needs a theory of institutions that focuses on their development and evolution. Borjas dodges the issue when he states that institutions can enter into neoclassical analysis as constraints on market choices. To reduce institutions to unexplained constraining parameters on market behavior is to shift the central causal factors to the periphery of the analysis. The truly important questions, Brown argues, are where did those institutions come from and what are they likely to do in the future?

Radical

Sam Bowles, the radical, asserts that the heart of Marxian economics is a theory of income distribution, in particular a theory of class distribution of income between profits and wages. However, Bowles argues as it has traditionally been formulated, the Marxian theory of income distribution has downplayed the role of exchange in determining differences among nations, ruling elites, workers, ethnic minorities, and sexes. Instead, traditional Marxian theory has treated class differences in income in a closed economy in a way that focused attention not on exchange relationships but on class relations in production. This allowed for an understanding of the generation of surplus labor time and its appropriation by a capitalist class in a closed economy. Marx had argued that opportunistically buying cheap and selling dear would not result in surplus labor time. However, Bowles points out, this only holds in a closed economy when exchanges between members of the capitalist class redistribute surplus among capitalists but do not create it. In an open economy, where interactions can occur between classes and nonclass groups such as the family, and between nations, exchange is important. Bowles proposes a neo-Marxian theory of exchange designed to highlight inequality arising from exchange as well as the traditional Marxian concept of inequality arising from production.

To illustrate the usefulness of such a theory, Bowles implicitly addresses a classical Marxian problem associated with Lenin's theory of imperialism. Do workers in advanced capitalist countries benefit from the power their country exercises over peripheral countries? In Bowles' model, in an open economy the amount of surplus product depends not only on the direct relationship between the exploiting class and the producers, but also on the relationship between producers and sellers outside this class relationship, relations with the family, and relations with one or more states. Imperialism, in its simplest form, can be thought of as an exchange relation between states where the exercise of world power allows the imperialist to exact a favorable exchange rate in trading with the periphery. At the same time it facilitates the interstate mobility of capital as it reduces the risks associated with investing capital in the periphery. How does this affect the income of workers in the imperialist country? By decreasing risk, imperialism supports the outflow of capital from the imperial center, thereby decreasing the center's demand for labor, and hurting the workers. On the other hand, by obtaining a favorable price for the goods produced in the periphery and sold to the center, imperialism may raise the standard of living of workers in the imperial center. This can happen directly by increasing the quantity of foreign goods workers can buy with their wages, or indirectly by cheapening the cost of domestically producing wage goods in the center. This would raise profits and attract capital to the imperial country. Capital inflows would raise the demand for labor and enhance its bargaining power. Thus, the effect of imperialism on the relative wages of workers in imperialist countries relative to wages in peripheral countries is ambiguous, depending on whether imperialism results in a net inflow or outflow of capital from the center.

More generally, Bowles' model establishes five ways in which the international economy may alter the domestic class distribution of income. Changing terms of trade associated with the exercise of power may change the wage/work-profit frontier, alter the various country rates of capital accumulation, shift the profitability of accumulation, shift the effective supply of labor and/or change the bargaining power of labor.

Traditionally, Marxian theories of class income distribution have been rooted in the relative power of classes in a closed economy. By opening his model to power relations between countries, Bowles is calling on Marxist economists to consider the effects of international exchange.

Summary of Perspectives On Income Distribution

Neoclassical economics in its human capital form presents a theory of earnings distribution that focuses on individual choices within the market. It regards institutions as exogeneous parameters constraining market behavior and altering market equilibriums. Institutionalists object to the notion that labor markets, left to themselves, generate full-employment equilibrium. The instability of aggregate demand combines with the rigidity of wages to create the long-term basis for institutions which do the actual job of matching worker to job and wages to both. Thus, the important focus of study should not be the minority of cases where individuals are free to choose among a wide array of meaningful options. Rather, one should concentrate on the social processes whereby individuals as members of social groupings are channeled into various roles and segments within the labor market. Radicals have long asserted that monopoly control over the means of production and class struggle determined the class division of wages and profits. However, Bowles would have radicals go beyond this to focus on exchange relations between various groupings within the context of an open economy. In doing so, he intends to borrow from what neoclassical economists have discovered about the effects of nonclearing and imperfect markets, rental and collective bargaining power, and contract enforcement costs. He also wishes to borrow from the institutionalist emphasis on business cycles and unemployment equilibria.

Racial Wage Gap

Neoclassical

While Borjas highlights the need to include labor demand factors into the neoclassical analysis of earnings distribution, Smith and Welch present an explanation of long-term trends in the male racial wage gap in the U.S. They emphasize human capital factors. In the long run, they argue, the long-term narrowing in the male racial wage gap is due to the gradual reduction in the educational gap separating white from black males in the labor market. Institutional factors must be considered. In particular, Smith and Welch point to the period of Reconstruction in the South which, for a time, slowed the long-term tendency for black education to approach the levels whites attain. For the generation of blacks who were denied education during that era, there was little progress toward earnings equality. But for the generations before and after this period, Smith and Welch find relatively steady progress toward racial earnings equality, which they associate with converging educational attainments. Business cycles, particularly the Great Depression, are seen as having influenced the racial pay gap in the short run. However, long-run trends are seen in the Smith-Welch analysis to be mainly a function of labor supply factors, particularly relative human capital attainments.

Institutional

Kiefer and Philips accept Smith and Welch's assertion that over the long run black men's earnings have approached white men's earnings. However, they object to attributing this trend to human capital factors and present an alternative explanation which asserts that the demands for labor during wartime were crucial in inducing employers to reach down through the labor market hierarchy to tap heretofore unused pools of black male labor. They find that employers used the relative education among blacks to ration jobs newly opened to blacks as a group, but that the level of black education relative to white education was not an important factor in opening up new segments of the labor market to blacks. The pressure of labor demand and the sense of wartime emergency were the crucial factors in breaking up traditional customs and rules that previously excluded black labor from Northern manufacturing.

Radical

Reich rejects both supply-based and demand-based explanations for long-term swings in black-white income ratios. Rather, he asserts that sociopolitical movements pressure existing institutions to change, which in turn eventually changes the relative earnings of blacks and whites. Reich focuses on the post–World War II period where he finds a trend in black-white male earnings which converge but at a slower and more uneven rate than the Smith-Welch data suggests. This is important because Reich argues that racial earnings gaps narrow in "bursts" associated with progressive political movements which emphasize racial solidarity. Furthermore, this convergence is at least partially reversible during periods of conservative rule and weak or divided labor movements. He interprets the post–1975 period as one of decline for solidaristic political movements and consequently as marking an end to black advancement in the labor market.

Summary of Perspectives on the Racial Wage Gap

Are male racial wages converging in the very long run? Smith and Welch have taken the historical record back farther than any other analysts to show that there has been a narrowing of the black-white wage gap. But there is still debate as to the causes of this convergence, its current rate of change, and prospects for further change. While Smith and Welch would have us focus our attention on educational policies and achievement, Kiefer and Phillips note the importance of rapid change during brief periods of war-induced labor shortages. Reich argues that the waxing and waning of political movements have been the key determinants of the rate of change. Study of the causes of racial wage changes is crucial to discovering the best policies for promoting racial equality.

Comparable Worth

Neoclassical

It is not surprising that, at a political level, Raisian, Ward, and Welch approve of the notion that wages should reflect and reward the productivity of individual workers. Some of the very first formulations of marginal productivity theory by J. B. Clark were expressly aimed at showing that in a competitive market factors of production were paid the value of their marginal product. Raisian, Ward, and Welch particularly believe that a worker's skills, effort, and responsibility should be fairly compensated. This is also not a surprising emphasis since the contribution of human capital theory to marginal productivity theory has been to show that the productivity of workers is at least in major part the result of their own efforts at accumulating human capital. Therefore, the efforts and acquired abilities of workers should be rewarded. Thus, Raisian, Ward, and Welch agree with what they take to be the goals of the comparable worth movement, the equitable compensation of workers with comparable productivities in comparable jobs.

However, these authors worry about the notion of replacing the market with an administrative mechanism in evaluating the worth of different jobs and workers. Along with most neoclassical economists, they believe that existing markets are relatively efficient institutions for allocating labor among competing uses. The market uses relative wages as cues for this allocation. If some government body administered wages, we would run the risk of massive inefficiency which would lead to lower output and consequently less to divide among those who contributed to production. There would be inherent problems in establishing administrative guidelines to enforce comparable worth. What characteristics of a job would go into a calculation of its worth? How would one measure these characteristics? If more than one characteristic is important, how would you weigh their relative importance? Finally, how finely should one break down job categories? These authors believe that the answers to these questions are essentially arbitrary and would lead to a revision of wage scales that would be costly both in terms of new direct wage payments and in terms of the efficiency losses associated with an arbitrary wage structure. They therefore reject administrative comparable worth programs on grounds of efficiency.

The authors also question the need for a comparable worth program simply on equity grounds. They note that well-known human capital variables can account for roughly half the wage gap between men and women. Thus, these differences do not reflect discrimination. Rather, the market indicates that the jobs women typically hold are not comparable to those held by men. In explanation of the remainder of the gender wage gap perhaps the market is picking up additional differences in jobs men and women hold, and we simply have not yet adequately identified and measured these real differences. In short, the market may not unfairly discriminate. It may be doing better at distinguishing real productive differences between jobs than our econometric models. In any case, the gap between men's and women's wages is narrowing faster than the public believes. While the aggregate gender wage gap is around 60 percent, this figure hides underlying trends toward wage equality that have generally been ignored.

Thus, these neoclassical authors agree that workers should be paid according to their worth as measured by their effort, skill, responsibility, and other attributes. But the market does a better job of making these comparisons than any administrative board could. To experiment with other means of compensation would be to tamper with the allocative efficiency of the labor market. Since the problem, if it exists, is going away faster than is generally recognized, these authors believe we should not risk efficiency losses for dubious equity gains.

Institutional

Mangum notes that in the real world, institutions are currently administrating wages and in one way or another making comparable worth judgments on a variety of jobs. This is especially true in the public sector and in internal labor markets in the private sector. These are areas of the labor market that are less susceptible to external competition, and while Mangum agrees with neoclassical economists who worry about tampering with the efficiencies of competitive labor markets, the institutional administration of wages is currently common where competitive markets are absent.

In contrast to Raisian, Ward, and Welch, Mangum believes that labor markets in the real world do discriminate. Given a cultural history of male power and female powerlessness in the economic and political spheres of American society, the mere existence of a wage gap between men and women is enough to make an institutionalist suspect discrimination. Thus, while the neoclassical authors are ready to give the benefit of the doubt to the market when econometrics cannot explain half of the gender wage gap, this institutionalist is ready to suspect the market, at least where it is less subject to competitive pressures.

For Mangum, the question becomes how to institute some remedies for suspected discrimination without hurting valuable institutions or market efficiency. The answer is one of gradualism and eclecticism. Mangum rejects economywide wage administration, but where institutions are administering wages anyway, through collective bargaining agreements or administrative policy, he feels it is appropriate to make these programs more explicit and to scrutinize these wage administrations for discrimination.

Radical

The radical, Hartmann, is essentially moderate in her proposal for comparable worth programs. She basically agrees with Mangum that comparable worth policies should not be economywide but rather firm-specific. In limiting the scope of comparable worth, she is not so much worried about efficiency losses as she is concerned with the political prospects for this reform. What makes Hartmann a radical is the belief that a modest comparable worth reform of the market would be a nonreformist reform. It would be revolutionary in its implications.

Underlying Hartmann's politics is the concept that within the broad boundaries of the political economy, women are worth as much as men to the reproduction of the system. Wage differentials between women and men create a false sense of inequality and power which hides true inequalities of class power. Thus, anything that leads toward erasing false distinctions between the sexes will lead to greater class solidarity between working men and women, with all the revolutionary potential that implies.

Hartman rejects the notion that is strongly held by most neoclassical authors and partially embraced by Mangum that wage differentials in labor markets act to efficiently allocate technically different labor inputs into the various jobs within the economy. Hartman believes that wage differentials for the most part reflect social differences among workers but not technical distinctions. Secretaries are not technically less important to social reproduction than are dentists, they are merely socially less powerful. Because Hartmann believes wage differences reflect social differences but not technical requirements, she is less worried about efficiency losses due to the implementation of comparable worth reforms.

Summary of Perspectives on Comparable Worth

What is the value of a worker to society? Does the market accurately measure and reward that person's worth? Are some groups of people shortchanged by the market, and would the situation be improved if government policy sought to discover and offset discrimination in the market? Raisian, Ward, and Welch make a good case that an economywide administrative effort to implement comparable worth programs aimed at narrowing the gender wage gap would be cumbersome and expensive. Mangum and Hartmann argue that in narrower spheres of the labor market, various governmental and corporate employers already use comparable worth programs. Both perceive employers as having much wider policy discretion in wage-setting than neoclassicists assume. Therefore both the institutionalist and the radical argue that piecemeal comparable worth programs that reconsidered the value of women's work would be fairer than current wage administrations which implicitly accept traditional notions of the relative value of women's and men's work.

International Division of Labor

Neoclassical

Reynolds and Seninger present the traditional neoclassical defense of free trade associated with the doctrine of comparative advantage. However, they feel that any effort to predict the evolving pattern of worldwide production and conse-quent international division of labor requires moving away from the traditional neoclassical understanding of international trade. They review variants of neo-classical trade theory which attempt to include dynamic economies of scale as a basis for understanding the pattern of international specialization. They argue that various national policies of targeted industrial support may in fact be rational from the standpoint of national, rather than international, efficiency and from the standpoint of profiting from imperfect competition rather than worldwide effi-cient production.

The authors accept the notion that developed countries and newly industrial-ized countries are in a battle over production shares rooted in the lower labor costs in the newly industrialized countries. They predict that developed countries will attempt to preserve their manufacturing base through protectionist trade policies, industrial promotion, and the outsourcing of some aspects of production to low-cost foreign ''production platforms.'' The newly industrialized countries, in turn, will seek to perpetuate their low-cost labor advantages while acceding to domestic pressures by allowing a moderate increase in domestic wages. The least developed countries may not be able to enter into this contest for shares in world manufacturing because they lack the various economies of scale and infrastruc-ture to compete. They may be forced into self-sufficient production at low levels of per capita income even though they would benefit from entering international trade in manufacturing goods.

While Reynolds and Seninger amend traditional trade theory in order to make its predictions of international trade and labor patterns more accurate, on the whole they take a traditional neoclassical stance. In the final analysis they believe that all countries benefit from freer world trade.

Institutional

Ray Marshall approves of a movement away from the traditional neoclassical notions of static comparative advantage. But he believes Reynolds and Seninger do not go far enough in abandoning neoclassical theory. He advocates an eclectic approach which focuses on the institutions of world trade and how their evolution affects the international division of labor. His paper concentrates on the reasons for the decline in American competitiveness on world markets and how that has affected the international division of labor. He lists six factors that have helped shift work away from the U.S. in the postwar period: (1) obsolescence of authori-tarian American management systems, (2) declining productivity growth, (3) slowdown in technological innovation, (4) high capital costs, (5) targeted industrial policies in other countries, and (6) passive economic policies in the U.S. In describing the effects of these changes, Marshall focuses on a comparison of the U.S. with Japan. He concludes that manufacturing and mining occupations have shifted away from the U.S. and Europe toward Japan and newly industrializing countries. High wage countries such as the U.S. will experience declining real wages unless new technologies, high quality human resources, or better management systems emerge to offset their existing disadvantages. To understand evolving patterns in the international division of labor and to devise policies to offset the declining standard of living that current trade patterns imply for the U.S. and Western Europe, Marshall argues that analysts must totally abandon the mechanistic theories of both the neoclassical and Marxist paradigms. He believes the pragmatism and descriptive traditions within institutionalism offer the best hope for constructing a more organic, synergistic, and cumulative picture of evolving world trade patterns.

Radical

Gordon believes that not only are the neoclassical and institutional insights regarding the evolving international division of labor off the mark, but also that most recent radical analyses have been mistaken. What Gordon rejects is the notion that the international division of labor is changing much at all. He presents evidence to suggest that the apparent shift in manufacturing shares toward Japan and newly industrialized countries is not really taking place. He argues that the stagnation in U.S. manufacturing employment is not due so much to increased price competition from abroad as it is to slower growth in domestic final demand in the U.S. Thus, what Gordon considers crucial in maintaining working-class standards of living in the U.S. is not trade policy but macroeconomic policy.

The radical political root of Gordon's argument is an effort to offset the notion that high wages inevitably lead to capital flight toward low-wage countries. He wants to defend the validity of U.S. workers struggling for higher standards of living. He believes that those who say there is a new international division of labor driven by high wage costs in advanced countries are wrong, and that their mistaken picture promotes passivity and fatalism on the part of American workers.

Summary of Perspectives on International Division of Labor

In a sense, all three papers struggle with the question of how to maintain American living standards in the face of increased world trade and traditional neoclassical comparative advantage theory. Reynolds and Seninger conclude that balanced multilateral trade would benefit everyone, including American workers. Marshall believes that greater attention to the institutions of production, management, and technology might continue to give U.S. workers a dynamic comparative advantage in world production. According to Gordon, the problem of American working-class living standards arises from long-term macroeconomic stagnation in the U.S. rather than from international competitiveness with newly industrialized countries.

In the coming decade are American wages inevitably going to decline relative to wages in newly industrialized countries? Will manufacturing increasingly be a Third World activity in the twenty-first century? In this set of papers, the neoclassical and institutional economists answer "yes" to both these questions. For the neoclassical authors, the greater efficiencies associated with balanced trade within this new international division of labor will offset any relative wage decline in the U.S. and lead to everyone being better off. The institutionalist doubts this conclusion and seems to suggest that without basic reforms in American production, the new international division of labor will lead to a lower standard of living for most workers in the U.S. and Europe. The radical doubts that any real shift in the international division of labor is taking place. He believes we are confusing long-term business cycle phenomena for permanent shifts in trade patterns.

Concluding Remarks

Labor economics is blessed with a richness in the questions it pursues, the evidence it gathers, and the policies it considers partly because it permits and encourages debate and cross-fertilization from three competing perspectives on the problems of labor. These controversies should not deceive the reader into believing that correct analysis in this area of economics is merely a matter of opinion. In fact, quite the opposite is true. The debate among adversarial paradigms forces each side to be more honest with its evidence, more careful with its arguments, and more modest in its conclusions. Furthermore, a certain borrowing takes place among these viewpoints, as when the radical, Bowles, seeks to include a variety of neoclassical theory of exchange in the Marxian theory of markets or when the neoclassical authors, Reynolds and Seninger, present a trade theory which includes the dynamic notions of comparative advantage that institutionalists have traditionally emphasized. Thus, each paradigm advances partly in response to and because of the advances of another, and each offers its own peculiar set of insights, valuable both for understanding and for policy prescription. However, the reader should not presume convergence or averaging of these three viewpoints. There are some very good scientific and political reasons why these paradigms are different and will remain so. Their ideological concerns are different, the way they set up questions is different, and what they consider to be adequate answers can differ. The neoclassicist inevitably advocates market competition as the solution to most ills. The institutionalist insists that knowledgeable tinkering can improve the functions of a generally satisfactory system. The radical is convinced more fundamental interventions and reforms are essential. Although this diversity in analysis and conclusions may be dismaying to some, this range of debate allows the reader to be not only a student of this subject but also a member of the jury.

INCOME DISTRIBUTION

PAPERS

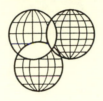

2

EARNINGS DETERMINATION
A SURVEY OF
THE NEOCLASSICAL APPROACH

George J. Borjas

Introduction

Few topics in modern labor economics have been more intensively researched than the question of why wage rates and earnings of individuals differ. The search for explanations of earnings inequality pervades the entire literatures of such diverse fields as human capital investments, labor market discrimination, compensating wage differentials, the behavior of labor unions, signaling and screening, and the role of incentives in determining effort and productivity.

Earlier schools of labor economists have, in fact, analyzed many of these questions. More often than not, however, ad hoc theorizing and even outright hostility to the basic insights of neoclassical economic theory characterized these studies.[1] In addition, the lack of a guiding theoretical framework left empirical results generated by these earlier schools stranded in a labyrinth of confusion, forever searching for a coherent interpretation.

The revolution in labor economics since 1955 amounts to nothing more than the introduction of the basic principles of neoclassical economic theory into the analysis of labor markets. In this literature two unifying principles are used to interpret labor market behavior: (1) all agents in the economy (i.e., individuals, firms, unions, governments) maximize a well-defined objective function; and (2) there exists a market equilibrium which balances the conflicting goals of the various players in the labor market.

George J. Borjas is Professor of Economics at the University of California at Santa Barbara and Research Associate at the National Bureau of Economic Research.

This paper surveys the literature that analyzes the earnings determination process within this framework. At the outset, I feel obliged to explain the objective of this survey. It is not a complete, chronological description of all (or nearly all) research done in this framework. Instead, the approach is to indicate what the neoclassical school teaches, where it leaves off, the connection (or lack of) between the theoretical implications and the empirical tests, and the interpretation of empirical results within the neoclassical framework. In short, I view this survey as a guide to the way of thinking of the neoclassical labor economists who are in the business of carrying out the research in this tradition.

The first few sections of the survey begin with the most successful of all neoclassical approaches to earnings determination: the human capital framework. This overview includes both the substantive content of the theory—in terms of testable implications—and the empirical tests of these insights. Perhaps the major flaw of this literature is its complete disregard for labor demand factors—in fact, for the entire firm as an entity—in analyzing the earnings determination process. The survey therefore continues with a discussion of how factor demand theory can shed light on the determinants of earnings inequality. Finally, the survey concludes with additional examples (e.g., discrimination, compensating differentials) of how the basic axioms of neoclassical theory lead to useful insights into the way the labor market operates.

Neoclassical Models of Human Capital Accumulation

The human capital approach, which has dominated the neoclassical literature on earnings determination for the last two decades, is based upon the theoretical models presented below.

The Ben-Porath Model

The key assumption in human capital models of earnings determination is that the individual can trade earnings today for increased earnings in the future. This concept forms the core of the early work of Mincer[2] and Becker[3] and lies at the heart of the most well-known model of human capital accumulation—the Ben-Porath model.[4] Since most of the literature follows the Ben-Porath framework, it is worthwhile to analyze both its contribution and its limitations. In this model, an individual has a human capital stock of k_t as of time t.[5] This stock measures the number of "efficiency units" that are available for rental to the labor market. The competitive market pays a constant rental rate R for each of these skill units. The Ben-Porath model makes no distinction among the different kinds of abilities or human capital (e.g., physical or mental) a single individual may have, nor is the model concerned with the differential value the market may place on these various abilities. In addition, by assuming R constant and predetermined, the model ignores the role of labor demand in the earnings determination process.

The individual is able to adjust his stock of human capital by allocating time to learning activities.[6] Let s_t be the fraction of time the individual allocates to these learning activities. The potential earnings of the individual are given by RK_t, while observed earnings are given by $RK_t (1 - s_t)$. The individual's objective is to maximize the present value of lifetime earnings. This quantity is given by:

$$W = \int_0^T e^{-rv} RK_t (1 - s_t) dv \tag{1}$$

where T is the (fixed) age of retirement from the labor market, and r is the individual's rate of discount.

The human capital accumulation process is described by the equations:

$$\dot{K}_t = Q_t - \delta K_t \tag{2}$$

$$Q_t = f(s_t, K_t) \tag{3}$$

where $\dot{K}_t = dK_t/dt$; Q_t is the flow of human capital accumulation at time t; and δ is the depreciation rate. Equation (2) states the simple fact that the net change in the human capital stock, $\dot{K}_t$, is equal to the new accumulation minus any depreciation of the existing stock. Equation (3) is the human capital production function.

The maximization of (1) subject to equations (2)–(3) has been found to be mathematically intractable.[7] The key stumbling block is the specification of the production function in (3). For purely technical reasons, it is necessary to make important mathematical and substantive assumption about the functional form of the production function. This "neutrality assumption" specifies the production function as:

$$Q_t = f(s_t \cdot K_t) \tag{3'}$$

so that only the "effective" amount of human capital used in learning ($s_t \cdot K_t$) enters the production process, and not the time input and the level of the human capital stock separately. The substantive content of the neutrality assumption lies in the fact that an increase in the capital stock—given neutrality—raises both the observed wage rate and the amount of "effective" time used in the learning process by the same percentage. Thus increases in K_t have a neutral impact on both the market wage and on the value of the capital stock used as an input in further learning. The neutrality assumption, in effect, makes the flow of human capital investments, and hence the marginal costs of human capital investments at time t independent of the *level* of the capital stock.

Using the neutrality assumption it is easy to illustrate the solution to the model as in Figure 2.1. At any point in time the neutrality assumption ensures that marginal costs of investments depend only on Q_t, the actual amount "learned" in

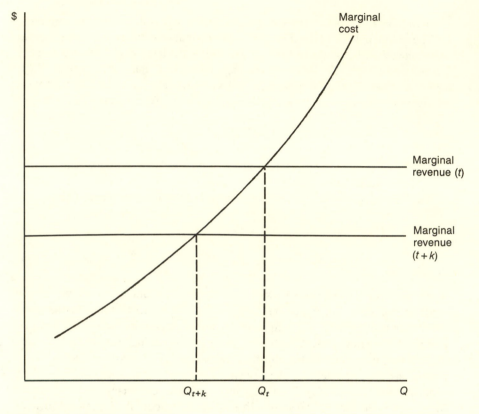

Figure 2.1. Ben-Porath Model

that time period. Hence marginal costs are constant over calendar time (i.e., are not a function of t). The marginal revenue of a dollar's worth of investment at any point in time τ is given by $\int_t^T Re^{-rv}dv$, and hence can be graphed as a horizontal line in Figure 2.1. At time τ the optimal investment of human capital is given by the intersection of marginal costs and marginal revenue, and since marginal revenue declines with calendar time, the flow of human capital investments will similarly decline over time. In addition, it can be shown that if Q_t declines over time, it is necessary that the amount of time allocated to human capital investments, s_t, also decline over time. The main theorems of the Ben-Porath model are, therefore, given by:

$$\frac{\partial Q_t}{\partial t} < 0 \text{ and } \frac{\partial s_t}{\partial t} < 0. \tag{4}$$

Two important points are worth making about these predictions. First, as Figure 2.1 makes obvious, the main factor generating these theorems is the fact that the marginal revenue curve is a negative function of calendar time. The marginal revenue of human capital investments declines because as the individual ages the existence of a finite (and constant) T implies that the payoff period to human capital investments is shorter. Thus the aging process is *solely* responsible for the predicted decline in the flow of human capital over the life cycle.

This result—as subsequent work by Ben-Porath[8] and by Mincer[9] indicated—cannot be empirically valid. For given rates of discount (say 10 percent), it is possible to calculate the marginal revenue of a dollar invested in human capital at age 20 (assuming the individual retires at age 65). The result is $9.89R$. Similarly, the marginal revenue of a dollar of human capital investment at age 40 is $9.18R$. Thus pure aging leads to about a 7 percent decline in the return of human capital investments over the relevant parts of the working life cycle! The aging process, therefore, cannot realistically predict the steep decline in human capital investments observed between, say, the schooling period and the middle of the working life.

A second and equally important limitation of the model is that both of its predictions are phrased in terms of changes in unobserved variables. Since neither the flow of human capital stock nor the amount of time allocated to human capital investments is directly observed, the validity of the Ben-Porath model cannot be tested directly. In a sense, the predictions of the Ben-Porath model are not scientifically "meaningful."[10] Moreover, it is incorrect to argue that these predictions bear a resemblance to the partially unobserved restrictions implied by the Slutsky conditions in the neoclassical consumer choice model. In that model observed data on consumption, prices, and income can, in principle, help disentangle the various effects so that the negativity of the price elasticity of demand can be established. In the Ben-Porath model, on the other hand, it is not possible to marshal existing data on human capital investments to test the basic predictions of the model. The only observed data even remotely available to test the model would be data on individual earnings over the life cycle, and the only prediction that the Ben-Porath model gives regarding these data is that earnings increase over the life cycle!

The Ben-Porath model explains earnings inequality among individuals in terms of differences in the parameters of the model; namely, the initial capital stock, the discount rate, the length of the working life, and the depreciation rate. In addition, the model generates inequality due to the aging process. That is, individual earnings will follow a systematic life-cycle pattern, and thus even otherwise identical individuals will have different earnings at different ages. This, in a sense, is one of the fundamental insights of the human capital model: the relevant unit of observation in earnings distribution studies is not annual earnings, but lifetime earnings.

The Ben-Porath framework has been expanded beyond the simple wealth maximizing model briefly summarized here. In this more general model, the individual is assumed to maximize a utility function defined over leisure and consumption, and human capital accumulation affects both earnings power and the efficiency of both investment and consumption activities.[11] The increasing complexity of these models[12] has not, however, generated additional implications regarding the determination of income inequality. Hence even though it is clear that the present value maximization of Ben-Porath is not ideal, the introduction of labor/leisure choices into the analysis adds little to our understanding of the earnings generation process.

The Supply and Demand for Human Capital

The Ben-Porath model focuses on explaining how the accumulation of human capital (and thus the rate of earnings growth) changes over the life cycle. A related model by Becker[13] provides a more direct link between the total stock of human capital and earnings inequality among individuals. In the Becker framework, the supply and demand functions for human capital determine the individual's optimal total accumulation of "learning." Figure 2.2 graphically illustrates the substantive content of the model. The supply curve S plots the rate of interest the individual must pay to finance human capital investments against the amount of human capital investment incurred. It is upward sloping because the individual would obviously exhaust the cheaper sources of finances (e.g., parents, government subsidized student loans) before continuing his investment. The more human capital investment the individual wishes to obtain, the higher the marginal cost of the investment.

The demand curve D plots the marginal rate of interest received on the investment as a function of how much investment is accumulated. The assumption that human capital investments are subject to the law of diminishing returns ensures that the marginal rate of return to human capital investments declines with the amount of investment.

The individual's optimal investment of human capital, q^*, is given by the intersection of the supply and demand schedules, while the individual's earnings are defined by:

$$W^* = \int_0^{q^*} [D(q) - S(q)] \, dq \qquad (5)$$

Note that the equilibrium condition in the model is the familiar first-order condition from any investment model: the (marginal) rate of return to human capital investment is equated to the rate of return in alternative investments.

In this framework income inequality is caused by shifts in the supply and demand schedules. Becker identifies the key source of variation in the demand curve as ability, and that of the supply curve as the family's financial resources. In addition, Becker proves the important theorem that if the variation in ability exceeds the variation in the supply schedule, the amount of earnings inequality in

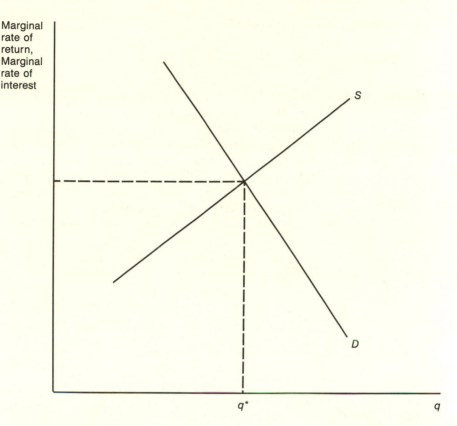

Figure 2.2. Becker Model

the economy will be less than the inequality in human capital stocks, while if the variation in ability is less than the variation in family backgrounds, the amount of inequality in earnings will exceed the inequality in human capital stocks.

This model has a strong intuitive appeal. It illustrates the role by which observable variables measuring family background and/or the individual's ability can generate differences in earnings across individuals. Although these types of variables are often included in "reduced form" earnings equations, little attempt has been made in the literature to directly estimate the structural equations underlying Becker's model. Obviously, the lack of data on the rates of interest and return of human capital and other investments (as well as the volumes of such investments) forms a major obstacle in the estimation procedure. Nevertheless, the labor supply literature has made important advances despite the analogous problem that reservation wages and market wages (for nonworkers) are also missing in the data.

The Human Capital Earnings Function

The Mincer Framework

The main empirical use of the aforementioned theoretical models has been the derivation of earnings functions that can be used to understand the role played by human capital accumulation in the generation of observed age/earnings profiles. The simplest way of bridging the theory with the empirical work would, therefore, be the imposition of a specific functional form on the Ben-Porath human capital production function, and the derivation of closed-form solutions to the earnings path generated by the model. The researcher would then fit this theoretical earnings profile to a data set containing earnings observations for every point in the life cycle (actually, the data is often composed of mean earnings by age of individuals in a cross section). The literature is, in fact, full of these types of empirical analyses.[14] Generally, however, these studies have not been successful in providing a good fit of the observed earnings profile, or reasonable estimates of the underlying parameters of the model. The failure of these studies is likely attributable to the imposition of arbitrary, and demonstrably false (in the case of the neutrality hypothesis), assumptions and functional forms on empirical age/earnings profiles.

A more successful approach to the study of earnings distributions is that of Mincer.[15] Mincer ignores the various assumptions and functional form restrictions that are implicit in the empirical applications of the Ben-Porath model and only uses the key substantive result of the model: individuals are more likely to invest in human capital at younger ages than at older ages.

The simplest derivation of this widely used earnings generating equation is as follows. Let E_t be the individual's earnings capacity at time t, and C_t be the level of investment costs at that time. (In terms of the Ben-Porath model $E_t = RK_t$, and $C_t = RK_t s_t$). The accounting identity relating current earnings capacity to past earnings capacity is given by:

$$E_t = E_{t-1} + r_{t-1}C_{t-1} \tag{6}$$

where r_{t-1} is the rate of return to human capital investment.

Define $k_t = C_t/E_t$. The variable k_t represents a "time-equivalent" measure of investment costs, conceptually similar to the variable s_t in the Ben-Porath model. Equation (6) can then be written as

$$\ln E_t = \ln E_{t-1} (1 + r_{t-1}k_{t-1}) = E_0 \prod_{i=0}^{t-1} (1 + r_i k_i) \tag{7}$$

where the last equality follows from recursing the system back to time 0. The transformation into logs yields:

$$\ln E_7 = \ln E_0 + \sum_{1=0}^{t-1} r_i k_i \tag{8}$$

using the approximation $\varrho = \ln(1 + \varrho)$ for small ϱ. Assuming that $k_t = 1$ for the s years of schooling; that the rate of return to schooling is r_s and to postschool investments is r_p; and defining observed earnings $Y_t = E_t - C_t$ yields:

$$\ln Y_T = \ln E_0 + r_s s + r_p \sum_{1=0}^{\tau-1} k_i - k_T \tag{9}$$

where τ indexes the number of years of postschool experience.

It is important to note that the Mincer earnings function given by (9) follows mechanically from the accounting identity in (6). Specifying a function for the path of the investment ratio, k_t, introduces economic theory into the model. In particular, the Ben-Porath model predicts that $\partial k_t / \partial t$ is negative, and a useful first-order approximation to this prediction is given by:

$$k_t = k_0 - \beta t. \tag{10}$$

Substituting the linear investment path into the earnings function (9) and converting the discrete sum into continuous form yields the Mincer earnings function:

$$\ln Y_T = \ln E_0 + r_s s + (r_p k_0 + \beta)\tau - \frac{r_p \beta}{2} \tau^2 \tag{11}$$

Log earnings are a linear function of years of schooling and a quadratic function of years of experience. The coefficients of these variables have the interesting interpretation of rates of return to school and postschool investments, and of the volume of human capital investments (in time-equivalents) accumulated by individuals. It is important to note, however, that in this simple formulation of the Mincer equation the model is underidentified.[16] That is, a restriction must be imposed on the parameters (e.g., the rates of return to school and postschool investments are the same) in order to identify all the parameters in the equation.

An interesting insight provided by the model is obtained by comparing the earnings path where postschooling investment exists with the earnings path of an individual who does not have postschool investments. These two alternative earnings profiles are illustrated in Figure 2.3. At the time of school completion, the individual's earnings capacity is given by E_s ($E_s = E_0 e^{rs}$). Positive levels of on-the-job training imply that an individual on leaving school will earn less than his "true" earnings capacity, but that over time his earnings will grow (as he captures the returns from the postschool investment). Postschool investments, therefore, have the important effect of steepening age/earnings profiles. Note that at $\hat{\tau}$ years of labor market experience the individual "overtakes" his earnings potential after the completion of school. Using the basic model summarized

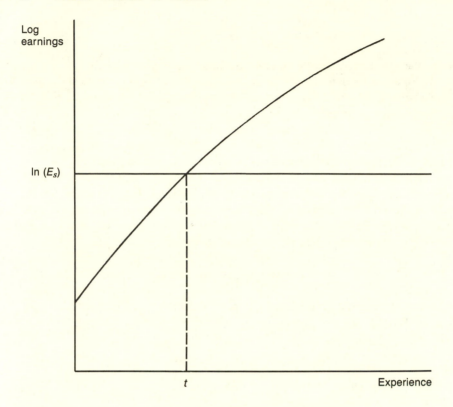

Figure 2.3. Effect of Postschool Investments on Earnings Path

above, Mincer shows that overtaking occurs at most $1/r$ years after the completion of schooling. Hence if $r = .10$, overtaking can be expected to occur within the first decade in the labor market.

This important insight leads to a major prediction of the human capital model: observed earnings and schooling will be more closely related at around the time of overtaking. Prior to $\hat{t}$ the costs of on-the-job training contaminate the correlation between earnings and schooling, which therefore does not truly reflect the full impact of schooling on earnings. After $\hat{t}$ the returns from on-the-job training contaminate the correlation. Thus if individuals differ in their rates of return the correlation between earnings and schooling will be maximized at around the mean age of overtaking. This prediction differs radically from that provided by a simple "luck" model of earnings determination, where prior events matter less as time elapses. It also differs significantly from predictions derived from models where schooling is only a signal allowing individuals to enter "good" jobs. Presumably as the employer observes the actual productivity of individuals the value of the schooling signal would decrease, and again the correlation between education and earnings would decline over the working life. Mincer's empirical work using the 1960 U.S. Census[17] finds that indeed the correlation between years of schooling and earnings is maximized at about 10 years after the average person in the sample enters the labor market.

The Mincer earnings function has, without doubt, become the most widely used empirical tool in labor economics—probably because this equation provides a simple, robust, and intuitive way of summarizing or describing data on earnings differences by schooling and experience.[18] In addition, as Mincer found in his study of the 1960 Census, the simple log specification explains about one-third of earnings differentials in annual earnings, and this fraction increases to about one-half once controls for labor supply are introduced into the model.

In addition, the Mincer framework provides a variety of insights and empirical predictions regarding other aspects of the income distribution such as skewness and the relationship between income inequality and age (or labor market experience). In fact, Mincer's original work investigates these relationship much more closely than it does the cross-section estimates of the earnings function. The literature contains little subsequent work on these additional implications of human capital theory despite the fact that two additional censuses are now available for this type of study.

The Schooling Model

An important special case of the human capital earnings function in equation (11) is that in which no postschool investments take place: $k_t = 0$ for all postschool years. This situation, which has come to be known as the "schooling model," has received a significant amount of attention in the human capital literature. This interest arises not only because of the intrinsic importance of schooling as a determinant of the earnings distribution, but also because the simpler schooling model allows a deeper understanding of what regression estimates of the human capital earnings function truly measure.

Mincer first derived the schooling model using a very different framework.[19] In particular, the salary received by persons receiving s years of schooling is Y_s, while the salary of persons receiving no schooling is Y_o. The competitive labor market will determine these salaries such that the present value of the earnings stream of the various alternatives is equalized:

$$\int_s^n e^{-rv} Y_s \, dv = \int_0^{n-s} e^{-rv} Y_0 \, dv \tag{12}$$

where the key assumption is that the length of the working life remains fixed regardless of the number of years of schooling received. That is, additional schooling leads to a corresponding increase in the retirement age.

The solution of this market condition leads to the earnings generating equation:

$$ln\ Y_s = ln\ Y_0 + rs \tag{13}$$

which is, of course, identical to that derived by the accounting mechanism above.

Using the basic schooling model, it is easy to see how the human capital model generates a positively skewed income distribution. In particular, if schooling is normally distributed in the population, the log-earnings distribution will be normally distributed. Hence earnings are log-normally distributed and the log-normal distribution is well known to be positively skewed.

Assuming that the rate of return to schooling and the amount of schooling are independent of each other (and are also independent of the level of initial earnings capacity) the log variance of earnings in the population is given by:[20]

$$\sigma^2(ln\ Y_s) = \sigma^2\ (ln\ Y_0) + \bar{r}^2\sigma^2(s) + \bar{s}^2\sigma^2\ (r) + \sigma^2\ (s)\sigma^2\ (r), \tag{14}$$

so that earnings inequality is a positive function of differences in the initial human capital stock, of the variance in the rates of return to schooling, of the variance in the distribution of schooling, and of the mean levels of both the rate of return and schooling. Though this type of decomposition (as well as the more complex analog based on the full Mincer earnings function) was quite popular at the time the model entered the literature,[21] it is unclear what interpretation can be attached to this type of result. First of all, the early literature interpreted the schooling model (as well as the more general human capital earnings function) as a ''structural'' regression equation, whose coefficients had a particular structural meaning—in terms of such factors as rates of return, investment volumes. It is unclear how to reconcile this interpretation of the equation with the mechanical derivation of an income inequality expression which explicitly treats the parameters of the regression model as random variables in the population. Often this discrepancy in the interpretation of the model was explained away by assuming that the regression model simply estimated averages over the population. But this raises the additional problem that if indeed initial earnings capacities and rates of return differed across individuals, the assumption that schooling was exogenous to the model was no longer tenable. It would be far more sensible to derive a structural model where the schooling level was endogenously determined by individual responses to initial conditions and rates of return.

This type of model was derived by Rosen,[22] and the implications of even this simple framework are far-reaching and have yet to be fully investigated. In particular, Rosen assumes that a ''hedonic'' wage/schooling relationship exists. This hedonic function is market determined, and the choice of an optimal schooling investment by individuals simply involves the choice of a point along this locus. The hedonic function is given by $Y(s, A)$, where A represents the individual's ability, which presumably shifts the earnings/schooling profile upward for more able individuals.

Assuming the absence of postschool investments, individuals wish to maximize the present value of earnings over the lifetime (which, for simplicity, can be assumed to be infinite in this context). This quantity is given by:

$$W = \int_{s}^{\infty} e^{-rv} Y(s, A) \, dv, \tag{15}$$

where it is assumed that zero earnings are received while the individual is enrolled in school. The maximization of (15) for the optimal level of schooling leads to the first-order condition:

$$\frac{d \ln Y(s, A)}{ds} = r \tag{16}$$

so that individuals equate the (relative)marginal gain of an additional year of schooling with the discount rate.

This solution to the model is illustrated in Figure 2.4. The market locus of earnings/schooling points is given by Y, and is assumed to be concave (in order to satisfy the second order conditions of the maximization problem). An iso-present value curve (holding W constant) can be calculated for the various schooling alternatives—and is defined by $\ln Y = \ln (rW) + rs$. The iso-present value function is linear and has a slope of r, the discount rate. The maximization of the present value of earnings requires that individuals equate their discount rate with the slope of the market-determined schooling/earnings locus.

Figure 2.4 makes clear the basic problem raised by this model for empirical analyses of the schooling mode: How are data in differences in schooling attainment and earnings generated? Clearly differences in either ability or in discount rates are necessary in order for schooling (and earnings) to have a nondegenerate variance in the population. If only the discount rate varies across individuals—i.e., ability is fixed—individuals will be located along the same schooling/earnings locus, so that a schooling model regression will simply identify the market locus. The resulting slope has no structural interpretation whatsoever, and, in particular, cannot be interpreted as the rate of return to schooling. If, on the other hand, individuals have the same discount rate, but vary in ability, the schooling/earnings profile is going to shift among individuals. The resulting schooling model regression can either be upward or downward sloping since it depends on whether more able individuals attain more or less schooling—a question that cannot be answered unambiguously within the context of the model since ability raises the returns to further schooling but also increases the current costs of going to school. The schooling model regression, in this context, does not identify any parameters of interest.[23]

The Rosen model thus implies that the schooling model regressions, which dominated the early phase of the human capital literature,[24] do not have any intrinsic interest since they do not estimate any of the important structural param-

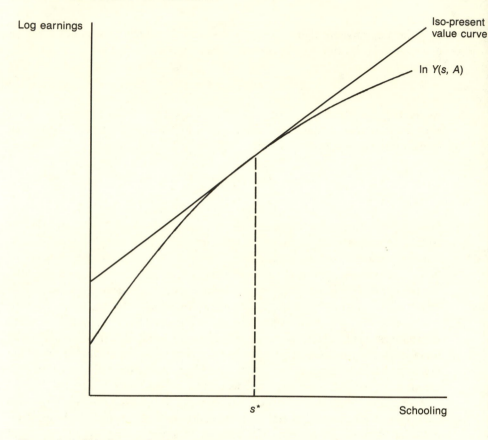

Figure 2.4. Solution to the Rosen Model

eters of the earnings determination process. Instead of the simple schooling equation, the Rosen model generates a two-equation recursive system:

$$s = g(A, r)$$

$$Y = f(s, A)$$

(17)

with the cross-equation restriction that $r = d\ln Y/ds$. Unfortunately, little research has been conducted on this more general model.

The Investment Decision

One major drawback of most empirical work reported in the human capital literature is the lack of direct tests of the basic premises or predictions of the theory. The most widely used human capital technique—the estimation of (*ln*) earnings function—does not truly present a basic test of the theory; rather it provides a framework for interpreting earnings differentials by schooling and experience. Recent papers[25] present important methodological breakthroughs that allow a direct test of the key premise of the schooling model: individuals choose the level of schooling that maximizes their present value of earnings.

In the Willis-Rosen framework the schooling decision is simplified to a college attendance decision (given that the individual has completed high school). Let Y_i^h be the earnings that individual i can obtain when he leaves school if he chooses to terminate his schooling with a high school degree, and g_i^h be the rate of growth the individual can expect over his lifetime given that choice. Similarly, let H_i^c be the earnings that the same individual i could obtain if he chooses to obtain further schooling and attend college, and g_i^c be the rate of earnings growth he will experience over the life cycle if he makes that choice. The present value of earnings associated with each of these options is:

$$W_i^h = \int_0^\infty \bar{Y}_i^h e^{-(r_i - g_i^h)v} \, dv \tag{18}$$

$$W_i^c = \int_0^\infty \bar{Y}_i^c e^{-(r_i - g_i^c)v} \, dv \tag{19}$$

where r_i is the individual's discount rate, s is the number of years of college, and for simplicity it is assumed that the individual lives infinitely. Note that equations (18) and (19) implicitly assume that all schooling costs are composed of foregone earnings.

Define $I_i = ln \, (W_i^c / W_i^h)$.. The individual attends college if $I_i \geq 0$. By using a first-order Taylor's expansion it can be shown that:

$$I_i = \alpha_0 + \alpha_1 \, (ln \, Y_i^a - ln \, Y_i^h) + \alpha_2 g_i^c + \alpha_3 g_i^h + \alpha_4 r_i, \tag{20}$$

with sign restrictions $\alpha_1 \geq 0$, $\alpha \geq 0$, and $\alpha_3 < 0$. Thus an individual is more likely to attend college: (1) the greater the differential between the base salaries resulting from the two options; (2) the faster the earnings growth he can experience if he does attend college; and (3) slower the earnings growth he can experience if he does not attend college. No prediction can be derived regarding the effect of the rate of discount on the college attendance choice.

These sign restrictions embody the basic content of the human capital hypothesis. Unfortunately, they are not easy to test since once a decision is made (attend college, or not), the data is generated only for the observed choice, and thus an individual who follows a particular educational path will not generate data under the alternative regime.

The solution to this problem follows from the use of the Heckman sample selection correction.[26] In particular, it can be assumed that all the variables in the model (earnings, earnings growth, and the discount rate) depend on vectors of various socioeconomic characteristics. If these equations are estimated consistently, it is then possible to predict what the earnings of, say, a high school graduate would be if he had obtained a college education, and what the earnings of a college graduate would be had he not attended college. These predicted data can then be used to estimate the structural choice equation (20). Surprisingly, and despite all the potential measurement and specification errors introduced by the multistage statistical analysis, Willis and Rosen find that all the sign predictions of human capital theory are confirmed by their analysis of college choice in the NBER-Thorndike data. This confirmation of the school choice model implies that persons who do not attend college do better by not attending than they would have done had they gone on to college. Similarly, persons who did attend college improved their situation by so doing (relative to the choice of stopping their schooling after high school diploma). Perhaps even more strikingly, the Willis-Rosen results show the existence of an important degree of comparative advantage in the college choice model. In other words, persons who did not attend college do better by not attending than college graduates would have done had they not attended college. Conversely, persons who attended college did better by attending than persons who did not attend college would have done had they attended. This important finding, of course, implies the existence of differential ability classes in the population. That is, persons who have a "knack" for doing work that presumably is best learned in college, do not have a "knack" for doing the kinds of jobs that are available to high school graduates (and conversely).[27]

This type of analysis provides the additional insight that commonly estimated rates of return to school—estimated across schooling and ability classes—are, at best, difficult to interpret. In particular, if a wealth-maximizing person chooses not to attend college, clearly the rate of return to further education after high school must be lower than alternative investments. At the same time, however, for persons who eventually did attend college, it must be that the rate of return to further schooling was at least as great as that of alternative investments. The simple regression of earnings on years of schooling, by mixing individuals at different ability levels, estimates a population average that presumably shows that an additional year of schooling is associated with an x percent increase in earnings. The results of the Willis-Rosen analysis, however, show that in a world with heterogeneous individuals the interpretation of x as a unique rate of return to additional schooling is not meaningful.

The Willis-Rosen framework, therefore, provides a conceptual and methodological avenue for further research on the human capital investment choice. This type of modeling and estimation provides a simple way of introducing the endogeneity of the human capital investment choice into the analysis. At the same time, however, this framework is not a panacea for all the unsolved problems of human capital theory because the empirical methodology used to correct for selection bias in labor market outcomes (i.e., earnings and earnings growth) is itself quite sensitive to the underlying technical assumptions.

Application of the Human Capital Model:
Job Mobility

One of the most serious substantive restrictions in the Ben-Porath model is the assumption that all training undertaken by the individual is general. This assumption, in effect, makes the remaining lifetime the relevant payoff period to the individual's investment. Since nothing is lost (or gained) when jobs are changed, the concept of a job has no relevance in the Ben-Porath context.

Rosen[28] first introduced jobs into the basic framework. He considers different jobs as offering different investment opportunities. Some jobs, in other words, are high-investment jobs while other jobs are low-investment jobs. If the individual's optimal behavior is to invest more in human capital at younger ages, then the relevant job career would be to start out in high investment jobs and switch to lower investment jobs as the individual ages. Although this model provides a provocative view of the labor turnover process, it is still quite restrictive since it ignores any interactions between the length of the job, the training content of the job, the probability of separation, and the rate of growth in earnings on the job.

Such interactions can be explicitly introduced into the model when Becker's concept[29] of specific training is taken into account. If some of the human capital obtained in the job is specific to that job (or perhaps specific to the occupation, or even to the labor market) then the individual and the employer will consider the potential gains or losses implicit in making such an investment. If the job is perceived to be a successful match both parties will want to invest in specific training, while if the match is perceived to be a failure, the incentives for investment in specific training decline correspondingly. (Kuratani's dissertation and the related work of Hashimoto[30] were the first investigations into the exact sharing of the investment costs and returns between employers and workers when specific training exists.)

Polacheck and Bartel and Borjas[31] conducted the generalization of the Ben-Porath model to account for the existence of specific training. Both of these papers provide the key insight that if human capital investments are partly specific and partly general, the Ben-Porath framework can only explain the behavior of investments in general training (and this result follows only if one assumes that specific and general training are separable in the production process). In the case of specific training the marginal revenue of the investment depends not on the remaining working life, but on the remaining expected time on the job. If the job is expected to last a long period of time the incentives to invest are increased for both the employer and the firm, and thus more investment will take place. On the other hand, if the job match is perceived as unsuccessful, little specific training investment will occur. Further, if general and specific training are complementary outputs—so that more or less of both types of investment are undertaken simultaneously—the expected length of the job will have a direct effect on the volume of general training itself. The key prediction from this analysis, therefore is that successful matches (i.e., longer jobs) will have more investment per time period, and thus wage growth (per unit of time) in longer jobs will exceed wage growth in unsuccessful jobs. This result implies that the age/earnings profile is likely to be steeper in longer, more successful jobs.

In addition, the introduction of specific training into the model suggests that the main Ben-Porath theorem that investment declines continuously over the life cycle is unlikely to hold in work careers characterized by job mobility. For instance, the recent interest in job matching models[32] suggests that young workers in the early phase of the working life cycle are shopping for the best job alternative, and hence are unlikely to make a long-term attachment to any particular job. Once the right job is found the individual has incentives to invest in on-the-job training (that is partly specific), and hence the rate of investment in these jobs may actually exceed the rate of investment in jobs that occurred early in the career.

The importance of job mobility as a determinant of earnings inequality, therefore, depends on the prevalence of job mobility in the economy and the rate with which workers eventually attach themselves to a "lifetime" job in the labor market. The work of Hall[33] finds that in the U.S. economy, job tenure in a particular firm is much longer than previously suspected. In fact, lifetime tenure is the norm rather than the exception in the labor market.

At the same time, studies of job separation rates[34] have found that turnover rates are quite high among particular groups of workers. The high probability of job separation for these groups suggests that strong disincentives may exist for both worker and firm to invest in a job match. In addition, these studies show a very strong negative relationship between the probability of job separation and job tenure. This result follows from the specific training model since individuals who have been in the job longer (and have presumably accumulated more specific capital) have more to lose from quitting, and employers have more to lose from laying them off. Controls for heterogeneity in the population (akin to the stayer and mover model[35]) cannot totally explain this finding.

Empirical studies have demonstrated that job turnover (or the prospect of job turnover) has an important impact on the earnings distribution. The work of Borjas[36] reveals that individuals who have been in the job a long time have significantly higher earnings than individuals who have had a more unstable job career. In addition, the slope of the earnings profile—which under the human capital interpretation measures the rate of investment on the job—is steeper in longer jobs than in shorter jobs. Work by Bartel[37] indicates that about 74 percent of all wage growth accumulated by white males is attributable to increases in earnings that occurred within the job and that only the remaining 26 percent is attributable to wage gains obtained by changing jobs. More generally, these studies illustrate that job tenure has a significant effect on individual earnings over and beyond the pure experience or aging effect.

Perhaps the most important application of the connection between specific training and the earnings distribution is the explanation of the male/female wage differential. In the seminal work of Mincer and Polachek and that of Polachek,[38] the importance of on-the-job training specific to the labor market is stressed. That is, investments undertaken by women in the labor market cannot be transferred over to the household sector, and vice-versa. The fact that a large number of married women interrupt their work careers to enter the household sector and raise a family implies that these women and their employers—prior to the interruption—have relatively low incentives for human capital investments. These low investment rates, combined with any depreciation of the human capital stock occurring while the woman is in the household sector, suggest that upon return to the labor force the woman will have a smaller capital stock to rent out to the market than men with a more continuous work career. These skill differentials will translate into earnings differences, and Mincer and Polachek estimate that about two-thirds of the wage differential between the sexes can be attributed to the intermittent work careers of women.

Although this finding has had a large number of detractors who detail a variety of technical sins[39] most of these critical studies do find that interrupted work careers—to some extent—have a major impact on the male/female wage differential.

In addition, the continuing application of the human capital model to the study of differences in male/female labor market behavior has generated a significant number of insights concerning other types of gender differentials. For instance, additional work by Polachek[40] has applied the basic framework to such diverse topics as the woman's choice of an occupation or of a college major. In these applications, the hypothesis that a fraction of on-the-job training skills are specific to the labor market is used to argue that women with intermittent labor market careers will want to invest in occupations or learn skills that can survive the household production period relatively intact. Polachek's studies show that measures of the depreciation rate of an occupation or a college major have an important effect on the occupational choice or college major choice of women.

It should be noted that the importance of interrupted work careers in the earnings determination process is not dependent upon the gender of workers. A study by Borjas and Welch[41] of the earnings of male military retirees finds essentially the same pattern. Military men are usually in their early 40s when they retire from the armed forces. Human capital skills that are learned in the military are likely to be partly specific to the military; hence when military retirees enter the labor market they are likely to be in a situation analogous to that of a married woman reentering the labor market after the household production period. And indeed, like women, military retirees have significantly lower earnings upon entering the civilian labor market than men who had continuous careers in the civilian labor market than men who had continuous careers in the civilian sector.

Also, like women, military retirees start catching up to (though never surpass) the earnings of their civilian counterparts, suggesting that retirees undertake a more intensive investment program than civilians at similar ages. The specificity of human capital investment, therefore, whether to the job, to the labor market, or to a particular sector of the labor market plays a major (and predictable) role in the determination of earnings inequality.

Wage Determination and Labor Demand

One of the major drawbacks of human capital theory is its complete disregard for the role of labor demand in earnings determination. Even though most economists know that prices are determined by the joint interaction between supply and demand, practically the entire human capital literature ignores this key insight. The earnings function is often viewed essentially as a "reduced form" equation even though variables on the right-hand side are usually given a supply interpretation.

The fact that labor demand also determines earnings—and thus affects earnings inequality—has become an important policy issue due to the large demographic shifts that have occurred in the U.S. labor market in the postwar period. These demographic shifts, which include the entry of the baby-boom babies into the labor market, the continuing increase in the labor force participation rate of married women, and the rapid increase in immigration rates since 1970, have led to a renewed interest in the role played by labor demand factors in earnings determination.

It is well known that profit-maximizing firms hire type i workers up to the point where the marginal productivity of a type i worker equals his wage. In general, this principle implies that the wage of a type i person will depend not only on the number of type i persons employed by the firm (labor market), but also on the numbers of other types of workers in the labor market. Empirically, this point is usually investigated by assuming a specific functional form for the production function. Typically, the production function used is the translog or the Generalized Leontief. Since it is much easier to see the link between wage determination and the labor demand framework using the Generalized Leontief production function, assume that:

$$\theta = \sum_{i, j} \gamma_{ij} (X_i X_j)^{1/2} \tag{21}$$

where θ is output, X_i is the quantity of the ith input, and the γ_{ij} are the technological parameters. The production function is (21) is linearly homogeneous and restricts the values of the technology parameters so that $\gamma_{ij} = \gamma_{ij}$.

The assumption that firms in the labor market maximize profits and face constant input prices leads to the following system of labor demand equations:

$$r_i = \gamma_{ii} + \sum_{j=i} \gamma_{ij} (X_j/X_i)^{1/2} \tag{22}$$

where r_i is the price of input i. The system of equations in (22) illustrates the usefulness of the Generalized Leontief assumption: wage equations are linear-in-parameters. Further, the functional form in (22) provides an intuitive understanding of the underlying process. In particular, the wage of group i, r_i, is affected by the number of type j individuals in the labor market per member of group i (X_j/X_i). Thus the relative quantities of other factors of production affect group i's wage through the technological parameter γ_{ij}. When group i is complementary with group j, increases in the supply of group j increase the wage of group i ($\gamma_{ij} > 0$). Conversely, when group i is substitutable with j, increases in the supply of group j decrease the wage of group i ($\gamma_{ij} > 0$). The parameter vector γ provides a complete description of the technological relationship among the n inputs. The system of equations in (22), therefore, provides the much-needed link between the wage determination process and labor demand theory.

There are, however, two major technical difficulties with analyses based on this labor demand framework (as well as the analogous studies that use the translog production function). First, it is common to assume that the supplies of the various inputs are inelastic, thus exogenous to the labor market.[42] The usual justification for this assumption is that the supplies of age-specific sex/race groups are essentially fixed at a given point in time. This argument, however, ignores the fact that even if the total stock of the inputs can be treated as fixed, its distribution across labor markets is likely to be guided by geographic wage differentials. Thus the study of how earnings determination is affected by labor demand conditions must take into account the supply decision of workers (just as the studies of wage determination using the human capital framework must take into account labor demand conditions).

A second problem with the framework summarized by the system of equations in (22) concerns the definition of the labor inputs themselves: What theoretical restrictions are imposed when the labor force is segmented across sex/race/ ethnic/immigrant groupings, and what are the empirical implications of these restrictions? Labor demand theory provides no guidance as to how labor inputs must be defined. Such guidance must come from a more fundamental study of how worker characteristics are distributed in the market, thereby defining a particular kind of "input." Although this type of research has been conducted,[43] little use of these theoretical models have been made in empirical applications of labor demand theory. Further investigation of this issue is likely to be the most fruitful avenue of research for combining the concept of human capital (and the theoretical framework of that literature) with the demand functions derived from the profit-maximizing behavior of firms. It is clear that until this synthesis is conducted neither the human capital literature nor the labor demand framework can claim to give a complete picture of the earnings determination process.

Despite these misgivings, empirical work utilizing the neoclassical labor demand framework has been quite successful in assessing the impact of demographic shifts in the labor market on the earnings and employment of the various labor inputs. For example, the work of Welch, Freeman, and Berger[44] shows that the size of the youth cohort has been an important variable in determining its earnings and employment behavior as the baby boomers entered the labor market. Although they use different methodologies and alternative data sets, these studies all find that the size of the youth cohort has an important negative impact on the earnings of young workers. Thus, the law of diminishing returns plays an important role in income determination.

Studies by Grant and Hamermesh, Berger, and Borjas[45] focus on the impact of the increase in the number of working women on the earnings of others in the labor market. These studies tend to find that the increasing labor force participation rate of women has played a major role in determining the earnings of men. In particular, it has significantly lowered the earnings of men, especially those of young men and black men, and thus has tended to reduce the extent of income inequality between the sexes.

Finally, Borjas and Grossman[46] have investigated the impact of the increasing flow of immigrants on the earnings of native-born men. These studies have found that immigrants have essentially no impact on the earnings of the native born, even among the minority native-born population.

Other Neoclassical Models of Wage Determination

The models and results presented above make up only a small fraction of the neoclassical literature on wage determination. An assortment of other hypotheses—within the neoclassical framework—have been proposed (or resurrected) and tested within the last two decades. These additional models include:

Compensating Differentials

The idea that jobs that differ in their characteristics should also differ in the wages offered dates back to Adam Smith. However, this hypothesis has been the subject of intensive empirical interest in recent years due to the availability of job characteristics in a number of data sets currently in use. Two important empirical studies in this tradition are those of Thaler and Rosen, which focuses on the compensating differentials induced by the risk of injury on the job, and the study of Abowd and Ashenfelter, which focuses on the compensating differentials induced by the instability of the job.[47] Both of these studies seem to support the compensating differential theory that jobs that are riskier, either in terms of injury or in terms of the probability that layoff will occur, offer higher wages.

However, the entire literature does not support the theory. Brown[48] recently surveyed many of the empirical studies in the compensating differential literature and he found that most of the job characteristics that would be expected a priori to have a particular effect on the wage, in fact, often have perverse or insignificant compensating differentials associated with them. There are at least two good reasons for the failure of these tests. First, even though the theory predicts compensating differentials for different kinds of jobs, it does not predict which jobs are "good" and which jobs are "bad." In other words, the economist cannot expect any guidance—except for his own tastes—as to which way the compensating differential should go. Secondly, it is unrealistic to assume that the entire population feels the same way about the characteristics of any particular job. If, indeed, tastes toward specific job characteristics do not have zero variance, the direction of the compensating differential will be determined not only by the supply of workers to that job, but also by the demand for these workers. Suppose, for example, that a few individuals love risk and thus are willing to pay to be test pilots. Since the demand for this type of worker is low, the compensating differential for test pilots may well be perverse even if almost the entire population dislikes that type of risk. Therefore, it seems that further advances in the role that compensating differentials play in determining the earnings distribution will require not only a fuller description of the job characteristics embodied in the job contract, but also an accounting of the supply and demand conditions for those types of jobs.

Education as a Signal

In the human capital model the association between schooling and earnings represents a fundamental relationship between the individual's productivity and his educational attainment. Models by Spence, Arrow, and Stiglitz[49] provide an alternative view of the positive correlation between schooling and earnings. In particular, if the individual's productivity is unobserved (or can only be observed at a relatively high cost, profit-maximizing employers have incentives to use screens or signals to filter out the truly productive persons. Schooling can provide such a signal.

The main result of these models is that a positive relationship will exist between schooling and earnings even if schooling does not directly affect the individual's productivity on the job. Thus regressions of the schooling model simply capture the fact that truly productive individuals have an incentive to invest in schooling in order to signal that they are truly productive and thus should receive higher wages.

Even though part of this literature views the signaling model as an alternative to the neoclassical tradition (as embodied by the human capital model), it is important to note that the signaling model is itself in the neoclassical mode. Signals (or screens) exist because both employers and individuals are income maximizers. In addition, some writers in this tradition argue that, in a sense, expenditures in education are socially wasteful since education does not increase productivity. Again, this is an incorrect interpretation of the substance of the model since even if education does not increase productivity, it does allow a better matching of jobs and individuals by levels of productivity. In the absence of the educational signal, mismatches would occur quite frequently and would lead to a decline in the output of the firm (and the economy). Thus education does serve a productive role even in the signaling context.

Despite intensive interest in these types of models at the time of their introduction, the signaling literature has not (as of yet) flourished. An important drawback to these models has been the difficulty researchers have had with deriving (and conducting) empirical tests of the key predictions of the theory.[50] Some studies[51] have even conjectured that the human capital model and the screening/signaling model are observationally equivalent. Thus it is still unclear whether the signaling hypothesis will live up to its early promise.

Labor Market Discrimination

Our understanding of the process of labor market discrimination has been increased substantially—at least conceptually—by the neoclassical approach. Since the seminal work of Becker,[52] the concept of "taste" discrimination has provided the basis of analysis for these issues. Becker's main hypothesis was that discriminatory behavior will be reflected in the price signals that market participants receive during a transaction. In the case where the employer discriminates against black workers, for example, the competitive money wage for black labor is r_b, but discriminatory behavior makes the perceived price of black labor $r_b (1 + d)$, where d is the discrimination coefficient.

This approach has proven quite useful in analyzing labor market discrimination.[53] The existence of employer discrimination in a competitive labor market leads to the empirically testable implications that: (a) the white wage will exceed the black wage, (b) firms will hire either only black labor or only white labor, and (c) discrimination is unprofitable, so that it will "wither away" in a competitive labor market.[54]

More recent models of discrimination[55] have applied the basic idea from the screening/signaling model to the study of racial wage differentials and postulate that in the absence of perfect information on the individual's productivity, profit-maximizing employers will utilize signals in order to guess the individual's productivity. One of the cheap signals employers can use is race, and as long as race is correlated with productivity the use of "statistical" discrimination will be optimal. As with the educational signaling model, this hypothesis has proven difficult to test empirically.

Despite the theoretical successes of this literature, the empirical studies of racial discrimination generally ignore most of these theoretical insights. In particular, it seems that the only concern of these studies is to start with the basic Mincer function, add a race dummy and other socioeconomic characteristics, and estimate the racial wage differential (holding all other factors constant). The coefficient of the race dummy variable, which is essentially the residual wage differential between blacks and whites, is then interpreted as discrimination. The conceptual problems with these studies are well known.[56] It is difficult to measure discrimination because the identification of the residual wage differential with discriminatory behavior is biased as long as productivity (or, more precisely, the socioeconomic vector which proxies for productivity) is incorrectly measured, and race is correlated with productivity.

A more useful approach to the problem would be to derive a structural model of discriminatory behavior and assess the impact of variables that shift the demand functions for black and white workers. These types of studies, while rare in the literature, do provide an understanding of the underlying behavior of labor market participants. Examples of these types of studies include those by Landes and by Ashenfelter.[57] In the Landes study, employer demand for blacks is assumed to be affected by the imposition of a fair employment law in the state. Landes finds that, indeed, the relative demand for black labor is higher in those states that impose this type of penalty on discriminatory behavior. Similarly, Ashenfelter analyzes the relationship between union power and discriminatory behavior by labor market participants and finds that in those types of unions where black workers can be used to increase union leverage over the firm, the racial wage differential declines.

Institutional Constraints

Finally, the neoclassical approach is often criticized for ignoring the institutional aspects of the labor market. There is nothing about the existence or importance of institutions, however, that contradicts the neoclassical approach, and, in fact, much recent work in the neoclassical tradition is concerned with emphasizing the constraints imposed on labor market interactions by the existence of such institutions as unions or governments.

The studies of union behavior by Freeman and Medoff, Lazear, Dertouzos and Pencavel, Ashenfelter and Bloom, Ashenfelter and Johnson, and Farber[58] consider alternative modes of union behavior and analyze how these forms of behavior interact in the labor market with profit-maximizing employers and utility-maximizing workers. In effect, equilibrium models of union behavior now exist, and these models have proven fruitful in understanding such issues as how arbitrators behave, the incidence and duration of strikes, the impact of unions on the productivity of the labor force, and the effect of unions on wage levels and wage growth.

Similarly, the recent marriage of models of neoclassical labor markets with public choice models of government behavior provides an important expansion of the neoclassical approach. These types of models have been helpful in understanding employment policies in the public sector. Studies by Borjas, Ehrenberg, and Ehrenberg and Schwartz[59] show that the earnings determination process for public sector workers cannot be understood unless the political environment in which the employer operates is modeled explicitly. Again, the existence of a well-defined goal for government and political units (i.e., maximizing the probability of reelection) provides a solid ground for further applications of the neoclassical approach.

Notes

1. Robert M. Fearn, *Labor Economics: The Emerging Synthesis* (Cambridge, Mass: Winthrop Publishers, Inc., 1981).
2. Jacob Mincer, "Investments in Human Capital and Personal Income Distribution," *Journal of Political Economy* 66, no. 4 (August 1958): 281–302.
3. Gary S. Becker, *Human Capital*, 2d. (New York: Columbia University Press for National Bureau of Economic Research, 1975). 4. Yoram Ben-Porath, "The Production of Human Capital and the Life Cycle of Earnings," *Journal of Political Economy* 75, no. 4 (August 1967): 352–65.
5. In this section, as in the original Ben-Porath framework, the distinction between general and specific human capital is ignored. Instead, all human capital is assumed to be general. See the section below on the application of the human capital model for a discussion of the importance of specific training.
6. In a more general model, the production of human capital would also depend on purchases of market goods. This trivial generalization of the model is ignored here since it does not affect any of the main implications of the analysis.
7. See, however, the recent work of Sherwin Rosen "A Theory of Life Earnings," *Journal of Political Economy* 84, no. 4, Pat. 2, (August 1976): 545–567. By formulating the maximum problem more in the spirit of the Mincer "accounting framework," Rosen finds that the technical problems introduced by non-neutrality are more manageable.
8. Yoram Ben-Porath, "The Production of Human Capital Over Time," in W. Lee Hansen, ed., *Education, Income, and Human Capital* (New York: Columbia University Press for National Bureau of Economic Research, 1970).
9. Jacob Mincer, "Comment," in W. Lee Hansen, ed., *Education, Income, and Human Capital* (New York: Columbia University Press for National Bureau of Economic Research, 1970).
10. See Paul A. Samuelson, *Foundations of Economic Analysis* (Cambridge, Mass: Harvard University Press, 1947).
11. See Robert T. Michael, *The Effect of Education on Efficiency in Consumption* (New York: Columbia University Press for National Bureau of Economic Research, 1972) for an early study of how human capital affects the efficiency of consumption. The theoretical basis for these effects is discussed in Gary S. Becker, "A Theory of the Allocation of Time." *Economic Journal* 75, no. 299 (June 1965): 493–517.
12. See, for example, Alan Blinder and Yorman Weiss, "Human Capital and Labor Supply: A Synthesis," *Journal of Political Economy* 84, no. 3 (June 1976): 449–72; James J. Heckman, "Estimates of a Human Capital Production Function Embedded in a Life-Cycle Model of Labor Supply," in Nestor E. Terleckyu, ed., *Household Production and Consumption* (New York: Columbia University Press for National Bureau of Economic Research, 1976); and James J. Heckman, "A Life-Cycle Model of Earnings, Learning, and Consumption," *Journal of Political Economy* 84, no. 4, Pt. 2 (August 1976): S11–S44.
13. Gary S. Becker, "Human Capital and the Personal Distribution of Income" (W. S. Woytinsky Lecture No. 1. University of Michigan, Ann Arbor, 1967) and *Human Capital*, 2d ed.
14. See, for example, William Haley, "Human Capital: The Choice Between Invest-

ment and Income," *American Economic Review* 63, no. 4 (December 1973): 929–44, and "Estimation of the Earnings Profile from Human Capital Accumulation," *Econometrica* 44, no. 5 November 1976): 1223–38; Charles Brown, "A Model of Optimal Human-Capital Accumulation and the Wages of Young High School Graduates," *Journal of Political Economy* 84, 2 (April 1976): 299–315; and Sherwin Rosen, "Income Generating Functions and Capital Accumulation" (Discussion Paper No. 306, Harvard Institute of Economic Research, June 1973) and "A Theory of Life Earnings."

15. Jacob Mincer, *Schooling, Experience, and Earnings* (New York: Columbia University Press for National Bureau of Economic Research, 1974).

16. Identification of the various parameters can be achieved by using alternative assumptions for the decline in the investment path and by introducing depreciation (see Mincer, *Schooling*, Chapter 5) or by more carefully modeling the role of time worked in the earnings function (Mincer, "Human Capital and Earnings," in A. B. Atkinson, ed., *Wealth, Income and Inequality*, [New York: Oxford University Press, 1980].

17. Mincer, *Schooling*, p. 57.

18. See Robert J. Willis, "Income Generating Functions" (State University of New York at Stony Brook, 1985, Mimeograph).

19. Mincer, "Investments in Human Capital."

20. See Mincer, *Schooling*, p. 27).

21. See, for example, Barry R. Chiswick, *Income Inequality* (New York: Columbia University Press for National Bureau of Economic Research, 1974) and, Barry R. Chiswick and Jacob Mincer, "Time Series Changes in Personal Income Equality in the United States from 1939 with Projections to 1985," *Journal of Political Economy* 80, no. 3, Pt. 2 (May/June 1972): S34-S66.

22. Sherwin Rosen, "Income Generating Functions, and "Human Capital: A Survey of Empirical Research," *Research in Labor Economics* 1 (1977): 3–39.

23. There exists a large literature that analyzes the impact of the ability bias on the coefficient of schooling in earnings regressions. The excellent survey by Zvi Griliches, "Estimating the Returns to Schooling: Some Econometric Problems," *Econometrica* 45, no. 1 (January 1977): 1–22, details all the various econometric biases and concludes, in a somewhat discouraging tone, that perhaps the value-added of these types of studies was not very large.

24. Culminating perhaps in the analysis by Giora Hanoch, "An Economic Analysis of Earnings and Schooling," *Journal of Human Resources* 2, no. 3 Summer 1967): 310–29.

25. Robert J. Willis and Sherwin Rosen, "Education and Self-Selection." *Journal of Political Economy* 87, no. 5, Pt. 2 (October 1979): S7--S36, and Lawrence W. Kenny, Lung-Fei Lee, G. S. Maddala, and R. P. Trost, "Returns to College Education: An Investigation of Self-Selection Bias Based on the Project Talent Data," *International Economic Review* 20, no. 3 (October 1979): 775–89.

26. James J. Heckman, "Sample Selection Bias as a Specification Error," *Econometrica* 47, no. 1 (January 1979): 153–62.

27. An early model applying the principles of comparative advantage to the earnings distribution is given by A. D. Roy, "Some Thoughts on the Distribution of Earnings," *Oxford Economic Papers* 3, no. 2 (June 1951): 135–46. In this prescient work, Roy foresaw practically all the important substantive insights of the sample selection literature.

28. Sherwin Rosen, "Learning and Experience in the Labor Market," *Journal of Human Resources* 7, no. 3 (Summer 1972): 326–42.

29. Becker, *Human Capital*, 2d ed.

30. Masatoshi Kuratani, "Specific Training, Employment Stability and Earnings Distribution in Japan" (Ph.D. diss. Columbia University, 1972) and Masanori Hashimoto, "Firm-Specific Human Capital as a Shared Investment," *American Economic Review* 71, no. 3 (June 1981): 475–82.

31. Solomon W. Polachek, "Differences in Expected Post-School Investment as a Determinant of Market Wage Differentials," *International Economic Review* 16, no. 2 (June 1975): 451–70 and Ann P. Bartel and George J. Borjas, "Specific Training and Its Effects on the Human Capital Investment Profile," *Southern Economic Journal* 44, no. 2 (October 1977): 333–41.

32. See Boyan Jovanovic, "Job Matching and the Theory of Turnover," *Journal of Political Economy* 87, no. 5, Pt. 1 (October 1979): 972–90.

33. Robert E. Hall, "The Importance of Lifetime Jobs in the U.S. Economy," *American Economic Review* 72, no. 4 (September 1982): 716–24.

34. See Jacob Mincer and Boyan Jovanovic, "Labor Mobility and Wages," in Sherwin Rosen, ed., *Studies in Labor Markets* (Chicago: University of Chicago Press for National Bureau of Economic Research, 1981).

35. See James J. Heckman, Heterogeneity and State Dependence," in Sherwin Rosen, ed., *Studies in Labor Markets* (Chicago: University of Chicago Press for National Bureau of Economic Research, 1981) and Mincer and Jovanovic.

36. George J. Borjas, "Job Mobility and Earnings Over the Life Cycle," *Industrial and Labor Relations Review* 34, no. 3 (April 1981): 365–76. See, however, the conflicting evidence in Katharine Abraham and Henry Farber, "Job Duration, Seniority, and Earnings," *American Economic Review*, June 1987.

37. Ann P. Bartel, "Earnings Growth on the Job and Between Jobs," *Economic Inquiry* 18, no. 1 (January 1980): 123–37.

38. Jacob Mincer and Solomon W. Polachek, "Family Investments in Human Capital: Earnings of Women," *Journal of Political Economy* 82, no. 2, Pt. 2 (March 1974): S76–S108 and Polachek, "Differences in Investment."

39. See, for example, Mary Corcoran and Greg J. Duncan,"Work History, Labor Force Attachment, and Earnings Differences Between the Races and Sexes," *Journal of Human Resources* 14, no. 1 (Winter 1979): 3–20.

40. Solomon W. Polachek, "Sex Differences in College Major," *Industrial and Labor Relations Review* 31, no. 4 (July 1978): 498–508 and "Occupational Self-Selection: A Human Capital Approach to Sex Differences in Occupational Structure," *Review of Economics and Statistics* 63, no. 1 (February 1981): 60–69.

41. George J. Borjas and Finis Welch, "The Second Career Earnings of Military Retirees," Unicon Research Corporation, August 1985.

42. See, for example, James H. Grant and Daniel S. Hamermesh, "Labor Market Competition Among Youths, White Women, and Others," *Review of Economics and Statistics* 63, no. 4 (August 1981), 355.

43. See, for example, Sherwin Rosen, "Substitution and Division of Labor," *Economica* 45, no. 2 (August 1978): 861–68 and Finis Welch, Linear Synthesis of Skill Distribution," *Journal of Human Resources* 4, No. 3 (Summer 1969): 311–27.

44. Finis Welch, "Effects of Cohort Size on Earnings: The Baby Boom Babies' Financial Bust," *Journal of Political Economy* 87, no. 5, Pt. 2 (October 1979): S65–S97; Richard B. Freeman, "The Effect of Demographic Factors on Age-Earnings Profiles," *Journal of Human Resources* 14, no. 3 (Summer 1979): 289–318; and Mark Berger, "The Effect of Cohort Size on Earnings: A Reexamination of the Evidence," *Journal of Political Economy* 93, no. 3 (June 1985): 561–73.

45. Grant and Hamermesh, "Labor Market Competition"; Mark Berger, "Changes in Labor Force Composition and Male Earnings: A Production Approach," *Journal of Human Resources* 18, no. 2 (Spring 1983): 177–96; and George J. Borjas, "The Demographic Determinants of the Demand for Black Labor," in Richard B. Freeman and Harry Holzer, eds., *The Black Youth Employment Crisis* (University of Chicago Press for National Bureau of Economic Research, 1986).

46. George J. Borjas, "The Substitutability of Black, Hispanic, and White Labor," *Economic Inquiry* 21, no. 1 (January 1983): 93–106; Borjas, "Demographic Determinants"; and Jean B. Grossman, "The Substitutability of Natives and Immigrants in Production," *Review of Economics and Statistics* 64, no. 6 (November 1983): 596–603.

47. Richard Thaler and Sherwin Rosen, "The Value of Saving a Life: Evidence from the Labor Market," in Nestor E. Terleckj, ed., *Household Production and Consumption* (New York: Columbia University Press for National Bureau of Economic Research, 1976) and John M. Abowd, and Orley Ashenfelter, "Anticipated Unemployment, Temporary Layoffs, and Compensating Wage Differentials," in Sherwin Rosen, ed., *Studies in National Bureau of Economic Research*, 1981). In addition, see the important theoretical advances made by Sherwin Rosen, in his analysis of the hedonic price model. ("Hedonic Prices and Implicit Markets: Production Differentiation in Pure Competition," *Journal of Political Economy* 82, no. 1 [February 1974]: 34–55). This interpretation of the Smith hypothesis ties together both heterogeneity in individual tastes in job characteristics as well as firm differences in the technology that produces these characteristics.

48. Charles Brown, "Equalizing Differences in the Labor Market," *Quarterly Journal of Economics* 95, no. 1 (February 1980): 113–34.

49. A. Michael Spence, *Market Signaling: Informational Transfer in Hiring and Related Screening Processes* (Cambridge, Mass: Harvard University Press, 1974); Kenneth J. Arrow, "Higher Education as a Filter," *Journal of Public Economics* 2, no. 3 (July 1973): 193–216; and Joseph E. Stiglitz, "The Theory of 'Screening,' Education, and the Distribution of Income," *American Economic Review* 65, no. 3 (June 1975): 283–300.

50. See, for example, Richard Layard, and George Psacharopoulos, "The Screening Hypothesis and the Returns to Education," *Journal of Political Economy* 82, no. 5 (October 1974): 985–98 and Kenneth Wolpin, "Education and Screening," *American Economic Review* 67, no. 5 (December 1977): 949–58.

51. John G. Riley, "Testing the Educational Screening Hypothesis," *Journal of Political Economy* 87, no. 5, Pt. 2 (October 1979): S227–S252.

52. Gary S. Becker, *The Economics of Discrimination* (Chicago: University of Chicago Press, 1957).

53. See, for example, the formalization of the Becker model by Kenneth J. Arrow, "The Theory of Discrimination," in Orley Ashenfelter and Albert Rees, eds., *Discrimination in Labor Markets* (Princeton, N.J.: Princeton University Press, 1973).

54. It turns out that this last prediction is invalid if the origin of the model is reversed. That is, if firms are nepotists toward white workers rather than discriminators against black workers. For details see Matthew S. Goldberg, "Discrimination, Nepotism and Long-Run Wage Differentials," *Quarterly Journal of Economics*, 97, no. 2 (May 1982): 307–19.

55. Arrow, "Theory of Discrimination," and Edmund S. Phelps, "The Statistical Theory of Racism and Sexism," *American Economic Review* 62, no. 4 (September 1972): 659–61.

56. See, for example, Solomon W. Polachek, "Potential Biases in Measuring Male-Female Discrimination," *Journal of Human Resources* 10, no. 2 (Spring 1975): 205–29 and Arthur S. Goldberger, "Reverse Regression and Salary Discrimination," *Journal of Human Resources*, 19, no. 3 (Summer 1984): 293–318.

57. William M. Landes, "The Economics of Fair Employment Laws," *Journal of Political Economy* 76, no. 4 (August 1968): 507–52 and Orley Ashenfelter, "Racial Discrimination and Trade Unionism," *Journal of Political Economy* 84, no. 3 (May 1972): 435–64.

58. Richard B. Freeman and James L. Medoff, *What Do Unions Do?* (New York: Basic Books, Inc., 1984); Edward P. Lazear, "A Competitive Theory of Monopoly Unionism," *American Economic Review* 83, no. 4 (September 1983): 631–43; James N.

Dertouzos, and John H. Pencavel, "Wage and Employment Determination Under Trade Unionism: The International Typographical Union," *Journal of Political Economy* 89, no. 6 (December 1980): 1162–81; Orley Ashenfelter and David E. Bloom, "Models of Arbitrator Behavior: Theory and Evidence" (Discussion Paper No. 1009, Harvard Institute of Economic Research September 1983); Orley Ashenfelter and George Johnson, "Bargaining Theory, Trade Unions, and Industrial Strike Activity," *American Economic Review* 59, no. 1 (March 1969): 35–49; and Henry S. Farber, "The United Mine Workers and the Demand for Coal: An Econometric Analysis of Union Behavior," *Research in Labor Economics* 2 (1978): 1–74.

59. George J. Borjas, "Wage Determination in the Federal Government: The Role of Constituents and Bureaucrats," *Journal of Political Economy* 88, no. 6 (December 1980): 1110–47; Ronald G. Ehrenberg, "The Demand for State and Local Government Employees," *American Economic Review* 63, no. 3 (June 1973): 366–79; and Ronald G. Ehrenberg and Joshua L. Schwarz, "Public Sector Labor Markets," Cornell University, July 1983.

52

3

INCOME DISTRIBUTION IN AN INSTITUTIONAL WORLD

Clair Brown

The issue of income distribution is historically tied to concerns about the standard of living, especially of the working class and the underclass.[1] The need to approach income distribution through the standard of living, is evident when the motivating question is the well-being of the various classes, which are defined and divided by their social and work roles. Incomes are directly tied to these roles, and the goods and services commanded by income outwardly mark each class in the society.[2] In this way, one's placement in the labor market simultaneously determines one's earnings, standard of living, and status.

Unequal access to resources provides the material basis for conflict among classes, conflict that is an ongoing process since inequality recreates itself with some minor deviations. Conflict between classes can occur directly at the workplace in the setting of wages and working conditions, in the society as disagreements over norms governing the standard of living, or in the political process as disagreements over the role of government. The primary function of the labor market is to ration people into the unequal job structure in such a way that workers remain productive and the structure is recreated over time. Government's function is to mediate the conflict in a way that preserves both social order and the social ordering.

In discussing an institutional theory of income distribution, this paper first

Clair Brown is Associate Professor of Economics and a member of the Institute of Industrial Relations at the University of California at Berkeley. The author appreciates the helpful comments from Lloyd Ulman, Marlene Kim, Teresa Ghilarducci, and Bill Dickens that improved this paper. Amelia Preece provided excellent research assistance. She is also grateful for the research support and staff support (especially Barbara Porter) provided by the Institute of Industrial Relations, University of California, Berkeley.

.plores the relationship between income distribution, class conflict, and the standard of living. In addition, the institutional model is contrasted to the neo-classical model. Then, the political implications of the institutional model are discussed (and briefly compared to the neoclassical model) in order to analyze the role of the government in forming the income distribution.

The Relationship Between Income Distribution, Class Conflict, and the Standard of Living

The Role of Income Distribution in the Economy

Class conflict is centered around *relative* differences in income, and an integral part of the conflict itself is deciding whether relative or absolute standards of well-being should be the basis for making policy. The capitalist/managerial class, which resists improvements toward equality, argues that absolute standards are the appropriate benchmark for judgment. Their position of being relatively well-off must be justified by a meritocratic world view, such as human capital theory, that rationalizes unequal labor market outcomes. The welfare class, whose standard of living would be improved by greater income equality, argues that relative standards are the appropriate benchmark for judgment, since poor people are painfully aware in their daily lives of the social exclusion that accompanies a standard of living below the norms achieved by the working class.

Prior to 1950, it did not make much difference whether one used a relative or absolute standard for judging well-being, and the accompanying prescription for a "living wage," since the income of the typical semiskilled wage earner's family was inadequate to meet a needs-based budget.[3] Economists assumed that families needed sufficient income to conform with prevailing standards, and they estimated "needs-based" budgets to derive the cost of a specified standard of living. For decades they found the wages of working-class men to be too low to maintain the well-being of a family of five.[4]

With enormous improvement in real incomes between the Depression years and World War II came a de-emphasis of absolute standards in societal evaluation of income adequacy and income distribution. After 1950, judgment of well-being was no longer tied to measuring needs-based standards since the large majority of the working class families had obtained a standard of living above the socially required minimum level. Instead, the focus shifted to the impact of the income distribution on motivation and efficiency. The assumption that people needed economic incentives (i.e., unequal labor market outcomes) to work hard and that capitalists required large returns in order to make investments led to the concept of efficiency and equality as trade-offs.[5] The processes were generally acknowledged to be highly complex, since many economists remained mindful that underemployment (not to mention unemployment) caused motivational problems and that total demand (rather than the profit rate) determined the growth path of the economy.[6]

Because of the dilemma posed by the assumed trade-off between equality and efficiency, economists tended to separate their prescription for production (by the market place) and for distribution (through taxes and other government programs). Even supporters of the market did not believe that distribution in accordance with marginal productivity was a *just* distribution.[7] However, economists heatedly disagreed about how much redistributional policies should be allowed to interfere with the functioning of the market. Interestingly enough, they seemed to place greater emphasis on growth as the level of affluence rose. Many economists had always argued against allowing large differences in material standards of living and against equating human welfare to money income.[8] But the argument that inequality played a positive role by increasing the size of the pie was now tempering that viewpoint.

In the absence of a better tool than recession to control inflation, the trade-off between efficiency and equity was seldom questioned. Unfortunately, the underlying class conflict precluded the political consensus needed to structure the economy to provide full employment without inflation and also to allow free collective bargaining. Traditional Keynesian policies were fairly successful in meeting the goals of this "uneasy triangle" of full employment, low inflation, and free collective bargaining[9] in the robust, Vietnam-war economy of the mid–1960s. The heightened conflict generated by rising energy prices in the mid–1970s proved to be more than traditional fiscal and monetary policies could handle. Nixon's halfhearted attempts at wage and price controls moderated inflation but did not resolve the underlying conflict. In the absence of the necessary consensus to restructure the economy with an incomes policy that would regulate the conflict, the government ended up accepting a higher rate of unemployment. In this case, efficiency arguments were convenient for justifying an inequitable income distribution that reflected unnecessary unemployment.

Assumptions of the Institutional Model

Since competitive markets produce full employment, unemployment as characteristic of the labor market has posed a major problem for economists. In the absence of an explanation for unemployment in a market economy, many economists (e.g., Keynes, Pigou, Solow) used social rule and custom to explain wage rigidity, which resulted in involuntary unemployment whenever aggregate demand fell below full capacity.[10] More recently, economists have explained unemployment within a market context by efficiency wage theory, where a worker's productivity depends on the wage rate (usually along with the unemployment rate and unemployment benefits).[11] These models result in the wage being close to the market-clearing wage. Economists have formulated efficiency wage models with both a material basis (e.g., shirking, nutrition, adverse selection, or labor turnover) and a sociological basis (e.g., gift exchange or morale). However, even the models with a material basis require social conventions to prevent the firm from setting up a more efficient wage structure (such as a hiring fee, fines or penalties for poor performance, seniority wages, piece rates, or firing of workers with low output). So we are still left with the wage structure (and involuntary unemployment) being formed by social rule and custom.

As long as we require institutions to explain labor market outcomes, we should ask if institutional forces or market forces are more powerful. In other words, should we study the earnings distribution as the outcome of a constrained neoclassical model or as the outcome of a dynamic institutional structure? The former approach sees market forces as the moving force that is only slightly disturbed by superimposed structural constraints.[12] The latter approach sees social rules and customs as the moving force, and the structure itself gives birth to and shapes the economic forces.

If one thinks of the labor market as a large castle with many floors—with a barren dungeon in the basement and gradually improving floor by floor until you reach an opulent penthouse on the top—then an institutionalist studies why the floors are so unequal, why certain families occupy each floor, and why so little mobility exists between floors. The neoclassical economist studies how people situate themselves *within* a given floor—in the dungeon, who sits on a wooden chair versus on the floor; who gets to use the jacuzzi in the penthouse. Of course the castle is constantly undergoing renovation, some of which is in response to the struggle between floors over use of resources. But the actions on the various floors must be coordinated, since structural renovations could bring down the castle.

As long as we need institutions to explain unemployment, then we should begin by assuming that unemployment is a characteristic of the labor market. In fact, the assumption that the labor market is characterized by unemployment and underemployment is at the heart of the institutional model (see Table 3.1). Although the exact definition of unemployment is a long-standing political issue, the state of unemployment is fairly easy to observe and measure. The controversial aspect of the definition is whether or not a person is "in the labor force," i.e., whether or not someone actually will accept a job at the prevailing wage if that individual is unemployed. The concept "at the prevailing wage" leads us to the issue of underemployment, which is much more difficult to define and to measure than unemployment. Of course, underemployment includes unemployment.

The institutional assumption of underemployment has two important implications. First, the absence of the full utilization of all workers' potential requires the rationing of workers into unequal positions in the labor market. Second, the distance from full employment determines the overall bargaining position of workers vis-à-vis capital. The rationing process is formed by the institutional structure within which the labor market functions.[13] Social rules and customs (i.e., institutions) perform the rationing process (i.e., the allocation of workers to unequal jobs), while the wage rate reflects the bargaining power and marks the

Table 3.1

Assumptions in Institutional and Neoclassical Models

Institutional model	Neoclassical model
Economy characterized by under-employment (and unemployment)	Economy characterized by competitive markets, which produce full employment
Allocation of workers within unequal job structure by rule and custom	Allocation of labor by price (wage)
Power relations important for establishing and enforcing institutions	Power is ignored since markets are competitive
Workers' productivity a result of command over resources, which reflects access	Productivity a result of individual human capital decisions
Social role forms behavior	Behavior reflects atomistic, idiosyncratic preferences
Total is more than the sum of the parts, whose functioning is conditioned by their interrelations	Total is the sum of essentially *equal* parts that operate independently

societal valuation of the job. The rules and customs that perform the rationing and prepare people for their work and social roles permeate all aspects of life. Since institutions provide the framework by which we view the world, we have difficulty in seeing and judging the institutional structure itself. In fact, our way of thinking embodies the institutional structure, which includes our system (or theory) of value.

The process begins with socialization and education of children, both within the family and in the school system, in which children learn the appropriate rules and customs that govern behavior and thinking. The rationing process—first through the educational system, then into the labor market—requires this socialization process in order for the rationing to occur automatically. For a black teenaged woman to become pregnant, a black teenaged man to leave high school and become unemployed, a white woman to receive a community college degree to become a secretary, and a white man to graduate from college to enter a management training program are neither "mistakes" nor "choices." These represent the unequal roles that members of these groups, divided by race and gender, play in our society.

Power relations within the systems are important for establishing and maintaining rules and customs, and thereby recreating relative outcomes. Since conflict is inherent in the system, institutions govern the resolution of ordinary conflict as well as order everyday life. The structure itself must be in slow but continual evolution in order to accommodate changing social and economic needs that reflect minor shifts in power among the unequal classes. The government plays an important role as mediator of conflict by legislatively changing the structure to facilitate and accommodate the various claims that become accepted as legitimate.

The income distribution is determined by the split between wages and unearned income (profits and rents) and by the distribution of wages. Unemployment primarily affects the split between wages and unearned income since it affects workers' bargaining power vis-à-vis capital.[14] Underemployment primarily affects the distribution of wages since it determines the range of productivity available in the job structure. As the level of unemployment grows, the amount of underemployment at jobs also grows as workers are bumped down.

Varying amounts of unemployment can exist, and the amount of unemployment allowed by the government reflects a complex aggregation of conflicting social needs. In a high pressure economy, such as during wartime, a high and growing level of employment results in an undermining of the rationing institutions as the need to ration diminishes. When inflationary pressures finally cause government to deflate the economy or to impose wage and price controls in order to restore capital's control over rising worker expectations, adjustment problems result as rationing is increased.

Because of job rationing, for a given level of skill and effort, a worker's productivity depends on his or her job, since the job determines the resources and power at the worker's command. This results from two phenomena—a large number of available workers possess the required skill and competence and can make the required effort for any given job; and most workers' talents are not fully developed or utilized by their jobs. Although it is true that most well-paying jobs require competent workers who work hard, the converse that all people who are competent and hardworking are well paid is *not* true. The rationing process is responsible for this distinction, which cannot exist in competitive labor markets.

A worker's productivity, comes with the job one is able to lead, and the job itself determines the development of the worker as it provides the acquisition of skills (primarily through experience or learning by doing) and contacts as well as the honing of the appropriate skills or personality. Most of this development occurs informally (i.e., through experience on-the-job and without any explicit training), but the results are both observable and valuable in terms of the worker's ability to gain access to higher paying jobs. This development of the worker, especially in connections, personality, and "learning the ropes," cannot take place outside of the job experience itself, and so initial access to the labor market is a required first step in a chain of potential job development. These consequences are irreversible since development of a worker makes the worker more productive and, therefore, more powerful. Some job chains are very short and do not provide much opportunity for worker development, while other job chains are long and provide extensive development.[15]

Labor market observers are sometimes confused by the fact that higher paid workers usually are more developed in terms of skills and job knowledge and have certain personality traits and many contacts. They conclude that these people deserve high wages for these reasons. However, this is true only if all people had been provided the opportunity for development through their jobs (as is assumed in competitive markets). In addition, people who are given access to jobs providing development, high wages, and job stability are not required to pay for this access (which is also assumed in a competitive market).

This view of the determinants of productivity contrasts markedly with neoclassical theory, which assumes that productivity resides with the worker as a result of human capital investment decisions (both in formal education and on-the-job training) and competition. In a competitive market the worker purchases differential productivity and, thus is not an unfair wage distribution. Unfulfilled human potential results from lack of motivation as opposed to lack of opportunity.

Each person has a social role as well as a work role, and these two roles must be well integrated in order for the individual (and the system) to function. The social role is assigned according to a child's sex and class position at birth, and the successful rearing of a child entails the proper preparation for the assigned social and work roles. The formal educational process reinforces the child-rearing practices at home and prepares the child in terms of skills, personality, and expectations for the available job access as well as for the correct social role.[16]

Personality traits (e.g., by gender) grow out of the social structure that prepares the child and places the adult. A person's work has a marked influence on her or his thinking and behavior. As Veblen said, "As he acts, so he feels and thinks."[17] The learned behavior ensures that the social and work roles are compatible.[18] If they are in conflict, then the structure must change to reintegrate the two roles. This type of conflict is evident in the demands being made on women to be full-time paid workers while still being responsible for child-rearing and family life. This conflict remains unresolved. Women are trying to restructure work life and family life so that gender roles are more equal in both sectors. Capitalist forces are trying to alleviate the labor market pressure on women through "special treatment" (e.g., part-time work, working at home, maternity leave) in order to retain them as unequal (i.e., lower paid) workers and to allow them to continue their function as provider of family life. These policies, which are not usually available to men, alleviate the pressure on men to shift some of their commitment and energy from work to family life.

The institutional assumption that social and work roles form behavior is in contrast to the neoclassical assumption that behavior reflects individualistic and idiosyncratic preferences, which cannot be accounted for[19] but can be observed in the wide array of differential labor market outcomes. In an ideal neoclassical world, tastes and abilities are two attributes that distinguish individuals, and these are usually implicitly assumed to be innate (i.e., genetic). The institutional world sees behavior and ability as shaped primarily by the economic and social structure. Although individuals do have innate differences in personality and abilities, these are small relative to the differences that are formed and rewarded by the system.

Recognition of the interrelatedness of the parts of the economy forms the basis for a holistic methodology practiced by institutionalists.[20] According to their principle of interrelatedness, each part of the economic system can be explained through analyzing its relation to the rest of the system.[21] Since the total is more than the sum of the parts, and since the functioning of each part is conditioned by its relationship to the whole, the institutionalists would not study a group of workers independent of their own social role or independent of the structure of the workplace and economy. To do so would be akin to describing someone's personality only when they are alone and excluding behavior with others.

In contrast, neoclassical economics sees the total as the sum of parts which operate independently. Because of competition and free choice, the parts are essentially equal. Neoclassical economists assume they can study each part in isolation from the whole without serious distortion of reality.

Political Implications and Practice

Assessment of Well-Being

The concept of using an individual's own evaluation of well-being, which is defined by observed behavior, is a fairly recent idea that became socially possible as the full-time adult male wage was sufficient to purchase basic requirements for food and shelter. As fulfilling the family's basic physical needs could be taken for granted, emphasis on individual free will grew and conflicted with the social structure within which physical needs, including reproduction, were being met. Assuming the social structure to be stable allowed the neoclassical model to focus exclusively on individual maximizing under free choice and to assume that observed outcomes were optimal. But in the presence of underemployment and a changing social structure, assuming observed outcomes are optimal is absurd. Such an assumption, however, plays an important social role in justifying, even requiring, the absence of government intervention to change the unequal outcomes.

Assessment of well-being, both for individuals and for the society, is more complex in the institutional world than in the neoclassical world. Judgments about individual choice must be made in the context of the actual income distribution and the requirements for social order. It is possible to make certain types of judgments concerning the resources needed for the physical well-being of individuals—nutrition, shelter, transportation, health care, clothing, recreation—which have a long tradition in the needs-based budget analysis. But as family income was increasingly spent to provide comfort and status rather than substance (or physical well-being), this approach became inoperative. It became necessary to use a new yardstick as majority of families surpassed absolute requirements of well-being.

Once absolute standards were met, the importance of relative differences became evident. The income distribution establishes the various standards of living by class, and income forms the material basis for social interactions (i.e., family, work, and societal transactions) through providing the material trappings of status and the symbols of one's social role. The social structure dictates the commodity requirements for various goals and status markings. In this way, the standard of living is intimately related to people's accepting their position in the job structure since their work role provides them with the income needed for their social role. Their labor market access and command over resources is congruous with the life-style provided by their income. Ways of improving access and command are unknown, even mystified. The prevailing ideology reassures workers that more command and greater access result from being more talented or more skilled or harder working without specific guidance on how to accomplish these ends.

The importance of using a relative yardstick to measure economic distance in such a world becomes clear. Even in the absence of differences in substance, the differences in comfort and status create a gulf in perceived well-being, which include both subjective judgments and objective measures of social integration. Higher standards of living allow more social integration, which in turn allows greater control over one's life and better ability to accomplish one's life goals. For example, higher income allows one to buy whatever is needed to accomplish a specific goal (e.g., a presentable house, an attractive yard, a fun birthday party). Of course, the standards for each of these goals vary by class. However, because there is less room for errors, it is more difficult to reach a lower standard with a lower income than to reach a higher standard with a higher income. Higher income allows one to make more "mistakes" in purchasing items—uncomfortable shoes, the wrong style dress, or too much fish—or in losing things. This flexibility reduces the stress related to material life. Although economists have limited skills in interpreting how living standards by class translate into social integration, we do have the tools for measuring the substance, comfort, and status components of the economic distance across classes.[22] These measurements allow us to judge the income distribution by its impact on the relative well-being across classes and to make policy decisions as to what type of income distribution is socially desirable.

The Role of Government

Since institutional theory assumes that the government plays a necessary and important role in creating the structure within which the economy functions, government is largely responsible for labor market outcomes. In a capitalist economy, government's most primitive role is the creation and preservation of private property, without which a private market economy cannot exist. Government's more developed role is to create and preserve the social rules and mechanisms by which people are prepared for and accept their social and work roles, without which an economy cannot function. The institutional structure exists to ensure social order through the creation and enforcement of rule and custom, to ensure social reproduction, and to provide a system of value. The daily conduct of business requires this institutional structure that provides "an environment of trust, understanding, and security."[23] In an institutional world, the idea of government "intervention" in the economy is absurd, since a modern industrial economy cannot exist without the structure created and maintained by the government.

Here we consider government's impact on income distribution through its impact on the earnings structure, the distribution of disposable income, the social infrastructure (i.e., the division between public and private goods), the industrial relations structure, and the level of unemployment. The government uses a variety of mechanisms for structuring the labor market, with some policies (generally instituted in response to workers' militancy or social unrest) used to ameliorate the unequal and harsh results of other policies. An obvious example in the U.S. is the use of unemployment insurance to help offset the financial burden of unemployment on the worker and to minimize the disruption of the economy by short-term unemployment instigated by the government to weaken labor's wage demands. Another example is Title VII of the Civil Rights Act of 1964 that declared illegal job market rationing on the basis of race, sex, religion, or nationality. The overall structure of unequal outcomes was not directly affected,[24] since the law attempted to change the rules by which the rationing was done so that race or sex did not place workers in unequal labor market queues. Backlash also occurs, and structure shifts to increase inequality of both money and power—such as the Tax Reform Act of 1981, the relative decline in social expenditures, and the interpretation of the National Labor Relations Act during the Reagan administration. Government policy evolves as it mediates conflict among the various classes (including political conflict on a global scale); the primary goal is the preservation of social order, which includes the preservation of the class structure.

In an institutional world, government regulation is not evaluated against an ideal benchmark, such as a "competitive market economy," since no such economy exists or can exist. Instead, institutionalists compare two possible structures—such as in an evaluation of government programs affecting the labor market as compared to the situation without such programs (for example, workers in a training program are evaluated relative to comparable workers not in the program). Attempts to dismantle the structure within which the economy functions can result in large transactions costs and economic chaos until anew structure evolves from the conflict. For this reason, deregulation is expected to lead to increased instability, uncertainty, and unemployment. An institutional world achieves full employment through a *more* structured economy. In contrast, a neoclassical world expects deregulation to decrease unemployment as it frees the market.

The difference between the institutional world and the neoclassical world in how to affect policy is profound. The institutionalists understand that the conflict is over how to shape the social structure, since institutions form economic outcomes. Marginal economic adjustments within the structure are trivial compared to changes that accompany the ongoing structural shifts. Shifting people around within a specific room within the castle is unimportant compared to making structural improvements in a floor or switching people between floors. Social changes generally give rise to resistance and an effort to reestablish the old ways. Above all, changes that threaten *relative* positions result in a high level of resistance and backlash since they require people to relinquish status and a favored position. People who desire a social structure with greater equality must be prepared to struggle since progressive change does not come naturally or easily.

A primary task of the social system is to resolve normal daily conflict and to maintain order. The inherent inequality of the economic system makes it potentially unstable, since the rules and customs that maintain order depend on people's acceptance of the inequality. Institutionalists' understanding of the fragile nature and essential role of the social structure usually leads them to favor policies of redistribution through government taxing and spending over more radical structural changes, such as workers' or state ownership of capital.[25] Maintenance of social order as a goal and a more equal distribution of income under capitalism clearly differentiated the older institutionalists from the Marxists.[26] While the Marxists predicted that socialism would produce increased equality *and* increased output,[27] the institutionalists predicted that increased output would *allow* increased equality since conflict over distribution of rising income was never as severe as conflict over distribution of falling income. With economic growth, it would be possible to relax rationing, and absolute differences in the material standards across class could fall without threatening relative position. Inequality could decrease without positions in the social order changing.

Even with these differences, however, Marxists and institutionalists both believe that higher output and greater equality go together. In contrast, neoclassical economists believe that government intervention to increase equality must decrease economic growth and output since interference with the competitive marketplace results in reduced efforts by workers and a misallocation of resources.

This brings us back to the basic difference between the institutional (including Marxian) and neoclassical theories of income distribution. In the neoclassical world, the income distribution reflects the outcome of individual choices in a competitive market; interference with the outcome has a social cost. In the institutional world, income distribution is part of the complex structure formed by society and, as such, it can be changed. A society's income distribution reflects how that society values class positions, and judgments about the income distribution must be made within an explicit social structure and value system.

Notes

1. See, for example, Paul H. Douglas, Curtice N. Hitchcock, and Willard E. Atkins, *The Worker in Modern Economic Society* (University of Chicago Press, 1923), chap. 9. The Marxian analysis of income and standards of living is presented by in Clair Brown and Joseph A. Pechman, eds., *Gender in the Workplace* (Washington, D.C.: Brookings Institution, 1987), 13–49.

2. The use of goods as an information system or as markers of social relations is discussed in Mary Douglas and Baron Isherwood, The World of Goods (New York: Basic Books, 1979). The use of goods as symbol is discussed by Mihaly Csikszentmihalyi and Eugene Rochberg-Halton, *The Meaning of Things* (Cambridge: Cambridge University Press, 1981). The importance of establishing the position of the person in the social context by economic transactions is discussed in Karl Polanyi, Conrad Arensberg, and Harry Pearson, eds., *Trade and Market in the Early Empires* (New York:: Free Press, 1957), chap. 5. Consumption used for participation in validating activities is discussed in Lee Rainwater, *What Money Busy: Inequality and the Social Meaning of Income* (New York: Basic Books, 1974), chap. 2.

3. Clair Brown, "Consumption Norms, Work Roles and Economic Growth" In Clair Brown and Joseph Peckman, eds., *Gender in the Workplace* (Washington, D.C.: Brookings Institution, 1987) 13–58.

4. Douglas, Hitchcock, and Atkins, chap. 9; Helen H. Lamale, "Changes in Concepts of Income Adequacy Over the Last Century," *American Economic Review* (May 1958): 291, 299; Carle C. Zimmerman, *Consumption and Standards of Living* (New York: D. Van Nostrand Company, Inc., 1936); and Rainwater.

5. "The differentials in income are meant to serve as incentives—rewards and penalties—to promote efficiency in the use of resources and to generate a great, and growing, national output" (Arthur M. Okun, *Equality and Efficiency: The Big Tradeoff* [Washington, D.C.: Brookings Institution, 1975], vii).

6. Robert Kuttner, *The Economic Illusion: False Choices Between Prosperity and Social Justice* (Boston: Houghton Mifflin Co., 1984 chap. 1), argues that full employment is essential for allowing the dynamic changes required by the economy in terms of technological innovation and the shifting of workers among industries. He argues that good economic performance requires (among other things) institutions that provide personal security and opportunity and minimize class conflict.

7. Okun, 41.

8. E. J. Urwich, *Luxury and Waste of Life* (London: J. M. Dent and Co., 1908); William A. Robson, *The Relation of Wealth to Welfare* (New York: Macmillan, 1925); Richard Tawney, *The Acquisitive Society* (San Diego, CA: Harcourt Publications, 1948).

9. Lloyd Ulman, "Unions, Economists, Politicians, and Incomes Policy," in Joseph A. Peckman and N. J. Simler, eds., *Economics in the Public Service* (New York: W. W. Norton, 1982).

10. See Robert Solow, "Theories of Unemployment," *American Economic Review* (March 1980): 1–11.

11. Earlier economists including Smith, Marshall, and Pigou tied efficiency to satisfaction of material wants (e.g., nutrition) since the worker was more productive if material wants were satisfied. See Zimmerman and Robert Cooter and Peter Rappoport, "Were the Ordinalists Wrong About Welfare Economics?" *Journal of Economic Literature* 22, no. 2 (June 1984): 507–30. Efficiency wage models are reviewed in Janet Yellen, "Efficiency Wage Models of Unemployment," *American Economic Review* (May 1984): 200–205.

12. In fact, some market economists view social norms or constraints as efficient responses to market imperfections. For example, upward-sloping age-earnings profiles (in

the absence of on-the-job training) produce appropriate work incentives. However, efficient employment contracts must then have hours requirements and restrictions as well as temporary layoffs. (Edward P. Lazear, "Agency, Earnings Profiles, Productivity, and Hours Restrictions," *American Economic Review* 71, no. 4 [September, 1981]: 607–20).

13. Peter B. Doeringer and Michael J. Piore, *Internal Labor Markets and Manpower Analysis* (Lexington, Mass.: Heath Lexington Books, 1971), chap. 1: 1–9.

14. See, for example, Michal Kalecki, "Political Aspects of Full Employment," in Kalecki, *Selected Essays on the Dynamics of the Capitalist Economy* (Cambridge: Cambridge University Press, 1971).

15. Michael J. Piore discusses how automatic, incidental learning on the job explains the construction of "mobility chains" in "Notes from a Theory of Labor Market Stratification," in Richard Edwards, Michael Reich, and David Gordon, eds., *Labor Market Segmentation* (Lexington, Mass.: D. C. Heath & Co., 1975), chap. 5.

16. Samuel Bowles and Herbert Gintis, *Schooling in Capitalist America* (New York: Basic Books, 1976).

17. Thorstein Veblen, *The Instinct of Workmanship and the State of the Industrial Arts* (New York: The Viking Press, 1937), 63. Veblen viewed the individual's personality as a reflection of the capitalist culture. He emphasized instinctive action, which requires consciousness and adaptation. Veblen used four basic instinct—the workmanship, the acquisitive, the parental, and idle curiosity. Instinctive drives establish habitual ways of thinking and acting, which take on institutional character and force. For Veblen, technological change was a major factor behind institutional change.

18. Michael J. Piore, *Birds of Passage* (Cambridge: Cambridge University Press, 1979), chap. 3 and Piore "Notes"; Rosabeth Moss Kanter, "The Impact of Hierarchical Structures on the Work of Women and Men," in Rachael Kahn-Hut, Arlene Daniels, and Richard Colvard, eds., *Women and Work*, (Oxford: Oxford University Press, 1982).

19. George J. Stigler and Gary S. Becker, "De Gustibus Non Est Disputandum," *American Economic Review* (March 1977): 76–90.

20. For some writers, this holistic methodological approach is the primary distinguishing characteristic of institutionalists as opposed to a world view. See Charles K. Wilbur with Robert S. Harrison, "The Methodological Basis of Institutional Economics: Pattern Model, Storytelling, and Holism," *Journal of Economic Issues*, 12, no. 1 (March 1978): 61–90.

21. Allan G. Gruchy, *Modern Economic Thought: The American Contribution* (New York: Prentice-Hall, 1947); Thorstein Veblen, "Why Is Economics Not an Evolutionary Science?", *The Place of Science in Modern Civilisation* (New York: B. W. Huebsch, 1919): 56–81.

22. Brown.

23. Okun, 32.

24. This attack on the rationing system did, in fact, undermine the structure of unequal outcomes, since it brought into public scrutiny the rules for rationing. The result was the "comparable worth" movement that directly attacked the rationing process.

25. Allan G. Gruchy, *Contemporary Economic Thought: The Contribution of Neo-Institutional Economics* (London: Macmillan, 1973): ix.

26. Although most of the better-known institutionalists were procapitalism (especially after the 1930s), many institutionalists were (and are) socialists.

27. Samuel Bowles, David M. Gordon, Thomas E. Weisskopf, *Beyond the Wasteland: A Democratic Alternative to Economic Decline* (Garden City, N.Y.: Anchor Press, 1983).

PART I

4

PROFITS AND WAGES
IN AN OPEN ECONOMY

Samuel Bowles

The capitalist class, Karl Marx observed, cannot make profits by exploiting itself; profits arise not because capitalists buy cheap and sell dear but because they pay labor less than its net product. The secret of profit making, Marx insisted, could be found through the study of class relations in production and in labor markets, not exchange relations in goods markets.

The classical Marxian emphasis on class relationships as the foundation of a theory of income distribution was a valuable antidote to earlier merchantilist conceptions, which focused on international exchange as the key to understanding profits. Not surprisingly, much of the subsequent Marxian theory of income distribution has been developed in the context of models that abstract from the international mobility of goods, credit, and labor.[1]

This reliance on closed economy models, however, is unfortunate, for it provides no theoretical basis for the integrated study of international rivalry and class conflict, and it obscures the manner in which the profit rate in any given national economy is significantly influenced by not only domestic but also global determinants. True, the owners of the means of production in a particular nation cannot make profits through the zero sum activity of exploiting themselves: but their exploitation of labor may be enhanced by buying cheap and selling dear on world markets. Indeed, as we shall see, their ability to pay labor less than its net

The author is Professor of Economics at the University of Massachusetts at Amherst. This essay owes much to the persistent questioning of labor activists and other participants in programs of the Center for Popular Economics in Amherst and Vancouver, as well as to the prodding of members of his seminars in macroeconomics and Marxian economic theory at the University of Massachusetts; He is also grateful to Authur MacEwan, Manuel Pastor, Jr., James Rebitzer, and John Willoughby for helpful comments.

product depends critically on the international terms of trade.

Nor is the tendency to ignore the international dimensions of the theory of income distribution necessary, for the relationship between international exchange and the distribution of income is quite readily modeled within the Marxian framework. In this essay I will propose a general model of this relationship.

The model is Marxian in inspiration: it represents the real wage and the intensity of labor as the result of class conflict between employers and workers, it focuses on the class distribution of income (rather than the size distribution), and it represents profits as the monetary equivalent of the surplus product, a residual category remaining after reproduction costs—wages and depreciation—are deducted from gross output.[2]

The approach adopted here is thus quite distinct from the conventional neoclassical models of income distribution and international trade. In this model agents are highly competitive, and they optimize, as in the neoclassical approach, but markets—and particularly labor markets—do not clear but rather are characterized by perpetual excess supply or unemployment. The critical determinant of investment is not domestic savings but rather the rate of profit relative to profit rates elsewhere in the world. Further, the treatment of international trade rejects the neoclassical fiction of mobile goods and immobile factors of production and makes global flows of capital and labor an integral part of the analysis.[3]

The approach is highly simplified, and is designed to illuminate the long-run dynamics of an open capitalist economy. Important questions concerning aggregate demand are set aside, as are the monetary aspects of international exchanges, taxation, and other state activities.[4]

I will begin by explicating the concept of the surplus product and its relationship to the terms of trade. I will then turn to the profit rate and the determination of wages and work intensity, and close with an analysis of the income distributional effects of the internationalization of economic activity and the exercise of power by a dominant state or states in the world system.

The Surplus Product and the Terms of Trade

A simple linear economic model defines the formal determination of the surplus product.

Consider an ''economy'' producing a single output, grain, which is both consumed and used as an input into grain production (as seeds, or possibly as feed for otherwise self-reproducing draft animals).[5] We denote the grain good by the script H (indicating home country production to distinguish it from goods produced externally). The input-output relations governing grain production are summarized by:

a_{HH} = the amount (fraction of a bushel of grain used
in the production of a (gross) bushel of grain, and

l_H = the hours of labor time used in the production of a
(gross) bushel of grain.

Note that l_H is the inverse of gross grain output per work hour, which may be written as the product of the intensity of labor and the efficiency with which labor effort is transformed into gross output, or

$$l_H = 1/de$$

where

d = the effort per hour of labor worked (work *d*one), and

e = the gross output of good H per unit of effort (the *e*fficiency of the production process).

Consumption levels of the producers are summarized by

b_H = the amount of grain consumed per hour of work done.

An assessment of the surplus producing capacities of this system of production (denominated in H-good units) shows that an hour of labor produces:

$$y_H = de - de(a_{HH}) = de(1 - a_{HH}) = (1 - a_{HH})/l_H \qquad (1)$$

and the surplus per hour of labor employed is:

$$s_H = de\,(1 - a_{HH}) - b_H = (1 - a_{HH})/l_H - b_H. \qquad (2)$$

Where the latter expression is negative or zero, the production of a surplus is impossible. Where surplus output is negative the economy may be termed nonreproducing or infeasible.[6]

An equivalent condition is expressed in terms of the amount of corn required directly and indirectly to produce a bushel of corn:

$$s_H > 0 \text{ iff } 1 - (b_H l_{LH} + a_{HH}) = 1 - M_{HH} > 0 \qquad (3)$$

where the term M_{HH} is the total amount of grain required to produce a bushel of (gross) grain output (including the grain input into workers consumption, as well as seeds).[7]

Let us now allow our model economy, like virtually all economies, to engage in exchange with other producers and sellers (designated by the subscript F) located in a different economy (one under the jurisdiction of a different nation state).

A good produced outside this economy is now assumed to be necessary to the production of the home good and is also part of the wage bundle. Thus

a_{FH} = the amount of the externally produced good used to produce one unit of gross output of the home produced good.

b_F = the number of units of the externally produced good acquired by the workers per hour of labor performed.

p = the number of units of good H necessary to exchange in order to acquire one unit of good F, also known as the terms of trade (p may be zero, of course, indicating tribute or plunder).

Assume that the two elements of the hourly wage bundle (the domestically and externally produced goods) are consumed in fixed proportions. The real wage (denominated in units of grain) is $b_H + pb_F$.

The production of one unit of gross output of good H now requires M_{HH} units of the H-good as well as M_{FH} units of good F where

$$M_{FH} = a_{FH} + b_F l_H.$$

The amount of good H necessary to acquire this amount of good F in exchange is obviously pM_{FH}.

The surplus per unit of gross output of good H produced (denominated in units of good H) is now $1 - M_{HH} - pM_{FH}$, the surplus per hour of labor time, s_H, is thus

$$s_H = (1 - M_{HH} - pM_{FH})/l_H$$

and the total surplus product (using the uppercase S to denote the aggregate) is

$$S_H = L_H(1 - M_{HH} - pM_{FH})/l_H \tag{4}$$

where L_H is the total amount of labor employed in the production of the home good.

It can be seen from this expression that:

$$S_H \geq 0 \text{ iff } (1 - M_{HH}) \geq pM_{FH} \tag{5}$$

or if and only if the domestic surplus is more than is required at the terms of trade p to acquire enough of the externally produced good to replace the imported inputs used or used up in production

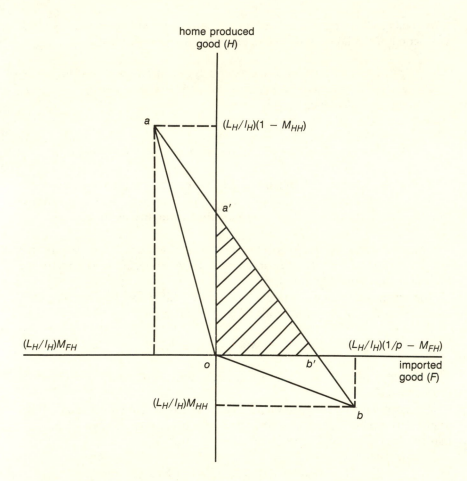

Figure 4.1. Surplus Production Possibility Set

The surplus producing capacity of the economy is represented in Figure 4.1. Surplus outputs are measured in the positive direction, while inputs are measured in the negative direction. The ray $0a$ is the vector of production and wage bundle coefficients representing domestic production.

The slope of the vector is $-(1 - M_{HH})/M_{FF}$, or the negative of ratio of the H-good surplus to the F-good inputs both expressed per unit of gross output. The total amount of labor employed, L_H, and the gross output per hour of labor hired, $l/(l_H)$ determine the length of the ray $0a$. The coordinates of point a indicate the surpluses of the H-good and the F-good generated when L_H worker hours are employed. The negative surplus of good F indicated at this point reflects the fact that the F-good used up in production is not being replaced. Point a is infeasible and hence not part of the surplus production possibility set: an economy producing at point a would be termed nonreproductive.

However, F-goods may be acquired by producing H-goods and exchanging them at the rate of p H-good per unit of F-good. The ray $0b$ represents this production and exchange opportunity; it may be considered a fictive production activity which hypothetically "produces" imports. It is identical to the ray $0a$ except that its "gross output" is $1/p$ units of F-goods rather than 1 unit of H goods. The line ab, with a slope $- p$, indicates the production and exchange opportunities at the terms of trade, p. The line $a'b'$ is the surplus production possibility frontier (SPPF): $0a'b'$ is the surplus production possibility set (SPPS). The level of the surplus, denominated in the H good is a'.

The condition for the existence of a surplus (equation 5) states that the slope of the production ray $0a$ must be steeper (in absolute value) than the exchange line (or SPPF) $a'b'$, or[8]

$$(1 - M_{HH})/M_{FH} \geq p. \tag{6}$$

Figure 4.1 does not tell us, of course, how the profit rate is determined: but it does tell us where to look to find out, and some of the likely international influences on the domestic profit rate. Thus, for example, we can trace the effects of an improvement in the terms of trade by simply rotating outward the surplus production possibility frontier, as is shown in Figure 4.2, thereby expanding the surplus production possibility set. The improvement in the terms of trade (fall in the real price of imports, p) is equivalent to a scalar improvement in the "productivity" of the fictive import producing sector of the economy.[9]

Profits, Wages and Work

Because variations in the level of aggregate demand (and hence in the level of capacity utilization) are not explicitly modeled here, it will simplify matters greatly at little cost if we assume a single year production period, so that all capital is circulating and none is fixed. Thus we can write the profit rate simply as the ratio of the surplus to the costs of production, or[10]

$$r = (1 - c)/c \tag{7}$$

where c is the cost (denominated in H-good units) of a unit of gross output:

$$c = M_{HH} + pM_{FH}. \tag{8}$$

Because the numerator of the profit rate is simply the point of intersection of

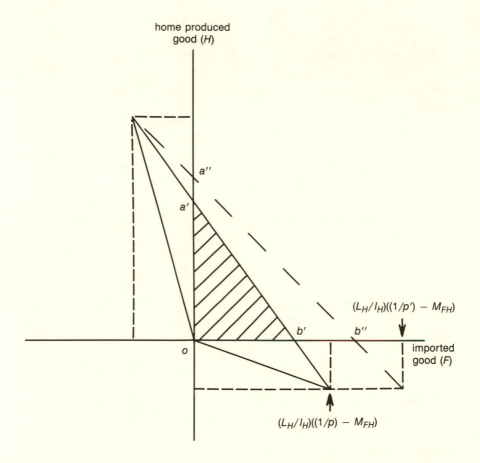

Figure 4.2. The Effect of an Improvement in the Terms of Trade

the vertical axis of Figures 4.1 and 4.2 with the surplus production possibility frontier for an economy arbitrarily scaled to produced a single unit of gross output, we can translate results from the surplus product analysis directly to results for the profit rate.[11] For example, it is clear from (7) and (8) that an improvement in the terms of trade (a reduction in p) will raise the profit rate. The increase in the profit rate is accounted for by the reduction in the real costs of both the wage bundle and the intermediate goods used in production.

Expressions (7) and (8) allow us to compile an exhaustive list of the determinants of the profit rate: the real wage bundle, the input-output coefficients, the amount of work done per hour, and the output per unit of work done—all of which make up the augmented input-out coefficients—and the terms of trade.[12]

Equations (7) and (8) also imply a well-defined relationship between the profit

Table 4.1

Determinants of the Profit Rate

b_F, b_H	The real wage bundle
e, a_{HH}, a_{FH}	Input-output coefficients
d	The intensity of labor (work done per hour)
p	The terms of trade

rate and the real wage per unit of work done. The expression for the profit rate indicates that for a given level of the input-output coefficients and the terms of trade, the profit rate will vary with the level of work intensity, d, and (inversely) with the wage bundle (b_H, b_F), an analogue to the more conventional real wage-profit frontier. Because the proportions of the wage bundle are assumed fixed, we can ignore the distinct components of the wage bundle and write b/d as an index of the real wage bundle per unit of work done. So as to focus on the interrelationship of domestic class conflict and international conflicts we will assume all of the determinants of the profit rate except b/d and p are exogenously determined and thus write what I will term the wage/work-profit relationship:

$$r = r(b/d, p, \ldots) \tag{9}$$

The rate of profit rate is thus determined in part through class conflict over the real wage and the intensity of labor. A critical determinant of working class bargaining power is the scarcity of labor, which I will represent simply as the ratio of labor hours employed to the potential labor force.[13] The potential labor force is itself variable, as high levels of labor demand will in the long run attract workers from other nations and noncapitalist forms of production internally (such as self-employment and domestic labor) and will generally foster cultural and institutional changes (in the structure of families and states, for example) facilitating increases in participation rates.

As the level of employment relative to the potential labor force rises—a depletion of the reserve army of the unemployed in Marx's terms—competition among employers for workers will intensify, and competition among workers for jobs will attenuate. Strikes and other forms of workers' collective and individual resistance to their employers demands will mount, along with the workers' own demands for better pay and a safer or less arduous pace of work. The result will be either an increase in the wage bundle, an improvement in working conditions reflected in a reduction in work intensity, or both.[14] Thus the wage/work bargain will be determined by j, the ratio of employment to potential employment, giving us what I will term—in honor of Marx's usage—the reserve army equation:

$$b/d = f(j, \ldots). \tag{10}$$

The level of demand for labor depends on the level of investment, which is itself a function of the rate of profit.[15] Let us assume that wealth holders throughout the world seek to invest their money at the highest expected return, regardless of location. The worldwide location of production will therefore respond more or less rapidly to the expected profit rate at each location.[16] It is plausible to represent the expected profit rate as dependent on the present profit rate and the degree of risk or uncertainty associated with it.[17] Thus representing the rate of growth of the inputs (including the wage goods) devoted to production as g, and labeling this interchangeably the rate of growth of the economy or the investment ratio, we have the employment function (11) and the investment function (12):

$$j = j(g, . . .) \tag{11}$$

$$g = g(r/\bar{r}, . . .) \tag{12}$$

where $\bar{r}$ is the rate of return in the rest of the world. For completeness we note that profits in the rest of the world move with the terms of trade, p, giving us the relationship $\bar{r} = \bar{r}(p, . . .)$.

The basic model of open economy growth and class conflict is represented by equations 9 through 12, combining the investment, employment, reserve army, and wage/work-profit functions. In Figure 4.3, the investment function in quadrant I (northeast) represents the relationship between the rate of growth of the economy, g and the profit rate. In quadrant II, the employment function is represented as a positive function of the rate of growth, but with employment always falling short of the potential labor force.[18] Quadrant III translates the resulting size of the reserve army to a class bargain concerning work intensity and the wage bundle. And quadrant IV is the wage/work-profit function.

By combing the employment, reserve army, and wage/work-profit functions we can write the profit rate as a function of the rate of growth of the economy in quadrant I, providing there is a convenient summary of two aspects of the model: profits as a function of growth and growth as a function of profits.

The wage/work level, profit rate, accumulation rate, and labor market scarcity indicated in Figure 4.3 are consistent, implying one and just one equilibrium; but there is no reason to expect this tidy result. Rather than explore the dynamic properties of this model here, however, I will illustrate some of the effects of the international economy on the distributional structure of this particular national economy.[19]

Internationalization of Capital and Class Conflict

We will explore two international influences on class conflict and the distribution of income: the exercise of world power by a dominant nation allows it to secure more favorable terms of trade, p, and at the same time facilitates the worldwide mobility of capital, in part by reducing the uncertainty and risk associated with

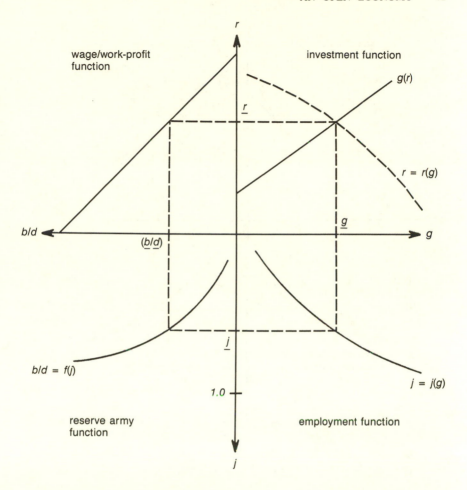

Figure 4.3. Overview of the Model

direct foreign investment in peripheral economies.[20]

If the wage bundle per unit of work done is constant, the proximate effect of an improvement in the terms of trade is simply an increase in the rate of profit.[21] The shift in the wage/work-profit relationship is indicated in Figure 4.4. Because the improvement in the terms of trade will lower profit rates in the rest of the world, thereby further raising the domestic relative profit rate, it will be accompanied by a rightward shift in the investment function. The increase in the rate of accumulation resulting from the increase in domestic profitability and the favorable shift in the investment function may be expected to deplete the reserve army and generate pressure for an increase in the wage relative to work done.[22]

If it were assumed—as many in the Keynesian tradition do—that domestic

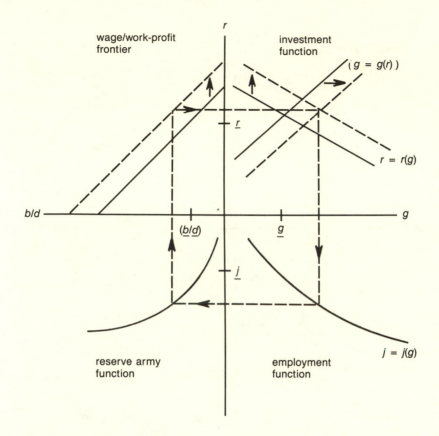

Figure 4.4. An Improvement in the Terms of Trade

Note: The dotted functions represent the new situation. The underbarred variables represent the initial values of the variables.

class struggle fixes the nominal rather than the real wage, then an improvement in the terms of trade would ceteris paribus raise the real wage, for the cheapening of imported wage goods (or goods indirectly used in the production of wage goods) would result in a reduction of the relevant consumer price index.[23] It is not obvious, however, why the real influences on the wage bargain should fix a nominal rather than a real quantity, and there is little empirical support for the strong form of money illusion applied by this variant of the model.

The internationalization of production accompanied by the global dominance of one or more capitalist states may reduce as well as argument the level of accumulation in the dominant countries. On the one hand, by making the entire world safer for private investment, it will reduce the degree of risk associated

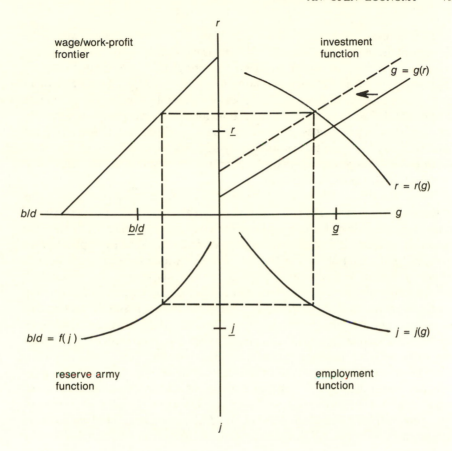

wage/work-profit
frontier

investment
function

$g = g(r)$

r

$r = r(g)$

b/d

$\underline{b/d}$

g

$\underline{g}$

b/d = f(j)

j

$j = j(g)$

reserve army
function

employment
function

j

Figure 4.5. Improved Investment Climate in Rest of World

with investment in the peripheral countries of the world system, thus tending to achieve a more nearly equal worldwide structure of expected profit rates through the relocation of production from the center to the periphery. On the other, by improving the terms of trade for the advanced capitalist countries (and still assuming no change in the real wage) it will raise profit rates in the advanced countries and lower them in the periphery, thus widening rather than narrowing the world spread of expected profit rates.

To summarize, the terms of trade effect will tend to raise the rate of accumulation in the dominant country. The ''making the world safe for private investment'' effect has the opposing impact, shifting the investment function to the left and resulting in a reduced level of accumulation domestically—and consequently a weakened bargaining position for domestic labor. This is illustrated in Figure 4.5.

The internationalization of economic activity will alter the slope as well as the position of the investment function. If capital is highly mobile internationally, the amount of investment in any given country may be a highly elastic function of the expected profit rate in that country relative to the analogous profit rates elsewhere in the world. Even if this mobility does not generate a common profit rate throughout the world, it will present each national economy with a very narrow range of feasible profit rates (or more precisely, profit rate expectations). In the limiting case of an infinitely elastic supply of funds there will be only one such profit rate that is reproducible in the long term.[24] The result is an infinitely elastic (horizontal) investment function.

In this case the unambiguously positive effect of an improvement in the terms of trade on domestic profits must be modified. The improvement of the terms of trade made possible by the international exercise of power will initially raise the profit rate in the dominant country, placing its profit rate (and by implication its expected profit rate) above the long-term rate at which the supply of funds is infinitely elastic. The relocation of world production toward this nation will continue until the profit rate is lowered or until some other aspect of the situation changes. In this case, as Figure 4.6 illustrates, the favorable shift in the terms of trade does not alter the profit rate in the long run, but raises the wage/work package and generates a rate of accumulation high enough to support the bargaining power of labor necessary to enforce this improved situation of workers.

A parallel effect of internationalization may be contemplated: labor supply may be internationalized. To make an extreme but illuminating case, assume that labor supply is highly responsive to changes in the wage/work package, and hence rises proportionally with labor demand, yielding a constant level of employment as shown in Figure 4.7.[25] In this case it is not the profit rate that is fixed by internationalization, but the wage/work package, for labor supply responds to labor demand in such a way as to maintain the bargaining power of the working class at a given level. Shifts in the terms of trade will generate changes in the profit rate, and hence in the rate of accumulation (assuming the investment function is not of infinite elasticity) which will then be accommodated by changes in the size of the potential labor force sufficient to offset the increased demand for labor and thus to maintain a constant wage-work package.

Finally, the more profit-rate-elastic is the investment function the more costly to workers will wage/work gains be in terms of employment losses. Thus a more open economy may reduce the wage-work package by shifting the relationship between the size of the reserve army and the bargaining strength of workers. It seems likely that the threat of losing ones job is considerably more ominous if the reason for job loss is capital flight or market penetration by external producers than the normal and presumably temporary cyclical movements of demand. Thus the internationalization of economic activity may have the effect of shifting the reserve army function in the third quadrant to the right, indicating a less favorable (to labor) wage/work bargain for a given labor market situation.

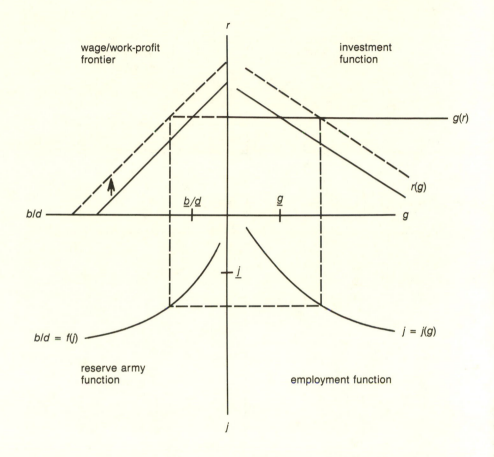

Figure 4.6. Improvement in the Terms of Trade: Global Hypermobility of Capital

Conclusion

A richer array of results and insights would no doubt be possible with a more complex model that accounted for monetary and aggregate demand aspects of the long-term growth problem. Nonetheless this simple model has identified five significant ways that the international economy may impact on the domestic class distribution of income: (1) shifts in the terms of trade affecting shifts in the wage/work-profit frontier; (2) shifts in the relative profit rates among the national economies that make up the world system, altering the rate of accumulation; (3) shifts in the profit rate elasticity of the accumulation function due to changes in the degree of global mobility of investment; (4) shifts in the level and wage/work elasticity of the potential labor force through variations in the conditions of international movement

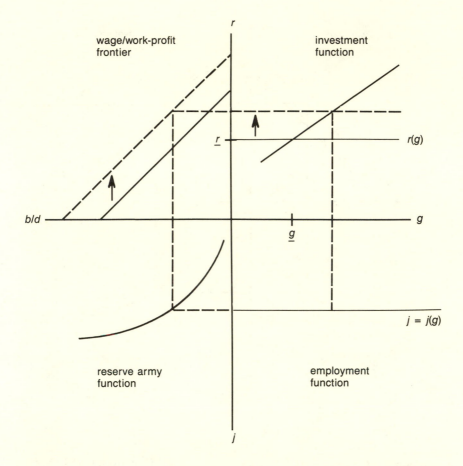

Figure 4.7. Improvement in the Terms of Trade: Global Hypermobility of Labor

of labor; and (5) shifts in bargaining power of labor due to the increased mobility of production.

The manner in which all of these effects interact is of course mediated not only through the individual and collective action of economic agents such as firms, individuals, and unions, but also through other forms of collective action, including military intervention, ideological leadership, and macroeconomic policies adopted by states. A significant advance in the theory of income distribution would be to model the manner in which these interventions and other forms of collective action may be considered endogenous to the income distribution problem. A second perhaps more modest project would be the careful international and historical comparative empirical estimation of the essential relationships identified in the model.

Notes

1. Open economy approaches to the study of class conflict within the Marxian tradition are hardly absent, as Lenin's theory of imperialism and the ample contemporary literature on dependency and unequal exchange testify.

2. The representation of profits as surplus product is purely heuristic and should be quite uncontroversial, for it amounts to little more than the statement that profits are value added minus wages. The representation of the wage-work relationship and the focus on classes are more uniquely Marxian in origin and play a more substantive role in the model.

3. The assumption of factor immobility which has been taken as the defining characteristic of international economic relations in the neoclassical tradition has long been questioned by those with a sense of the history of capitalism as a global system in which labor and credit are recruited on a world scale. See, for example, J. H. Williams, "The Theory of International Trade Reconsidered," *Economic Journal* 39 (June 1929): 195–209. If labor and capital as well as goods are internationally mobile, one might reasonably wonder what it is that distinguishes nations in the analysis that follows. The relatively limited mobility of labor and the existence of distinct states are the most obvious answers, suggesting that this approach is formally analogous to a hypothetical model of segmented labor markets with a distinct state for each labor segment.

4. I will address the issue of aggregate demand in a subsequent paper.

5. I assume that labor power is homogeneous, and that there are no nonreproduced means of production and no joint production.

6. The surplus product is generally a heterogeneous collection of outputs of distinct goods. But it may be aggregated and denominated in units of either labor or any nonluxury good. The units adopted for this purpose reflect the presuppositions of the theory rather than mathematical or economic analytical necessity. The conventional measurement of the surplus product in labor time units—surplus labor time—reflects the Marxian focus on the centrality of the labor process in understanding economic structure and dynamics. However, no particular purpose would be served here by expressing the surplus in labor time units.

7. This result is readily generalized to the multigood case: where M, the augmented input-output matrix, is composed of coefficients measuring the direct input requirements of production as well as the inputs required to pay the wage bundle required to hire the labor necessary to produce a unit of output in each sector. The maximal eigenvalue of M is an inverse measure of the surplus producing capacities of the economy, an eigenvalue of unity indicating the infeasibility of a surplus and an eigenvalue greater than unity indicating the nonreproducibility of the economy. See Andras Brody, *Proportions, Prices, and Planning: A Mathematical Restatement of the Labor Theory of Value* (Amsterdam: North Holland, 1968). This result may extend to the open economy case by representing imports as indirectly produced through the production and export of home-produced goods.

8. The production of the F-good domestically can also be represented in this quadrant; its production ray—constructed analogously to $0a$—would allow a comparison of the SPSS with and without international exchange.

9. A reduction in any input coefficients of M will—by a theorem of Frobenius—lower the maximal eigenvalue of M and hence raise the general profit rate. See Luigi Passinetti, *Lectures on the Theory of Production* (New York: Columbia University Press, 1977.) Thus the improvement in the terms of trade augments the profit rate in exactly the same manner that neutral technical progress will—in the absence of other changes—raise the profit rate.

10. The time structure of production implied is this: wages and other expenses are paid at the beginning of the production period and revenues on sales are received at the end. Profits are calculated as a percentage of labor as well as material costs.

11. The profit rate itself may also be represented in Figures 4.1 and 4.2 by defining a composition of the surplus (a point on the SPPF) such that the proportions of the surplus are identical to the composition of the inputs of the economy. The ratio of surplus to inputs will thus be identical for both goods and equal to the profit rate.

12. Where domestic production comprises a multiplicity of goods and where the import activity is represented in the augmented input-output matrix simply as pm, where m is the vector of export good coefficients, these are the terms that determine the magnitude of the maximal eigenvalue of M.

13. The potential labor force exceeds the number actively looking for work and those working, for it is defined to include all who would seek work if the economy were operating at full employment.

14. This interpretation of the determination of the real wage and work intensity receives empirical support for the U.S. economy in T. E. Weisskopf, "Marxian Crisis Theory and the Rate of Profit in the Postwar U.S. Economy," *Cambridge Journal of Economics* 3, no. 4 (1979): 341–78; Juliet Schor and Samuel Bowles, "Employment Rents and the Incidence of Strikes," *Review of Economics and Statistics* 62, no. 4 (November, 1987), 584-92; T. E. Weisskopf, David Gordon, and Samuel Bowles, "Hearts and Minds: A Social Model of U.S. Productivity Growth," *Brookings Papers on Economic Activity* 2 (1983): 381–450; James Rebitzer, "Unemployment, Long-term Employment Relations, and Productivity Growth," *Review of Economics and Statistics* 62, no. 4 (November, 1987); and Michele Naples "The Unraveling of the Union-Capital Truce and the U.S. Industrial Productivity Crisis," *Review of Radical Political Economics*, 18, nos. 1 and 2, (spring-summer 1986): 110–31.

15. This is a drastic simplification of employment determination, but it does capture much of the important long-run influences on employment. The relationship of the profit rate to the rate of accumulation is explored econometrically in Andrew Glyn, "The Oldest Relationship—Profitability and the Rate of Accumulation" (Oxford University, 1986, mimeo) and in Thomas Weisskopf, David Gordon, and Samuel Bowles, "A Conflict Theory of Investment" 1986, mimeo.

16. This long-run model assumes that the global relocation of production in response to differential profit rates, determines employment. If employment were determined in a Keynesian manner, by aggregate demand and the average product of labor, a more complex determination would be required. For example, the outward mobility of capital (ceterus paribus implying a reduction in the rate of growth of the domestic capital stock) requires that the capital-exporting country run an export surplus to effect the capital transfer. This will increase demand for labor in the capital-exporting country. But in a highly open world economy in the long run world demand and the country's competitive position in the world will determine the level of employment in each country. Needless to say, few if any economies exhibit this extreme degree of openness.

17. The proposition that the rate of accumulation in each country is responsive to profit rates elsewhere is supported in a number of recent empirical studies. See Tim Koechlin, "The Location of U.S. Direct Foreign Investment" (University of Massachusetts, 1987, mimeo); Edwin Melendez, "The Social Structure of Accumulation and the Postwar Boom in Puerto Rico" (Doctoral diss., University of Massachusetts, 1985). There is considerable evidence that domestic savings and investment are highly correlated across countries, suggesting to some that capital mobility is relatively limited. See Martin Feldstein and Charles Horioka, "Domestic Savings and International Capital Flows," *Economic Journal* 90 (1980): 314–29, and the subsequent literature referred to in Jeffrey Frankel, Michael Dooley, and Donald Mathieson, "International Capital Mobility in Developing Countries vs. Industrial Countries: What Do Savings-Investment Correlations Tell Us?" (Working Paper No. 2043, National Bureau of Economic Research. But if savings is not exogenous but rather (and more plausibly) strongly determined by income,

which is itself investment driven, this inference is unwarranted. Similar cautions apply to the presumed exogeneity of state policy.

18. The implication—that full employment is precluded as a long-term characteristic of the capitalist economy—is based on a conflict theory of the production process which entails nonclearing labor markets as an equilibrium result. See Samuel Bowles, "The Production Process in a Competitive Economy: Marxian, Walrasian, and NeoHobbesian Models," *American Economic Review* 75, no. 1 (March 1985): 16–36; and Samuel Bowles and Robert Boyer "Labor Discipline and Aggregate Demand: A Macroeconomic Model," *American Economic Review* (forthcoming), May 1988.

19. The analysis of the dynamic properties of the model would be a pointless and perhaps misleading exercise without consideration of a number of excluded elements, notably the endogenous interventions of the state in the distributional process.

20. In an illuminating paper, Thomas Riddell has demonstrated a strong relationship between U.S. military power and the U.S. terms of trade: "Testing Hypotheses about Military Spending" (Smith College, 1985, mimeo). Arghiri Emmanuel and the unequal exchange school explain the terms of trade largely in terms of differences in wages relative to labor productivity; these in turn may be explained in part by dominant country support for authoritarian antilabor social institutions in the peripheral countries. A general model of the determination of the terms of trade integrating firms' choice of optimal markups and optimal labor control strategies with variations in macroeconomic conditions and inter-state conflicts is presented in Samuel Bowles, "Price Wars: Contested Global Exchange and Contradictory Optimizing Rules" (University of Massachusetts, 1986, mimeo). These approaches—stressing military power and nonclearing markets—may be contrasted with the standard neoclassical determination of the terms of trade. See R. Findlay, "Fundamental Determinants of the Terms of Trade," in S. Grassman and E. Lundberg, eds., *The World Economic Order: Past and Prospects* (London: Macmillan, 1981).

21. The relationship between the terms of trade and the profit rate is demonstrated econometrically in Samuel Bowles, David Gordon, and Thomas Weisskopf, "Power and Profits: The Social Structure of Accumulation and the Profitability of the Post-War U.S. Economy," *Review of Radical Political Economics* 18, nos. 1 & 2 (Summer 1986): pp. 132–162.

22. This result differs from that of R. K. Sah and J. E. Stiglitz ("The Economics of Price Scissors," *American Economic Review* 74, no. 1 (March 1984): 125–38), who in their consideration of a series of propositions concerning the internal terms of trade in a closed two sector economy, find that an improvement in the terms of trade for the sector that employs labor will result in a larger surplus for that sector only if it lowers the real wage of the workers who are employed there. The difference is due to the assumed autarky of their economy and their use of domestic product market clearing (in a closed economy) to determine the real wage.

23. If imports are strictly luxuries which do not enter directly or indirectly into the workers' wage bundle, the real wage will be unaffected.

24. Of course the rates may differ from country to country depending on wealth holders' perceptions of the relative riskiness of investment in each country.

25. I will ignore the effects of changes in the terms of trade on the standard of living of workers in the rest of the world and the consequent effects on international labor supply.

PART I

COMMENTS:

Clayne Pope, Brigham Young University

These three papers by Professors Borjas, Bowles, and Brown represent markedly different views of the determinants of the distribution of income. This is to be expected since the distribution of income and wealth is the focus of much of the attack on capitalism. Moreover, the economics of distribution is one of the least developed areas of economic theory. As one reads papers representing three views of distribution economics with virtually no intersection of ideas, one naturally wonders whether or not economics will ever produce any convergence of thought in this area. This comment will discuss each paper in turn and then review the common empirical ground on which convergence should be sought— although it would be naive to expect such activity.

Professor Borjas' paper is a useful survey of some aspects of labor economics over the past three decades. Labor economics has certainly been one of the most "fertile" areas of economics with reintroduction of demographic behavior, spinning off of the new household economics, development of very important econometric techniques to solve problems of selection bias, presentation of an analytical framework to consider the economics of discrimination and, most importantly, development of a rich human capital model with schooling, on-the-job training, specific and general investment. Professor Borjas draws on most of these developments in his paper and makes many of the developments more accessible to economists not specializing in labor economics.

What is the essence of the surveyed material? There are two methdological guides. Agents maximize and markets equilibrate. This is certainly pure and undiluted neoclassical economics applied to individual and household behavior. Most of this analysis has been formed as an exercise in investment. Individuals choose varying amounts of schooling and on-the-job training, both of which are costly to obtain. Markets equilibrate by bringing the present value of earnings for alternative strategies into balance so that the net earnings streams from going to school or not going will be the same for a person with given characteristics. The most important caveat to the market equilibrium is the possibility that individuals will not be able to borrow sufficiently to reach equality of return for human and nonhuman capital. That is, the marginal return for some individuals will be higher on human capital than other assets.

What evidence exists to substantiate the basic model? Borjas argues, and I leave the challenge to other authors in this volume with a comparative advantage in attacking neoclassical models, that some empirical evidence supports the model. He views the age pattern of investment in human capital as weak evidence, but is more enthusiastic about the Mincer test at the overtaking point and the Willis-Rosen evidence that both those choosing college and those choosing not to attend were maximizing earnings. The accumulated empirical evidence does seem to support the proposition that individuals consider schooling and training as investment. Whether or not markets are bringing rates of return into equilibrium seems more open at this point. That is, the importance of the institutional constraints of the capital market appear unmeasured.

What are the implications of the neoclassical labor model for the distribution of economic well-being? Here Borjas deserts us to consider other interesting dimensions of labor economics such as job turnover, specific human capital and age profiles, and compensating differentials. But, amateurs in neoclassical labor economics really need to know how the human capital model guides thinking about and measuring of the distribution of economic well-being. Borjas does mention one implication: he observes that, because of investment in human capital, lifetime rather than annual earnings is the relevant unit to observe.

The discussion contains the most important implication of the model but does not highlight it as it should. In the neoclassical model, markets perform a leveling function, which reduces inequality. If the returns to a particular form of schooling are high, individuals will invest and the return will fall toward normal. Returns to education in general will be reduced to the return on other forms of capital. As long as an attribute may be acquired, the market forces drive the return to that attribute to the costs of acquisition.

What then will be the sources of inequality of lifetime earnings? Unfortunately, there is not much direct emphasis on this in the survey, although Becker's Woytinsky lectures, which are discussed briefly in Borjas' paper, point the way. Inequality will largely come from differing costs of acquisition of income-related attributes and from the returns to characteristics that are fixed and may not be discarded or acquired—such as ability, family background, initial location, cohort size, sex, and race. In short, rents accrue to these fixed characteristics. The size of the rents may be changed by the individual's choices about investment in human capital and shifts in labor demand. For example, technological change has probably increased the rent to intelligence and reduced the return to physical strength. Nevertheless, the rents pertain to the fixed characteristic and will not be eliminated by market forces. The other critical factor in addition to rents to fixed characteristics is the uneven access of individuals to capital for investment in human capital.

Much has been done since Becker's Woytinsky lectures to measure the effect on income of rent-producing characteristics such as ability, family background, race, or sex. Perhaps these studies were omitted from the survey because they do not represent the neoclassical model where individuals maximize and markets equilibrate. But that is precisely the point. Once one accepts a model where individuals maximize and markets equilibrate, attention relative to the distribution of economic well-being will be directed away from choices where the market will level returns and toward the non-choice elements of the story, which the market will not level. Professor Borjas' survey is an interesting discussion of the neoclassical theory choice-making, but, in my view, does not help us to understand the implications of the theory for income distribution.

The Bowles paper poses the following question: How is the Marxian model of the expropriation of surplus labor time altered by assuming the economy to be part of a world capitalist system? The paper first sets up a standard model in the Marxist tradition and then extends that model to consider the key issue of the effect of trade on the rate of profit and the real wage. Except for the obvious point that if the real wage is constant, an improvement in the terms of trade increases the rate of profit, the modeling stops short of this real issue.

The critical problem in Marxist models is the determination of the wage. When one considers physical characteristics such as life expectation or nutritional status, then the wage necessary for reproduction of the labor force has an empirical base that can be grafted to the model. The rise of the real wage from the early nineteenth century to the present forced abandonment of an empirically based reproductive wage. However, once the wage is "socially determined" or equal to "some customary norm" to use Professor Bowles' terms, it is not possible to simply take that wage as a datum. Rather, the real wage should be endogenous to the model.

The most interesting part of this paper is the discussion of the effect of international capital flows. In Professor Bowles' view, these flows affect the bargaining power of labor and increase or decrease the real wage and, therefore, the rate of profit. Imperialistic flows of capital out of advanced countries will reduce the demand for labor and weaken its bargaining power in those countries. Presumably the effect is opposite in the dominated country. Use of imperialistic power to improve the terms of trade will increase the rate of profit in the advanced country, causing a capital inflow that will increase the real wage so that labor benefits from the imperialistic adventures of the country. Capitalists also benefit so both capital and labor are sharing the "superprofits" from the power to control the terms of trade. The stability of the system hinges on equal rates of profit across countries. This discussion raises the question of the effect of domestic capital flows. Do rates of profit equalize across industries, firms, and states? If so, such flows would act as a constraint against expropriation of the surplus by capital. All of these issues go back to the basic problem of the determination of the wage—a lacuna in Marxian theory that needs attention.

There appear to be two key elements in Professor Brown's institutional theory of distribution. Unemployment and underemployment always exist, so jobs must be rationed by a mechanism other than price. Jobs, not individuals, have product so that institutional structures rather than individual behavior are the key to the model. The ebb and flow of unemployment determines the split of product between capital and labor. The continual underemployment means that good jobs must be rationed by institutions since wages and competitive markets are assumed to be ineffective at this task. Professor Brown's paper does not clarify the way in which social institutions perform this rationing task although the nature of this rationing is central to the determination of the distribution of earnings. Once the jobs have been filled, the lucky individuals with good jobs develop and appear to be competent and productive while equally competent people are left underemployed. A puzzle in this description does not explain why individuals are given access to jobs rather than being required to pay for that access. Surely, entrepreneurs would like to pay less to its employees if possible. Why do they not do so or hire the underemployed at a lower wage? A description of the institutional theory needs to deal with this lack of information.

One of the central elements of the institutional description of the distribution of income is the attachment of productivity to jobs rather than individuals. This is a seductive notion. Economists would like to think we would have the same product as more notable economics professors if only we were tenured at a more prestigious department. Unfortunately, such departments remain wedded to the neoclassical notion that productivity is embedded in the individual. It is difficult to accept the view that all or even most productivity differences are associated with the job rather than the individual. Yet, there is something to the notion that some productivity comes out of position. Hierarchy is a familiar and evidently useful form of organization in many though not all contexts. Certainly, positioning of individuals within a hierarchy is partially stochastic. Hierarchy has some effect on job productivity although I would be hesitant to ascribe it a dominant role in the explanation of productivity.

From the viewpoint of an economic historian, one argument in Brown's paper seems particularly doubtful—that the income of a typical semiskilled wage earner was inadequate to meet a "needs-based budget" prior to 1950 but was adequate after that time. Historical indications show that the real wage rose rather steadily in the U.S. from the early nineteenth century to the present. Indices of physical well-being such as life expectation and nutritional status also were rising for much of this period, certainly for all of the twentieth century. So-called needs usually are defined relative to the general population. The institutionalist story does not require this argument nor acceptance of a Dusenberry view of income in contradistinction to the more relative view of income. These points simply detract from the argument.

At various points in the Brown paper, there is a comparison of institutional theory with neoclassical theory, but the comparisons usually are rhetorical and misstate the neoclassical model. A description of that model as regarding every-one as equal at age 18 will be a shock to a lot of people who have worked long and hard, if not always successfully, to remove the influence of ability and family background from the measured effect of education on earnings. Gary Becker might be surprised to learn that neoclassical theory concludes that "unfulfilled human potential is not seen as a serious problem, since it results from lack of motivation as opposed to lack of opportunity." Becker has looked to differential access to investment funds as a primary consideration in explaining both cross-sectional and intergenerational inequality. To say that "income distribution re-flects the outcome of individual choices in a competitive market" in a neoclassi-cal world does not do justice to the emphasis that neoclassical theory places on the operation of the market itself on the outcome and on the importance of nonchoice elements. The characterization of the neoclassical model in this paper is certainly a straw man.

What do these three approaches to distributional economics have in common? Very little at this point. The neoclassical model emphasizes individual maximiza-tion and achievement of market equilibrium. The Marxist model emphasizes labor production of a surplus and its capture by capitalists. The institutional model focuses on the creation of a viable and consistent social structure to ration scarce jobs. The common ground of the three approaches appears to be limited to the use of words and some numbers to talk about the same phenomena—jobs and wages.

Consensus should be sought through the empirical record. Advocates of each view should be required to make their story consistent with satisfactory explana-tions of historical and contemporary patterns in the distribution of earnings, income, and wealth. Some of the important empirical patterns that should disci-pline all three views of distributional economics include:

1. *Rising real wages.* The most striking economic phenomenon of the past two centuries is the unprecedented rise in real wages and associated increase in well-being measured by almost any index.

2. *Constancy of labor's share.* Shares of output received by inputs have varied over time, but most of the change has involved land and capital, with labor generally maintaining its proportion. None of the three viewpoints adequately explains this phenomenon.

3. *Long-run pattern of inequality.* Distributions of income display remark-able stability over decades, but there is a long-run pattern that seems general. During the process of development, inequality rises for a time and then declines. This pattern, referred as the Kuznets' "U," holds for the U.S. as well as other countries.

4. *Substantial economic mobility.* Both contemporary and historical studies point to substantial occupational mobility. Mobility within wealth and income distributions is also quite impressive. Models emphasizing class and institutional barriers must be reconciled to this documented mobility.

5. *Importance of family background.* Most studies measuring the effect of family background conclude that it accounts for a significant portion of the variance in earnings, income, or wealth. Given the economic importance of family background and intergenerational transfers, models need to incorporate family behavior to explain patterns of inequality and mobility successfully.

6. *Substantial intergenerational mobility.* The limited number of studies of the economic position of parents relative to their children document regression toward the mean in the distributions of income and wealth.

These and other empirical findings should form the basis for modeling the distributions of earnings, income, and wealth with consensus sought through empirical verification of proposed explanations. Acceptance of any of the three views of distribution presented should be contingent on the ability of any view to accommodate the empirical facts. Obviously, it is unlikely that the debate over distribution will be conducted on empirical ground as long as these three ideologies continue to influence and divide participants.

Robert S. Goldfarb, George Washington University

In the version of her paper given at the conference, Clair Brown sets forth one feature of the institutional model as "the assumption that the labor market is characterized by unemployment and underemployment." She goes on to argue that the assumption of underemployment implies "rationing of workers into unequal positions. . . . The rationing process is formed by the institutional structure. . . . Social rules and customs (i.e., institutions) perform the rationing process. . . ." I cannot comment on the aptness of this description of the institutional model, since I do not know whether it would be accepted by most analysts who call themselves institutionalists. My comment instead concerns an analytical bridge between a neoclassical framework and Brown's stress on rationing of job positions. Such bridges or connections are worth recognizing because such recognition can lead to sharper understandings of shared features and crucial discrepancies between analytical frameworks. Indeed, developing such understandings would seem an important aim of this conference.

Recent work in labor economics by individuals who must in the context of this conference be called neoclassical has focused on the firm's staffing problem in the presence of uncertainty about applicant productivity on the job and applicant propensity to quit. Where productivity per period is uncertain and employee quitting is costly to the firm because of the existence of hiring and training costs, staffing strategies that raise applicant quality or lower the quit propensities of the applicant pool may be cost minimizing. One line of analysis[1] bases such a strategy on the idea that the productivity of particular applicants cannot be easily ascertained by the firm, but a higher wage results in a higher quality (average productivity) applicant pool because individuals' acceptance wages are correlated with their productivity. Since not all firms will need labor of higher quality, not all firms will use this "high-wage" strategy. That is, some firms will be high wage and have applicant queues, while others will not.

Another line of analysis that can produce high-wage firms with queues starts from Walter Oi's[2] stress on hiring and training costs. Once these costs are recognized, it can be shown that firms with sizable hiring and training costs and quit rates sensitive to wage levels may find it cost minimizing to pay wages above the level needed to obtain enough applicants. So long as the higher wage reduces turnover costs (through reducing quits) by more than it raises the wage bill, it will be cost minimizing to offer the higher wage. A large body of literature implies the existence of some high-wage firms with applicant queues.[3]

Several comments abut this framework are in order. First, a recent review article by Janet Yellen of what she calls "efficiency wage models of unemployment" identifies several other lines of analysis that have some firms setting "high" wages.[4] Second, the idea that some but not all firms are high wage is consistent with casual empiricism about the labor market and such nonneoclassical analyses as the dual labor market hypothesis. Moreover, Albert Rees's classic article[5] explaining screening devices (a type of rationing rule widely observed in "the real world") as a way employers have of coping with uncertainty about applicant quality *presumes* a world in which some firms have excess applicants and must screen out some of them. Thus, Rees's analysis—and the very existence of screening devices—only makes sense in a world where some firms are so attractive that they draw excess applicants; such firms must by definition be paying wages above those needed to attract "just enough" applicants.

Thus, neoclassical analysis of a world with turnover costs and uncertainty about applicant quality suggests that some firms will set "high" wage levels, producing applicant queues at these firms. This provides an important point of contact with Brown's institutional analysis. She stresses the existence of underemployment and "rationing of workers into unequal positions." But that is quite consistent with the neoclassical "high-wage firm" scenario. If some firms with desirable high-wage jobs have applicant queues, then those jobs will indeed have to be rationed! Thus, this imperfect information neoclassical framework has rationing of "good" jobs, just as Brown's institutional framework requires. Moreover, since good jobs are rationed, those turned away from the firms with good jobs could certainly be called "underemployed" if they could have done the job at the high-wage firm but end up in less attractive jobs.

Brown's institutional model stresses that "social rules and customs (i.e., institutions) perform the rationing process." While some neoclassical literature is totally silent on how the rationing is done, work such as Rees's 1966 article tries to relate the widely observed institutional rationing rule known as a screening device to underlying behavior consistent with cost-minimization in the face of uncertainty. In any case, this bridge between the Brown and the neoclassical high-wage framework does suggest two important issues of interest to both lines of inquiry: (1) Since both frameworks recognize rationing of jobs, what more concrete theoretical results can each produce about what kinds of rationing devices are used, and how do those theoretical results check out empirically? (2) If information on actual rationing devices at actual high-wage firms or groups of firms could be collected, each framework could see how well it could do at explaining why those particular rationing devices were in fact chosen (this is in the spirit of Rees's 1966 article). This second issue in particular indicates the usefulness of finding out how actual firms actually do make these rationing choices.

Notes

1. See, for example, Andrew Weiss, "Job Queues and Layoffs in Labor Markets With Flexible Wages," *Journal of Political Economy* (June 1980): 526–38. Weiss's work builds on George Akerlof's stress on the effects of asymmetric information on the way that markets operate; see Akerlof's "The Market for 'Lemon's': Quality Uncertainty and the Market Mechanism," *Quarterly Journal of Economics* (August 1970): 488–500. In the Weiss case, a productive worker not hired by a high wage firm cannot successfully offer to work at a lower wage, because the firm will view his lower-wage offer as an indication that he is a lower-productivity "lemon."

2. Walter Oi's original article is "Labor as a Quasi-Fixed Factor," *Journal of Political Economy* (December 1961): 538–55. That article does *not* focus on the wage-setting implications of hiring and training costs.

3. Among many articles that do are S. C. Salop "Wage Differentials in a Dynamic Theory of the Firm," *Journal of Economic Theory* (August 1973): 321–44; J. Pencavel, "Wages, Specific Training, and Labor Turnover in U.S. Manufacturing Industries," *International Economic Review* (February 1972): 53–64; and D. Hamermesh and R. Goldfarb, "Manpower Programs in a Local Labor Market: A Theoretical Note," *American Economic Review* (September 1970): 705–9.

4. Janet Yellen, *American Economic Review* (May 1984): 200–205.

5. Albert Rees, "Information Networks in Labor Markets," *American Economic Review* (May 1966): 559–66.

Bruce Elmslie, University of Utah

Professor Brown's fine paper has three expressed purposes which she develops within an institutional framework of income distribution. First, "the relationship between income distribution, class conflict, and the standard of living is explored [by] looking at the role of income distribution in the functioning of the economy." Second, she addresses "the political implications of the institutional model." And third, she compares the "assumptions of the institutional and neoclassical model." In this comment I will focus on the second purpose, describing the political implications of the model to show a conflict between the institutionalist's assumptions on how government uses its power, and the policy conclusions the institutionalist advocates, specifically those to ensure full employment.

Professor Brown clearly states the important role government plays in determining market outcomes when she writes "since institutional theory assumes that government plays a necessary and important role in creating the structure within which the economy functions government is largely responsible for labor market outcomes." Government's role "is to create and preserve the social rules and mechanisms by which people are prepared for and accept their social and work roles. . . ." This function of government to create an atmosphere that allows people to accept social and work roles takes many forms. One is the preservation of social and class distinctions through the protection of property rights. It also takes the form, in times of full employment, of decreasing levels of employment by generating unemployment and underemployment "in order to restore capital's control over rising workers expectations." Thus unemployment is "instigated by the government to weaken labor's wage demands."[1] We see that in an institutionalist world, government uses unemployment to preserve the class structure and thus the social order. This is a major goal of government in a capitalist economy.

In a capitalist economy, unemployment is accepted by the institutionalist as an effective and socially useful means of preserving the social order by preserving the subordination of labor to capital. As Kalecki argued, "The assumption that a Government will maintain full employment in a capitalist economy if it only knows how to do it is fallacious."[2] This point of view, to which Professor Brown clearly adheres throughout most of her paper, is suddenly dropped when she states that "full employment is achieved in an institutional world through a *more* structured economy." This full employment is "achieved" by a grand contradiction indeed. To ensure full employment we must rely on the two groups in society that will always oppose it. Professor Brown states that "the Institutionalists predicted that increased output [increasing levels of employment] would allow increased equality." But she has already stated that government will not allow periods of high output to continue for long periods of time. On the one hand we are to rely on the further integration of government and business to gain the stability necessary for full employment to be possible while, on the other hand we know that these groups will never advocate policies designed to achieve long-term levels of full employment. This is a contradiction that growth cannot solve.

I have tried to show that a flaw exists in the internal logic of the Professor Brown-style institutionalist model. She argues, using a Kaleckian framework, that it is not in the interests of either government or industry to ensure full employment under capitalism. Unemployment is used as a tool by government "to weaken wage demands." With this established, Professor Brown contradicts herself by arguing that full employment will be achieved "through a more structured economy." The term "structured" is taken to mean an economy in which government and industry are integrated to formulate market outcomes, because "in an institutional world, the idea of government "intervention" in the economy is absurd, since a modern industrial economy cannot exist without the structure created and maintained by the government.''

The contradiction that full employment is to be ensured by a reliance on a structured economy composed of two forces that don't want and will not accept full employment must be solved in one of two ways: (1) Drop the essentially correct assumption that capitalist governments generate systematic unemployment to dampen wage demands and defuse ''workers' militancy.'' (2) Drop the assumption that ''structured'' capitalism can and will generate long-term levels of full employment.

Because of the inherent instability of capitalism acknowledged by disposing of the second assumption, capitalism must, in the long run, move to some form of socialism or fascism. Given the current political reality, the latter possibility seems most likely. I sincerely hope that Professor Brown's ''structured economy'' somehow holds together long enough for today's political reality to change.

Notes

1. This line of argument is extremely close to Kalecki's analysis of the political business cycle. He writes that ''the maintenance of full employment would cause social and political changes which would give a new impetus to the opposition of the business leaders. Indeed, under a new regime of permanent full employment, 'the sack' would cease to play a role as a disciplinary measure. . . . Strikes for wage increases and improvements in conditions of work would create political tension.'' He then reiterates that ''The workers would 'get out of hand' and the 'captains of industry' would be anxious to 'teach them a lesson.' '' Michal Kalecki, ''Political Aspects of Full Employment,'' *Selected Essays on the Dynamics of the Capitalist Economy* (Cambridge, England: Cambridge University Press, 1971): 140–141, and p. 144 respectively.

2. Kalecki, 138.

RACIAL WAGE GAP

PAPERS

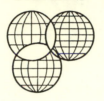

PART II

5

RACIAL DISCRIMINATION
A HUMAN CAPITAL PERSPECTIVE

James P. Smith and Finis R. Welch

At its core, the human capital approach to race is quite simple. It is a skill-based theory that asserts that if you want to understand the racial wage gap and the way it is changing, you must understand why the races differ in marketable skills and how skill differences change over time. In part, allegiance to theories determines research emphasis and dictates where one decides to devote scarce research energies and resources. Those of us with a human capital emphasis spend much of our research time worrying about how to more accurately measure skills and how markets translate those skills into earnings. In essence, the human capital approach is a belief that skills matter. Economists who attend different churches are betting that exploring the reasons for the lack of mobility between sectors or the constraints imposed by institutions represents the key to further progress on the economics of race.

Theories that attract interest don't claim to be able to successfully resolve all puzzles and answer all questions. The human capital approach to race is certainly no exception. Its current explanatory scope is incomplete; it also confronts major empirical regularities that appear contradictory to its main themes. The importance of the issues and a sense that the challenges may be amenable to resolution through continued research are what attracts us to this topic. And the occasional successes sustain continued effort.

In this paper, we claim that the skill-based theory has made significant recent advances in resolving three long-standing challenges to its validity. These challenges are (1) its ability to explain long-term historical trends in black-white

James Smith is a Senior Economist at the Rand Corporation; Finis Welch is associated with the Unicon Research Corporation and the University of California at Los Angeles.

income differences, (2) its reliance on schooling as its primary empirical weapon, and (3) its contention, counter to the secondary labor market view, that once starting conditions are taken into account, blacks and whites face similar career job prospects.

This paper can probably best be described as an autobiographical survey. We rely almost exclusively on our own past and current research to make our points and document our claims. This reliance should be taken as evidence of ease of access and not as a slight on the considerable volume of valuable work done by others. We also consciously try to demonstrate the value of the human capital approach solely on its own merits; we ignore the ability of failure of other theories to account for similar phenomena.

The paper is divided into five sections. The first presents a brief summary of existing literature relating to the three challenges listed above. Next, we present some new evidence of time series trends in racial income disparities derived from the 1940–80 census micro data files. The final three sections deal sequentially with the three challenges confronting a human capital approach to race.

Background

Three basic problems with the human capital approach to race have surfaced. The first, and perhaps most fundamental, is that the long-term relative income and relative skill series seemed inconsistent. Until the acceleration in black incomes during the mid–1960s, it is argued that, at best, black incomes barely kept pace with those of whites. In contrast to this stability in relative racial incomes, there has been a steady long-term convergence in skills. This skill convergence is especially apparent if we use education to proxy human capital. A number of studies consistently showed a continuous narrowing of racial education differences throughout the twentieth century. This apparent contradiction between the relative skill and income series cast serious doubt on the historical applicability of the human capital perspective applied to race.

The other two problems disputed the empirical importance and relevance for blacks of human capital's two empirical constructs—education and on-the-job-training. Early empirical studies consistently showed an almost minuscule effect of schooling on black earnings.[1] This pessimism was deepened later by the work of Coleman, Jencks, and others,[2] suggesting that manipulating school attributes had little impact on student performance. If schools had little economic payoff for blacks, the situation was far worse when attention shifted to job investments. Here, there was no dispute. All empirical studies indicated that the incomes of black males increased with age at a significantly slower rate than those of whites. In summary, the minor historical relevance of human capital seems consistent with contemporary data indicating that investments in skill—either in school or on the job—were not a reliable vehicle for black economic mobility.

Ashenfelter first pointed out the historical problem with contemporary human capital studies of race:

> Where does this leave us? In my view, it leaves us with a considerable puzzle. Attributing the steady increase in relative earnings to the gradual increase in their skills (as measured, say, by schooling) requires an explanation of why the gradual increase in skills of black men had so little effect on their relative earnings before the mid 1960s.[2]

The basic issue raised by Ashenfelter is simple. With each successive birth cohort in this century, racial differences in education levels narrowed, until a 3.5-year gap for those born between 1907–16 had been reduced to only a 1.1-year advantage for white men born between 1947–51. Using education as the index, the human capital disadvantage for blacks has continuously narrowed. But Ashenfelter argued that before 1960 there was little change in relative incomes by race. The documentation of the income side of the argument is fuzzy. But post–World War II data does show little appreciable rise in relative incomes of black men until the mid–1960s. The evidence before 1948 was largely circumstantial. But the scanty evidence that did exist, and certainly a reading of the masterworks, indicated long-term stagnation in black economic status.

Two prominent scholars, Robert Fogel and Stanley Engerman, state at the end of *Time on the Cross*:

> It appears that the life expectations of blacks declined by 10 percent between the last quarter century of the antebellum era and the last two decades of the nineteenth century. The diet of blacks deteriorated. Studies of the diet of black sharecroppers in the mid–1980s indicate that they were protein- and vitamin-starved. The health of blacks deteriorated. Sickness rates in the 1890s were 20 percent higher than on slave plantations. The skill composition of the black labor force deteriorated. Blacks were squeezed out of some crafts in which they had been heavily represented during the slave era and were prevented from entering the new crafts that arose with the changing technology of the last half of the nineteenth century and the first half of the twentieth. The gap between wage payments to blacks and whites in comparable occupations increased steadily from the immediate post-Civil War decades down to the eve of World War II. It was only with World War II that this trend reversed itself. And it is only during the last fifteen years that the reduction in the differential has accelerated to an extent that equality in wage payments for blacks and whites in comparable occupations seems once again in sight.[3]

In a similar vein, after summarizing the post–Civil War history of blacks, Gunnar Myrdal concluded:

The picture of the economic situation of the Negro people is dark. The prospects for the future—as far as we have been able to analyze the trends until now—are discouraging.[4]

The earliest cross-sectional attempts at a human capital explanation for racial income differences were also not encouraging. Morton Zeman's 1955 dissertation, a detailed and careful analysis of the 1940 census, served as the standard empirical reference until the micro-level 1960 census tapes became available. Whether the added skill involved an extra year in school or another on the job, Zeman reported that black-white income ratios declined by one-third of 1 percent for every 1 percent rise in white income. The elimination of racial differences in schooling or age would have reduced the southern racial income gap by less than one-quarter and that in the North by about 5 percent. Essentially, Zeman's work implied that giving blacks the same amount of schooling as whites would do little to alter racial income disparities. The problem, rather, was different pay for the same skill and differential racial payoffs to acquiring more skill.

Throughout the 1950s, events appeared to confirm Zeman's research. Studies based on the 1950 and 1960 censuses indicated that, if anything, there may have been a deterioration in the relative economic position of blacks. The initial micro-level studies based on the 1960 census, such as those by Hanoch and Thurow[5], did little to amend this view. Their work once again painted a consistent picture of low returns to schooling for blacks as well as a sharp deterioration in relative black economic potential over job careers. In light of these findings, economic literature concentrated on reasons for racial differences in the value of skill. On the schooling dimension, market discrimination against black skilled labor was advanced to explain declining black-white income ratios with schooling. On the job investment side, discrimination-based theories dominated, either using the language of denying blacks access to jobs with human capital growth (for human capital advocates) or simply confining blacks to secondary labor markets.

The human capital perspective had a partial resurgence during the late 1960s and early 1970s. Micro analysis based on the 1967 and 1970 censuses indicated that rates of return to education, especially at upper schooling levels, appeared as high for blacks as for whites. In addition, reanalysis of the 1960 census revealed that first-generation studies had significantly understated rates of return to education for blacks.[6] On the issue of job-related investments, Welch pointed out that cross-sectional data showing declining black-white income ratios with age may not reflect life-cycle factors at all if changes across birth cohorts are larger for blacks than whites. There was evidence that over recent years, black male incomes did not fall behind those of comparable whites as their careers evolved, lending some support to a cohort interpretation of the cross-sectional deterioration of relative black incomes with age.[7]

These studies are not completely persuasive. Their major limitation is that they were confined to the 1960s and 1970s, a period that many regarded as unique in terms of sustained improvement in black incomes. This recent human capital work left unresolved the apparent long-time contradiction between the skill and income series. Alternative explanations that were unique to the last two decades were put forward. Regarding education, it was argued that the pro-skill bias of affirmative action pressures might account for the rise in black schooling coefficients. Similarly, affirmative action pressures to promote blacks in a nondiscriminating fashion may indicate that the race neutral career wage growth of the last two decades was unique to this time period.

New Evidence on the Racial Wage Gap

There is increasing recognition that the resolution of the debates about the sources of black-white income differences lies not with the examination of contemporary data. Instead, there is far more scientific promise in data from earlier periods of American history, such as two prominent explanations for the narrowing of the racial income gap—affirmative action[8] and the labor market withdrawal of low-income blacks[9]—that both rely on events unique to the 1960s and 1970s.

Monitoring the long-term evolution of racial income disparities makes events unique to our own day less seductive explanations. Moreover, data that span half a century or more allow us to better evaluate theories in terms of their relative historical importance. The recent release of the micro data files from the 1940 and 1950 censuses makes such an effort possible, while still maintaining labor economists' insistence on high-quality nationally representative data. In this section, we summarize some of our recent work based on the micro-data files of the 1940–80 U.S. censuses.

Table 5.1 depicts our estimates of black-white male weekly wage ratios from each of the decennial census tapes.[10] Ratios are listed for five-year intervals of years of work experience,[11] and the final row contains relative wages aggregated across all experience classes.

Table 5.1 points to a very impressive rise in the relative economic status of black men over this forty-year time span. Between these forty years, black male wages increased 52 percent faster than those of whites. In 1940, the average wage of black men was only 43 percent of the average for whites. By 1980, it was 73 percent.

The pace at which blacks have been able to narrow the wage gap is far from uniform. The largest improvement occurred during the 1940s, a decade that witnessed a 25-percent expansion in the relative wages of black men.[12] These advances slowed considerably during the 1950s, when the narrowing of racial wage disparities was quite modest. The years after 1960 signalled a return to more rapid wage growth among black men. During both the 1960s and 1970s, the rise in black wages was more than 10 percent higher than for whites.

We have contrasted the average black and white worker—but such comparisons do not address the question of whether all segments of the black community

Table 5.1

Black Male Wages as a Percentage of White Male Wages: 1940–1980

Years of market experience	Census years				
	1940	1950	1960	1970	1980
1–5	46.7	61.8	60.2	75.1	84.2
6–10	47.5	61.0	59.1	70.1	76.6
11–15	44.4	58.3	59.4	66.2	73.5
16–20	44.4	56.6	58.4	62.8	71.2
21–25	42.3	54.1	57.6	62.7	67.8
26–30	41.7	53.2	56.2	60.6	66.9
31–35	40.2	50.3	53.8	60.0	66.5
36–40	39.8	46.9	55.9	60.3	68.5
All	43.3	55.2	57.5	64.4	72.6

Source: Public use tapes of the decennial censuses 1940–80.

Table 5.2

Extent of Overlap between Black and White Income Distributions

	% of black men whose income exceeds white income			% of white men whose income exceeds black income		
	bottom quarter	median	top quarter	bottom quarter	median	top quarter
1980	56	29	10	87	70	45
1970	45	22	5	90	78	57
1960	38	12	1	92	81	66
1950	36	12	2	92	82	66
1940	31	8	1	95	84	70

shared in this economic resurgence. While average white incomes are well in excess of those achieved by the average black, income distributions of the black and white populations have always overlapped. Table 5.2 summarizes the extent of this overlap. The left-hand side of the table measures the proportion of black men with income exceeding three critical values in the white income distribution—the bottom quartile, the median, and the top quartile. For example, 29 percent of black men had incomes larger than the average (median) white man in 1980. The right-hand side of the table indicates the fraction of white men with incomes that exceed the same critical values within the black income distribution.

The complete set of overlap statistics are displayed in Figure 5.1, where the graphs resemble and indeed are close analogs to Lorenz curves. Each line designates the fraction of one population (vertical axis) whose incomes exceed the indicated quantile (horizontal axis) of the population against which it is plotted. The lines below the diagonal plot black people against white income. For example, by extending a vertical line up from the 50th percentile, the first graphed line shows that in 1940 only about 8 percent of the black men had incomes that exceeded the white median. Conversely, the lines above the diagonal plot white people against black income quantiles. Extending the 50th-percentile line shows that in 1940 about 92 percent of the whites had earnings above the black median. We call line pairs like those for 1940 dominance plots, cross-cumulatives, or simply left-handed Lorenzes.

Notice that the 45° line implies coincident distributions. A cross-sectional that is everywhere below the 45° line shows that the distribution whose population is referenced by the vertical axis is inferior in the sense that the cumulative lies everywhere to the left of the corresponding distribution for the population whose quantiles are indexed on the horizontal axis.

There is unambiguous convergence toward equality only when the dominance plots shift inward toward the 45° line. Otherwise, if dominance plots for one period intersect those for another, indexes can disagree as to whether or not there has been movement toward equality.

The degree to which the two income distributions overlapped in 1940 was quite small. If income is the measuring rod, black and white men were indeed divided into two separate and unequal societies in 1940. In that year, only one in every twelve black men earned incomes larger than the average white. The view from the other side was equally stark. Among white men, 70 percent had incomes exceeding the top quarter of blacks.

Figure 5.1 indicates that, although racial income distributions are by no means identical, they have converged dramatically across these forty years. For example, on both sides of the diagonal, our relative Lorenzes shift sharply inward. By 1980, 29 percent of working black men had incomes above the median white, more than triple the proportion forty years earlier and double that of 1960.

Figure 5.1 indicates that race has progressively become a less important determinant of earnings. Table 5.3 summarizes the extent to which blacks made economic progress at different segments of the complete income distribution. Incomes of black men at each percentile of the black income distribution were calculated relative to the incomes of white men at the same percentile of the white income distribution. No matter what their original position in the income distribution, virtually all parts of the black population participated in the economic resurgence over this forty-year period. The principal exception was blacks within the bottom 10 percent, who gained relative to the lowest incomes whites, but the size of their wage improvement is much smaller than that of those in other percentile segments.[13]

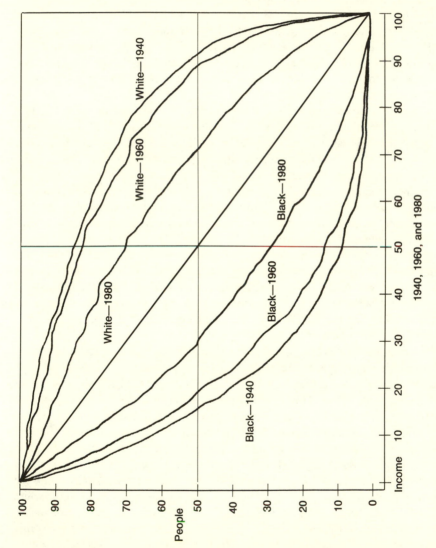

Figure 5.1. Black and White Income "Percentiles"

Table 5.3

Percentage Increase in Black-White Annual Income at Selected Percentiles: 1940–1980

Percentile	Percent increase	Percentile	Percent increase
2	4.8	60	54.9
4	8.4	70	57.4
6	30.7	80	49.0
8	36.9	90	46.2
10	48.1	92	50.6
20	48.2	94	48.1
30	50.2	96	51.6
40	45.2	98	54.7
50	45.5		

Black-White Income Ratios over the Long Term

Because of their preference for large micro-data sets, labor economists concentrated on the post–1960 years in their analysis of race. Until recently, economic historians specialized in the slavery period and on the turbulent transitions during the postbellum era. That left the eighty-year span between 1880 and 1960 largely unexplored, even to the extent of knowing the basic facts of what was happening to the relative economic status of racial groups. These eighty years not only constitute three-quarters of entire postslavery black history; they also represent the key to understanding alternative explanations for long-term changes in black economic status.

The relative income series presented in the previous section covering the forty years between 1940 and 1980 already goes a long way toward ending reliance on post–1960 trends. It demonstrates that the belief that the improvement in black relative income was purely a post–1960 trend is a false one. Between 1940 and 1960, black male incomes increased 28 percent faster than those of whites. The relative income ratio of 58 percent in 1960 is far in excess of the 44 percent in 1940. The notion of pre–1960 black stagnation is simply not valid.

While valuable, adding the twenty years between 1940 and 1960 does not come close to describing the full postslavery era. The primary data problem in tracing out a long-term relative income series is that income questions were first asked in the 1940 census. Nationally representative income data of reasonable quality simply does not exist before 1940. Of necessity, we must then rely on more indirect methods to trace out the full series.

James Smith recently compiled estimates that were derived from the occupational distributions of the work force published by the census. These distributions

Table 5.4

Estimated Black-White Male Income Ratios by Birth Cohorts

Birth cohort	Census years									
	1890	1900	1910	1920	1930	1940	1950	1960	1970	1980
1956–60										.653
1951–55										.625
1946–50									.646	.624
1941–45									.608	.610
1936–40								.571	.583	.573
1931–35								.561	.582	.593
1926–30							.555	.555	.577	.583
1921–25							.542	.546	.571	.554
1916–20						.501	.532	.537	.562	.583
1911–15						.488		.536	.562	
							.516			
1906–10					.509	.480		.526	.548	
1901–05					.500	.482		.524		
							.508			
1896–1900				.515	.498	.483		.519		
1891–95					.494	.478	.503			
1886–90					.492	.469	.501			
				.494						
1881–85					.481	.465				
		.488								
1876–80					.458	.445				
1871–75					.452					
	.472	.463		.387						
1866–70					.438					
1856–65	.454	.451								
1846–55	.435	.428								
1836–45	.417	.398								
1826–35	.397									
All Ages										
10–75	.433	.442	.455	.476	.479	.474	.516	.542	.590	.611
Ages 20–64	.439	.449		.484	.486	.479	.522	.543	.585	.605

were available by race, sex, and age for all decennial censuses from 1890 onward. Occupations were first aggregated into a consistent set of 133 categories. Each occupation was then assigned a race, sex, and age-specific average income based on mean incomes derived from the 1970 census. Smith's occupation-based income series is presented in Table 5.4.

Focus on the time-series swings in the average racial income ratio (over all age groups) in each census year that are described in the final two rows of the table. According to this occupation-based index, the relative income status of black men rose from 1890 to 1920, remained relatively constant between 1920 and 1940, increased sharply during the 1940s, and ended with the steady and significant post–1960 rise in relative black incomes.[14] Table 5.4 indicates not only that black-white income ratios rose after 1960, but also that the 1960 income ratio is clearly larger than that prevailing throughout the 1920–40 period, and that the 1920–40 ratios exceeded the ratio of 1890. The table pushes this relative income series back to 1890, leaving the twenty years after the Civil War still unaccounted for. But the sharp deterioration with age in relative black incomes in the 1890 and 1900 cross-section is a strong clue that occupational-based black-white relative income ratios rose between 1870 and 1890. For example, assume that 1890 age-specific black-white ratios of men in the labor market prevailed at earlier ages. Assume further that older workers in 1870 and 1880 had the identical relative wage ratio (.397) as those 55–64 in 1890. In that case, the relative income ratios for those 20–64 was .420 in 1880 and .409 in 1870.

Obviously, the relative income series in Table 5.4 differs from the common belief that the long-term relative economic status was stagnant. This series suggests that from 1870 to 1920 there was a gradual but significant improvement in relative black male incomes (from .409 to .484). Between 1920 and 1940, however, the relative income series indicates a slight deterioration in relative black incomes. As we have seen, both the occupation-based and actual income series show sharp improvement in black economic status after 1940.

If Smith's occupation-based estimates are reliable, trends in relative skills (human capital) must explain three basic trends in relative income by race: (1) the long-term, 120-year gradual increase in relative black economic status; (2) the period of retrogression that occurred between 1920 and 1940; and (3) the post–1940 acceleration in the rate of improvement in black incomes.

Racial Education Differences

Schooling Completed

It may be surprising that until recently we did not even know what the post-Civil War trends in racial education differences were. The twentieth-century trends were well documented, and there was a tendency to simply extrapolate those trends back to the Civil War. That extrapolation turns out to be extremely misleading. Table 5.5 lists post–Civil War levels of average schooling completed by five-year birth cohorts. To highlight differential secular trends, Table 5.6 shows racial differences in school completion for each birth cohort.[15]

The 120-year post–Civil War period turns out not to be a simple story of steady and constant narrowing of human capital differences between the races, as one would expect backward extrapolation of twentieth-century data. For those born in this century, the underlying trend was indeed one of convergence. Similarly, racial differences in mean schooling levels diminished sharply for both sexes

Table 5.5

Mean Schooling Levels by Birth Cohorts

Birth cohort	White males	Black males	White females	Black females
1951–54	12.64	11.82	12.70	12.24
1946–50	12.68	11.93	12.45	11.86
1941–45	12.32	11.25	12.14	11.33
1936–40	12.00	10.46	11.81	10.89
1931–35	11.09	9.78	11.52	10.37
1926–30	11.38	9.11	11.33	9.87
1921–25	11.14	8.44	11.12	9.03
1916–20	10.74	7.65	10.80	8.36
1911–15	10.15	6.75	10.37	7.70
1906–10	9.72	6.26	10.02	7.16
1901–05	9.19	5.72	9.45	6.46
1895–1900	8.74	5.42	8.96	6.03
1891–95	8.18	4.96	8.42	5.52
1886–90	7.74	4.72	8.11	5.13
1881–85	7.56	4.38	7.95	4.67
1876–80	7.44	4.11	7.88	4.27
1871–75	7.22	3.56	7.58	3.59
1865–70	7.07	3.06	7.45	2.89
Pre–1865	6.76	2.37	7.13	2.00

Source: Smith (1984).

during the first quarter century after the Civil War. Matters took a different course, however, for the generations born between 1886 and 1905. During this period, racial disparities in school completion expanded for males and stabilized for women. This twenty-year reversal has had important implications for the economic history of blacks right to the present.

Table 5.6 suggests that a convenient way of understanding the history of black schools is to separate that history into three distinct subperiods. The initial post-Civil War phase of convergence (1865–85) during the Restoration Era, the period of divergence (1886–1905) during the Restoration period, and finally, the more recent narrowing of schooling differences during the twentieth century.

In each of these subperiods, a unique set of political and economic events shaped the ability of blacks to expand the amount of schooling they could achieve and to improve the quality of that schooling. Because of these events, the amount of progress blacks were able to make relative to their white contemporaries in their schooling accomplishments differs in each of these three periods, and these differences go a long way toward explaining the relative economic progress of blacks.

Table 5.6

Racial Difference in Mean Schooling Levels
(Additional Years of Schooling of Whites)

Birth cohort	Men	Women
1951–54	.83	.46
1946–50	.75	.60
1941–45	1.07	.81
1936–40	1.54	.92
1931–35	1.91	1.15
1926–30	2.27	1.47
1921–25	2.71	2.09
1916–20	3.09	2.44
1911–15	3.41	2.69
1906–10	3.46	2.86
1901–05	3.46	3.00
1896–1900	3.32	2.93
1891–95	3.23	2.90
1886–90	3.02	2.98
1881–85	3.18	3.28
1876–80	3.33	3.62
1871–75	3.67	4.00
1865–70	4.01	4.55
pre-1865	4.39	5.13

Source: Smith (1984).

Since schooling of black slaves was prohibited by law, it is not surprising that the period after the Civil War was one of improvement. Black schooling began on a large scale in the first two decades of the Civil War. Financed by northern philanthropic organizations and the Freedman's Bureau, schools for black children were constructed throughout the South. Between 1870 and 1880, the number of black children in school rose by 500 percent, and the proportion of the young in school increased from 9 percent to a third. Although black and white children in the South attended separate schools, these schools may have been more equal in the ten years after the Civil War than they would be for some time.[16] Table 5.6 shows that black schooling levels rose by more than two years compared to pre–Civil War levels. Racial progress in the division of skills during this period is indicated by a narrowing of black-white differences in schooling by almost a year and a half for men and more than two years for women.

During the next twenty years, 1886–1906, there was a temporary setback as the human capital of blacks, as measured by years quantity and quality of schooling, fell behind that of whites. This subperiod roughly coincides with the erosion of black political power in the South as the forces of disfranchisement worked

Table 5.7

Racial Difference in Length of Schooling Completed

Birth cohort	White men		Black men	
	Go on	Complete high school	Go on	Complete high school
A. School continuation probabilities for elementary school graduates				
1916–20	83.1	59.7	75.6	41.2
1906–10	70.4	44.7	65.7	32.4
1896–1900	58.6	36.2	57.0	29.2
1886–90	49.8	31.3	54.3	30.8
1876–80	44.0	29.0	51.4	29.1
B. Increase in average schooling by year of birth				
	North	South	North	South
1888–1908	2.30	1.75	2.09	2.01
1908–28	1.64	1.58	1.78	1.98

Source: Smith (1984), p. 689.

their way through the system. But events in the North were of equal import in causing the reversal.

Public high school education was widespread in the North. The speed at which white high school attendance and completion became common during this sub-period is illustrated in Table 5.7, which lists school continuation propensities based on elementary school graduation.

Across the span of years that covers those born in 1886 to those born in 1916, the fraction of white males who continued their education beyond elementary school rose dramatically. By the birth cohort of 1916, more than 8 in 10 white male elementary graduates continued in school, and 60 percent would earn their high school diplomas—almost double the rates that existed thirty years earlier. In contrast, these high school completion rates were stable (at around 30 percent) among blacks between 1886 and 1910.[17] Table 5.7 also illustrates the lead taken by the North in the development of the public high school. Between birth years 1888 and 1908, the largest increases in mean education were achieved by north-ern-born whites. In contrast, for those born between 1908 and 1928, the largest schooling gains would be among southern-born blacks.

Political developments in the South also played a role in causing this period of reversal. A number of scholars[18] have demonstrated the link between reduced schooling opportunities for blacks and the erosion of black political power during the Restoration Era. This impact on black schooling took a variety of forms, including a shift of education funds from black schools to those attended by whites and a sharp divergence in the quality of black and white teachers. With the return to office of conservative Democrats in the elections of 1876–77 and the end of Reconstruction, whatever equality had existed between black and white southern schools began disappearing. This process accelerated with disfranchisement. Therefore, events both in the North and South contributed to the retrogression of black schooling shown in Table 5.6.

Trends in the twentieth century are widely known. Table 5.6 shows that as each new generation of blacks and whites born in this century arrived in the labor force, the difference in schooling achieved by race continued to decrease. Data also clearly indicate improved relative quality of black schools in the twentieth-century.[19]

School Quality

Secular trends in years of schooling completed are, of course, only part of the story. We need to know what the schooling was able to buy in terms of enhanced market earnings. This brings us to the issue of school quality. The economic mobility of blacks was, and unfortunately continues to be, severely constrained by the inferior education open to them. Even judged by the standards of the time, the quality of southern black rural schools in the late nineteenth and early twentieth century was often abysmal. Teachers were poorly trained, the school a dilapidated one-room building, transportation facilities for the large distances students had to travel almost nonexistent, and books so scarce that they had to be shared among many.

The consequences of this inferior education show up clearly, even with such rudimentary indicators as attendance rates, the length of the school term, and illiteracy. Even as late as 1920, the average black school term was only four months long—three-quarters of that of whites; only two-thirds of black school-aged children attended school on a typical day (the corresponding white figure was 75 percent); and black teachers had classrooms of fifty-six students compared to thirty-two pupils per teacher in white schools. In 1920, more than a fifth of the black population was illiterate, five times the rate of whites. Even among black school-aged children, one in seven was illiterate.[20]

The only bright side to this dismal portrait is that the relative quality of black schooling has improved significantly throughout this century.[21] There is no serious dispute about the broad twentieth-century trends in relative quality of black education. The debate centers on the ability of blacks to translate their improving education into a significantly higher economic status.

This is another instance in which reliance on post–1960 data has severely limited our ability to discriminate among alternative hypotheses. In the remainder of this section, we report on our recent estimates of schooling coefficients.[22]

Using the 1940–80 U.S. census files, we obtained estimates for each race of the proportional increase in weekly wages associated with an additional year of schooling.[23] Given our regression specification, separate estimates exist for each of eight experience intervals from all five Census tapes.

Table 5.8, which lists black-white differences in estimated education coefficients for men, highlights some very dramatic secular changes by race. Of the forty entries in this table, there is but one instance where trends in the returns to schooling favored whites (the 1–5 experience interval between 1950 and 1960). In all other cases, there was a persistent narrowing of racial differences in schooling coefficients. The result of this forty-year persistence is that the magnitude of change became quite large. For example, among those in their first five years of work in 1940, white men's income increased 5 percent more than did black men's for each additional year of school attended—that is 20 percent more than black men's as a result of attending and completing college. This white advantage declined as each new cohort of workers entered the labor market. In fact, among men who first entered the labor market during the 1970s, the income benefits blacks received from schooling now exceed those of white men.

There are alternative explanations for the occurrence of this racial convergence in education coefficients. The Civil Rights movement and the associated legislation during the 1960s is one obvious cause. A number of studies[24] demonstrated that black male college graduates were one of the primary beneficiaries of affirmative action pressures. Consistent with this view, the racial convergence in education coefficients was larger in the 1970s than in the 1960s.

However, affirmative action is not the whole story nor, for that matter, a large part of it. Table 5.8 also indicates that the general pattern of rising relative returns to black schooling emerged long before the Civil Rights activism of the 1960s. Indeed, these rising relative black returns characterize the entire twentieth century represented in Table 5.8. Therefore, we must search for causes that lie far deeper in black American history than contemporary political movements.

A subtle pattern which emerges from Table 5.8 offers an important clue to what these underlying causes might be. The cross-sectional pattern in every census suggests that black-white differences in education coefficients expand as we move from less to more experienced workers. This expansion is consistent with a life-cycle perspective where black skilled labor is denied access to jobs with significant career wage growth. Alternatively, it may reflect cohort-styled effects where the relative returns to schooling are permanently higher for younger generations of black workers.

Table 5.8 strongly supports the second interpretation. Instead of black schooling coefficients declining relative to those of whites across actual life cycles (as implied by the cross-section), precisely the opposite occurred. Thus, the root causes of the improvements in relative black returns apparently lie within long-term improvements in black schooling across birth cohorts that enabled blacks to translate an incremental year of schooling into more income.

Table 5.8

Racial Difference in Education Coefficients Arranged by Birth Cohorts

Median year of work cohorts	Years of work experience							
	1–5	6–10	11–15	16–20	21–25	26–30	31–35	36–40
1902								4.50
1907							4.86	
1912						4.88		3.60
1917					5.03		3.49	
1922				4.82		3.05		3.35
1927			4.07		4.30		3.43	
1932		3.77		2.88		2.64		2.66
1937	5.13		2.21		2.58		3.11	
1942		2.25		1.84		2.50		2.08
1947	2.06		1.99		1.68		1.73	
1952		1.63		1.42		1.34		
1957	3.12		0.88		1.27			
1962		0.75		−0.47				
1967	2.02		−0.47					
1972		−1.18						
1977	−1.09							

Source: See Smith-Welch (1985).

Are the long-term racial relative income and relative skill series inconsistent? We believe not. First, refer to the skills indexed only by quantity of schooling (Tables 5.5 and 5.6). Both of the two historical periods of clear racial convergence in education—the first twenty-five years after slavery and the twentieth century—show steady across-cohort improvement in the relative income of black men. In contrast, consider 1920–40, the subperiod in which no strong across-cohort trends exist in relative income of blacks. During those years, men born within the era of education retrogressions were passing through the labor market (see Table 5.4). Table 5.4 also demonstrates that the rate of improvement for blacks accelerated among younger cohorts. This acceleration makes sense in light of the speedup in racial convergence in education levels during this century.

If we then add our results on school quality from Table 5.8, we show that since 1940 a significant increase in the relative economic gains from schooling took place—most likely due to improving school quality. In our view, the post–1940 acceleration in relative black male incomes mirrors a corresponding acceleration in relative black human capital. This acceleration in human capital results from both dimensions of skill—an improvement in the relative quantity and quality of black schooling. In conclusion, far from being inconsistent, we believe that evidence suggests that the long-term relative income series is closely correlated with the long-term racial trends in human capital.

Work Careers and Wage Growth

From the beginning, the human capital tradition has emphasized the acquisition of skills both in schools and on the job. Just as the initial cross-sectional studies suggested little economic payoff to blacks from investments in schooling, these studies also cast doubt on the empirical importance of job training in affecting black men's earnings. A widely held view is that blacks' relative career prospects are much inferior to those enjoyed by whites. According to this view, initial racial wage disparities are compounded over time as blacks fall successively behind white workers as their careers proceed. This section summarizes some recent evidence that relates to this controversy.

One pattern that characterizes all five census years in Table 5.1 is that black-white wage ratios decline with years of work experience. For example, in 1950, among men who had spent 36–40 years in the labor market, black wages were 47 percent of whites. Contrast this with the 62-percent ratio among men in their first five years of work experience in 1950. For a long time, the cross-sectional decline in wage ratios with experience, as in Table 5.1, was the principal aggregate level statistical evidence that lead to widespread scientific and popular acceptance of a particular theory of labor market discrimination. According to this theory, an important mechanism of discrimination is that blacks were systematically denied access to jobs with more favorable future prospects or greater wage growth.

We now know that such cross-sectional data, however, do not speak directly to life-cycle realities for any group of workers. Men who have more labor market experience in any calendar year are also members of older generations. The 47-percent ratio for the 36–40 experience interval, for example, may be lower than the 62-percent ratio for the first five years of experience in 1950 because the more experienced workers were born thirty-five years earlier. Relative to their contemporary whites, these older blacks had less schooling and attended poorer quality schools than blacks would thirty-five years later.

The almost exclusive, although then necessary, reliance on cross-sectional data in first- and even second-generation studies of race differences in earnings meant that unambiguous tests of these alternative hypotheses remained elusive. There was no dispute in any camp that cross-sectional data indicated a quite severe relative wage deterioration with age. The debate was exclusively over interpretation of agreed-upon facts. Cross-sectional data could never resolve this debate over assigning a life-cycle or cohort (reverse age) interpretation. Moreover, initial studies that took the empirical resolution of this debate as their goal[25] were not completely persuasive. This work was largely confined to the 1960s and early 1970s; a period of rapid black economic progress that many viewed as quite unique. And there were other confounding forces, including the implementation of the major Civil Rights employment legislation.

These limitations of recent studies also illustrate the value of analyses of earlier periods of American history. The following conclusions are based upon a painstaking analysis of published census data and of the recently released micro-data files of the 1940 and 1950 census.

The only series of racial income differences stratified by age that spans the twentieth century and relies on national samples is presented in Table 5.4.[26] By reading across the rows in the table, we can follow the actual experience of all labor market cohorts born in this century, as well as partial segments of careers for men born in the nineteenth century.

If we consider men who entered the labor force during the twentieth century (for example, those born after 1886), black-white income ratios did not decline over life cycles. Among men born before 1886, the table does provide evidence of a less rapid career income growth for black men, although obviously not as pronounced as the cross section would predict.

The ratios in the table can only detect life-cycle decay in the relative economic status of blacks that originates in movement across occupations. It was necessary to use occupational-based income statistics because of the absence of any reliable and nationally representative historical income data. One of the great advantages of the recently released 1940 and 1950 census data is that we can now monitor actual long-term career evolution.

Table 5.9 isolates the actual labor market experiences of labor market cohorts by rearranging the items in Table 5.2. This arrangement involved centering the original data by the initial year of entry into the labor market. For example, men in their first five years of work in 1940 first entered the labor market, on average, in 1938. Among these men, blacks earned 46.7 percent as much as whites. By 1950 these same men had spent 10–15 years in the labor market; blacks in this cohort now earned 58.3 percent as much as whites. By reading across any row in Table 5.9, we can follow the actual life-cycle path of relative wages of the labor market cohorts indexed in the first column.

The message of Table 5.9 is unambiguous. In contrast to the cross-sectional implication of deterioration in the relative economic status of blacks across labor market careers, the reality is that, if anything, black men actually improved their situation relative to whites. They narrowed the gap between their incomes and those of their white contemporaries as their careers evolved in virtually every instance depicted in Table 5.9. The cross-sectional decline in each census year that characterized Table 5.2 is not the result of any increasing life-cycle differentiation by race. Instead, improvement in the quality of black workers relative to white workers across successive birth cohorts accounts for the cross-sectional decline.

Conclusions

We have evaluated three objections to a human capital emphasis to racial differences in economic outcomes. The first posits that historical relative income and

Table 5.9

Black Male Wages as a Percentage of White Male Wages by Labor Market Cohort

Median year of initial labor market work	Census years				
	1940	1950	1960	1970	1980
1978					84.2
1973					76.6
1968				75.1	73.5
1963				70.1	71.2
1958			60.2	66.2	67.8
1953			59.1	62.8	66.9
1948		61.8	59.4	62.7	66.5
1943		60.0	58.4	60.6	68.5
1938	46.7	58.3	57.6	60.0	
1933	47.5	56.6	56.2	60.3	
1928	44.4	54.1	53.8		
1923	44.4	53.2	55.9		
1918	42.3	50.3			
1913	41.7	46.9			
1908	40.2				
1903	39.8				
All	43.3	55.2	57.5	64.4	72.6

Source: Public use tapes of the decennial censuses 1940–80.

relative skills series are inconsistent. This objection is based on assumptions about the value of long-term skill and income series that turn out to be false. Far from being inconsistent, recent estimates of these two series suggest that relative long-term trends in relative income by race are a product of racial secular trends in skill.

The other two objections discount the importance of human capital's two main empirical constructs—education and job investments. Our work suggests that racial differences in education, both in terms of quality and quantity, can explain the major long-term cycles in relative incomes by race. Finally, when actual average career wage growth of black and white men is compared, we find that men of both races enjoy similar career prospects in this respect.

Notes

1. It is worth mentioning that the most often cited of these studies were University of Chicago dissertations, hardly an unsympathetic source (see Morton, Zeman, "A Com-

parative Analysis of White–Non-White Income Differentials'' (Dissertation, University of Chicago, September 1955); and Giora Hanoch, ''Personal Earnings and the Investments in Schooling'' (Ph.D. dissertation, University of Chicago, 1965).

2. Orley Ashenfelter, ''Comment on Smith-Welch, 'Black/White Male Earnings and Employment: 1960–1970,' '' in Thomas Juster, ed., *The Distribution of Economic Well-Being*, National Bureau of Economic Research, Studies in Income and Wealth, no. 41 (Cambridge: Ballinger, 1977): 297.

3. Robert Fogel and Stanley Engerman, *Time on the Cross* (Boston: Little, Brown and Co., 1974): 261.

4. Gunnar Myrdal, *An American Dilemma* (New York: Harper and Brothers, 1944): 380.

5. Hanoch, and Lester Thurow, *Poverty and Discrimination* (Washington: The Brookings Institution, 1969).

6. Apparently, due to the use of group data or an age control rather than experience. James P. Smith and Finis Welch, ''Black-White Male Wage Ratios: 1960–1970,'' *American Economic Review* (June 1977): 67, 323–38.

7. Finis Welch, ''Education and Racial Discrimination,'' in Orley Ashenfelter and Albert Rees, eds., *Discrimination in Labor Markets* (Princeton: Princeton University Press, 1974); and Smith and Welch, ''Black-White Male Wage Ratios.''

8. Richard B. Freeman, ''Changes in the Labor Market for Black Americans 1948–1972,'' *Brookings Papers on Economic Activity*, 1, 1973: 67–120.

9. Richard Butler and James Heckman, ''The Impact of Government on the Labor Market Status of Black Americans: A Critical Review,'' in *Equal Rights and Industrial Relations* (Industrial Relations Research Association, The University of Wisconsin, 1977): 235–81.

10. Our numbers are ratios of arithmetic means of weekly wages. Income is defined as the sum of wages and salary and self-employment income. Weekly wages are calculated as income divided by weeks worked. Our sample consists of men 16–64 years old who are U.S. citizens and who did not live in group quarters. We imposed a number of additional sample restrictions. We excluded men (1) who worked less than 50 weeks in the previous year and are now attending school; (2) who worked twenty-six weeks or less in the previous year; (3) who were in the military; (4) who were self-employed or working without pay if they were not employed in agriculture; (5) whose weekly wages put them below the following values: 1940 = $1.50, 1950 = $3.25, 1960 = $6.25, 1970 = $10.00, 1980 = $19.80; (6) whose computed weekly wages put them above the following values: 1940 = $125, 1950 = $250, 1960 = $625, 1970 = $1250, 1980 = $1875; (7) in the open-ended upper-income interval who did work at least 40 weeks last year. In addition, in the 1950 census only sample line people (who were asked income questions) were included.

11. Years of market experience is defined as current age minus assumed age at leaving school. The mapping from years of schooling completed and school-leaving age is as follows: ed. 0–11 = age 17, ed. 12 = age 18, ed. 13–15 = age 20, ed. 16 or more = age 23.

12. Throughout this paper, the 1940 statistics include only wage income because in the 1940 census individuals were asked only the amount of their wage and salary incomes. In addition, we know whether they had fifty dollars or more of other income, but not the amount. Those men without any wage income are not included in our 1940 sample. As a result, the 1940 sample is not strictly comparable to the other census years. However, the trends we describe are not affected to any large degree by this limitation. For example, if we similarly restrict the 1950 sample to men with positive wages and base the wage ratio only on wage income, our aggregate wage ratio in 1950 would be 59.0. This is even a larger wage improvement for blacks than we measure in Table 5.2.

13. A word of caution is necessary. Our conclusions are confined to working men. As such, our statistics are a good barometer of economic changes in the workplace. A more pessimistic conclusion would emerge, especially about the black poor in the last decade, if we had examined the distribution of family income or the withdrawal of many low-income blacks from the labor market. We limit our attention to male incomes because family income changes confound changing labor market realities with the increasing problems in maintaining the black family.

14. These decade-by-decade comparisons are necessarily made against the backdrop of major historical upheavals that can easily dwarf the type of slowly evolving forces that we argue were reshaping black America. For example, the Great Depression could easily have overwhelmed the factors at issue in this paper, for blacks surely bore more than their proportional share of its burdens. Thus, the 1940–1980 comparison in Table 5.1 could easily suppress the slow economic evolution we emphasize here.

15. These tables are derived from Smith, "Race and Human Capital."

16. See Welch, "Education and Racial Discrimination," and Stanley Lieberson, *A Piece of the Pie* (Berkeley: University of California Press, 1980).

17. Note that black progression rates were initially higher than those of whites—at that time those black who reached the eighth grade were clearly a very select group. Later in the twentieth century, progression rates for high school graduates to college were also higher for black men, a reflection of a similar phenomenon.

18. See Horace Mann Bond, *The Education of the Negro in the American Social Order* (New York: Prentice Hall, 1934); Welch, "Education and Racial Discrimination; and Lieberson, *A Piece of the Pie*.

19. To cite but two examples, in 1920 black youths attended school only two-thirds as many days per year as white students, but by 1954, there were no real black-white differences in days attended. Similarly, in 1920, teachers of black students had 1.75 times as many pupils as the average teacher in the country. By 1954, this difference had been reduced to 1.18. Welch, "Education and Racial Discrimination" gives a more complete summary.

20. This statistic is for black males aged 15–19. See Smith, "Race and Human Capital."

21. See especially Welch, "Education and Racial Discrimination."

22. The details are contained in James P. Smith and Finis Welch, "Closing the Gap: Forty Years of Black Economic Progress," R 3330 DOL (Rand Corporation, February 1986).

23. The other explanatory variables included in these regressions were residence in the South, (SMSA—Standard Metropolitan Statistical Areas), and central cities of these SMSAs.

24. For one example, see Smith and Welch, "Affirmative Action and Labor Markets." See also Jonathan Leonard "The Impact of Affirmative Action on Employment," *Journal of Labor Economics*, 2, no. 4 (October 1984): 439–463.

25. Welch, "Education and Racial Discrimination" and Smith and Welch, "Black-White Male Wage Ratios."

26. See Smith, "Race and Human Capital."

6

RACE AND HUMAN CAPITAL
AN INSTITUTIONALIST RESPONSE

David Kiefer and Peter Philips

Introduction

Theories that are long-lived and widely accepted in labor economics share five characteristics. First, at their analytical core, they are elegantly simple ideas susceptible to clear expression and popular understanding. Second, properly articulated these core ideas are capable of wide applications yielding reasonably useful predictions or a verisimilitude that is descriptively appealing. Third, they speak to questions of policy or social action. Fourth, lasting theories typically resonate with some underlying ideological tendency that has a significant tradition and following within the profession and society at large. Finally, good theories carry with them research agendas that induce us to look in some areas and not in others for further understanding of issues that concern us.

Human capital theory is one such entity in labor economics. At its heart this theory is basically simple. It says that we all get out of the market wages associated with the productivity we bring to the market and any individual's productivity can be shaped by the choices he or she makes. The market sorts people out and pays them differing wages based on their differing productive abilities. Most of any one person's productive abilities are acquired through learning at school or on the job. These acquired skills are human capital accumulated by individuals who chose to pay the direct and indirect costs that learning entails. In short, workers develop their own productivity and bring it to the job— that is what the employer is buying when he pays out wages. An often unstated, underlying assumption of this theory is that, in the long run at least, the pattern of

David Kiefer and Peter Philips are members of the Economics Department at the University of Utah.

acquired skills will create the structure of wage differences. This presumes what one might call a Say's Law of labor markets: the supply of human capital creates its own demand. In other words, in the long run, people will know what kind of skills the market wants, and these skills will be utilized when accumulated. Unemployment is not a long-run problem.

The application of human capital theory to racial wage differences is a major demonstration of the theory's usefulness. James Smith's[1] extension of this effort to the explanation of long-run trends in the male racial wage gap in the United States is a major achievement within the confines of human capital theory. By positing that the narrowing racial schooling gap should lead to a narrowing racial wage gap and then by showing that in the case of males a considerable past correspondence between racial schooling differences and racial wage differences exists, Smith has made an appealing descriptive case for the theory. Smith's work also predicts that a continued narrowing of racial schooling differences, especially in the area of quality differences, should lead to a continued narrowing of the male racial wage gap. The policies implied by this theory relate to schooling rather than market intervention. According to Smith's analysis, racial social inequality has existed and may continue to exist. But the source of this social inequality lies in schooling, and perhaps the culture of learning, but not in the labor market. The labor market in Smith's world distinguishes between people based on their skills and not their race per se. A correlation between skills and race is a problem of educational policy, not labor market policy. This perspective harmonizes with a longstanding ideological tradition in economics that sees markets as an equalizing force in society. At the root of human capital theory is the notion that there is nothing in the operations of the market that prevents people from choosing the amount of human capital they wish to acquire. The market, itself, distinguishes among people based only on their human capital and natural abilities—which are innate. One may choose to redistribute income to offset innate differences among workers but this should be after the market is allowed to distribute workers efficiently through wage differentials in order to maximize the production one intends to redistribute. Thus, social inequality may come from unequal access to schooling or differences in innate abilities, but the market will typically reward people according to their merits and not according to social or racial status. Finally, human capital theory applied to historical trends in the racial wage gap asks us to look more closely at the question of quality measures of schooling as well as a separating out of labor market experience by age cohorts once the majority of human capital has been accumulated prior to entering the labor market. It does not encourage us to look at labor demand issues nor the particularities of labor market institutions, technology, group conflict, or class conflict as essential elements in the operations of the labor market itself.

Many feel that institutionalist labor economics fails the first test of a powerful theory in that it is not susceptible to a simple, clear formulation. However, the heart of institutionalist wage differential theory is captured by John Dunlop's[2] dictum that in the long run, the structure of wages is determined by the pace and pattern of economic development. If in human capital theory the direction of causation runs from individual choices to labor supply to the market, in institutionalist theory historical causation runs from the requirements of industrial development to the demand for labor to the structure of wages, to the allocation of workers among jobs. In human capital theory, the worker brings his skills to the job. In institutionalist theory, the job makes the man and consequently, skills are embedded in the job. In human capital theory, the skills workers have determine how they are allocated among jobs. This can be correlated with race, but it is not racism per se. In institutionalist theory, in most parts of the labor market, people can fairly quickly "come up to speed" in whatever job is made available to them. People are allocated among the jobs available through the pecking order of a social hierarchy which has overt and conflictual racist and sexist determinants embedded in custom. In the long run, the jobs made available to particular groups in the labor market may change due to pushes and pulls on the labor force that are rooted in the pace and pattern of uneven economic development. Marked shifts in the demand for laboring groups may upset the accustomed process that allocate particular social groups within the labor market to particular job groupings.

With the exception of the upper tier of the primary labor market, formal education is not a skill-conferring process. Rather, it is part of the overall social process of channeling particular groups of people into particular types of jobs. If Harvard Business School were to suddenly enroll only highly talented black females, corporate America would not soon be run by black females. Rather, the status of Harvard Business School would immediately plummet. Differences in educational credentials within a group of workers may serve as a means of sorting out job access within that group. But across noncompeting groups within the labor market, a variety of customary channeling devices prevent large-scale educational convergences between noncompeting groups to lead to full-scale wage convergences or equal access to jobs between those groups.

This institutionalist way of thinking brings with it its own ideological baggage and policy prescriptions. The market is fundamentally shaped by labor demand. Customary racist and sexist labor allocation processes are strongest when unemployment is high and jobs are scarce. Consequently, a concern for unemployment is appropriate and macroeconomic stimulation is to be considered. Furthermore, because in most cases workers do not bring their productivities to the job, the labor market allocative function is not an efficiency function matching skills attached to workers to the right job. Rather, the labor market is involved in questions of equity by determining which class of workers will attain preferred jobs with preferred skills and rewards attached to those jobs. Thus, market intervention for the sake of equity is appropriate and long-term questions of efficiency are not put at risk by programs of comparable worth or racial quotas in hiring. The underlying ideological presumption of the institutionalist is that the market, like other aspects of society, is fair game for those who wish to add a little more equity to the world. This contrasts with the neoclassical human capital viewpoint where one may wish to reform the school but leave alone the presumedly competitive labor market.

Causes of Trends in the Racial Income Gap

James Smith[3] begins his analysis of long-term trends in the male racial wage gap by developing an index of the black-white wage ratio based on changes in the relative occupational distribution of blacks and whites over time. This procedure extends our knowledge of trends in the racial wage gap back fifty years from 1940 when the first income data by race was collected in the U.S. census to 1890 when the first occupational data by race and age was collected. He applies the human capital explanation of racial wage differences to this new data by noting the historical correlation between decreases in the schooling gap and decreases in the racial income gap. Although Smith presents his arguments by an insightful use of cohort by decade cross tabulations, they can be summarized in a regression model (model A in Tables 6.1 and 6.2). Adult formal education being of relatively minor importance, the racial schooling gap, S, is taken as fixed for a particular age cohort after they enter the labor market and throughout their adult lives. Sixty observations are available from Smith's Tables 3 and 12 relating education to his constructed racial wage gap index. Also thirty-seven observations on the actual racial income gap from 1940 to 1980 are available from Smith's Table 14. These dependent observations may be used to compare the performance of Smith's constructed index with actual income observations. Model A in Table 6.1 provides this comparison, as does the correlation between the occupational index and post–1940 observations. The estimation results in Table 6.1 support Smith's interpretation of the causal relation between schooling differences and income differences by race.

Institutionalists would explain movement in the racial income gap not from the vantage point of differential supply of labor skills but from the pattern of economic development as it affects the options particular laboring groups face. Over the period Smith investigates, the institutionalist might expect that a considerable proportion of the total variation in racial income ratios could be explained by the migration of southern rural blacks to urban areas, particularly in the manufacturing North. This migration would be seen as the result of a search by northern manufacturers for new supplies of labor (especially during wartime emergencies and the coincident cutoff in the supply of foreign immigrants) and a decline in the viability of southern black tenant farming. Furthermore, the institutionalist would expect that sustained periods of tight labor markets associated with economic growth and changes in the structure of the economy would result in epochal changes in the accustomed channels of labor allocation. During these periods, disadvantaged groups of workers may permanently move up in the pecking order of laboring groups by creating footholds in occupations heretofore

Table 6.1

Imputed Racial Income (R̂) Regressions: 1890–1980
(Standard errors in parentheses)

	Human capital model (A)	Institutional model (B)	Expanded model (C)
Constant	63.55	63.63	64.45
Schooling gap (S)	−0.341*		−0.247*
	(0.016)		(0.026)
Percent blacks southern rural (M)		−2.051*	−0.717*
		(0.143)	(0.168)
R²	0.884	0.775	0.910
Observations	60	60	60

*denotes statistical significance at the 95 percent level.

Correlation coefficients

	R̂	S	M	time
R̂	1.000			
S	−.941	1.000		
M	−.883	.823	1.000	
time	.873	−.883	−.905	1.000

Notes:
R̂ is Smith's occupational index of the black-white income ratio, written as a percentage and disaggregated by birth cohort for men.
S is the white-black gap in years of schooling for men as a percentage of white schooling for each cohort.
M is the percentage of all black men in that cohort living in Mississippi.

closed to them. Model B in Tables 6.1 and 6.2 presents a simple form of the alternative institutionalist explanation of the same dependent variables. Smith's racial income index from 1890 to 1980, and actual observations of the male racial income ratio from 1940 to 1980. A large proportion of the total variation in Smith's index for 1890 to 1980 can be associated simply with the migration of blacks out of the rural South. This migration explanation does less well for the actual observations of racial income ratios from 1940. Still over half of what Smith explains with the schooling gap can be associated with out-migration of blacks from the rural South.

Smith or other human capital theorists would find this result unsurprising. After all, the Smith index merely traces the relative movements of blacks and whites throughout the occupational structure. In 1890, the beginning of our

Table 6.2

Racial Income (R) Regressions: 1940–80

	Human capital model (A)	Institutional model (B)	Expanded model (C)
Constant	77.55	73.63	77.62
Schooling gap (S)	−0.815*		−0.808*
	(0.067)		(0.108)
Percent blacks		−4.057*	−0.623*
southern rural (M)		(0.698)	(0.692)
R²	0.801	0.477	0.795
Observations	37	37	37

*denotes statistical significance at the 95 percent level.

Correlation coefficients

	R	S	M	time	R̂
R	1.000				
S	−.898	1.000			
M	−.701	.776	1.000		
time	.743	−.699	−.898	1.000	
R̂	.913	−.899	−.886	.874	1.000

Notes:
R is the black-white income ratio, written as a percentge and disaggregated by birth cohort for men.
Also see notes to Table 6.1.

analysis, blacks in the rural South were heavily concentrated in agriculture. Thus, out-migration on the right-hand side of the equation is the mirror image of blacks moving into new occupations on the left-hand side of the equation. This being true, the results in Table 6.1 and 6.2 tell us that the debate over the causes of movement in the racial wage gap from 1890 to 1980, and to a lesser extent from 1940 to 1980, can be shifted to a discussion of the causes of black out-migration from the rural South. The human capital theorist must maintain that southern blacks were pulled from the rural South by the opening of new job opportunities in the North and in the urban South. More importantly, the human capital theorist must maintain that a key cause of these new job opportunities is rooted in the convergence of the educational gap between southern rural black males and the overall white male population. This convergence, in the human capital view, would have made southern rural black males increasingly attractive to employers who would open up heretofore unoffered job opportunities. The institutionalist must counter that black-white relative educational credentials were not a significant determinant of black out-migration from the rural South. Rather, it was rooted in events beyond the educational decisions of blacks as a group.

Migration Modeled

Historians of the black migration from the South to the North in the period under study have typically discussed causes in terms of pushes and pulls of the overall economy—factors that are amenable to the institutionalist viewpoint. In terms of pull factors, the growth of northern manufacturing, particularly during wartime booms, and the cutoff of foreign immigration are often cited as inducing black migration North. In terms of push factors, in the post–World War II period, the decline in southern tenant farming associated with the mechanization of southern agriculture and the expansion of viable farm size has often been understood as a modern enclosure movement forcing blacks off the farms and into urban areas. This kind of structural scope and historical argument leaves little scope for schooling and even less cope for individual worker choices.

Both the institutionalist and human capital preconceptions about black migration from the rural South can be modeled and tested with regressions. In Table 6.3, we present various models for the movement of black males out of the state of Mississippi. Mississippi was selected as an index of overall black movement out of the rural South because during most of 1890 to 1980, it was a predominantly rural, relatively nonindustrialized state with a proportionately large black rural population. The independent variable used to measure black out-migration is the change over the census decade of Mississippi black men by age cohort as a percentage of all black men of that age cohort in the U.S.

Model A in Table 6.3 reflects an institutionalist notion of the origins of black migration north. The decennial percentage change in black men by age group in Mississippi relative to the U.S. black male population is seen as a function of the sustained demand for workers as measured by the average unemployment rate of the previous decade, the availability of the workers just ahead of blacks in the social pecking order (measured by average foreign immigration over the previous decade as a percent of the total labor force), and the exclusion of blacks from southern rural agriculture as measured by the percentage of all black farmers in Mississippi who were tenant farmers. Age is also entered as an independent variable reflecting the notion that younger people tend to be the ones who migrate while older folk are more firmly rooted in their locale. All these variables turn out to be statistically significant while just over half of the total variation in our measure of black net out-migration is explained by these institutionalist variables.

Education is sometimes mentioned by historians as a factor in the movement of blacks out of the rural South. However, the argument is typically presented in a form that coincides with the institutionalist notion of noncompeting groups. Historians have noted that when blacks do leave, it is not only the younger blacks

Table 6.3

Migration (ΔM) Regressions
(Standard errors in parentheses)

	(A)	(B)	(C)	(D)
Constant	4.538	2.461	1.593	1.812
Unemployment	−.0896*	−.0809*	−.0790*	−.0793*
rate (U)	(.0216*	−.0214*	−.0215*	−.0217*
Foreign	−.8046*	−.5693*	−.3547	−.4191
immigrants (I)	(.1834)	(.2085)	(.2696)	(.3415)
Age (A)	−.0739*	−.0513*	−.0533*	−.0518*
	(.0112)	(.0151)	(.0143)	(.0152)
Tenant Farmers	.0116*	.0133*	.0206*	.0182
(F)	(.0046)	(.0045)	(.0060)	(.0098)
Relative		.9270*		.3495
schooling (RS)		(.4286)		(1.1224)
Black-white			−.0251*	−.0165
schooling (MS)			(.0113)	(.0297)
R²	.510	.539	.541	.534
Observations	63	63	63	63

*denotes statistical significance at the 95 percent level.

Correlation coefficients

	ΔM	U	I	A	F	RS	MS
ΔM	1.000						
U	−.217	1.000					
I	−.241	−.293	1.000				
A	−.585	.000	.000	1.000			
F	−.030	.250	.414	.000	1.000		
RS	.605	−.037	−.478	−.590	−.363	1.000	
MS	.448	−.052	−.716	−.342	−.705	.863	1.000

Notes:
ΔM is the change in M (see notes to Table 6.1) between censuses.
U is the national unemployment rate, averaged over the preceding decade.
I is foreign immigrants as a percentage of the labor force, averaged over the preceding decade.
A is average cohort age.
F is black tenant farmers as a percentage of all black farmers in Mississippi.
RS is the schooling ratio for a particular cohort of Mississippi blacks compared to average schooling among all Mississippi blacks.
MS is schooling for Mississippi blacks as a percentage of the national average of white schooling for each cohort.

that are more likely to migrate, but also the better educated. The human capital argument is that as blacks narrow their educational disadvantages relative to whites, they improve their relative job opportunities. An institutionalist has difficulty accepting that argument, but believes that as one black male improves his educational credentials relative to other black males, he improves his job opportunities relative to other blacks. Educational credentials within the confines of a noncompeting group can serve as a device for ordering the labor hierarchy within that group. It is only across noncompeting groups, such as between black and white males, that the institutionalist doubts the power of education to determine hierarchy. In Model B of Table 6.3 this notion of the role of education is entered into the institutionalist explanation of black out-migration. The measure used is the median educational attainment of each black age cohort in Mississippi in time t relative to the average median educational attainment for all black male age cohorts in Mississippi in time t. This within-group relative education variable is found to be significant, while all the previous institutionalist variables retain their significance.

The human capital notion of the role of education in black out-migration may be substituted for the institutionalist idea. This is done in Model C of Table 6.3. By calculating the ratio of the median educational attainment by age cohort for Mississippi black men in time t relative to the U.S. white population, a proper measure of black male human capital in Mississippi relative to their white competitors in the economy as a whole can be constructed. This human capital objection to the institutionalist model is substituted for the institutionalist measure of the role of black education in Model C of Table 6.3. It turns out that this new variable (MS) is negatively correlated with foreign immigration. The later variable loses its significance in Model C. With the inclusion of a true human capital variable for black-white differences, Model C of black out-migration can be given a fairly consistent human capital interpretation. As the racial schooling gap narrows, opportunities open for southern rural blacks. With their new skills relative to whites, they are more attractive to employers in urban areas and in the North, and these southern rural black males respond by migrating to these new opportunities. The supply of competing labor groups is relatively unimportant. Fluctuations in unemployment can effect variations in out-migration but not the overall trend. Indeed, because the unemployment variable can only fluctuate and not trend, the real role of unemployment is to mask long-term trends. The young are the ones who leave because older rural blacks have more personal as well as physical investments in the local region. Thus, age is really another aspect of the human capital argument. Blacks also move North as exogenous technology undermines some southern rural farming opportunities. The key here is the term exogenous. Rather than viewing the decline in tenant farming as an endogenous result of the development of the economy (the institutionalist viewpoint), the human capital theorist sees farm mechanization and increased farm size in the South as an exogenous negative shift in the opportunities faced by rural southern blacks. The opportunity set faced by these blacks would be even less had they not, over time, narrowed the racial educational gap, which in turn enhanced their alternatives to tenant farming.

Thus, the human capital and institutional models stand side-by-side in explaining the movement of blacks throughout the occupational structure. The difference in numbers is insignificant—not enough to force us to choose one viewpoint over the other. The choice, however, is significant. One viewpoint would have you reform schooling, perhaps, but leave the market alone. The other would present the market, both at the macro and micro levels, as an appropriate object for reform by those interested in greater social equality.

Further Prospects For the Racial Income Gap

Arguments about the cause of past trends in the racial wage gap may be trivial if all can agree that the aggregate racial income convergence that Smith and Welch document will continue and perhaps accelerate. The following comparison of the neoclassical and institutional perspectives on further prospects for the racial income gap uses actual income by race and education for males as recorded for the years 1939 and 1979 in the U.S. census. A neoclassical story is told first, and using the same data, an institutionalist counterproposal is then presented. Both admit the possibility of a future convergence of the racial income gap. However, the neoclassical prospects for convergence hinge on future improvements in the quality of black education relative to white, while the institutionalist worries about an apparent barrier to black improvement within labor market segments where aggregate black improvement has come from the entry of blacks into the lower echelons of previously all-white segments of the labor market.

The Neoclassical Story

The neoclassical explanation for the racial pay gap focuses on differences between individuals in relation to the forces of market competition. Employers are believed to be under a competitive compulsion to ferret out the productivity differences among prospective workers and to hire and pay workers accordingly. At an empirical level, much emphasis is given to differences in formal education among workers as an index of actual productive differences. Sustained and successful schooling is believed to be generally correlated with positive worker attitudes and abilities. Consequently, schooling is a convenient measure of the more general concept of human capital. If systematic differences in pay exist between blacks and whites, the neoclassical story asks us to first look for quantitative differences in the amount of schooling received by each group. If, controlling for the quantity of schooling acquired by race, racial pay gaps persist, the neoclassicist would first look for qualitative differences in schooling not captured by mere years in school. If a residual pay gap still persists, then this theorist would consider the possibility of discrimination. On the whole, the neoclassical story expects existing racial pay gaps to narrow both because educational differences between blacks and whites are narrowing and because, over time, one would expect the force of market competition to greatly reduce the effects, if any, of racial discrimination.

An empirical version of the neoclassical story can be exemplified by comparing the racial pay gap between black and white males in 1939 and 1979. Figure 6.1 shows the ratio of black male annual median income to white male annual median income for the year 1939. The racial pay gap is shown in relation to years of school attained by adult males divided into five age cohorts from 25 to 29 year-olds to 55 to 64 year-olds. In all cases, for the same level of schooling whites received a greater annual income than did blacks. The gap was narrowest where no schooling was attained by either race. The existence of a racial pay gap where no formal schooling was involved could be attributed to the market's discount for inferior informal training within the black household or it could be said to measure racial discrimination within the labor market in 1939. Figure 6.1 shows that as individuals began to take on formal schooling, the racial pay gap widened. Some neoclassical theorists would take this as a sign of inferior black education during a period of widespread educational segregation. Others would probably attribute at least some of the decline to increased discrimination in areas of the labor market where educated labor found jobs. It is possible but not often argued within the neoclassical framework that this lower return to schooling for blacks reflects an innate racial learning inferiority. Thus, within the neoclassical tradition there is room for debate over the existence and extent of racial discrimination with the labor market, the existence and extent of unequal natural abilities by race, and the accuracy of school years attained as a measure of an individual's accumulation of human capital.

Few, if any, neoclassical analysts would expect the relation found in 1939 between the racial pay gap, on the one hand, and schooling and age, on the other, to obtain forty years later. The well-known convergence in the racial educational gap since 1939 would lead one to expect at least a partial convergence in the racial pay gap. Not only have differences in the average years of formal schooling narrowed in the last forty years, but also the end to de jure and some de facto segregation in most schools would lead one to expect a narrowing in the qualitative differences between the educations received by blacks and whites. Furthermore, if discrimination exists, one would expect its effect to diminish over time. The neoclassical analyst looking at Figure 6.1 would be quick to point out a systematic stacking by age of the lines representing age cohorts. The general pattern revealed in the figure is one in which the racial pay gap is widest where the age cohort is oldest while the pay gap narrows as the age cohort is younger. In the neoclassical story this means that the more recent black entries into the adult male labor market in 1939 were hurt less by either inferior schooling and/or labor market discrimination.

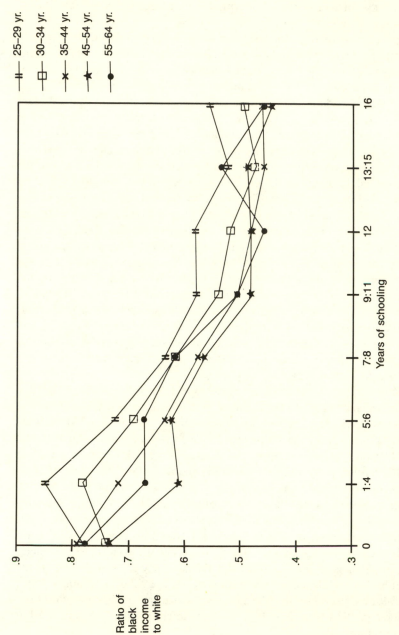

Figure 6.1. Male Racial Pay Gap by Schooling and Age: 1939

Source: U.S. Department of Commerce, *Statistical Abstract of the United States, 1950* (Washington, D.C.: GPO, 1950), Table 135, 115. The original source was Department of Commerce, Bureau of the Census, *Population-Special Reports,* Series P-46, no. 5. The schooling data for these individuals was for the year 1940 but the income they were asked to report was for 1939.

Figure 6.2 presents largely the same data for 1979. Notice, however, that an additional younger age cohort (18 to 24 year-olds) and an older age cohort (65 years and up) have been added to the display, and the amount of schooling recorded has extended from 16 to 19 years. Figure 6.2 would lead most neoclassical storytellers to feel satisfied with the predictive consistency of their theory over a forty-year span. They would point out three things. First, the downward trend of the age cohort lines observable in 1939 are gone in 1979. This is consistent with the belief that educational desegregation in the intervening period had reduced the qualitative differences in black and white education. It also casts doubt on the proposition that blacks as a group are less capable of learning. Second, generally speaking the stacking of pay gap lines by age cohort observed in 1939 has been repeated in 1979. For high school graduates and above, the pay gap is widest for the oldest cohort and narrowest for the youngest cohort. This is again a sign that the educational gap is narrowing the racial pay gap. Older age cohorts possess older vintages of human capital that were accumulated when quality differences between the education of blacks and whites were very real. Thus, a college degree for a black born in 1914 or before was substantially inferior to the one available to whites at the time. Consequently, even in 1979, these blacks are burdened with a severe but nondiscriminatory market discount on their educational credentials. Newer vintages of black human capital minted as quality differences in racial education converged show a smaller discount on black educational credentials. Some liberal neoclassicists might also wish to interpret the demise of a widening racial pay gap as education increases as the partial result of competition forcing out discriminatory hiring practices. Figure 6.3 illustrates the third point of the neoclassicist. Here Figure 6.2 is repeated with a few modifications, the most important of which is the addition of the youngest age cohort reported in the 1939 data.[4] Those who were born from 1910 to 1914 and therefore were 25 to 29 years old in 1939, make up a significant proportion of the 1979 age cohort ''65 and up.'' Notice that the racial pay gap by education attained by this age cohort had not significantly changed in forty years. This is both further evidence of the vintage human capital phenomena and evidence justifying optimism about future trends in the racial pay gap. The age cohort represented by 25 year-olds in 1939 and 65 year-olds in 1979 could not redo the qualitative dimensions of their vintage of human capital, and consequently the relative positions of these individuals did not change significantly over the forty years between labor market entry and retirement. However, this would lead one to have stronger confidence that the improved positions of younger blacks observable in the display of 1979 data in the Figure 6.2 would persist in the future, leading to an aggregate narrowing of racial pay differences. Without making too much of it, liberal neoclassical storytellers might also add that the slight narrowing (around 5 percent at each level of education except 0 to 7 years) between 1939 and 1979 in the racial pay gap observable in Figure 6.3 for the 1910 to 1914 generation may be attributed to a decline in labor market discrimination.

130

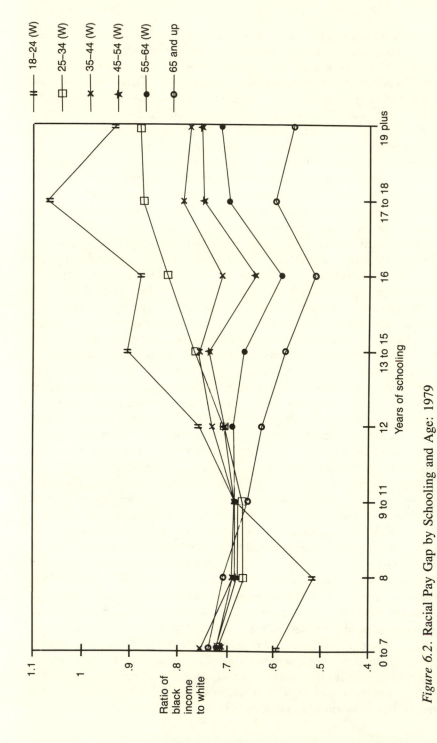

Figure 6.2. Racial Pay Gap by Schooling and Age: 1979

Source: U.S. Bureau of the Census. Census of 1980, vol. 1, *Characteristics of the Population* (Washington, D.C.: GPO, 1980), Table 296, 1–451, 452, 455, 456.

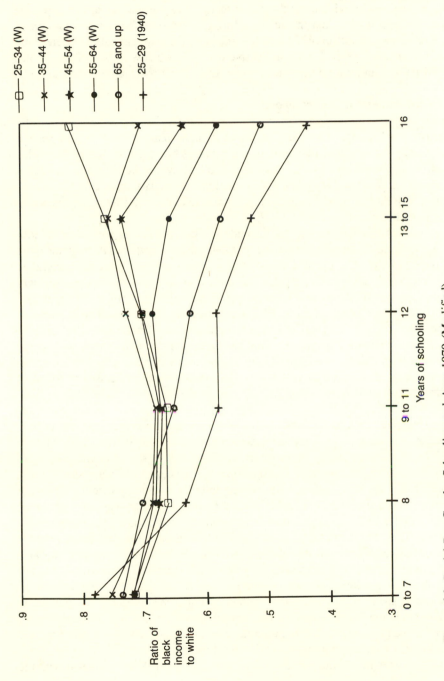

Figure 6.3. Racial Pay Gap by Schooling and Age: 1979 (Modified)
Source: See notes to Figure 6.1 and 6.2.

Thus, in its emphasis on quantitative and qualitative differences in human capital among individuals as the major factor in explaining racial pay gaps, the neoclassical story is optimistic regarding the prospects for an elimination of racial economic inequality. As older vintages of human capital are retired and newer vintages formed, real productive differences between blacks and whites will narrow and the market racial wage differential will narrow accordingly.

An Institutional Counterproposal

Institutional stories describe pictures of a labor market divided into several relatively separate and independent segments. While there is debate over what causes segmentation in labor markets and over how the barriers between labor market segments might change over time, institutionalists agree that within each labor market segment the relation of formal schooling and work experience to income differs.

The institutionalists sees the secondary labor market as consisting of jobs requiring rudimentary skills and commitments that are acquired through the mere process of growing up in society. Skill requirements are typically general in character and not specific to particular industries or firms within the secondary labor market. Workers move from job to job and from employer to employer with little long-term job attachment. Wages are low and, relative to other segments of the labor market, they do not improve either with formal education or with accumulated work experience. This sector of the economy employs socially disadvantaged workers which includes disproportionate numbers of recent immigrants as well as minority groups who have been the object of various forms of discrimination.

In the institutionalist picture, a better paying primary labor market is divided into two sectors. A lower tier contains jobs associated with blue-collar manufacturing work as well as some service-sector work such as construction. Formal education is not a major requirement in this sector of the economy. Skills are learned on the job, and a high proportion of the needed skills are specific to a particular firm or industry. Promotional job ladders within particular firms are common as a means of conveying needed firm and industry-specific skills and, according to some, as a method of dividing and better managing an attached work force. Thus, the institutionalist expects that within the lower tier of the primary labor market, wages and income will rise with age and seniority. There may also be some improvement in income associated with increased schooling in this tier of the primary labor market. However, this is more a reflection of school-acquired social status and contacts than of enhanced productive capabilities. Workers in the lower tier of the primary labor market find jobs through family, ethnic, neighborhood, and social connections. Certain levels of schooling are associated with maintaining and utilizing those connections.

The upper tier of the primary labor market contains jobs associated with the designing, supervising, financing, and marketing of production. These typically white-collar male jobs exist in both the manufacturing and service branches of industry. Here formal schooling is quite important and improvements in income should be clearly associated with both formal schooling and work experience. For many jobs in the upper tier of the primary labor market, workers are attached to their profession but not to their employer—promotion often comes by switching employers. For other jobs in this tier, promotion is association with rising in the bureaucracy of one corporation.

Thus, the secondary labor market shows much labor turnover, little in the way of internal labor market, compact wage differentials between occupations and within firms, and from the individual's standpoint, relatively little pay improvement with increased schooling or work experience. The lower tier of the primary labor market has limited labor turnover as workers contract with one firm and then move up within that firm. Relative to the secondary labor market, average wages in the lower tier of the primary labor market are higher and more dispersed. Returns from on-the-job experience are associated both with the learning of skills and the management of labor. The return from increased schooling is a reflection of and correlates with other social connections that got these workers into the firm's entry jobs in the first place. The upper tier of the primary labor market has the highest average wages and shows the best returns from formal education, which not only provides the social contacts of the ''old school tie'' but increasingly also the technical skills required in this sector of the labor market. Pay improves in this sector with work experience either via a promotional job ladder internal to the firm or wage increases associated with switching firms.

Figure 6.4 shows annual average income by schooling and age for black and white males in 1939. These data are the basis for the racial pay gap displayed in Figure 6.1. Both blacks and whites of all ages who had no schooling in 1939 appear to be in the secondary labor market of the institutionalist's story. Pay is low and there is little in the way of improvement with age. Clearly blacks with only 1 to 4 years of formal schooling are also entirely in the secondary labor market as their incomes do not improve either with age or education. Indeed, relative to whites, in 1939 blacks with even up to 15 years of formal schooling show relatively little return to either schooling or age as a proxy for on-the-job experience. In comparing the slopes of income-education lines for 1939, only blacks with a college degree show a return to education matching the improvements whites experience with increased education past the eighth grade. No blacks show an improvement in pay associated with age to match that of whites who have any schooling at all. Thus, in 1939, blacks appear to be in the secondary labor market, trapped in bottom-rung jobs in the lower tier of the primary labor market (which are in effect secondary jobs) or, in the case of black college graduates, limited to jobs in the upper tier of the primary labor market where career promotional trajectories are foreshortened. Whites with some education (either 1 to 4 or 5 to 6 years of schooling) appear to be able to enter the lower tier

134

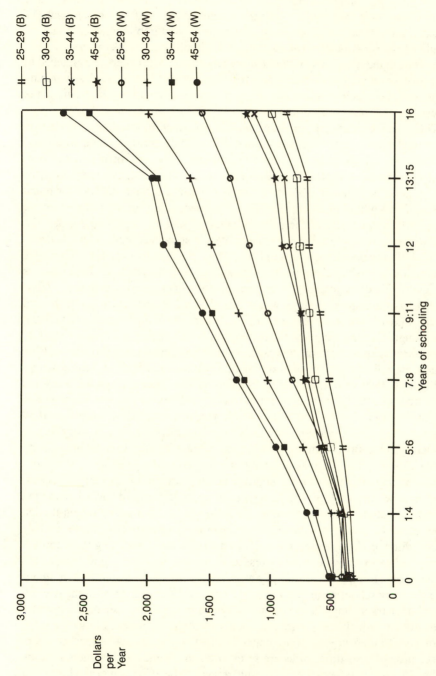

Figure 6.4. Income by Schooling, Age: White and Black Males; 1939

of the primary labor market where pay improves with age and schooling. Graduating from the eighth grade seems to mark the dividing line between the lower and upper tiers of the primary labor market in 1939 as this shows the most marked improvement in pay with increased education for 25 to 29 year-old whites. For age cohorts that entered the labor market earlier, the educational standard dividing market segments was probably lower, since throughout the twentieth century credentials inflation has altered the relation of education to labor market access.

Male income by schooling, race, and age for 1979 is presented in Figure 6.5. While the overall relation of income to schooling and age by race in Figure 6.5 appears similar to that for 1939 in Figure 6.4, several aspects have been altered. To best see the changes brought by forty years, Figures 6.6 and 6.7 overlay data from both 1939 and 1979 on the same display. In these two figures income is represented by index numbers where for each year, 1939 and 1979, the income received by black men in the 45 to 54 age cohort and with the lowest level of education shown is set to 1.0. All other incomes are then divided by this base income to show changes in relative incomes by education and age for each year on the same y axis. On the x axis, the years of schooling categories had to be adjusted in two cases. For the 0 to 7 years category in 1979, we have associated the 1939 category of 5 to 6 years of schooling; and for the 8 years category in 1979, we have associated the 1939 category of 7 to 8 years of schooling. Finally, in these two figures we present only the age cohorts beginning with the 25 year-olds and 45 year-olds in order to show the span of income that comes with increased age. All other age cohorts fall within the boundaries described by the incomes with education of these two age cohorts. With these adjustments made, Figures 6.6 for black males and 6.7 for white males present the closest comparison, given available data, of changes in the relationship between income, schooling, and age by race over forty years.

Beginning with figure 6.6, income returns to age and education for blacks with very little education has not changed at all in forty years. For blacks with an eighth grade education or less, relative increases in income due to either increases in age or education follow the same pattern in both 1939 and 1979. For the age cohort beginning with 25 year-olds, the pattern set in 1939 holds true up through the eleventh grade in 1979. The institutionalist sees this as evidence of tracking into the secondary labor market. In 1939, almost all blacks landed in the secondary labor market. In 1979, almost all blacks with less than a complete high school education also were headed for the secondary segment, where returns to education or on-the-job tenure are relatively limited. In Figure 6.6, the patterns established in 1939 break for blacks with a twelfth grade education. In 1979 a sharp upward increase in income correlates with receipt of the high school diploma. For the institutionalist, this is evidence that, unlike in 1939, some blacks were entering the lower tier of the primary labor market.

In the forty years between 1939 and 1979, the educational boundary of the primary and secondary labor market has shifted—a process some have called

136

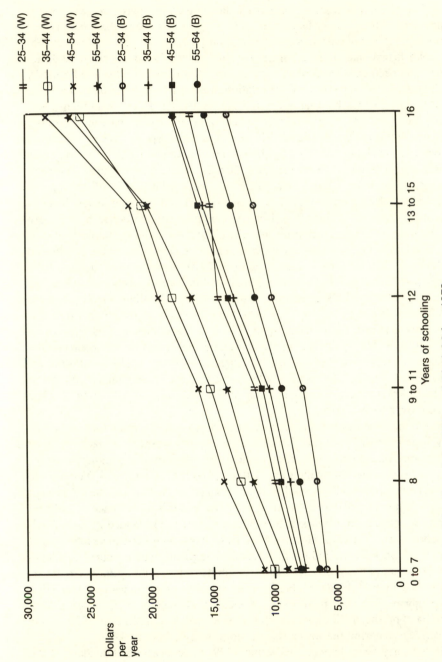

Figure 6.5. Income by Schooling, Age: White and Black Males; 1979
Source: See note to Figure 6.2.

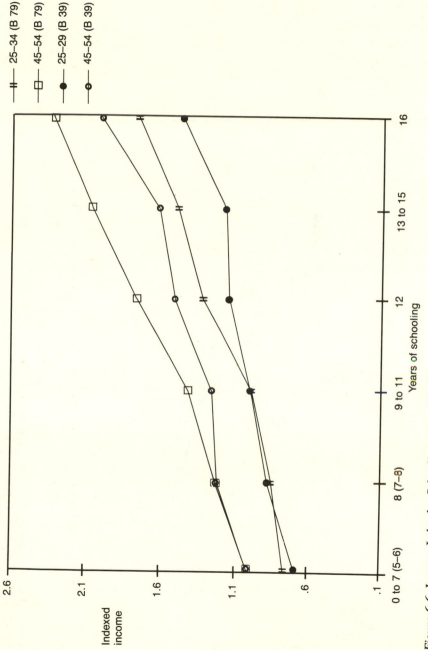

Figure 6.6. Income Index by Schooling, Age (Blacks)
(In each yr., 45–54 (B) with no school = 1.0)
Source: See notes to Figures 6.1 and 6.2.

138

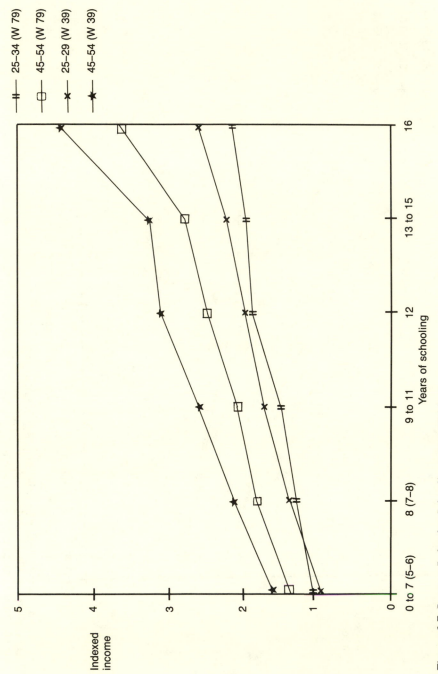

Figure 6.7. Income Index by Schooling, Age (Whites)
(In each yr, 45–54 (B) with no school = 1.0)
Source: See notes to Figures 6.1 and 6.2.

credential inflation. This can be seen most clearly in Figures 6.4 and 6.8. For whites in 1939 (Figure 6.4), the educational boundary between the primary and secondary labor market appears to be more or less marked with the receipt of 5 to 6 years of schooling. That is where there are not only return to age but also an upward break in the pattern of increases in income with increases in education. In 1979 (Figure 6.8), for the white male 25 to 34 year-old age cohort, the upward break in the income-education pattern occurs with receipt of a high school diploma. Thus, in 1939, almost all blacks and whites with four years or less of schooling found themselves tracked into the secondary labor market. In 1979, all blacks and whites with less than a high school diploma found themselves trapped in the secondary labor market. To a certain extent, this represents a leveling out of hiring criteria by race over forty years. However, the racial wage gap in the secondary sector has not changed in the intervening forty years. In Figure 6.1 for 1939, the racial wage gap is around 75 to 80 percent for those with no schooling, which surely includes blacks and whites who are only in the secondary labor market. The declining wage gaps in 1939 for from 1 to 15 years of schooling are due to the fact that whites with these levels of education are in the various tiers of the primary labor market, while blacks with these levels of education remain trapped in the secondary labor market. Racial incomes by education in 1979 (Figure 6.2) show basically the same pay gap for the secondary market as they did in 1939 (i.e., all whites and blacks with less than a high school diploma) the racial pay gap is still around 75 percent. The apparent improvement between 1939 (Figure 6.1) and 1979 (Figure 6.2) in the relative income position for blacks with from 1 to 11 years of education is due to the confinement of whites with these educational credentials to the secondary labor market. The secondary labor market itself appears to have remained unchanged in that it rewards blacks with three-fourths the income it pays its white members.

If this institutionalist story of the secondary labor market is correct, then a question arises. The secondary labor market is described by institutionalists as that sector of the overall market where firms are small, entry is easy, and product markets are highly competitive. This is precisely the sector of the economy where believers in the leveling hand of competition would expect the most convergence in racial wage gaps due to economic discrimination. In some indirect fashion there has been a leveling. In 1939, blacks in the secondary labor market had much better educational credentials than whites. Now their educational credentials are the same. Yet at each level of education in the secondary labor market, blacks still earn only roughly three-fourths what whites earn. Unless one is ready to assert the natural inferiority of blacks, the persistence of constant racial wage gaps in the secondary labor market raises series questions about the alleged leveling effect of competition on discriminatory labor market practices.

Like the secondary labor market, the primary labor market has experienced credential inflation and a leveling of educational entrance criteria by race. The lower tier of the primary labor market appears to pull in both blacks and whites

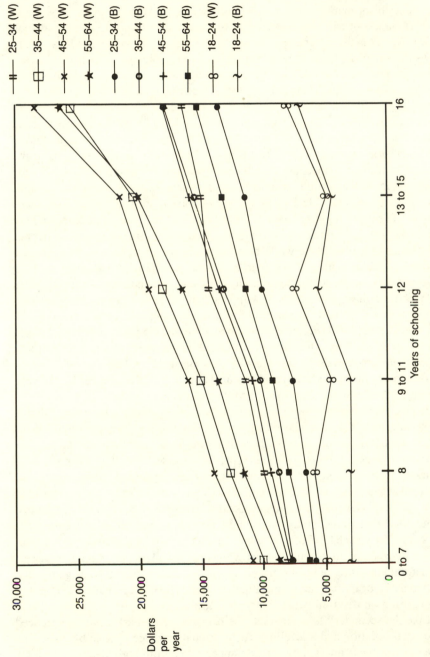

Figure 6.8. Income by Schooling, Age: White and Black Males; 1979 (Modified)
Source: See note to Figure 6.2.

with 12 to 15 years of schooling. The upper tier of the primary labor market recruits college graduates. The opening of these markets to educated blacks is reflected in Figure 6.6 by the upward divergence in the 1979 black income path by education and age relative to the black income path for 1939. In contrast, credential inflation and the opening of primary markets to blacks appear to have lessened the advantages of a high school or college degree for whites. In Figure 6.8 the income educational path for whites in 1979 diverges downward from the path observed in 1939. Taken together, the upward climb experienced by educated black labor and the downward decline experienced by educated white labor in the primary labor market between 1939 and 1979 has led to the racial pay gap convergence found in comparing Figures 6.1 and 6.2. Structurally, this has come about through an opening of primary labor markets to educated blacks and a reduction in the returns to education experienced by educated whites. It is not evidence that within any one market, blacks are treated more evenly than they once were. Indeed, in the secondary labor markets where blacks once were almost entirely found, no improvement of pay gap of three-fourths is visible. In the primary labor market lower tier (12 to 15 years of education) the pay gap in 1979 is also around 75 percent and even that is only for the youngest age cohort. Only in the upper tier of the primary labor market into which college graduates and postgraduates enter do we observe a pay gap narrower than 75 percent in 1979 (Figure 6.2). For college graduates and above in the 25 to 34 year age cohort in 1979, the racial pay gap is in the 80 to 90 percent rage. This is not due so much to a dramatic improvement in black incomes in this area as it is due to an erosion in the return to education for young whites with college degrees (Figure 6.8). A possible interpretation of this decline in white but not black wages for young college graduates may involve credential inflation and affirmative action. Whites in 1979 with advanced degrees may have been finding it increasingly difficult to enter the primary, upper tier labor market. The force of affirmative action criteria in some sectors of the upper tier may have allowed blacks to continue to enter at least for a while. Consequently, the white wage for college graduate represents more a mixture of upper- and lower-tier primary wages lowering the average young white college graduate wage and leading to an apparent convergence in racial wages for young male workers in the upper tier of the primary labor market. Thus in each sector of the labor market, primary-upper tier, primary-lower tier, and secondary, it may well be that the racial pay gap has not changed in forty years.

For the neoclassical economist, convergence in the racial pay gap is simply a matter of education, willingness, ability, and time. To the extent that the racial educational gap converges, to the extent blacks and whites display similar ambitions relative to the labor market, to the extent that blacks and whites are innately blessed with similar abilities, then it is only a matter of time until market competition eliminates the racial pay gap. For the institutional labor economist, labor market structure, the social channeling which distributes groups of workers across and within those labor market segments, and the pushes and pulls placed on labor market structure by the uneven pattern of economic development are key to understanding trends in racial pay gaps. While racial pay gaps may converge, it is not a simple or inevitable matter, nor is it best left to the automatic workings of the market. The current existence of racial pay gaps by education is not a fair outcome of market action nor is the elimination of these pay gaps automatically a future outcome of market action given the convergence of racial educational credentials. Thus, for the institutionalist, the existence of racial pay gaps by education is a justification for labor market intervention by government.

Conclusion

Economists often work from within theoretical paradigms of the economy. Paradigms are useful; first, because they provide a framework within which the economist can tie an analysis of a particular problem to an overall description of the economy. Second, paradigms present the economist with a logic of causation which provides a standard of consistency with which to judge any particular analysis. Finally, and probably most important, by drawing a picture of the overall economy and general rules of causation within it, paradigms suggest to the economist what to look for in a particular situation. Thus, theoretical paradigms allow an economist to explore new situations purposefully with a sense of direction and an idea of what one might find. The usual business of economic science is reconciling existing theory with surprises and anomalies cast up by a new situation. Only very slowly does an accumulation of anomalies force fundamental changes in the paradigm itself.

Even though economists must work from within paradigms, there is no necessity to be ignorant of or unable to replicate other paradigmatic approaches to a particular concern. Reference to but one paradigm in one's research is a refuge taken only by lovers of complacent consistency. It is dogmatic. Comparison across paradigms is not useful in the naive hope that a simple test will confirm one and disprove the other. Nor is it useful to compare across paradigms in the expectation of some straightforward synthesis of the two. Paradigms by their nature tend to live separate lives for very long periods. Rather, the comparison across paradigms is useful for the anomalies they present to each other, anomalies that do not naturally arise from within the internal logic and imagination of a particular paradigm.

In this study of how the neoclassical and institutional paradigms might view the causes of and prospects for the racial wage gap, each approach offers to the other an anomaly that might not be internally generated. For the neoclassical paradigm, the institutional story offers the question of why, in the secondary labor market where firms are most competitive, have racial wage gap by education not changed in forty years? Indeed, why does it appear that within any one sector of the labor market, racial wage gaps do not seem to narrow and that the narrowing of the income gap across the white and black male populations seems to come from a redistribution of blacks across sectors rather than from improvements for blacks within sectors? In turn, the neoclassical story presents to the institutionalist paradigm questions concerning education and entry into labor market segments. Why is it that blacks, who were excluded from all but the secondary labor market in 1939, are now finding access to all major labor market segments? If this is not primarily due to a narrowing of the qualitative and quantitative differences in education by race, what pushes and pulls generated by the development of the economy have allowed for this entry? The modeling of black out-migration from the rural South gives a partial explanation of this movement. But this explanation is less relevant to the post–1960s period.

Labor economics is more fortunate than many branches of economic science. Typically, competition between paradigms within a science leads to discrediting all but one theoretical overview. In most branches of economic science the neoclassical paradigm predominates, and its victory has been sustained not solely by dispassionate logic and test, but also by advocacy, ideology, and institutional politics. We are among the fortunate in labor economics because the battle between paradigms is still going on. While this may bring to our discipline a certain degree of discomfort and partisanship in debate, it also allows us a perspective unavailable in those branches of economics that no longer read the minority reports of insurgent viewpoints.

Notes

1. James P. Smith, "Race and Human Capita," *American Economic Review* 74, no. 4. (September 1984): 685–98.

2. John T. Dunlop, "The Task of Contemporary Wage Theory," in J. T. Dunlop, ed., *The Theory of Wage Determination* (London: MacMillan and Company Ltd., 1957): 27.

3. Smith, "Race and Human Capital."

4. Three other modifications in Figure 6.2 need mention. First, years of school reported have been truncated to 16 to correspond to the 1939 data display. Second, the youngest 1979 age cohort has been dropped. Third, and most important, the schooling frequencies do not quite correspond. For the 1979 category 0–9 years of schooling, we have taken the 1939 average of the three groups—no schooling, 1 to 4 years, and 5 to 6 years schooling. For the 1979 category 8 years of schooling, we have used the 1939 category 7 to 8 years.

The 18 to 24 age cohort which is not available for 1939 but is available for 1979 has been excluded from the discussion. It shows the narrowest racial wage gap of all in 1979. However, the pay level for this cohort is substantially lower than any of the other age cohorts. We take this as an indication that these youths, especially the whites, are not yet involved with their adult labor market career trajectories. The fact that a 19-year-old white studying to be a dentist and a 19-year-old black enrolled in technical college work side-by-side at a hamburger stand after school is not an indication of future trends in adult racial pay gaps.

PART II

7

POSTWAR RACIAL INCOME DIFFERENCES
TRENDS AND THEORIES

Michael Reich

Introduction

Progress in race relations in the United States historically has occurred in concentrated bursts, rather than through a gradual and continuous evolution. These bursts of progress often have been followed by periods of regression that diminished but did not totally erase the previous advances. The abolition of slavery in 1861 and the Reconstruction Era of the postbellum years offer the most dramatic cases of such bursts of progress. The Reaction Era that began in 1877 and the subsequent rise of Jim Crow offer an equally dramatic illustration of a period of regress. More recently, World War II and the Civil Rights era of the 1960s provide important examples of concentrated bursts of progress, each followed by some reaction.

This pattern of progress followed by regress invites explanation. Through an analysis of black-white income differences in the post–World War II era, I attempt such an explanation for the postwar period. Conventional wisdom notwithstanding, I show that black-white income ratios exhibit a long-swing pattern, with a period of upward trends followed by one of declines. I suggest that neither the supply-based nor the demand-based analyses of conventional economics provides an adequate explanation of the postwar patterns of black-white income differ-

The author, a member of the Economics Department at the University of California at Berkeley, is grateful to S. William Segal for excellent research assistance and to the Institute of Industrial Relations, University of California, Berkeley, for generous research support.

ences. I argue that an account that stresses the rise and fall of sociopolitical movements pressing for institutional change provides a superior explanation.

Consider first the burst of progress that occurred during the upheavals of World War II—a time, most historians agree,[1] during which blacks first made major economic advances. Weaver writes:

> [The] changes in a period of four years [1940 to 1944] represented more industrial and occupational diversification for Negroes than had occurred in the seventy-five preceding years.[2]

Income data from the 1940 and 1950 censuses indeed indicate the dramatic extent of this progress. During the 1940s the median income of urban black males relative to that of urban white males rose by a fifth, nearly twice the increase recorded during the 1960s. Comparable increases were recorded for black females.[3]

Sitkoff's explanation of these advances is of interest to labor economists. Like many other historians before him, Sitkoff does not refer to the gains in educational attainment of blacks in this period, for these were modest; nor to equalizing effects of increasing competitiveness in labor or product markets, for wartime labor and procurement policies make it arguable whether these occurred; nor to the great wartime expansion of demand for labor, for blacks at first did not share in increased employment; nor to government intervention, for President Roosevelt at first opposed equal employment policies.

Instead of looking to such traditional labor economists' variables, Sitkoff assigns the credit to a solidaristic sociopolitical movement, led by blacks but encompassing a coalition with organized labor, white liberals, and white radicals. Constructed painstakingly during the 1930s, this coalition successfully pressured the government in 1941 to open wartime production employment to blacks and to establish, for the first time in U.S. history, nondiscriminatory hiring as official government policy.

Many accounts of the implementation of this new policy document employers' resistance to altering the color line.[4] Even under the pressure of wartime, the government's antidiscrimination efforts proved effective only when the civil rights and labor movements joined with the federal government to press employers to hire blacks, Sitkoff's choice of explanatory variables for this important episode thus seems persuasive.

The postwar era constitutes the period of main interest here. Sitkoff's account, I shall suggest, is instructive for economists attempting to understand the racial dynamics of the postwar era. In this period the major political and civil upheavals of the late 1950s, 1960s, and early 1970s demolished the separatist and unequal practices that had characterized race relations in the United States since Reconstruction ended in Reaction in 1877. With its major progress toward racial justice and equality in political and civil affairs, this period deserves to be called the

Second Era of Reconstruction in U.S. history.

Progress toward racial justice and equality in the economic dimensions of employment and income has not followed such a dramatic trajectory. Blacks no longer are concentrated in the sharecropping agrarian South, which has virtually disappeared, nor in the very lowest paid industrial and domestic employment that had comprised their northern job ghetto before World War II. A much larger proportion of blacks are employed in either the capitalist or government sectors of the economy, many in professional and managerial occupations.

On the other hand, and contrary to much popular and scholarly opinion, progress toward racial equality within the capitalist and government sectors has been severely uneven. Increasing unemployment, declining labor force participation rates, and increasing inequality among blacks constitute one set of indicators of unevenness. Changes in the black-white income ratio over the period constitute another. Among men, most of the increase in black-white income ratios was concentrated in the 1960s and early 1970s, with no visible improvement since 1975. Among women, racial progress looks more dramatic: since the early 1970s black and white female incomes have come close to equality. This apparent improvement, however, must be weighted against the continuing inequality between women and men and the considerable postwar divergence in black and white family patterns.

More worrisome is in the 1980s many of these indices show signs of worsening. And under President Reagan the political direction of the federal government on racial matters is once again reversing. The Reagan administration has attacked existing government antidiscrimination programs in schooling, employment, housing, and even voting rights. The Second Reconstruction has clearly ended, and we are already well into a Second Era of Reaction.

How are these contradictory developments to be understood? Why are the outcomes of the 1980s so different from those of the 1940s and 1960s? Do traditional labor economic variables or sociopolitical movements of the type Sitkoff described better explain the ebb and flow of racial progress in the postwar era?

I take up these questions by examining postwar trends and theories concerning male racial economic inequality. The discussion is limited to the case of males both because racial inequality among men has proven more intractable and because the analysis of female racial inequality would require (to an extent that the male racial case does not) an analysis of male-female relations and family structure that is beyond the scope of this work.

I first show how sectorally disaggregated data on racial inequality revise popular images of continued racial progress. I then consider alternative theories of racial inequality in capitalist societies characterized by free markets and liberal-democratic governments. The main theories, in my view, break down not into neoclassical, institutional, and radical, but into conservative neoclassical, liberal neoclassical, and radical-institutional. Against neoclassicals I argue that

racial inequality need not disappear even under conditions of perfectly competitive markets. Changes come about not because of economic development or
political freedom per se, but because sociopolitical movements arise that undermine and then restructure the existing institutions and norms of economic and
political relations. A radical-institutional conception of the capitalist economic
and political process is better equipped to explain recent patterns of change and
continuity in race relations.

Racial Income Trends: What Is to Be Explained?

Census data show that in the postwar period the median annual income of black
males has risen from a level averaging about 55 percent that of whites in the late
1940s to 63 percent in the early 1980s. (See Table 7.1) The annual aggregate
figures show considerable short-run cyclical fluctuation, but they seem to suggest
modest but permanent relative improvement since the war for black men. This
optimistic conclusion is not inescapable, however. Table 7.1 also reveals that
most of the improvement occurred during the late 1960s and that no improvement
has occurred since 1975. Equally important, the familiar aggregate figures of
Table 7.1 obscure as much as they reveal. The published median and mean
income statistics, for example, exclude those with zero incomes during the year;
estimates suggest that about half of the observed improvement in the table may
just reflect the declining labor force participation of blacks relative to whites.[5]
Moreover, disaggregations by different economists of the data underlying Table
7.1 show contrasting patterns. Some find even greater progress, while others find
much less. Explanations for these patterns are just as diverse.
Economists of the supply-side human capital school frequently have argued that
racial income data, when disaggregated by age, schooling attainment level, and
gender of family ''head,'' show even *more* progress than the aggregate figures of
Table 7.1 and that advances in racial equity in schooling in recent decades best
explain this racial economic progress.[6] Many demand-side oriented economists
agree that much racial progress has been made, but suggest that growth in the
demand for black labor, assisted by governmental antidiscrimination efforts, is
primarily responsible. The demand-side view accepts the importance of increased
schooling of blacks, but suggests that schooling gains represent a response to
improved opportunities.[7]
  Whether the ultimate cause falls on the demand or the supply side, gains
attributable to improvements in black schooling undoubtedly are significant. But
how much black economic progress is really shown in data disaggregated by
schooling and age? And how much of the gains can be attributed to human capital
variables? Smith represents perhaps the most impressive attempt to measure the
importance of schooling variables.[8] However, the evidence marshalled in this
article is not conclusive.
  One important question simply involves correct reporting of the data. Put

Table 7.1

Ratio of Nonwhite to White Median Income
Postwar United States

Year	Nonwhite families	Black families	Nonwhite Males	Females
1945	.56		n.a.	n.a.
1946	.59		.61	n.a.
1947	.51		.54	n.a.
1948	.53		.54	.49
1949	.51		.49	.51
1950	.54		.54	.49
1951	.53		.55	.46
1952	.57		.55	n.a.
1953	.56		.55	.59
1954	.56		.50	.55
1955	.55		.53	.54
1956	.53		.52	.58
1957	.54		.53	.58
1958	.51		.50	.59
1959	.52		.47	.62
1960	.55		.53	.70
1961	.53		.52	.67
1962	.53		.49	.67
1963	.53		.52	.67
1964	.56	.54	.57	.70
1965	.55	.54	.54	.73
1966	.60	.58	.55	.76
1967	.62	.59	.59	.78
1968	.63	.60	.61	.79
1969	.63	.61	.59	.85
1970	.64	.61	.60	.92
1971	.63	.60	.61	.90
1972	.62	.59	.62	.95
1973	.60	.58	.63	.93
1974	.64	.60	.63	.92
1975	.65	.61	.63	.92
1976	.63	.59	.63	.95
1977	.61	.57	.61	.88
1978	.64	.59	.64	.92
1979	.61	.57	.65	.93
1980	.63	.58	.63	.96
1981	.62	.56	.63	.92
1982	.62	.55	.64	.92
1983	.62	.56	.63	.90
1984	.62	.56	n.a.	n.a.

Sources: U.S. Bureau of the Census, ''Income of Families and Persons in the United States,'' *Current Population Reports*, P-60 Series (Washington, D.C.: various years).

aside a number of important problems with the official data on income and race that I cannot explore here[9] and examine the two pictures presented in Panels R and S of Table 7.2. The two panels of this table compare my own calculation of black-white male incomes by age and schooling level (Panel R) with that of Smith (Panel S). My sources for each year are the published decennial census volumes. Smith's sources vary: 1940 and 1950 data are taken from published decennial census volumes, 1960 and 1970 data from micro-data decennial census tapes, and the 1980 data from the current population survey tapes.

Smith's figures show dramatic improvements in racial equality over the period 1940 to 1980. My figures, however, show a much more modest gain, with 1940 estimates slightly higher than Smith's, 1950 estimates considerably higher, and 1980 estimates considerably lower. Much improvement, according to both Smith's and my figures, occurred during the war decade of the 1940s. But the gains between 1960 and 1980 look quite different. In these years the black-white income ratio among college graduates in my table rose, on average, only one-third as much as Smith's.[10]

One might reply that even the Reich panel in Table 7.2 demonstrates substantial racial progress over these decades. There are, however, other compelling grounds to question further the extent and rhythm of postwar black economic progress. Other indices show stability or decline in black males' relative economic position.

The Persistence of Racial Inequality

Disaggregations of black-white male income data by the characteristics of economic sectors rather than the human capital attributes of individuals, reveals not more but substantially *less* progress than is shown in the postwar aggregate data. This sectoral analysis is developed in Tables 7.3 to 7.7, which disaggregate the national black-white male income data by public versus private sectors, urban-rural differences, regions, metropolitan areas, and detailed industries.

Within each of these sectors black-white differences in traditional supply-side variables, such as years and quality of schooling, age, and experience diminished over this period. At the same time, substantial pressure from the civil rights movement and from governmental efforts to reduce discrimination increased the relative demand for black labor within these sectors. Consequently, a traditional supply-and-demand framework would predict improvements in the relative incomes of blacks within sectors as well as in the nation as a whole.

The public-private disaggregation is presented in Table 7.3. Both decennial census and annual current population survey data are shown, because annual data are available only since 1967. The decennial data on black-white male earnings ratios show increases between 1949 and 1969 within both public and private sectors, mirroring the national trends in Table 7.1. The annual data show that improvement in the national private sector black-white earnings ratios ended in the mid–1970s and that declines have occurred in the 1980s. Public sector figures

Table 7.2

Alternative Estimates of Black-White Male Mean Annual Income Ratios 1940–80
Panel S: Smith

	Census year				
Birth cohort	1940[a]	1950[b]	1960[c]	1970[c]	1980[d]
Years of schooling = 8–11					
1946–55					73.2
1936–45				72.8	76.4
1926–35			65.9	69.7	75.1
1916–25		68.4	68.6	69.9	82.6
1906–15	57.8	64.0	63.8	72.0	
1896–1905	51.8	62.5	61.0		
1886–95	51.6	63.0			
1876–85	51.7				
Years of schooling = 12					
1946–55					75.1
1936–45				74.6	79.0
1926–35			65.1	70.3	72.0
1916–25		68.7	63.8	64.9	78.6
1906–15	55.3	61.6	57.8	65.0	
1896–1905	49.0	54.0	49.0		
1886–95	47.1	52.2			
1876–85	44.0				
Years of schooling = 16 +					
1946–55					88.5
1936–45				76.7	82.9
1926–35			62.5	78.0	79.1
1916–25		63.4	52.9	59.5	70.9
1906–15	49.6	53.4	45.7	54.9	
1896–1905	42.6	50.9	43.7		
1886–95	40.2	48.4			
1876–85	40.6				

Source for Panel S: From James P. Smith, "Race and Human Capital," *American Economic Review* (September 1984).
[a]Derived from tables in Zeman, using 1940 Census.
[b]1950 U.S. Census Special Reports, "Education," table 12.
[c]1 in 100 decennial U.S. Census (computer tape).
[d]1980 *Current Population Survey* (computer tape).

Table 7.2 (continued)

Panel R:Reich

Birth cohort	Census year				
	1940[a]	1950[b]	1960[c]	1970[d]	1980[e]
Years of schooling = 8–11					
1946–55					69.7
1936–45				69.9	70.9
1926–35			65.2	67.7	69.7
1916–25		76.9	66.7	67.6	70.9
1906–15	55.5*	61.2	64.0	66.7	
1896–1905	51.0	64.7	62.4		
1886–95	48.4	71.1			
1876–85	50.9				
Years of schooling = 12					
1946–55					73.1
1936–45				72.8	71.4
1926–35			66.6	67.6	69.3
1916–25		66.0	65.2	63.9	66.3
1906–15	54.7*	57.4	59.4	61.2	
1896–1905	48.5	53.0	53.7		
1886–95	48.1	54.1			
1876–85	46.0				
Years of schooling = 16 +					
1946–55					79.9
1936–45				77.3	67.5
1926–35			64.5	64.2	62.9
1916–25		64.7	58.4	57.2	57.3
1906–15	52.2*	60.6	54.4	51.7	
1896–1905	47.1	60.7	51.6		
1886–95	44.8	57.1			
1876–85	46.1				

*Weighted average of birth cohorts 1906–10 and 1911–25.

Sources for Panel R:

[a]Ratios of wage and salary median income, excluding farm areas. Calculated from *Census of Population, 1940*, "Special Reports," Series P-46, no. 5.

[b]Means calculated from distributions in *Census of Population, 1950*, "Special Reports," Series no. 5B, Education, table 12.

[c]Means calculated from distributions in *Census of Population, 1960*, "Final Report," Series PC(2)-5B, Educational Attachment, table 6.

[d]*Census of Population, 1970*, vol. 1: *Characteristics of the Population.* Pt. 1: "U.S. Summary," Section 2, table 249.

[e]*Census of Population, 1980*, vol. 1, chap. D: "Detailed Population Characteristics." Pt. 1: "U.S. Summary," table 296.

for this period suggest no trend between 1967 and 1975 and a relative decline for black men since the mid–1970s.

Table 7.4 examines trends for the urban United States, the urban South, and the urban non-South. For these sectors relative median income ratios can be calculated from each of the decennial censuses since 1940. During the 1940s the relative income of black males increased substantially in both the urban South and the urban non-South. Decreases throughout the urban United States occurred during the 1950s. Between the 1960 and 1970 censuses the relative income of black men improved in the urban South while it deteriorated in the urban non-South. Between 1970 and 1980 the black-white income ratio declined in both the urban South and the urban non-South. Progress in the urban South ended sometime after 1969, while regress in the urban non-South has been continuous since 1949.

A further disaggregation into four regions is shown in Table 7.5. Income data by race and region (but not by urban-rural) are available for each year since 1953. In the Northeast, the Midwest, and the West no trend is visible between the mid–1950s and the late 1970s. In two of these regions, the Northeast and the Midwest, black men have fallen farther behind white men since 1979; in the West, a small gain is registered in these years. The biggest gains since the mid–1950s again occurred in the South. However, improvement in this region seems to have ended by 1972.

Racial income data on particular metropolitan areas exhibited in Table 7.6 reveal a similar pattern. This table also draws from the decennial census data available for the years since 1949. (Adjustments to the 1979 data were made to maintain comparability with previous years. Census methods and questions regarding racial classification changed in 1980, with consequential effects on white median income calculations for metropolitan areas with large Hispanic populations.) According to Table 7.6, black-white male incomes ratios rose slightly between 1949 and 1979 in southern metropolitan areas, but fell considerably more in non-Southern metropolitan areas. A more detailed tabulation (not shown in Table 7.6) of the forty-eight largest metropolitan areas in the United States further generalizes this finding.

A final disaggregation examines trends for detailed industries, covering forty-nine private-sector industries for which consistent decennial census data for the period could be obtained. As Table 7.7 shows, in 1979 the average black-white male earnings ratio among these detailed industrial sectors was exactly the same as in 1949. Some gains occurred during the 1960s and small declines in the 1950s and 1970s.

Taken together, the sectoral analysis in these tables suggests that some of the national improvement for black males registered in Table 7.1 occurred because of declines in inequality within economic sectors. But most of the improvement resulted from shifts in the sectoral composition of the economy rather than

Table 7.3

Black-White Male Median Annual Earnings Ratios, Public and Private Sectors

Year	Public sector	Private sector
1949	.73	.58
1959	.77	.56
1969	.77	.65
1967	.70	.59
1968	.76	.62
1969	.69	.62
1970	.76	.62
1971	.73	.63
1972	.70	.64
1973	.68	.64
1974	.69	.65
1975	.73	.66
1976	.74	.66
1977	.68	.65
1978	.62	.65
1979	.68	.66
1980	.64	.64
1981	.67	.66
1982	.68	.63
1983	.66	.62

Public sector: civilian government employees.
Private sector: nonfarm wage and salary employees.
Sources:
1949 to 1969 from decennial censuses:
Census of the Population, 1950, "General Social and Economic Characteristics," table 142.
Census of the Population, 1960, "Subject Reports: Industrial Characteristics," table 27.
Census of the Population, 1970, "Subject Reports: Industrial Characteristics," table 44.

1967 to 1983 from annual March Current Population Surveys, *Current Population Reports*, P-60 series: no. 60, table 9; no. 66, table 46; no. 75, table 52; no. 80, table 57; no. 85, table 58; no. 90, table 60; no. 97, table 67; no. 101, table 67; no. 105, table 55; no. 114, table 55; no. 118, table 55; no. 123, table 59; no. 129, table 61; no. 132, table 58; no. 137, table 54; no. 142, table 54; no. 146, table 54.

Table 7.4

Relative Median Income of Black Males in the Urban U.S., Urban South, and Urban Non-South, 1939–79

Years	Urban U.S.	Urban South	Urban Non-South[b]
1939[a]	.496[b]	.446[b]	.664
1949[c]	.600	.533[b]	.726
1959	.583	.512	.701
1969	.640	.605	.688
1979	.620	.592	.672

[a]Wage and salary income of males, eighteen to sixty-four years old.
[b]One or both medians calculated by linear interpolation by the author.
[c]Data for 1949 are for nonwhites.
Sources: For 1939 to 1969 see Michael Reich, *Racial Inequality: a Political-Economic Analysis* (Princeton, N.J.: Princeton University Press, 1981): 50.
Data for 1979 are from U.S. Bureau of the Census, *Census of Population, 1980*, "General Social and Economic Characteristics, U.S. Summary," table 128; and from *Census of Population, 1980*, "Detailed Population Characteristics, U.S. Summary," part 1, section B, table 332.

because of declining inequality within sectors. The national data obscure the continuities in racial inequality within the major urban areas where blacks are now concentrated.

The collapse of the low-income sharecropping South and the associated black out-migration play a major role in these sectoral shifts. Contrary to conventional wisdom, out-migration from the *rural* South did not end in the early 1960s—as late as 1970, 17.3 percent of all blacks and 10.3 percent of all whites still resided in the rural South.[11] The growth of government employment, which paid blacks higher salaries than the private sector, also generated significant intersectoral shifts and raised the observed national ratios.

Within economic sectors, both public and private, the relative position of black males has displayed a modest upward curve, followed by a modest downward one, with little permanent improvement. This pattern suggests that a long-swing mechanism may be at work in the capitalist and government sectors of the economy.

In short, these postwar trends in black-white income differences among blacks raise many interesting questions, and not just for supply or demand theorists. The human capital approach may not explain the limited progress evident in these tables. But can other theoretical approaches do any better? With the trends in the tables in mind, let us turn to the discussion of alternative theories of racial inequality.

Table 7.5

Nonwhite-White Male Median Income Ratios by Region, 1953–83

Year	Northeast	Midwest	South	West
1953	.75	.75	.42	.68
1954	.78	.74	.40	.52
1955	.79	.88	.40	.68
1956	.73	.77	.42	.79
1957	.70	.76	.42	.76
1958	.73	.77	.39	.73
1959	.72	.78	.33	.69
1960	.76	.76	.37	.73
1961	.73	.72	.38	.78
1962	.67	.71	.44	.75
1963	.72	.74	.44	.79
1964	.74	.76	.46	.76
1965	.69	.75	.47	.74
1966	.71	.76	.49	.69
1967	.75	.84	.49	.77
1968[a]	.77	.82	.52	.78
1969	.76	.82	.54	.69
1970	.78	.82	.52	.75
1971	.73	.82	.52	.78
1972	.70	.79	.56	.79
1973	.77	.80	.56	.76
1974	.72	.81	.55	.74
1975	.75	.77	.56	.80
1976	.69	.73	.57	.74
1977	.72	.74	.57	.67
1978	.78	.72	.57	.73
1979	.74	.74	.61	.70
1980	.66	.69	.59	.76
1981	.68	.69	.60	.73
1982	.71	.74	.57	.75
1983	.67	.61	.56	.78

[a]1968 data for black/white ratios.
Source: U.S. Bureau of the Census, *Current Population Reports*, P-60 series, various years.

Table 7.6

Nonwhite-White Male Median Income Ratios, Selected SMSAs, 1949–79[a]

	1979[a]	1969	1959	1949[b]	Percent change 1949–79
North & West					
Chicago	.642	.713	.678	.714	− 10.1
Cleveland	.668	.718	.701	.702	− 4.8
Detroit	.629	.738	.685	.808	− 22.1
Los Angeles	.781	.726	.684	.704	10.9
New York	.682	.712	.677	.678	0.6
Philadelphia	.607	.689	.662	.686	− 11.5
Pittsburgh	.615	.638	n.a.	.729	− 15.6
San Francisco	.665	.686	.726	.712	− 6.6
St. Louis	.563	.583	.581	.632	− 10.9
Average	.650	.689	.674	.707	− 8.1
South					
Atlanta	.571	.531	.481	.520	9.8
Baltimore	.580	.631	.626	.630	− 7.9
Birmingham	.532	.515	.488	.581	− 8.4
Dallas	.608	.550	.476	.505	20.4
Houston	.640	.551	.511	.554	15.5
Memphis	.491	.583	.467	.484	1.4
New Orleans	.535	.507	.511	.557	− 3.9
Washington, D.C.	.594	.610	.573	.627	− 5.3
Average	.569	.560	.517	.557	2.1

[a] 1949 to 1969: 14 years and older. 1979: 15 years and older.
[b] 1949 data is for the Standard Metropolitan Area (SMA).

Sources:
1949: *Census of the Population, 1950*, "Characteristics of the Population," table 185.
1959: *Census of the Population, 1960*, state volumes, table 133.
1969: *Census of the Population, 1970*, state volumes, table 192.
1979: *Census of the Population, 1980*, "General Social and Economic Characteristics," tables 59, 130, 136, 142, 148, 154. Hispanics who classified themselves as neither white nor black are included among whites to provide comparability with previous years.

Table 7.7

Black-White Male Earnings Ratios[a] for Detailed Industries,[b] 1949–79

Year	Unweighted averages, 49 industries
1949	.712
1959	.670
1969	.742
1979	.712

[a]Ratio of nonwhite to white median annual earnings for males in the experienced civilian labor force.

[b]Manufacturing, transportation, communication, and utilities. Sample of 49 detailed (three-digit) industries covers all industries for which comparable data are available for each year. See Michael Reich, *Racial Inequality: a Political-Economic Analysis* (Princeton, N.J.: Princeton University Press, 1981): 53–58 for industry listings.

Sources:

U.S. Bureau of the Census, *1980 Public Use Microdata Sample Tapes*.

U. S. Bureau of the Census, *Census of the Population, 1970*, "Detailed Characteristics, U.S. Summary," 1973.

U.S. Bureau of the Census, *Census of the Population, 1960*, "Industrial Characteristics," V. PC(2)-7F, 1967.

U.S. Bureau of the Census, *Special Reports*, "Industrial Characteristics," PID-15 Series, 1955, Table 2.

U.S. Bureau of the Census, *Census of the Population, 1950*, "U.S. Summary," vol. 1, 1953, Table 133.

Theories of Racial Inequality

How can we understand the persistence of racial inequality in a society such as the modern United States? Unlike the eras of southern slavery or debt peonage and unlike contemporary South Africa, blacks and whites today work in a capitalist economy that is premised upon free labor mobility. Unlike the era of Jim Crow, blacks and whites today live in a liberal democratic polity that is premised upon one-person, one-vote principles. Government policy, moreover, explicitly prohibits discrimination based upon race and attempts, through affirmative action programs, to remedy past racial inequalities. Schooling, moreover, is supposed to be equally available to all, and racial differences in schooling have narrowed dramatically. With such liberal economic and political institutions, the continuing reality of racial inequality demands explanation.

This conference is premised on the assumption that economists can address broad questions from one of three major intellectual approaches—neoclassical, institutional, and radical—the three "worlds" of labor economics represented here. Among economists the discussion of racial inequality can be categorized into three major approaches. In my view, however, these approaches divide differently from the three worlds division—they correspond not so much to such scholarly divisions as to political ones.

A conservative neoclassical approach regards competitive capitalism as the best cure for racism and attributes the persistence of racial inequality to noncompetitive market structures and to extramarket phenomena, notably the family and the state (including the educational and welfare apparatuses). A liberal neoclassical approach takes a less sanguine view of the effects of competitive markets upon racial inequality, has been mainly silent with regard to the family, and has been more sanguine with regard to the efficacy of liberal government interventions. The third approach combines the institutional and radical "worlds" of economics and emerges from a radical approach to economics that has been developed in the past fifteen years, during which, in my view, there have been greater similarities than differences between radical and institutional approaches.

In recent years radical economists have developed theoretical tools and analyses to study capitalist economies. For the first time, a Marxist microeconomics has been developed that is distinct from the neoclassical approach, and a Marxist-institutional approach to macroeconomics has been created that is distinctive from both traditional and Marxist macroeconomic theory. These efforts have contributed significantly to our understanding of capitalist economies.[12]

I draw upon these recent innovations in radical economics to develop further a political-economic analysis of racial inequality. In order to contrast the contending positions clearly, I first review the conservative and liberal neoclassical approaches. I then outline the approach to capitalist economies that forms the core of the radical theory.

The Conservative and Liberal Neoclassical Approaches

On the subject of race, neoclassical economics speaks not with one voice, but two. The conservative neoclassical approach sees competitive markets as the great dissolver of racial discrimination, eliminating all differences in factor returns that are not related to differences in individual productivity or preference (such as for leisure, hazardous work, present vs. future consumption, or risk aversion). The persistence of racial inequality is then attributed either to imperfections in market competition (in which case "pure" discrimination can persist) or to extramarket phenomena, particularly government and family structures and policies that may disadvantage blacks. According to this view, if competitive markets are operating, governmental efforts can only hurt blacks—whether by intention, as in the era of Jim Crow, or despite benevolent intentions, as in the current conservative view of governmental antipoverty, welfare, and affirmative action policies as constituting in effect a "government plantation" analogous to the plantations of the cotton era.

The liberal neoclassical view, by contrast, takes a less sanguine view of markets and a more sanguine view of government policy. Markets do not eliminate discrimination because of difficult-to-eradicate imperfections—such as information and personnel costs—and feedback effects. Alternatively, markets might eliminate discrimination but the time period involved is so great as to constitute effective market failure and to justify governmental policies.

Since I have elsewhere presented a detailed discussion and critique of these two neoclassical approaches I confine myself here to a single summary comment: both conservative and liberal neoclassical approaches ignore conflict and power and consequently contain inadequate accounts of markets and governments.[13] (I leave aside here their treatments of the family.) Alternative approaches to markets and government, which build upon the institutional and radical traditions to examine changing structures of power, can better aid our understanding of the dynamics of racial inequality.

The Radical Approach to Racial Inequality

The radical view of the capitalist economy builds upon two institutional specifications which together distinguish the concept of the capitalist economic process from that of the competitive market process developed in the Walras-Arrow-Debreu tradition.[14] First, the distribution of property in the means of production is highly concentrated, so that most households are dependent upon labor incomes.[15]

The second institutional specification, related to the first but not reducible to it, states that the labor market is of necessity a market of incomplete contracts. Employers cannot purchase workers with a definite flow of labor services in the way that they can purchase a capital good with a technologically specified flow of capital services. The purchase of labor time does not determine the flow of labor services because workers are conscious human agents who pursue goals that differ, at least in part, from those of their employers.

These goals are not limited to the pace of work or the extent of compensation; they also include the desire to obtain meaning and identity through work and through social relationships at the workplace. These goals are pursued through both individualistic and solidaristic practices, the mix varying greatly in degree. Such practices, which can coexist with competition among workers, are inherent in workplace relationships. Consequently, for capitalist production to be profitable, a set of managerial practices must be adopted by employers to extract work from workers at an average product wage less than the average product of labor. This specification of the problem of extracting work from workers distinguishes radical theory from traditional neoclassical theory.[16]

The two institutional specifications of the radical perspective can be combined with assumptions of competitive market conditions with flexible wages and no information, monitoring, or personnel costs to generate surprising results: Involuntary unemployment and wage inequality between black and white workers (of equal productivity and preference characteristics) can persist in competitive equilibrium. The presence of unemployed workers outside the workplace and the presence of wage differences among black and white workers inside the work-place (as well as out) constitute sources of employer power over individual and collective action by employees.[17] It is through this power that employers are able to profitably extract work from workers.

The theory thus states that racial wage differentials are profitable to individual employers and will not be completed away, even if employers are not the direct agents of racial discrimination. The theory also predicts that interracially solidaristic practices by workers will be associated with less racial inequality, higher wages for all workers, and lower profits for employers.

Such a theory is difficult to test empirically. Nonetheless, the empirical work that has been performed is consistent with the theory, but not with neoclassical approaches to discrimination. I have already reviewed the persistence of racial income differentials in the face of equalizing pressures in the capitalist sector of the economy. My previous econometric research using detailed industry data also supports the radical theory. I found that black-white wage ratios are positively associated with greater unionism, higher white wages, and lower profit rates.[18] Similar research across metropolitan areas using size distribution of income data comes to similar conclusions.[19]

Institutional Variation

This view of the capitalist economic process rejects the conservative neoclassical view that competitive capitalism provides the best cure for racism, or that capitalists constitute a progressive historical force opposing racism. At the same time, the opposite concept, that capitalism needs racism, also seems inadequate. Capitalist can benefit, both individually and in the aggregate, from racial inequality. But there are a complex set of possible relationships among capitalism, government policy, and racial inequality. In both the economic and the political realms, progressive coalitions can alter structures of power and in fact, race relations vary considerably among the advanced capitalist nations. The range on racial issues goes from the more egalitarian, such as Sweden, Denmark, and the Netherlands, to the most brutal, such as South Africa, with the United States and the rest of Western Europe somewhere in between.

To comprehend this particular variation we must see it as part of a more general historical reality. There are many different kinds of capitalisms, with no single path of development discernible among them. A satisfactory theory of capitalism needs to be able to encompass and explain these differences.

With several colleagues I have elsewhere sketched an institutional theory of the sources of historical variations in capitalist countries.[20] This theory emphasizes the importance of the institutional environment that surrounds the capitalist accumulation process. The institutions that form this environment together constitute what we call the social structure of accumulation. The rise and decline of a social structure of accumulation is correlated with long swings in economic activity and delineates successive stages of capitalist development. A new social structure of accumulation emerges when a complex and lengthy struggle among classes and groups is resolved and a new governing coalition is able to institute its reform program.

I cannot in this paper develop a full analysis of the relationship between race relations and the social structure of accumulation. Instead, I present some schematic remarks concerning the dynamics of postwar race relations and their connection to the fluctuations of the postwar social structure of accumulation.

To begin, consider the role of racial issues in the construction of the postwar limited capital-labor accord, which constitutes a central element of the liberal postwar social structure of accumulation. The limited accord between organized labor and capital emerged from the 1940s' resolutions of labor struggles that had been waged since the 1930s. A relatively egalitarian approach to race relations by the industrial unions proved to be a critical variable in these struggles.[21] Earlier attempts to organize industrial workers had foundered largely on the divisive factor of race, as many employers of blacks, such as Henry Ford, well knew.

The formation of a durable multiracial coalition among U.S. industrial workers therefore constituted a key innovation in the early successes of the CIO, whose strength certainly would have been much diminished had this breakthrough in race relations not occurred. The CIO's experience contrasts especially with the record of other New Deal era reforms, none of which significantly changed the lives of blacks for the better.

Both blacks and white workers in the industrial unions gained enormously from the CIO's efforts. Blacks particularly benefited from the CIO opposition to racial segregation and the policy of disproportionately raising the wages of unskilled workers. The experiences of this period show that race and class issues can be combined in struggles without sacrificing the integrity of either. Bringing them together resulted not in divisiveness or a longer list of demands, but in a progressive coalition whose whole was greater than the sum of its parts.

The changes of the 1930s were continued by the late 1940s as the limited capital-labor accord became solidified. A key turning point occurred in 1948 when the labor movement's campaign to extend unionization to the largely unorganized South failed dismally, primarily because of a decision not to challenge the pattern of southern race relations. The labor movement's failure to challenge race relations in the South marked the point beyond which labor could make no further gains. Progress in race relations proved critical in the formation of the CIO, and regress in race relations proved critical in its containment.

Under the capital-labor accord, blacks inside the industrial sector had made some gains. But the majority of blacks remained outside, either in what we now call the secondary sector of the labor market or outside the wage-labor sector altogether, trapped in the sharecropping economy of the agrarian South. The exclusion of most blacks from the limited capital-labor accord soon generated pressures upon it. From 1957 on, a mass civil rights movement gathered steam, initially in the South where its attention centered on the dismantling of legal segregation and disfranchisement.

At first the movement had little impact upon the capitalist sector, where blacks still mainly provided a supply of low-wage labor to employers. But by the late 1960s this structure began to change, as the combined effects of the civil rights movements and the booming demand for labor succeeded in opening many primary sector jobs, blue collar and white collar, to black workers. Blacks became much more heavily represented in the traditional working class than ever before, and at a rate of change much greater than in any period since World War II. Equally important, the black consciousness movements of the period transformed the expectations of black workers, who no longer formed a docile low-wage labor supply.

In the 1960s and 1970s, the civil rights movement also ignited other courses, including feminist, antiwar, environmental, and labor struggles. Collectively, and in conjunction with other contemporary developments, these movements contributed to the decay of the capital-labor accord and other key elements of the postwar social structure of accumulation. By the early 1970s the collective strength of coalitions of the labor movement combined with various social movements had grown considerably. The concomitant decline in the strength and power of capital first became highly visible in the aftermath of the 1973 oil crisis, when much of the burden of adjustment for higher energy prices fell upon capital, and in the deep 1974–75 recession, when labor, minorities, and women were able to maintain their relative position while capital again proved surprisingly weak.

By the mid–1970s economic pressure—inflation and slower growth in real wages—were beginning to be felt by many whites as well as blacks, placing strains upon interracial alliances. At about the same time capital began a systematic counteroffensive to restore its former power. In this counteroffensive two racial factors were of great benefit to capital and contributed to the end of the period of black advancement.

First, visions of a greater social good and of greater racial equality to be brought about through the collective action of multiracial coalitions were repeatedly challenged and defeated. The process by which this occurred was complex. Challenges were frequently organized by capital, as in the furor over the very limited affirmative action employment programs in place in the 1970s (recall the hysteria over the Bakke case). Many conservative, liberal, and radical whites in all layers of American society at the time saw further racial progress as a zero-sum game, played at white expense, and they therefore participated actively in these challenges.

The econometric evidence in *Racial Inequality* established that a nonzero-sum game, based on class rather than race conflict, could have been played. But by the 1970s, the 1930s' conception of the integration of race and class issues through a broader reform process was largely absent from existing understandings and programs. As a result whites and blacks lost an opportunity for progressive reform that would have benefited both.

A second racial element of the capitalist counteroffensive also contributed both to the end of the period of advancement for blacks and to the reestablishment of capitalist power in the labor market. By the late 1960s employers began to recognize that blacks were no longer a source of docile and cheap labor. This shift in the character of the black labor supply should be understood primarily in terms of the heightened consciousness of blacks developed by the civil rights movement and only secondarily as resulting from the growth of transfer payments (in part also a result of the civil rights movement). In any case, employers began actively to recruit and to switch to new labor supplies, mainly Latinos already in the United States and new immigrants from Latin America, the Caribbean, Asia, the Pacific Islands, and elsewhere. These groups became a major source of new labor supplies for the private sector. At the same time, the growth of government, which had been the fastest growing employment sector for blacks, slowed substantially. The twofold reduction in the demand for black labor explains declining black employment to population ratios in this period. (No expansion in black labor supply occurred when transfer payments were reduced in the 1980s.) Employers succeeded in reestablishing low-wage employment, which grew rapidly, but a remarkably small percentage of these jobs were filled by blacks.

The result of the capitalist counteroffensive is clear: the rise of competition among all and social meanness toward disadvantaged groups. Was this not a preview of the drama that we now know as the broader conservative political shift of the past decade?

Conclusion

I conclude that progress and regress in race relations do not depend in a simple manner upon traditional labor economic variables unmediated by considerations of power and conflict. In the prewar and the postwar eras progress in race relations has depended upon the development of interracial class and multiclass coalitions and the ability of such coalitions to conceptualize and effect progressive reform programs that would transform black-white relations from perceived zero-sum games into nonzero-sum games. High rates of economic growth can create permissive conditions for such coalitions and nonzero-sum games to develop. But the extent to which they are effective depends upon power relations that are not themselves reducible to traditional economic variables.

The improvement in the relative position of black men in the 1960s was not just the product of high rates of economic growth as James Tobin argued at the time. It was also directly connected to the sociopolitical movements pressuring for change in that decade. These movements did not succeed in creating a nonzero-sum game based upon class rather than race conflict. As a result, little was left of these movements by the early 1970s. As a further consequence, existing pressure upon the capitalist and government sectors to maintain affirmative action and other such programs soon further eroded, ushering in the current era of reaction.

In this paper I have tried to convey the differing pictures of postwar trends in racial income differences that emerge from data on the nation as a whole and from individual sectors. The sectoral approach shows that some improvements have taken place, but mainly for reasons other than exogenous shifts in supply (human capital) or demand variables. Little secular progress is apparent, however, within the capitalist sector of the economy, as improvements have been followed by retrogression. I have suggested that the dynamics of sociopolitical movements and power relations explain both the improvements and the retrogressions.

In making the argument that black-white relations are determined more by sociopolitical movements and institutionalized power relations than supply and demand variables in markets, I recognize at least three considerations that must be addressed to render the argument more cogent.

First, as a simple queue theory of the labor market suggests, the rate of economic growth and the consequent state of labor market tightness will affect black-white employment and income ratios. In recent decades the black unemployment rate has remained approximately double that among whites, with only a slight tendency for the ratio to increase during recessions and decrease during expansions. Consequently, as the overall unemployment rate falls, unemployment among blacks falls roughly twice as fast as among whites. At the same time, skill differentials in wages narrow during economic upturns, disproportionately affecting blacks because they are more likely to hold lower-paid jobs. Although these phenomena pertain to short-run cyclical movements, similar effects apply for long-swing movements—labor demand conditions do play some role in determining black-white income ratios.

Second, while I have stressed the importance of political movements and the outcomes of power conflicts, I have not provided an analysis of the developmental path of these dynamics. Economic variables may play a role here too. For example, it has often been posited that rapid economic growth produces more rapidly rising expectations, increased capacities for collective organization, and increased efficacies of collective action. Such considerations suggest that the development and consequences of sociopolitical movements are not exogenous variables, and may themselves in part be the product of economic variables traditionally analyzed by economists.

Both of these modifications to my argument, which are a return to the traditional analytic categories of economics, are turned upside down by the final modification.

If the rate of economic growth affects the relative demand for black labor and conditions the dynamics of collective action, it must also be recognized that the growth process itself is not independent of income distribution and power relations. The crisis and slowdown of the world capitalist economy in the 1970s and 1980s indeed occurred because of the declining share and power of capital and subsequent attempts by capital, at both the microeconomic and macroeconomic levels, to regain its previous position. Both supply and demand variables reflect power and conflict processes that have affected black-white income differences.

I have attempted to outline some of the differences between conservative or liberal neoclassical approaches, on the one hand, and a radical-institutional or (to use a term I much prefer) a political-economic approach, on the other. Of these, it is the political-economic approach that seems better suited to comprehend the rise and decline of racial economic justice in our era.

Notes

1. See, for example, Robert Weaver, *Negro Labor: A National Problem* (New York: Harcourt, Brace & Co., 1946) and Harvard Sitkoff, *A New Deal For Blacks* (New York: Oxford University Press, 1978.

2. Weaver, *Negro Labor*, 78.

3. Michael Reich, *Racial Inequality: A Political-Economic Analysis* (Princeton, N.J.: Princeton University Press, 1981): chap. 2.

4. See, for example, August Meier and Elliott Rudwick, *Black Detroit and the Rise of the UAW* (New York: Oxford University Press, 1979).

5. In a period of declining black labor force participation rates (relative to whites) official statistics on the relative earnings of blacks contain a well-established upward bias. Depending upon racial trends in nonlabor incomes, racial income trends may also be biased upward over time. This issue has been addressed for earnings by William A. Darity ("Illusions of Black Economic Progress," *Review of Black Political Economy* [Winter 1980]: 153–168), Charles Brown ("Black/White Earnings Ratios Since the Civil Rights Act of 1964: The Importance of Labor Market Dropouts" [National Bureau of Economic Research Working Paper No. 617, 1981], and Saul D. Hoffman and Charles R. Link ("Selectivity Bias in Male Wage Equations: Black-White Comparisons," *Review of Economics and Statistics* [May 1984]: 320–24.

6. See James P. Smith and Finis R. Welch "Black-White Male Wage Ratios: 1960–1970," *American Economic Review* (June 1977: 323–38; James P. Smith "Race and Human Capital," *American Economic Review* (September 1984); and Glen G. Cain, "The Economic Analysis of Labor Market Discrimination: A Survey" (Institute for Research on Poverty Special Report No. 37, University of Wisconsin, Madison, 1985).

7. Richard B. Freeman, "The Changing Labor Market for Black Americans, 1948–72," *Brookings Papers on Economic Activity* (1973): 67–120, and "Time Series Evidence on Black Economic Progress: Shifts in Demand or in Supply" (Harvard Institute of Economic Research Discussion Paper No. 32, 1978) and Charles Brown, "Black/White Earnings."

8. Smith, "Race and Human Capital."

9. Two separate issues are pertinent here. First, the definition and method of measurement of race changed between the 1970 and 1980 censuses. In the same decade the size of Hispanic, Asian, and Pacific Islander population groups grew significantly. I have found (see "Long-Run Trends in Racial Economic Inequality" [forthcoming] that the change in census definitions substantially reduces some measurements of racial income differences, particularly those for many major metropolitan areas.

Second, the concept of money income and incomplete reporting of income to both the decennial census and the *Current Population Survey* imply likely biases in racial income trends, but the direction of bias is not transparent. See Daniel R. Fusfeld and Timothy

Bates 1984 *The Political Economy of the Urban Ghetto* (Carbondale, Ill.: Southern Illinois University Press, 1984) chap. 9.

10. I would also question the completeness of the human capital explanations. Cross-sectional data usually show, as in Table 7.2, that black-white income ratios for particular schooling groups decline with increasing age. Some have interpreted this decline as the result of ongoing discrimination, particularly in career promotions; others as the result of segmented labor markets. Human capital theorists attribute this pattern to the lower relative quality of black schooling in earlier decades—the so-called vintage effect. One cannot doubt the improved relative quality of black schooling since the 1930s and earlier. However, Smith's contention ("Race and Human Capital" and Smith and Welch, "Black-White Male Wage Ratios") that the quantity, quality, and vintage of human capital accounts for much of the variation in black-white income ratios over time is not so persuasive.

First, the results seem to hold mainly for college-educated blacks; much smaller improvements in income are found for lower schooling groups. Since improvements in quality occurred at all schooling levels, the divergent trends in earnings seem to confound the human capital explanation. Second, as I have already mentioned, the extent of improvement is not clear, and even Smith's data show continuing unexplained black-white income differences. Third, cohort data show that black-white income ratios rose over time well after the cohorts completed their schooling. Since blacks in these cohorts are not likely to have received more on-the-job training or experience over their careers than whites, the continuing increases in relative incomes must have been due to other than human-capital-related explanations. Fourth, several researchers (Saul D. Hoffman, "Black-White Life Cycle Earnings Differences and the Vintage Hypothesis: A Longitudinal Analysis," *American Economic Review* [December 1979]: 855–67; Edward Lazear, "The Narrowing of the Black-White Wage Gap Differentials is Illusory," *American Economic Review* [September 1979]: 553–64; and Greg Duncan, "Recent Trends in the Relative Earnings of Black Men" [Survey Research Center, University of Michigan, 1981].) have used longitudinal data sets to obtain more appealing tests of the vintage hypothesis than is possible from moving cross-sectional data. Their results often contradict the vintage hypothesis and support the segmented labor market or promotion discrimination hypotheses. Fifth, historical research in progress by Gavin Wright ("Race and the Labor Market in Virginia, 1900–1926" [Department of Economics, Stanford University, 1984]) has shown shown that prewar trends in racial wage differentials were often related not to human capital variables but to institutional variables such as the extent and type of labor union power. Finally, changes in the extent of schooling and the returns to schooling themselves reflect institutional variables not analyzed by human capital theories. (Henry M. Levin ["Education and Earnings of Blacks and the Brown Decision" (Institute for Research on Educational Finance and Governance Report 79-B13, Stanford University, 1979)] provides a cogent alternative account emphasizing the role of the civil rights movement.) For all these reasons, human capital approaches seem incomplete as explanations of either past or present trends of racial inequality.

11. Reich, *Racial Inequality*, 63.

12. See Herbert M. Gintis, "The Nature of the Labor Exchange and the Theory of Capitalist Production," *Review of Radical Political Economics* (Summer 1976): 36–54; Reich, *Racial Inequality*; Michael Reich and James Devine "The Microeconomics of Conflict and Hierarchy in Capitalist Production," *Review of Radical Political Economics* (Winter 1981): 27–45; David M. Gordon, Richard Edwards, and Michael Reich, *Segmented Work: Divided Workers* (New York: Cambridge University Press, 1982); Samuel Bowles, David M. Gordon, and Thomas E. Weisskopf, *Beyond the Waste Land* (New York: Anchor Doubleday, 1983); Samuel Bowles and Richard Edwards, "Theoretical Developments in Radical Political Economy" (Paper presented at the American Economic

Association meetings, Dallas, Texas, 1984); Samuel Bowles, "The Productionn Process in a Competitive Economy: Walrasian, Neo-Hobbesian and Marxian Approaches," *American Economic Review* (March 1985): 16–36; and Samuel Bowles and Richard Edwards, *Understanding Capitalism* (New York: Harper and Row, 1985).

13. Reich, *Racial Inequality*, chap. 3.

14. Ibid., chap. 5.

15. For documentation, see Richard Edwards, Michael Reich, and Thomas E. Weisskopf, *The Capitalist System*, 3d ed. (Englewood Cliffs, N.J.: Prentice-Hall, 1986).

16. Recent neoclassical literature on the employment relations shows greater signs of similarity, but substantial differences remain. See Reich and Devine, and Bowles, *Understanding Racial Capitalism*.

17. Reich, *Racial Inequality*, "Microeconomics of Conflict," 204–15.

18. Ibid., 300–303.

19. Ibid., chap. 4 and 7.

20. Gordon, Edwards, and Reich, *Segmented Work*; Michael Reich, "Capitalist Development, Class Relations and Labor History" (Paper presented at the conference. "The Future of Labor History: Toward a Synthesis," Northern Illinois University, 1984).

21. Reich, *Racial Inequality*, chap. 5; Meier and Rudwick, *Black Detroit*.

PART II

COMMENTS:

Samuel Rosenberg, Roosevelt University

I like these papers. Individually, each is extremely interesting and informative; taken together, they are fascinating. Fundamentally, each asks the same basic question—What is the nature and extent of male racial differences in the labor market? Each uses information from the decennial censuses. Yet, their underlying theoretical frameworks substantially differ as do their quantitative findings. Not surprisingly, each writer is able to argue that the results support his position. The "facts" speak in three different voices and are unable to settle the competition between paradigms.

Smith and Welch, in a very ambitious venture, investigate male racial wage and income differentials from 1890 to 1980. They argue that blacks have made substantial relative progress due to improvements in the quantity and quality of their schooling. I contend, however, that they exaggerate the relative gains of blacks, overemphasize the role of human capital, and do not adequately treat dual labor market theory, the only alternative hypothesis they choose to investigate.

Smith and Welch claim to be comparing the average black and white worker. This is not the case. They exclude from their sample those who worked twenty-six weeks or less in the year prior to the census survey. This selection criterion truncates the lower tails of the black earnings and occupational distributions to a greater degree than the white ones. To the extent this occurs, the black-white earnings or income ratios will be biased upward at any point in time. In addition, if this truncation becomes more serious over time, as I believe it does, the relative gains of blacks will be exaggerated.

For most of the time period under consideration, blacks and whites were equally likely to be in the labor force. This situation began to change during the 1960s when the black male labor force participation rate began falling faster than the white one. In 1979, the white male labor force participation rate was 78.6 percent while that of blacks was 71.9 percent. Thus, by 1980 many blacks, who likely would have been earning low wages had they been working, were no longer included in the Smith and Welch analysis.

In addition to being less likely to participate in the labor market, blacks are more likely to be unemployed. And in recent times the average unemployed black worked fewer weeks per year than the average unemployed white. This difference in weeks worked widened during the 1970s. In a study of males aged 20 to 40 years in 1964, 1972 and 1978, Levy finds that in 1964 and 1972 unemployed blacks and whites worked on average approximately twenty-nine weeks in the previous year. But in 1978, unemployed blacks averaged only twenty-four weeks worked in the previous year while whites averaged thirty-three weeks.[1] It is likely that the average unemployed black in 1980 worked even fewer weeks in the previous year than in 1978 since the aggregate unemployment rate rose from 6.1 percent to 7.1 percent.

Thus, Smith and Welch include the typical unemployed black and white male in 1960 and 1970 but likely exclude the typical unemployed black, but not white, in 1980. In short, by explicitly ignoring those who have dropped out of the labor force and likely excluding the average unemployed black, Smith and Welch exaggerate the extent of relative progress made by blacks since the mid–1960s. Reich, who includes all males earning some income, not surprisingly finds considerably lower black-white mean annual income ratios for 1980 than do Smith and Welch.

Smith and Welch's analysis of income ratios based upon occupational position also potentially overstates the relative gains of blacks. Their measure of relative income changes only when the distribution of blacks and whites across occupations shifts over time. At the beginning of the time period, blacks are concentrated at the bottom of the occupational hierarchy while whites are more likely to be at the top. When a group is at the bottom of a given hierarchy, it is more likely to move up if it moves at all. The opposite holds for a group at the top. Thus, virtually by definition, Smith and Welch's measure of occupational progress would be expected to show relative gains for blacks. A more correct way to investigate trends in occupational mobility would be to study whites and blacks holding the same job at the beginning of the relevant time period and then to determine the extent of occupational progression over the period.[2]

The truncation of the black employment distribution and the problem with the occupation-based index both point to less relative black progress than Smith and Welch argue has occurred. Blacks have made gains since 1940, but there has not been the "steady and significant post–1960 rise in relative black incomes" that they claim.

The occupation-based black-white income ratio has its largest improvement from 1940–50 and 1960–70. The gain during 1970–80 is half of what it was in these two earlier periods and is totally due to the entering of the youngest cohorts into the labor market and the exiting of the oldest cohorts. In fact, several of the younger cohorts—those born in 1946–50 and 1936–50—show substantial declines in the relative standing of blacks, and the cohort born in 1941–45 shows no improvement. This, by the way, is prior to taking into account the upward bias intrinsic to their methodology.

The extent to which the gains made by blacks is primarily due to improvements in human capital is open to question. Racial differences in mean schooling levels have narrowed. Yet, since 1965 the labor force participation rates of blacks below the age of 35 have significantly dropped while they have risen for whites. Levy's work shows unemployed blacks between the ages of 20 and 40 having worse labor market experiences than similarly aged blacks in earlier years. The same does not hold for whites. Smith and Welch demonstrate a relative deterioration in the occupational standing of younger blacks in the 1970s.

These phenomena probably are due to the overall worsening of labor market conditions in the 1970s. In addition, the high levels of aggregate demand during World War II and the late 1960s, together with the civil rights movements of the times, help explain the progress of blacks during the 1940s and 1960s.

Pointing to the importance of general labor market conditions raises the corollary issue of the role of labor market structures—which Smith and Welch ignore.[3] They argue that the dual labor market theory, a theory of labor market structures, is unable to explain the labor market trends they find.

They test the dual labor market theory incorrectly by assuming all blacks work in the secondary labor market and all whites are found in the primary labor market. Yet all empirical works on segmented labor markets have shown that while blacks may be more likely to be in the secondary labor market than whites, many blacks hold primary sector positions and many whites work in the secondary sector.[4] Thus, rather than assessing dual labor market theory, they are merely investigating differential racial experiences in the labor market.

They argue that once starting positions are taken into account blacks and whites face similar career prospects. This, they claim, is counter to dual labor market theory. But they do not control for beginning in the primary or secondary labor markets, however defined. In addition, their sample selection criterion likely eliminates many who would have been working in the secondary sector.

Smith and Welch do not give adequate attention to labor market structures, while they are crucial for Philips and Kiefer as they are for Reich. Philips and Kiefer lucidly present the similarities and differences between a human capital approach and an institutionalist approach to racial wage inequality. They analyze the racial pay gap in 1939 and 1979 and find evidence supporting each perspective. They lean toward the institutionalist explanation.

Philips and Kiefer divide the labor market into three segments—secondary, lower primary, and upper primary—based on differential returns to schooling and work experience. There is no return to schooling or experience in the secondary sector. Age and seniority are important determinants of wages in the lower tier of the primary market, though there is some return to schooling. Formal schooling plays its greatest role in the upper tier of the primary labor market where there are also returns to work experience.

They analyze the incremental returns to schooling and age for blacks and whites in 1939 and 1979 and, based on the pattern of returns, place blacks and whites in each of the three segments. They argue that the relative gains of blacks from 1939 to 1979 can be explained primarily by more blacks gaining access to primary sector positions and more whites finding themselves in the secondary market and in the lower tier of the primary market. But Philips and Kiefer find that the racial pay gap within each sector "has not changed in forty years." Racial discrimination within each segment of the labor market remains a serious problem.

They very creatively place their results within a labor market segmentation framework. But, at times Philips and Kiefer go too far. They try too hard to claim that their findings are consistent with labor market segmentation theory. They attempt to rationalize anomalous findings; all economists do. But their rationalizations can be used to question their interpretations of other results thought to be supportive of labor market segmentation theory. They make life-cycle judgments based on cross-section data at a point in time.

Rather than explicitly characterizing occupations as being secondary, lower primary, or upper primary, they base their segmentation schema on income levels and incremental returns to schooling and age. By so doing, they avoid the criticism that their segmented labor market typology is an arbitrary one. But they do not conclusively demonstrate that the differences that they claim represent segmented labor markets are significant, either statistically or otherwise.

Their theoretical discussion correctly points out that the wage equations for the primary sectors should be upward sloping with respect to schooling and experience while that for the secondary sector should be flat with respect to these human capital variables and below the others at most points. But in their interpretation of their results they emphasize only the incremental returns to schooling and age.[5] For example, in 1979 they place all blacks and whites with less than a high school diploma in the secondary labor market. Yet many of these whites are earning as much or more than similarly aged blacks with substantially more years of schooling who are placed in the primary sectors. And they may continue to do so over their careers. Some of these whites may, in fact, be working in primary-type positions.

Philips and Kiefer are aware that some groups may be misclassified by their segmentation criterion. For example, they find that in 1979 the racial pay gap narrows to the 80–90 percent range for 25 to 34 year-olds who have attained at least a college degree. They assert that many young white college graduates may be holding lower tier primary positions. To the extent this is occurring, the average income level for young whites in the upper tier of the primary labor market will be biased downward, resulting in an apparent but not real convergence in racial wages in this sector. With this supposition, they then conclude that the racial pay gap has not changed in over forty years in each of the three segments of the labor market. But, there could just as easily have been a misclassification of workers in the secondary and lower primary sectors, resulting in an apparent but not real stability in the racial pay gaps over the past forty years.

Their methodology does not allow them to adequately deal with questions of intersectoral mobility, barriers to which are a central component of labor market segmentation theory. Philips and Kiefer argue that "in 1979, all blacks and whites with less than a high school diploma found themselves trapped in the secondary labor market." They base this conclusion on cross-section data showing returns to education for different age groups in 1979. But "being trapped" connotes remaining in the secondary labor market throughout one's working life. Philips and Kiefer's assertion from cross-section data at one point in time requires assuming that the current employment experiences of older blacks are useful predictors of the future employment prospects of younger blacks. This is quite a heroic assumption, one I do not feel comfortable making. Longitudinal data are needed to study occupational mobility.

Philips' and Kiefer's argument concerning the stability of the racial pay gap within each sector of the labor market and the importance for relative black progress of increased access to the primary labor market is consistent with Reich's analysis. Reich finds less racial progress than do Smith and Welch and argues that little, if any, improvement has taken place since the early 1970s. The black gains that have occurred have been due more to "shifts in the sectoral composition of the economy rather than because of declining inequality within sectors." His sectoral breakdown differs from that of Philips and Kiefer but his message is the same.

He provides the outlines of a political-economic approach for understanding contemporary trends in racial economic inequality. Although his explanations are provocative, I do not totally agree with them. He wishes to deemphasize the traditional economic variables focused on by economists and bring to the forefront the role played by social-political movements. But in doing so, I believe he has underestimated the importance of economic factors.

Significant black economic progress occurred during World War II and the late 1960s. Black economic gains during the war are attributed to the pressure placed on the federal government by the March on Washington movement, not to the great wartime expansion of demand for labor. Yet even by the summer of 1942, a year after the creation of the Fair Employment Practice Committee and the issuance of an executive order banning discrimination in defense industries and government, blacks composed only 3 percent of the war-production work force. Only by the fall of 1944 were they more than 8 percent, slightly less than their overall proportion in the labor force.[6] In addition, at this time black war workers were much more likely than whites to be found in areas classified as experiencing acute labor shortage. According to Robert Weaver, economic necessity was by far the most important factor in influencing the timing and extent of black participation in war industries.[7]

While the March on Washington coalition did exist, relations were not always smooth between blacks and organized labor. There were many instances where white males went on strike over the hiring and promotion of blacks. While they occurred in the early part of the war mobilization, they became more prevalent as more blacks were hired or promoted in defense industries. In addition, there were strikes by blacks against racial discrimination: overall, there were fifty strikes in 1943 and fifty-seven strikes in 1944 over racial questions.[8]

Reich's analysis of the late 1960s is more correct. He attributes the black gains to the combined effects of the civil rights movements and the booming demand for labor. He claims these interracial alliances were unable to survive the economic pressures of the mid-1970s and the capitalist counteroffensive. While basically true, my impression is that Reich overestimates the role played by the capitalist counteroffensive and underestimates the racism of white workers and the extent to which further racial progress had, in fact, become a zero-sum game by the mid-1970s. (At least it had become a zero-sum game for the relatively short run.)

In conclusion, the works of Smith and Welch, Philips and Kiefer, and Reich are extremely provocative treatments of past trends in male racial inequality. What are their implications for black progress in the future? Smith and Welch would argue that the continued elimination of racial differences in education would lead to further declines in racial inequality. But these racial education differences are not continuing to be eliminated. In fact, during the 1980s minority enrollment in colleges has been declining.[9] Philips and Kiefer would not leave the matter to the automatic workings of the market as would Smith and Welch. Rather they would call for labor market intervention by the government to eliminate racial discrimination in the secondary and primary labor markets. But as Reich argues, an interracial alliance pressuring the government would be required for such policies to be implemented. Unfortunately, such an alliance does not appear to be forming and I therefore believe the message of all of the papers, given the current political-economic environment, is that racial inequality will continue to exist for many years to come.

Notes

1. Frank Levy, "Changes in Employment Prospects for Black Males," *Brookings Papers on Economic Activity*, 2, 1980: 513–37.

2. For a discussion of the importance of holding initial occupational position constant and then analyzing occupational mobility, see Sam Rosenberg, "Occupational Mobility and Short Cycles," in Frank Wilkinson, ed., *The Dynamics of Labour Market Segmentation* (London: Academic Press, 1981): 229–40; and "Racial Differentials in Younger Male Occupational Mobility Over the Business Cycle: 1966–75," *Proceedings of the 38th Annual Meeting, IRRA*, Madison, WI: IRRA, 1986: 391–99.

3. Their occupation-based index assumes a rigid wage structure from 1890 to 1980. Human capital accumulation does not affect the wage structure. At best it influences the rate of passage through the occupational hierarchy. Given the importance of this index for their analysis, it is surprising they ignore issues of labor market structure.

4. See, for example, Sam Rosenberg, "Male Occupational Standing and the Dual Labor Market," *Industrial Relations* 19, no. 1 (Winter 1980): 34–49; and Russell W.

Rumberger, and Martin Carnoy, "Segmentation in the US Labour Market: Its Effects on the Mobility and Earnings of Whites and Blacks," *Cambridge Journal of Economics* 4, no. 2 (June 1980): 117-32.

5. For a very interesting discussion of the limitations of the incremental formulation for defining labor market segmentation see Paul Ryan, "Segmentation, Duality and the Internal Labour Market," in Frank Wilkinson, ed., *The Dynamics of Labour Market Segmentation* (London: Academic Press, 1981): 3-20.

6. Robert C. Weaver, *Negro Labor: A National Problem* (New York: Harcourt, Brace & Co., 1946).

7. Ibid., 92.

8. Don Q. Crowther and Ruth S. Cole, "Strikes in 1943," *Monthly Labor Review* 58, no. 5 (May 1944): 927-47; Don Q. Crowther and Ruth S. Cole, "Strikes and Lockouts in 1944," *Monthly Labor Review* 60, no. 5 (May 1945): 957-73.

9. Edward B. Fiske, "Minority Enrollment in Colleges is Declining," *New York Times* (October 27, 1985): 1, 30.

Richard Butler, Brigham Young University

These three papers have, at least with respect to their empirical content, a very similar focus—they are concerned with the *Growth of Male Wage and Salary Income*. They are not so much concerned with presenting evidence on the wage gap in any particular year as they are in seeking whether or not the human capital model provides a reasonable explanation of why relative wages are changing over time. I think their focus is appropriate for this conference, but we must be aware that we are ignoring some other very dramatic changes in the economy with respect to average hours worked, labor force participation rates, unemployment rates, and the occupational distribution. Unfortunately, unless one is very careful, these other trends can make the interpretation of trends in the relative wages very difficult. It's that difficulty to which I'll aim my remarks. That is, what do we learn about these paradigms from the empirical data presented?

In order to focus my remarks I start with the most common regression in labor economics.

$$\ln E^i = \alpha_0^i + \alpha_1^i S^i \tag{1}$$

where E^i and S^i are the earnings and formal schooling of the ith group (i denotes a particular race in a particular year). Then black wage growth between two periods (say 1960 and 1970) can be decomposed as follows:

$$\ln E^{70} - \ln E^{60} = (\alpha_0^{70} - \alpha_0^{60} + (\alpha_1^{70} - \alpha_1^{60})S^{70} + \alpha_1^{60}(S^{70} - S^{60}). \tag{2}$$

That is, earnings change as the intercepts change, as the returns to schooling varies (that is, because of the term $(\alpha_1^{70} - \alpha_1^{60})S^{70}$), or because the leveling of schooling has changed (the term $\alpha_1^{60}(S^{70} - S^{60})$). What strikes me as odd in all these papers is that the focus is on the $(\alpha_1^{70} - \alpha_1^{60})S^{70}$ component of wage growth. This term, it is argued, reflects respectively "changes in the quality of schooling" (Smith/Welch), "changes in the political environment" (Reich), or "changes in segmented labor markets" (Kiefer/Philips). While there is no clear unambiguous interpretation of the term $(\alpha_1^{70} - \alpha_1^{60})S^{70}$ the last term on the right-hand side, $\alpha_1^{60}(S^{70} - S^{60})$ clearly represents a "pure" human capital effect—how much observable improvements in formal schooling contribute to wage growth. And since all these papers address the relevancy of the human capital model, it seems strange to me that none examines the empirical relevance of this last term. For example, if it accounts for 60 percent of wage (or relative wage) growth that surely indicates something different about the human capital interpretation of wage growth than if it only accounts for 6 percent of the growth.

A careful examination of Table 5.1 in Smith and Welch seems to indicate that more than just human capital seems to be shaping the trend of relative wages. Consider the trends of relative wages of a given cohort—recalling that formal schooling has already been completed. Note that the 1–5 market experience cohort in 1940 represent the same individuals (or at least represents the same vintage of workers) as the 11–15 market experience cohort in 1950. For this group relative wages increased from 46.7 percent to 58.3 percent (see also Table 5.9). Six such intracohort comparisons are available between each decennial census, and what is striking about these changes is their cyclical pattern. All six comparisons increase between 1940 and 1950, as well as between 1960 and 1970. Five out of six increase between 1970 and 1980, while five out of six decrease between 1950 and 1960. These regularities are not readily explained by the human capital model. Neither is the secular growth exhibited over time—since formal schooling is constant, why should wages increase unless blacks are receiving more on-the-job training than whites (this seems implausible), or there is a sample selection process taking place, or some other secular forces are at work?

To Smith and Welch's Tables 5.2 and 5.3, and Figure 5.1, I would juxtapose similar inequality measures of educational attainment. These are very interesting tables, but they do not tell us anything about the relevancy of the human capital model in contributing to the decline of income inequality. The most convincing evidence they present on behalf of the human capital model is given in Table 5.4. I will point out a further anomaly with that table, the resolution of which, I believe, further tends to reinforce their conclusion. Comparison of Table 5.6 and Table 5.4 shows a decrease in the quantity of schooling (Table 5.6, 1890–1905) precedes a decrease in the relative wages of blacks (1920–40). The direction of that impact seems correct; the size does not. For while the increasing spread in the surplus schooling of whites in 1890–1905 is small relative to the decrease in other years (Table 5.6), the percentage decreases in relative wages in 1920–40 (reflecting the 1890–1905 reversals) are much larger than the percentage increases subsequently. Why? The answer lies in the figure giving black-white relative educational expenses in South Carolina. The U-shaped pattern is obvious, with

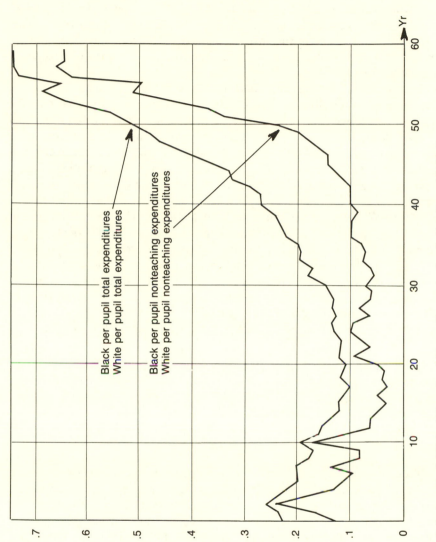

Black per pupil total expenditures
White per pupil total expenditures

Black per pupil nonteaching expenditures
White per pupil nonteaching expenditures

Relative Black/White Educational Expenditures in South Carolina, 1900–60

blacks receiving only one-tenth the aid that whites received around 1917. So not only is the *quantitative* dimension of relative schooling changing, but the *qualitative* dimension is changing even more. When the qualitative dimension is taken into account, it is not surprising that—as, indeed, the human capital model would predict—the 1920–40 decreases would be large compared to subsequent increases in relative wages.

Finally, I have a few concerns about the results in Table 5.8. The first concern was outlined in my discussion of equation (2) above: why examine only the returns to schooling, when only the *pure* human capital effect (the last right-hand term of the equation has an unambiguous interpretation)? The other concern is somewhat more technical. I understand the need to impose some sample criterion in order to keep the data as "clean" as possible, hence the truncation of those with very "high" and very "low" wages. But in real terms, the upper truncation on real weekly wages increased rapidly to 1970, then decreased significantly in 1980 (in 1967 dollars, these values are $298 [1940], $347 [1950], $705 [1960], $1,075 [1970], and $698 [1980]). Why this pattern of truncation? Could anything be done to assure us that sample selection doesn't become a serious problem?

While the theoretical contrast between the neoclassical and institutionalist models in the Kiefer/Philips paper is clear, I am not confident that the empirical research allows us to say much about either paradigm, let alone allow us to differentiate between them. Their equation associated with Table 6.1 can be written in the context of my equation (1), by replacing my S with $\ln S$ as

$$\ln\left(\frac{E^B}{E^W}\right) = B_0 + B_1 \ln\left(\frac{S^W}{S^B}\right) + B_2 \ln S^B \tag{3}$$

$$\text{where } B_0 = (A_0^B - \alpha_0^W)$$
$$B_1 = \alpha_1^W$$
$$B_2 = (A_1^B - \alpha_1^W).$$

The omission of the last term in the right-hand side of equation (3) forces the returns to black and white schooling to be the same at every point in the sample and probably seriously biases the results, given the detailed analysis by Smith and Welch. Another type of human capital model (namely, the human capital model of migration) has individuals acquiring "locations" to increase wages rather than acquiring job "skills." This model reverses the causality in equation (B) of Table 6.1, but includes the same variables—so how can the equation be viewed as a contrast to the human capital model? Finally, the general applicability of the Mississippi index (using the percent of black men living in Mississippi) concerns me—not only in Tables 6.1 and 6.2, but also in Table 6.3. More discussion of the relevance of Table 6.3 to the neoclassical/institutionalist debate would probably be helpful, especially since the dependent variable measures a different vintage of workers in year t than it does in $t - 10$.

Finally, it would be useful for the reader to realize that Kiefer/Philips, in the pedagogical spirit of their paper, are treating the 1939, 1979 cross-section age/income profiles as if they represented the *life-cycle earnings* of those workers. They do not, of course. The vintage of workers matters: a 60-year-old in 1939 (or 1979) is not the same as a 20-year-old in the same year and will not face the same earnings profile. Had Kiefer/Philips replicated Table 5.9 of Smith/Welch by educational cohort, the empirical results would have been much more relevant to the theoretical discussion.

I have three comments on the empirical evidence presented by Professor Reich. First, since Professor Reich argues that it is the shifting of blacks from lower- to higher-paying sectors that drives up their average wages (given the Smith/Welch results), I think that it would be appropriate to do a simple accounting decomposition of overall relative wage growth to check out this assertion. Second, such an accounting may be useful because, rather than shifting sectoral weights, the difference between Professor Reich's results and the Smith/Welch results may be that they use weekly wages while Professor Reich uses annual earnings or annual income. Annual *earnings* introduces labor supply into the comparison, while annual *income* introduces not only labor supply, but also a host of clouding trends in family size and needs-based government programs. (Incidentally, the increase since the early 1960s in needs-based programs strongly suggests that the trend of racial income may be biased downwards over time—rather than upwards as some have suggested. In order to "refute" the human capital explanation of relative wage growth with these data (Tables 7.3–7.7), Professor Reich would probably need to augment this information with data on the relative labor supply of blacks, showing how the trends in wages and hours worked contradicted the human capital paradigm. Finally, what is learned from Tables 7.4–7.7 is that there has been a decline in relative earnings in industrialized urban areas (in *annual* earnings/income). But what does this have to do with the human capital model? What, for instance, has happened to (relative) educational attainment in those areas? I am afraid that without additional information some might prematurely discount these findings as another example of selective migration—the younger, more highly educated blacks leaving the urban areas.

In conclusion, let me hastily add that I enjoyed reading all of the papers and hope that future, careful examination of the data may help resolve the empirical importance of these alternative ways of looking at trends in relative black wages.

COMPARABLE WORTH

PAPERS

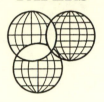

8

IMPLEMENTING COMPARABLE WORTH

CONCEPTUAL ISSUES AND IMPACTS

John Raisian, Michael P. Ward and Finis R. Welch

Introduction

Pay equity is a concept with which few would disagree. The notion that wages should reward a worker's skill, effort, and responsibility is at the heart of the American market system of compensation. The comparable worth movement, however, is an attempt to supplant the market by proposing alternative pay mechanisms based on a subjective scoring of abstract job attributes. The rejection of traditional market principles is motivated by the perceived failure of the market process, as well as existing antidiscrimination laws, to close the wage gap between men and women and to reduce the occupational segregation of the sexes.

The wages of working women in the United States have averaged about 60 percent of the wages of working men, with little apparent progress for several decades despite women's increased commitment to the labor market as evidenced by the surge in their labor force participation rates.[1] Part of the wage differential is explained by differing amounts of labor market experience between men and women and by differing intensities of commitment to the labor force. A report on comparable worth by the U.S. Commission on Civil Rights points out that:

John Raisian is Associate Director of the Hoover Institution, Stanford University, Stanford, California. Michael Ward is Vice President of Welch Associates in Los Angeles, California, and Finis Welch is Professor of Economics at UCLA and President of Welch Associates.

The 1983 pay ratio, when based on annual earnings of mostly full-time workers, was 63.6 percent, and is 72 percent when based on hourly wages. If only full-time workers between 20 and 24 years old are considered on an hourly basis, the earnings ratio is 89 percent. Women aged 25 to 34 years old earn 80 percent of what their male counterparts earn, and women over 35 earn about 65 percent of the average hourly wage of the counterpart male population.[2]

Thus, even among full-time workers, men work more hours per week than women,[3] and the age pattern evident for the wage gap points to differential accumulations of labor market experience. In another study, we find that after men and women have been out of school just six years, women have worked 1.6 years (or 30 percent) less than men; after sixteen years out of school, women average only half as much labor market experience as men.[4] Generally, empirical studies suggest that at least half of the wage gap is attributable to observed differences in labor market characteristics.

Another attribute of the labor market is that four out of five working women are in occupations where women account for at least 70 percent of all workers. This is a key factor for the emergence of the comparable worth doctrine. Treiman and Hartmann[5] state that, ". . . not only do women do different work than men, but also the work women do is paid less, and the more an occupation is dominated by women, the less it pays." Thus, there are two prominent components of the wage equality issues: (1) wage parity within occupations, and (2) wage parity across occupations. The Equal Pay Act of 1963 is designed to address "equal pay for equal work," and proposed comparable worth legislation is targeted to attain "equal pay for comparable worth," allowing for pay comparisons across occupations.

In our study, we attempt to empirically differentiate between (1) a general proposition that women are paid less than men, and (2) a narrower proposition that women are paid less than men *because* they work in jobs dominated by women. In so doing, we critically evaluate comparable worth methodology and its anticipated impacts, depending upon which of the above propositions are emphasized in the implementation of the comparable worth doctrine.

Comparable Worth Methodology

The goal of comparable worth advocates is to have wages in an occupation be determined by a vector of job attributes; i.e.,

$$W_j = f(A_{1j}, A_{2j}, \ldots, A_{kj}) \tag{1}$$

where W_j denotes the wage in the jth occupation, and the A's denote a series of scores on k job attributes.[6] Operationally, the first step is to decide on the appropriate functional form of the wage-job-attribute relation. This choice is certainly arbitrary and not based on science or fact. In our presentation, we subject this relation to a log-linear form; i.e.,

$$\ln W_j = a_o + a_1 A_{1j} + a_2 A_{2j} + \ldots + a_k A_{kj} \tag{2}$$

where the a's represent the attribute weights or parameters to be determined.

It is then necessary to make a number of critical judgments (aside from functional form) in order to operationally utilize (2):

(a) How does one measure abstract attributes like skill, effort, and responsibility?

(b) How many attributes are to be included in the framework?

(c) How are the weights to be established?

(d) How does one insure objective "bias-free" procedures?

With regard to the measurement of attributes, it is conceivable that ordinal comparisons could be agreed upon, but the idea of assigning cardinal values to attributes like "skill" is completely arbitrary.[7] Furthermore, a decision to weigh skill units differently than responsibility units represents another arbitrary action. Consequently, it is impossible for the process to be objective; it can only be subjective. In terms of being bias-free, a judgment of any kind becomes solely a subjective opinion. Moreover, the complexity of the problem increases enormously as either the number of occupations or the number of job attributes increases.

Finally, it is easy to see that the comparable worth scheme completely supplants supply and demand. If two occupations are judged to be comparably worthy, the wages are set independent of occupational preferences on the part of workers or input demands on the part of producers. Without a price mechanism to alleviate potential excess demands and supplies, one expects to observe queues, discriminating choice behavior, or unofficial side payments.

A sense of the measurement problem is afforded from an analysis of occupational characteristics contained in a review by the Committee on Occupational Classification and Analysis of the *Dictionary of Occupational Titles* that describes the procedures used by the Department of Labor to rate jobs.[8] Each of approximately 12,000 job classifications in the dictionary is carefully evaluated on the basis of forty-six characteristics. There are three "worker functions" that are part of the forty-six characteristics. Their definitions, taken verbatim from the dictionary, are as follows:

Data: Information, knowledge, and conceptions, related to data, people, or things, obtained by observation, investigation, interpretation, visualization, and mental creation. Data are intangible and include numbers, words, symbols, ideas, concepts, and oral verbalization.

People: Human beings; also animals dealt with on an individual basis as if they were human.

Things: Inanimate objects as distinguished from human beings, substances or materials; machines, tools, equipment, and products. A thing is tangible and has shape, form, and other physical characteristics.

To say the least, each of these defined characteristics is vague. It is not at all apparent what is to be measured. Despite this ambiguity, evaluators are given the task of assigning each of the more than 12,000 jobs scores ranging from 0–6 for *Data*, 0–8 for *People*, and 0–7 for *Things*.

Added guidance is given to evaluators as to the precise assignment of scores. With regard to *People*, as well as the other two characteristics presented here, a high score represents a low level of complexity. A value of eight implies ''taking instructions or helping,'' where ''helping applies to 'non-learning' helpers,'' and ''no variety of responsibility is involved.'' At the other extreme, a value of zero implies ''mentoring: dealing with individuals in terms of their total personality in order to advise, counsel, and/or guide them with regard to problems that may be resolved by legal, scientific, clinical, spiritual, and/or other professional principles.'' The value descriptions for *Data* and *Things*, not to mention the other forty-three attributes, are similar in nature to *People*. The vagueness of these job characteristics and value definitions attests to the inherent difficulty in pinning down meaningful and objective numeric valuations of job worth. Although this effort represents one of the most careful attempts to organize job characteristics on a large scale, such a task simply cannot be meaningfully undertaken from the perspective of judging wage equality.

Wages, Job Characteristics, and Occupational Segregation

Despite the insurmountable difficulties in measuring job attributes for use in comparable worth schemes, existing job evaluations are available to illustrate pay equity mechanisms. The Committee on Occupational Classification and Analysis matched the 12,099 job titles in the *Dictionary of Occupational Titles* to the 591 three-digit occupational categories designed for the 1970 census.[9] Weighted averages of each of the forty-six scores were computed to derive analogous scores for each three-digit occupation. Most of the forty-six job traits and functions are found to be highly redundant statistically and, thus, multiple-item scales of the major underlying dimensions were developed using factor analysis. Four interpretable factors emerge: substantive complexity, motor skills, physical demands, and undesirable working conditions. Together, these four factors account for about 85 percent of the total variation of scores using all forty-six attributes.

The March 1982 Current Population Survey (CPS) is utilized to compare these attribute scores with wages and female representation by occupation. This CPS sample contains 1970 census occupation codes (three-digit) and allows the four job attribute scores to be linked to the sample. Two variables are constructed for each three-digit occupation: an average hourly wage rate, and the percent of workers (in the occupation) who are women. The hourly wage variable is defined as wages and salary in 1981 divided by the product of weeks worked in 1981 and usual hours worked per week. The wage variable can be computed for 53,743 individuals covering 410 three-digit occupations. However, many of the occupations have relatively few observations available to compute the wage and female representation variables. We decided to eliminate occupations from further consideration if there were less than thirty individual observations within an occupation. This procedure left 247 occupations in our analysis sample, representing 51,854 individuals; thus, information was discarded on 1,889 individuals, covering 163 occupations (an average of 11.6 observations per omitted occupation).

Selected descriptive statistics on the variables of interest are presented in Table 8.1. Scores on each of the job attribute variables range as follows: substantive complexity, 0.3 to 10.0; motor skills, 2.2 to 10.0; physical demands, 0.0 to 10.0; and undesirable working conditions, 0.0 to 4.7. The average hourly wage for a typical occupation is $8.14 (in 1981 dollars), and the typical occupation in our sample has 40.3 percent women. The range of hourly wages across occupations runs from $1.87 to $23.46, and the representation of women in an occupation ranges from none to 100 percent. The frequency variable measures the number of individuals that are part of the occupation in our sample. A typical occupation has 210 individuals associated with it, with a range running between 30 (by constraint) and 2,570.

In 1982, total civilian employment numbered 99.527 million, of which 43.256 million were women—43.5 percent. We use this percentage as a cutoff for describing ''men's jobs'' and ''women's jobs.'' That is, an occupation whose representation of women is less than the economywide average of 43.5 percent is termed a male occupation, and vice versa for a female occupation. Table 8.1 also contains descriptive statistics for male and female occupations. On average, male occupations score higher than female occupations in each of the four job attribute categories. The typical male occupation has about 15 percent women, whereas the typical female occupation has about 73 percent women. Moreover, the average wage in a typical male occupation is $9.47 compared to $6.46 in a typical female occupation—68 percent of the wage for the typical male occupation.

Correlation coefficients between selected pairs of the occupational characteristics are presented in Table 8.2. The only job attribute variable that has a high correlation with female representation in an occupation is the physical demands index; jobs requiring greater physical demands are concentrated in male-dominated occupations. The only job attribute variable that is highly correlated with observed average wage levels in an occupation is substantive complexity. Finally, there is a definite negative relation between the average wage level observed for an occupation and the percentage of workers who are women within the occupation, an empirical verification of the stylized fact pointed to by comparable worth advocates.

Table 8.1

Descriptive Statistics for Occupational Characteristics*

Occupational characteristic	Mean	Standard deviation	Minimum	Maximum
All occupations (247 observations)				
Substantive complexity	4.25	2.23	0.3	10.0
Motor skills	5.18	1.77	2.2	10.0
Physical demands	2.04	2.38	0.0	10.0
Undesirable working conditions	0.32	0.83	0.0	4.7
Percent female	40.3	32.9	0.0	100.0
Wage	8.14	2.96	1.87	23.46
Frequency	210	298	30	2,570
Male occupations (138 observations)				
Substantive complexity	4.41	2.31	0.3	10.0
Motor skills	5.44	1.72	2.2	9.9
Physical demands	2.95	2.70	0.0	10.0
Undesirable working conditions	0.40	0.94	0.0	4.7
Percent female	14.7	13.4	0.0	43.1
Wage	9.47	2.92	3.55	23.46
Frequency	196	283	30	2,570
Female occupations (109 observations)				
Substantive complexity	4.06	2.13	0.4	8.6
Motor skills	4.85	1.79	2.3	10.0
Physical demands	0.90	1.13	0.0	6.9
Undesirable working conditions	0.22	0.67	0.0	4.7
Percent female	72.7	18.3	44.2	100.0
Wage	6.46	2.02	1.87	11.95
Frequency	228	316	30	2,276

*Means and standard deviations are calculated using occupational magnitudes not weighted by cell size. A male occupation is defined as one having less than 43.5 percent women within the occupation; a female occupation is defined as one having greater than 43.5 percent women. The percent of total employment who are women economywide is 43.5 percent.

Sources: Ann R. Miller, Donald J. Treiman, Pamela S. Cain, and Patricia A. Roos, eds., *Work, Jobs, and Occupations: A Critical Review of the Dictionary of Occupational Titles* (Washington, D.C.: National Academy Press, 1980): Appendix F, and 1982 Current Population Survey.

Table 8.2

Correlation Coefficients between Selected Occupational Characteristics

Occupational characteristic	Percent female	Wage
Substantive complexity	−.12	.68
Motor skills	−.18	.13
Physical demands	−.53	.04
Undesirable working conditions	−.11	−.15
Percent female	1.00	−.54

Sources: Ann R. Miller, Donald J. Treiman, Pamela S. Cain, and Patricia A. Roos, eds., *Work, Jobs, and Occupations: A Critical Review of the Dictionary of Occupational Titles* (Washington, D.C.: National Academy Press, 1980): Appendix F, and 1982 Current Population Survey.

Selecting Weights for Job Attributes

Among the 147 occupations in our analysis sample, only three sets of occupations have attribute scores that are identical for each of the four attributes. These occupations are presented in Table 8.3. Bank tellers and medical secretaries have identical scores, both are female-dominated occupations, and the secretaries are observed to earn (on average) over 12 percent higher wages. In principle, comparable worth methodology would call for equality of wages. Another comparison involves legal secretaries and other secretaries (i.e., nonlegal and nonmedical). Both are female-dominated occupations, and legal secretaries are observed to earn (on average) nearly 10 percent higher wages. Again, despite identical scores for each of the job attributes, these workers earn different wages, differences that are not attributable to male or female dominance within the occupation.

In order to compare occupational categories according to degree of female representation, the attributes must be weighted and summed to obtain a single total score. Occupations can then be compared according to their total attribute scores. There are two ways of generating attribute weights: (a) *ad hoc* determination, and (b) regression of market wages on the job attributes. First, consider an *ad hoc* set of weights; namely, suppose each of the weights is equal to one, such that a unit of one job attribute (e.g., substantive complexity) is worth a unit of any other job attribute (e.g., motor skills). Indeed, there is no objective reason for justifying this set of weights; however, there is no objective reason that could be offered for any other set of weights (with the possible exception of market-determined weights, to be discussed subsequently).

Noteworthy comparisons using this scheme are presented in Table 8.4. For example, physicians, athletes, and roofers have identical total scores. Physicians receive relatively high scores for substantive complexity and motor skills, whereas roofers score highest on physical demands. If this scheme were adopted, it

Table 8.3

Occupations with Identical Attribute Scores*

Census occupation	1	Attribute scores 2	3	4	Percent female	Hourly wage
Bank tellers (301)	5.6	8.2	0.0	0.0	89.9	4.98
Medical secretaries (371)	5.6	8.2	0.0	0.0	100.0	5.60
Legal secretaries (370)	5.5	8.3	0.0	0.0	100.0	6.44
Secretaries NEC (372)	5.5	8.3	0.0	0.0	99.3	5.88
Machine operatives —not specified (692)	2.0	5.2	1.8	0.6	38.0	6.85
Miscellaneous operatives (694)	2.0	5.2	1.8	0.6	38.3	6.32
Operatives —not specified (695)	2.0	5.2	1.8	0.6	38.7	7.18

*Attribute scores 1–4 refer to the job attributes of substantive complexity, motor skills, physical demands, and undesirable working conditions respectively. Numbers in parentheses refer to three-digit census occupation codes for 1970. NEC is a census abbreviation meaning "not elsewhere classified."

Sources: Ann R. Miller, Donald J. Treiman, Pamela S. Cain, and Patricia A. Roos, eds., *Work, Jobs, and Occupations: A Critical Review of the Dictionary of Occupational Titles* (Washington, D.C.: National Academy Press, 1980): Appendix F, and 1982 Current Population Survey.

would force wages to be the same for the three groups, even though currently there are pronounced differences; physicians earn nearly two-and-a-half times what athletes earn and nearly twice what roofers earn.

Another comparison involves registered nurses, bank tellers, secretaries, and police—all of whom have total attribute scores within a tenth of a point. Both bank tellers and registered nurses are female-dominated occupations and yet the nurses earn 75 percent more than the bank tellers. In the case of police and bank tellers, police earn 89 percent more than the tellers. Police, however, are mostly men and bank tellers are mostly women. Does one conclude the existence of sex bias in this situation, especially in light of the other evidence on wage differences where sex bias cannot be claimed? Other suspicious comparisons include real estate agents and garbage collectors, library assistants and accountants, dishwashers and university teachers, carpet installers and psychologists, and gardeners and computer programmers. In many cases, the female-dominated occupation has wages that exceed the male-dominated occupation despite the equality of total attribute scores.

It would seem that a comparable worth scheme that assigned equal weights to the four job attributes would lead to rather radical adjustments in the existing occupational structure of wages. Another method for weight determination in-

Table 8.4

Occupations with Similar Total Attribute Scores When All Weights Are Unity*

Census occupation	1	Attribute scores 2	3	4	Total	Percent female	Hourly wage
Physician (065)	8.9	9.9	0.8	0.0	19.6	15.1	15.88
Athlete (180)	5.4	7.2	6.9	0.1	19.6	47.9	6.48
Roofer or slater (534)	3.1	6.5	10.0	0.0	19.6	1.0	8.12
Registered nurse (075)	6.1	6.6	1.0	0.0	13.7	94.9	8.73
Bank teller (301)	5.6	8.2	0.0	0.0	13.8	89.9	4.98
Secretary (372)	5.5	8.3	0.0	0.0	13.8	99.3	5.88
Police (964)	4.1	5.3	4.4	0.0	13.8	7.5	9.39
Real estate agent (270)	5.3	3.3	0.0	0.0	8.6	53.0	9.06
Garbage collector (754)	0.3	3.6	4.6	0.2	8.7	2.0	5.95
Library Assistant (330)	3.5	4.2	2.1	0.0	9.8	82.4	4.55
Accountant (001)	6.9	2.9	0.0	0.0	9.8	40.1	10.00
Dishwasher (913)	0.6	3.0	2.7	4.6	10.9	31.7	3.55
University teacher (140)	7.8	2.9	0.2	0.0	10.9	38.5	11.11
Carpet Installer (420)	3.4	7.4	1.7	0.0	12.5	1.0	6.35
Psychologist (093)	8.5	3.9	0.0	0.1	12.5	52.5	9.67
Gardener (755)	1.2	3.7	7.1	0.0	12.0	6.6	5.43
Computer programmer (003)	7.4	4.3	0.3	0.0	12.0	34.6	11.12

*Attribute scores 1–4 refer to the job attributes of substantive complexity, motor skills, physical demands, and undesirable working conditions respectively. Numbers in parentheses refer to three-digit census occupation codes for 1970. The total attribute score is simply a summation of the four individual attribute scores.

Sources: Ann R. Miller, Donald J. Treiman, Pamela S. Cain, and Patricia A. Roos, eds., *Work, Jobs, and Occupations: A Critical Review of the Dictionary of Occupational Titles* (Washington, D.C.: National Academy Press, 1980): Appendix F, and 1982 Current Population Survey.

volves regressing observed wages on the attribute scores similar to the specification outlined in equation (2) above. The regression coefficients would then provide estimates for each of the a's. The hypothesis maintained by comparable worth advocates, however, is that wages in an occupation are discriminately affected by sex composition. Consequently, the specification in (2) should be modified to allow for systematic differences in wages due to occupational segregation.[10] We control for sex-based wage differences by estimating the following specification:

$$\ln W_j = a_o + a_1 A_{1j} + a_2 A_{2j} + a_3 A_{3j} + a_4 A_{4j} + b(\%FEM)_j + c(CON)_j \qquad (3)$$

where %FEM denotes the percent of an occupation's workers who are women and CON denotes an added effect regarding female concentration. Specifically, the latter variable is defined as $CON = (FEM)(\%FEM - 44)$, where FEM is a dummy variable equal to one if the occupation is represented by more than 44 percent women, and zero otherwise.

Other analysts[11] have postulated a specification similar to (3), but without the variable CON. In this situation, %FEM is interpreted as capturing the sex bias in wages attributable to occupational segregation. We maintain that this variable instead represents, for the most part, an observation that women earn less than men in the labor market, independent of occupational employment. To illustrate this point, suppose all women earn wages that are 60 percent of their male counterparts, holding the other attribute scores constant. The upshot of this is that an occupation with all women will earn 60 percent of an occupation with all men. Furthermore, an occupation with half men and half women will have an average wage that is 80 percent of an occupation with all men. Thus, the coefficient on %FEM can be negative and significant as a result of women earning less than men generally, and not necessarily because women are concentrated in occupations that are, by-and-large, different from those of men.

At the other extreme, it could be maintained that men and women earn identical wages (on average) within an occupation, implying that a negative relation between wages and %FEM across occupations (holding job attributes constant) is indicative of sex bias. Thus, the key piece of information required to shed light on this issue is the degree to which wages vary between men and women within occupations as compared to across occupations. In our earlier study,[12] using individuals rather than occupations as units of observation, we estimated two regressions of log wages on (a) a female dummy variable and, (b) a female dummy variable as well as separate dummy variables for each of the three-digit occupations. From the first regression, we find that the female-male wage ratio is 0.65; from the second regression, we find that the ratio closes to only 0.71. The latter magnitude means that women on average earn 71 percent of the wages earned by men *within* any given occupation. In other words, only 17 percent of the wage gap is closed if wages are equalized across occupations, and 83 percent of the wage gap is attributable to wage differences within occupations. This information substantiates our claim that %FEM is indicative of general wage differences between the sexes, not of across-occupational concentration effects.[13]

The purpose of introducing the variable CON is to account for the possibility of wages being further depressed as a result of occupational segregation. Notice that the variable can take on values between 0 and 56. It is zero for all male-dominated occupations and is positive for all female-dominated occupations, increasing in a one-to-one fashion with %FEM. For a given set of attributes, the relation between

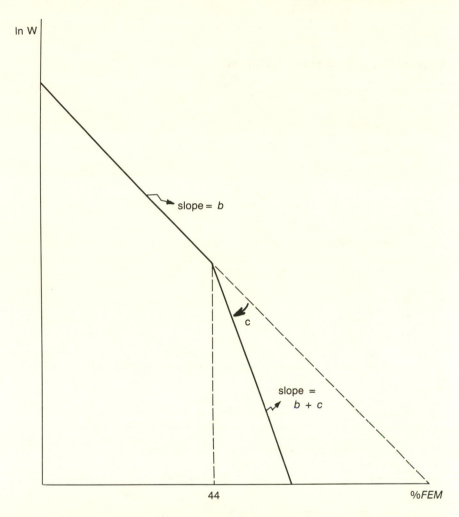

Figure 8.1. Structure of the Wage-Concentration Relation

log wages and %*FEM* is exhibited in Figure 8.1. Assuming the coefficients on both %*FEM* and *CON* are negative, the relation has two linear segments connected at the value of %*FEM* = 44. The slope of the segment to the left of 44 percent is equal to b, and the slope to the right of 44 percent is equal to $b + c$. Thus, b can be interpreted as the effect of whether women earn less than men in general, and c can be interpreted as the effect of whether women earn less than men *because* they are concentrated in "women's jobs." We think this is an important point in the comparable worth controversy because it provides some information relating to the source of wage discrepancies.

Regression estimates for three related specifications are presented in Table

Table 8.5

Wage Regression Parameter Estimates*

Explanatory Variable	Specification		
	1	2	3
Substantive complexity	—	.09659	.10004
		(14.52)	(17.02)
Motor skills	—	.00800	.00754
		(1.02)	(0.97)
Physical demands	—	−.00629	—
		(0.81)	
Undesirable working conditions	—	−.01101	—
		(0.68)	
Percent female (%FEM)	−.00304	−.00559	−.00501
	(2.23)	(4.56)	(4.94)
Female concentration (CON)	−.00671	−.00063	−.00118
	(2.81)	(0.33)	(0.66)
Constant	2.23919	1.82907	1.78399
	(62.97)	(25.36)	(31.30)
R-square	.361	.715	.714

*The independent variable is the natural logarithm of the average wage in an occupation. There are 247 occupations in the sample. Numbers in parentheses are absolute values of regression coefficients divided by standard errors.

Sources: Ann R. Miller, Donald J. Treiman, Pamela S. Cain, and Patricia A. Roos, eds., *Work, Jobs, and Occupations: A Critical Review of the Dictionary of Occupational Titles* (Washington, D.C.: National Academy Press, 1980): Appendix F, and 1982 Current Population Survey.

8.5. In the first specification, wages are regressed exclusively on *%FEM* and *CON*. Both regression coefficients are found to be negative and significant, suggesting that women have low wages generally and that wages are proportionately lower as a result of occupational concentration. The magnitude of the general effect suggests that women earn wages that are 26 percent lower than men and that the typical female occupation (i.e., 73 percent female) will have a wage that is 16 percent lower than the typical male occupation (i.e., 15 percent female). Taking both effects together, the typical female occupation has a wage that is 31 percent lower than the wage of its male counterpart; thus, the effect of occupational concentration represents a significant marginal effect.[14] However, no other considerations for the existence of wage differentials are taken into account—i.e., in this case, job attributes are not held constant.

In the second specification, job attributes are included with *%FEM* and *CON*; this is the specification outlined in equation (3). The regression coefficients on the job attributes represent the market's attempt to evaluate these factors for given values of *%FEM* and *CON*. Substantive complexity is by far the most important variable. The estimated weights for physical demands and undesirable working conditions are perverse since they are negative (though they are not significantly different from zero). It is not intuitive to expect that jobs with greater physical demands and/or more unpleasant working conditions will command lower wages, other things being equal.[15] Consequently, these two job attributes were dropped from the third regression specification, in which 71 percent of the observed variation in log wages can be explained by variations in the two job attributes, substantive complexity and motor skills, along with %*FEM* and *CON*. Dropping the other two job attributes has virtually no effect on the explanatory power of the model, though having substantive complexity and motor skills as part of the model does increase its explanatory power from 36 percent of wage variability to 71 percent.[16]

Notice the relative weights of substantive complexity and motor skills: the former job attribute has a weight more than 13 times greater than the latter. Consequently, it takes only one-tenth of a unit of substantive complexity to compensate for 1.3 units of motor skill.

The most intriguing result of these regressions is that the effect of occupational concentration (holding job attributes constant) is negative but negligible. The average wage of the typical female-dominated occupation is only three percent lower than the typical male-dominated occupation as a result of the occupational concentration effect.[17] Since the coefficient on %*FEM* represents a general wage differential between the sexes separate from occupational representation, the implication is that women earn 39 percent less than men, that the average wage for the typical female occupation is 25 percent lower than the wages for the typical male occupation, and that the total difference between these typical occupations expands to only 28 percent when considering the occupational concentration effect as well.

Implementation of Comparable Worth

Helen Remick has described comparable worth as being ". . .for many, a vague concept aimed at correcting. . .systemic sex bias in wages."[18] We interpret comparable worth as a mechanism designed to reduce across-occupation wage variability that is statistically correlated with female representation within an occupation. Other investigators have pointed to %*FEM* as an occupational concentration effect.[19] Instead, we view *CON* as a more appropriate indicator of occupational concentration with %*FEM* measuring the general degree to which wages vary between the sexes. Because comparable worth means different things to different people, however, it is certainly plausible that a structure could be proposed to close the wage gap and, if it goes beyond strict occupational concentration effects, so much the better from the standpoint of comparable worth advocates.

Obviously, the method of implementation chosen can appreciably affect the results in terms of wage adjustments and aggregate costs. We pursue two simulations of comparable worth implementation. First, suppose that the target is only the effect of occupational concentration—in our view, the stated conceptual point of emphasis by the advocates. Given our empirical structure, this amounts to adjusting upward everyone's wage by 1.18 percent for every ten percentage points that %FEM exceeds 44 percent—based on the coefficient estimate for CON. This adjustment would lead to an increased wage bill of 1.5 percent, and reduce the observed occupational wage gap between the typical female and male occupations by 7 percent.[20] While the 1.5 percent figure might appear to be small, the 1982 wage bill for wage and salary workers economywide amounted to approximately $1.5 trillion—1.5 percent of this magnitude yields $22.5 billion. Given the inflation and employment growth that has occurred since 1982, this increment would amount to approximately $28 billion today.

The second adjustment involves a compensation for both CON and %FEM effects. That is, in addition to the above adjustment, suppose that all wages of women are raised by 65 percent.[21] It might seem that this adjustment should involve raising the wages of all individuals, men and women, by around 5 percent for every ten percentage points that %FEM exceeds zero—based on the coefficient estimate for %FEM. Since we have demonstrated, however, that %FEM is measuring a general male-female wage difference and not an occupational concentration effect, this adjustment would perpetuate the wage gap.[22]

It is worth noting that the second wage adjustment does not take into account the known differences in labor market experience and labor force attachment between men and women alluded to earlier. Consequently, raising every woman's wage by 65 percent results in an overcompensation. In any event, such an adjustment would lead to increasing the wage bill by 25.7 percent and would reduce the observed occupational wage gap between the typical female and male occupations by 81 percent.[23] The gap is not closed totally because women's occupations are assigned lower levels of the job attributes substantive complexity and motor skills and they account for the remainder of the wage gap. The more than 25 percent wage bill increment would amount to around $385 billion in 1982 dollars and $482 billion today, given inflation and employment growth.

There is one important endogenous factor built into these kinds of schemes—namely, the number of occupations that are utilized. The 1970 census classification lists 591 different occupations; our CPS sample utilizes only 247 of the 591 because of sample size considerations. Despite being a seemingly large number, there is substantial heterogeneity of job titles within an occupation. For example, occupational code 231 represents sales managers and department heads in retail trade, but it includes department supervisors, division heads, floor supervisors, floor walkers, aisle managers, and ushers, representing an occupational hierarchy within itself. Thus, as the number of categories increases and the descriptions of jobs narrow, one expects greater across-occupation wage variability and less within-occupation variability.

As an illustration, suppose that every individual is unique and belongs to a separate occupation. In our analysis sample, the number of observations expands from 247 to over 50,000, %*FEM* becomes a dichotomous variable that is equivalent to indicating the sex of the worker, and *CON* must be dropped because of underidentification (i.e., *CON* is perfectly colinear with %*FEM*). By definition, all male-female differences in wages become the target of comparable worth because they are defined as differences across occupation. Unless the expansion of occupations leads to compensating adjustments in job attribute scores, such an action is expected to result in progressively greater wage adjustments. The implication is that, as the number of occupations is expanded, comparable worth implementation is more likely than the first adjustment to have an impact similar to our second simulated wage adjustment.[24] Thus, another subjective judgment comes into play prior to the implementation of a comparable worth mechanism— namely, the appropriate level of occupational detail.

Conclusion

Comparable worth methodology is aimed not at insuring equality of labor market opportunity, but at insuring equality of labor market outcomes. Even if this were a desirable public policy, the comparable worth solution is arbitrary and subjective. Meaningful measurement of abstract job attributes for hundreds, if not thousands, of occupations is impossible. The task of defining all relevant job attributes to be measured compounds the problems, and the weights to be assigned to the job attributes are not easily justified, although comparable worth proponents often look to the market for a source of help. Finally, the decision of where to draw the line when it comes to describing occupations is not one that is based on objective fundamentals. These are problems that have as much to do with inherent biases of those who will make these decisions as they do with the technical ability to make meaningful judgments.

What is wrong with wanting to close the pay gap between men and women? Women earn wages that are 60 percent of those earned by men. *Observed* differences in productivity-related worker traits explain at least half of this gap. There is no simple explanation for the remainder of the gap, which is commonly assumed to be attributable to discriminatory behavior on the part of market participants. However, it could as easily be due to differing *unobserved* productivity-related traits, compensation for differing conditions of work, and/or uncoerced occupational preferences for some type of work. Comparable worth schemes proceed on the presumption of discrimination in their undertaking of wage adjustments and, at the same time, eliminate the price mechanism within the labor market as a primary means of resource allocation. There is nothing wrong with wanting to eliminate discrimination but we need to be sure that is what we are doing—and not limiting our ability to efficiently allocate human resources.

Despite the gloom and doom portrayed by comparable worth advocates, there are significant signs of progress in recent years with regard to women's labor market patterns. In 1960, about two out of five women between the ages of 20 and 64 were in the labor force. Today, the number is three out of five. Women are gradually catching up to men in their stock of labor market experience, and this is gradually being translated into wage convergence.[25] Currently, men and women are graduated from college in almost equal numbers but, as recently as twenty years ago, men were twice as likely as women to obtain a college degree. Perhaps more importantly, new cohorts of women are choosing college majors in specialties other than traditionally female subjects. And recently women workers are shifting away from female-dominated jobs and toward previously male-dominated jobs.

The choice to pursue comparable worth methodology is a rather fundamental one. Today, we have a system where decentralized decisions by labor market participants dominate the process of wage determination. Comparable worth schemes would replace this process with centralized determinations of wages at the risk of substantial inefficiencies in the allocation of human resources. Given the facts and uncertainties surrounding this issue, we are convinced that a national mandatory implementation of the comparable worth idea would produce more harm than benefits.

Notes

1. James P. Smith and Michael P. Ward (*Women's Wages and Work in the Twentieth Century* [Santa Monica, Calif.: Rand Corporation, 1984]) maintain that there has been substantial progress in wage convergence between the sexes and that the observed constancy is attributable to compositional changes in the female labor force. Wage ratios are calculated for *working* men and women. During the last thirty years, the number of working women has grown enormously, with the new entrants and reentrants having relatively little labor market experience and lower than average education. As a result, these new entrants and reentrants have tended to hold down the average wage for all working women, disguising what would otherwise have been an upward trend in women's wages relative to men's. However, while progress is evident in these results, the wage gap is still substantial.

2. U.S. Commission on Civil Rights, *Comparable Worth: An Analysis and Recommendations* (Washington, D.C.: U.S. Commission on Civil Rights, 1985): 14.

3. Among full-time workers, men outnumber women 1.8 to 1. However, among part-time workers, women outnumber men 2.2 to 1—see John Raisian, Michael P. Ward, and Finis Welch, *Comparable Worth: Issues, Evidence, and Impacts* (Los Angeles, Calif.: Welch Associates, 1985).

4. See *Ibid.*

5. Donald J. Treiman and Heidi I. Hartmann, eds., *Women, Work, and Wages: Equal Pay for Jobs of Equal Value* (Washington, D.C.: National Academy Press, 1981): 28.

6. It is uncertain whether advocates think of W_j as the wage to be paid to all individuals in the jth occupation, or the average wage to be paid in the occupation that allows for a distribution of wages across individuals based on other factors (with the exception of sex per se). It is the latter interpretation to which we tend to give credence.

7. Moreover, the idea of comparing and scoring jobs independent of the individuals

holding the jobs is not a natural one to many economists.

8. Ann R. Miller, Donald J. Treiman, Pamela S. Cain, and Patricia A. Roos, eds., *Work, Jobs, and Occupations: A Critical Review of the Dictionary of Occupational Titles* (Washington, D.C.: National Academy Press, 1980).

9. See *ibid*, Appendix F.

10. To our knowledge, Treiman and Hartmann in *Women, Work, and Wages* were the first investigators to suggest this methodology. There is also an alternative that regresses observed wages on job attributes only, but only for a nondiscriminated group (e.g., white men). The weights that are generated could then be applied to all demographic groups. The weakness of this alternative approach is that, if jobs differ substantially by demographic group, the weights estimated for the nondiscriminated group may not be truly pertinent to the others.

11. E.g., Teiman and Hartmann, *Women, Work, and Wages*.

12. Raisian, Ward, and Welch, *Comparable Worth*.

13. Added features of male-female wage differentials within occupations and associated human capital characteristics are the subject of our ongoing research.

14. To determine the general wage effect between men and women, one computes $\exp\{(100)\,(b)\}\, -\, 1$; this calculation yields the wage difference between totally male and totally female occupations. Occupations having both men and women are interpreted as having the same wage differential between men and women, but a smaller occupational differential given the presence of men in the occupation. The wage difference between the typical male and female occupations attributable to the general wage effect is calculated as $\exp\{(73\, -\, 15)(b)\}\, -\, 1$. The total difference in wages between typical male and female occupations is given by $\exp\{(73\, -\, 15)(b)\, +\, (73\, -\, 44)(c)\}\, -\, 1$.

15. Using a linear specification of wages (rather than log wages) on job attributes and %*FEM* for 1970 census data on 499 occupations, Donald J. Treiman, Heidi I. Hartmann, and Patricia A. Roos, "Assessing Pay Discrimination Using National Data," in Helen Remick, ed., *Comparable Worth and Wage Discrimination* [Philadelphia, Pa.: Temple University Press, 1984] also estimate a negative weight for physical demands; their estimate for undesirable working conditions is positive though insignificant.

16. We do not mean to infer that subjective job attributes are appropriate measures to include as explanatory variables. Our hypothesis is that substantive complexity is probably correlated with such human capital variables as education.

17. The magnitude for the concentration effect alone is calculated as $\exp\{(73\, -\, 44)(c)\}\, -\, 1$.

18. "Major Issues in a Priori Applications," in Helen Remick, ed., *Comparable Worth and Wage Discrimination* (Philadelphia, Pa.: Temple University Press): 99.

19. See, for example, Treiman and Hartmann, *Women, Work, and Wages*.

20. For each three-digit occupation in our sample, we can compute a wage bill as being the average wage times the number of workers in the occupation (i.e., the frequency variable). An aggregate wage bill is generated by summing all of the occupational wage bills. For female occupations, the average wage is adjusted upward. Using the same process, new occupational wage bills can be generated and summed to arrive at a new aggregate wage bill that can be compared to the existing wage bill magnitude. To estimate the effect of the adjustment on the wage gap between typical male and female occupations, two simple regressions were estimated: (a) log wages on the female occupation dummy variable (*FEM*), and (b) adjusted log wages on *FEM*, where adjusted log wages are ln W + .00118 (*CON*). The regression coefficients on *FEM* for (a) and (b) respectively are −.3859 and − .3520. The first coefficient indicates that the typical female occupation has a wage that is 32 percent lower than the typical male occupation. The second coefficient indicates that this differential falls to 29.7 percent after making the wage adjustment, representing a closing of the gap by 7 percent.

21. Recall that the implicit wage gap between men and women was calculated to be 39.4 percent, or $\exp\{(100)(-.00501)\} - 1$; i.e., in general women earn 39.4 percent less than men. To determine the percentage increment to be applied to a woman's wage, the following calculation is pertinent: $\exp\{(100)(.00501)\} - 1$ which amounts to 65 percent.

22. Remember, however, that increasing every women's wage by 65 percent is equivalent to raising the average wage in an occupation by 5 percent for every ten percentage points that %FEM exceeds zero.

23. In this situation, adjusted log wages are given by $\ln w + .00501 \, (\%FEM) + .00118 \, (CON)$. A regression of these adjusted wages on FEM yielded a regression coefficient of $-.0615$, implying that the typical female occupation has a wage that is 6 percent below a typical male occupation. Relative to the 32 percent gap that exists without any adjustment (see note 20), this wage increment represents a closing of 81 percent of the gap.

24. As the level of occupational detail expands, and the across-occupation wage variability increases, the coefficient on %FEM must be interpreted more as an occupational concentration effect and less as a general male-female difference. The consequence is that wage adjustments that include %FEM as a consideration becomes more appropriate from a comparable worth perspective.

25. See Smith and Ward, *Women's Wages and Work*.

PART III

9

COMPARABLE WORTH:
THE INSTITUTIONAL ECONOMIST'S
APPROACH

Stephen L. Mangum

The comparable worth debate is drawing much attention. The purpose of this paper is not to list the pros and cons of the comparable worth idea or to take a position in the debate. Rather this paper attempts only to outline the approach that an institutional economist would take in examining the issue. This does not imply however that all calling themselves institutionalists would subscribe to every idea expressed here.[1] Beginning with a brief discussion of the institutional approach in general, this paper poses some questions the institutionalist would raise in the comparable worth debate and sets forth how such an economist would seek answers to these questions. Some thought is also given to how an institutionalist might fare in the debate and to policy actions which might be proposed.

Who is the Institutionalist?

After reviewing writings of the founding institutionalists, Jerry Petr has suggested ten "fundamentals of an institutional perspective on economic policy."[2] According to Petr, the institutionalist approach to economic policy is values driven, process oriented, instrumental, evolutionary, activist, fact based, technologically focused, holistic, nondogmatic, and democratic. While the other economic paradigms, the neoclassical and radical viewpoints, share some of these points, distinctions do exist.

The author is a member of the Faculty of Management and Human Resources at Ohio State University.

One fundamental and perhaps overriding difference between the paradigms is that while the neoclassical and radical perspectives have their deus ex machina (their theoretical structures that absorb, analyze, and respond to any issue in a consistent way), the institutionalist perspective has no single philosophical anchor. The neoclassical economist views economic actors as utility or profit maximizers, and/or cost minimizers who rationally weigh costs and benefits in determining what actions to take. In a market setting their individual actions interplay freely to determine societal outcomes. The radical economist, on the other hand, analyzes power relationships and finds motivations for human interaction in class strife and class friction.

The institutionalist, in contrast, does not have an all-encompassing, fixed analytical framework from which to analyze the world. He has no black box. The institutional economist is first and foremost eclectic, recognizing the importance of market forces, but at the same time concerned with the historical, institutional, and social forces that limit the role and influence of markets. Not trusting the use of one general purpose ideology or tool to analyze all economic problems, the institutionalist believes that institutions matter; that the rules of the work place are influenced by the existing technology, product and labor markets, and political power; that different institutional structures produce different results; and that the validity of any analysis depends upon understanding existing institutional forces. Lacking any confining ideology the institutional economist is a tinkerer, the loose cannon on the deck that slides from side to side with the waves, trying to glean insight from other economic paradigms and "noneconomic" disciplines as the issues evolve. He spurns as unrealistic and as inducing blindness attempts to seek one universal explanation of all events, and concentrates on finding "typologies or patterns of actions."[3] The effort is to describe, predict, and prescribe— goals shared with the other perspectives.

The institutionalist is an integrative approach, recognizing the interdependence of economic, social, and institutional phenomena. The institutionalist is political scientist, lawyer, sociologist, psychologist, and anthropologist as well as economist. If not a practitioner,, he consorts with practitioners and has great respect for the knowledge and judgment that involvement breeds. Learning where the levers of power are and how they work, the institutionalist tends to be an interventionist. The institutionalist's world view might be summarized by Gunnar Myrdal's remark: "I came to see that there are no economic, sociological, or psychological problems, but just problems, and they are mixed and composite."

For reasons suggested above it is difficult to speak of *the* institutionalist's perspective on any issue. Perhaps then, this paper is better titled *an* institutionalist's perspective. Institutionalists are a mixed lot, some having more natural affiliation to the neoclassical perspective, others move comfortable with the radical perspective. Still others, some of the best known, have successfully avoided labels and seem to move comfortably between the perspectives, drawing together different viewpoints and pieces of evidence in the search to describe, predict, and prescribe.

Comparable Worth Defined

There is considerable definitional confusion about the meaning of the term "comparable worth." One has only to review recent characterizations by the U.S. Commission on Civil Rights[4] and the countercomments of the General Accounting Office[5] and comparable worth advocates to document the confusion. Definitions abound from the perception that "whenever two jobs are of equal worth to the employer, they should be paid equally" to "equalization of pay on jobs of equal worth to the employer after accounting for all legitimate compensable factors such as seniority and merit." Whatever definition one entertains, there is at least one fundamental issue—how to measure the worth of a job to the employer.

Measuring Worth

I suspect most institutional economists (if not all economists) initially would approach the question of measuring worth by reviewing the tenets and predictions of the basic market model, the philosophical home of the neoclassical economist.[6]

The market economist finds the explanation of every price, including the price of labor, in the interaction of supply and demand. The explanatory power of this formulation is universal because everything that conceivably impacts upon price can be theoretically incorporated into the conceptual constructs of supply and demand functions. To implicitly understand the firm's decision processes relative to the employment relationship, the market economist uses the concept of marginal revenue product (MRP)—a measure of the addition to a firm's total revenue resulting from the employment of additional labor units, a concept built on the assumption that as additional labor units are added to a fixed stock of equipment and raw materials, output from the marginal labor unit will eventually decline. Assuming employers prefer more profit to less profit, it follows that the firm will add labor units to the production process as long as the resulting addition to total revenue exceeds the resulting addition to total production costs. To add labor beyond that point would violate the assumption of preferring more profit to less, as would failing to add labor until that point is reached. Since the worth of an employee to a profit-seeking employer is that which the employee's effort adds to the employer's profit (and since all employees are assumed to be interchangeable), the conceptual construct of MRP, the labor demand function, registers for each employment level the worth to the employer of each interchangeable employee. At any wage/employment combination of that conceptual construct each employee receives comparable worth, that is the individual's worth to the employer comparable to every other employee producing an equal addition to total revenue.

The conceptual construct of a labor supply function shows the number of workers willing to offer themselves for employment (or the number of labor hours offered) at any particular wage rate. Everything affecting the decision to work or not is conceptually incorporated into this supply function. The individual decides what pay he or she must receive to accept the job. Built into that judgment are such factors as the individual's preference for income and leisure, the relative attractiveness of alternative job opportunities, the necessary return on the investment required to obtain the skills of the job, and an estimate of the future prospects from accepting the job. In other words, each point on the supply function defines what the job is worth to each of the many potential employees or, in the case of a single individual, what it would be worth to a particular worker to supply a particular amount of labor.

Hence the wage/employment relationships of a demand function show the worth of various levels of labor input to the employer and combinations on a labor supply function show how much a job is worth to each of a number of employees. Points on a labor demand function are measures of comparable worth to the employer; points on a labor supply function are a measure of worth to the employee willing to supply labor hours at that wage given alternatives and constraints. Where the supply and demand functions intersect is a wage/employment combination where the number of workers being sought in an occupation at a particular wage and the number of individuals seeking work in that occupation at the same wage are equal. Thus, in the market economist's terms, where the market clears is a point where the worth of a job to the employer is the same as the worth of the job to the employee. This point was made a few decades ago by F. Y. Edgeworth who said:

> In short we must understand with the term "equal work" some clause importing equal freedom in the choice of work. There are thus presented two attributes: equality of utility to the employer as tested by the pecuniary value of the result and equality of disutility to the employee as tested by his freedom to choose his employment. These two attributes will concur in a regime of perfect competition.[7]

Therefore, to the market economist, the ostensible objectives of the comparable worth movement are either already accomplished or well on their way toward accomplishment. The cited result does not hinge on profit maximization. As long as more profit is preferred to less profit and as long as the employer makes decisions which lead in that direction, there will be pressures toward the point where the wage equals the marginal revenue product. That most products are jointly produced by different types of workers means the employer will be making judgments about the relative contributions of more than one job to a single product. Some jobs will have no more than a loose connection to any product. Nevertheless, the profit-seeking employer must make judgments about job worth in product market terms—"what does the job contribute to whatever it is we sell in the marketplace and to our bottom line?"

The worker, on the other hand, is paid at least the minimum he considers the job to be worth or the job would not be accepted. The job may not pay what the worker thinks it should but by the very acceptance of the job the worker manifests that the job is more attractive than the other alternatives available (including the alternative of no employment). The worker is being paid the job's worth compared to other alternatives—its comparable worth—just as management is paying what it considers worthwhile compared to not having the job done.

Some Institutionalist-Styled Questions

Market economics suggests comparable worth is achieved when markets work according to the assumptions of perfect competition. With market model predictions in hand the institutional economist would look at the world and discover some facts not necessarily inconsistent with, but certainly suspect in, the world of pure markets. Among these facts are:

- the apparent clustering of women in certain occupations of the occupational structure
- the existence of an earnings gap between full-time, full-year male and female workers with similar years of education
- 30 to 50 percent higher earnings in traditional male occupations than in predominantly female or integrated occupations[8]
- the persistence of the male-female wage gap over time
- the significant reduction in occupation segregation during the 70s but the stability of the wage gap over the period[9]
- the inverse relationship between average annual earnings by occupation and the percentage of females in the occupation[10]

The comparable worth question and the distance between "reality" and the expectations of the pure market model would prompt the institutionalist to pose general questions such as:

1. Why may the predictions of the market model not be reached?
2. What in the institutional structure may contribute to producing the observed results and how do these institutional forces operate?
3. How desirable is an outcome consistent with the concept of comparable worth?
4. If the decision is made to move toward comparable worth, how do we get there and still allow valued institutions to function?

Pursuit of the first two questions leads the institutionalist to more specific questions, such as:

- What are the wage-setting mechanisms through which women's wages are established?

- How are tastes and preferences formulated?
- What is the process of wage and salary administration that is suppose to produce the equality between pay and marginal revenue product and how does it work in practice?

In pursuing answers the institutionalist does not limit the search to any one philosophical viewpoint. It is not enough to charge exploitation on the one hand or to assume the market has correctly valued worth on the other. Rather, the institutionalist examines the entire list of possible explanations—those presented by neoclassical economics, radical economics, and "non" economics. Among the explanations that would be explored are:

- The clustering of women into certain occupations (often characterized by low human capital investment) due to individual and family unit choices made *freely* based on such factors as marital status, child care responsibilities, and expectations of work force attachment."[11]
- A set of customs, traditions, and institutions exogeneously yielding lower pay and more limited choices to women, structuring economic incentive so as to yield the observed behavior.[12]
- Blatant exclusion of women from certain high paying, high prestige jobs.[13]
- Segregation by firm rather than or in addition to by occupation.[14]
- The lack of convergence in skill and wage disparities between men and women in the labor force in contrast to the narrowing of population skill and wage disparities between men and women.[15]
- Widespread noncompetitive economic forces—government, public institutions, regulated monopolies.
- Degradation of "women's" work.[16]
- Segregation via internal labor market structures, promotion ladders, structured mobility ladders.[17]
- Social and self-stereotyping, sex role segregation, value systems, "the latent slavery in the family. . .where wife and children are slaves of the husband."[18]

Wage Setting Practices

While neoclassical general equilibrium models tend by nature to be ahistorical and built upon assumptions of atomistic, individualized decision making, institutional analysis focuses on the *reality* of the labor market and on institutionalized or social patterns of behavior. Recognition of societal actions raises the possibility of institutional discrimination rather than, or in addition to, individualized acts of discrimination—the possibility of binding societal constraints within which processes of individual free choice occur.[19]

The search for institutionalized patterns leads the institutional economist to spend considerable effort examining wage setting mechanisms. This exploration is fueled by the latent practitioner in the institutionalist and the belief that a thorough understanding of institutions is fundamental to description, prediction, and prescription. One product of the exploration of practice is the institution-alist's concept of segmented markets[20] and of the distinction between internal and external labor markets.[21]

The institutionalist finds that firms rely on the external market for pay setting purposes when market signals exist but that because of demand for firm-specific skills within the job structure of individual firms, the labor market does not always work as hypothesized in pure market theory, and consequently other mechanisms for wage setting emerge. Firm specific skills require on-the-job training for their acquisition. On-the-job training requires job security for the trainer to be willing to impart acquired, unique skills to the trainee. Security involves, among other things, the establishment of rules and customs governing relative pay, job promotion, and the settlement of internal disputes. Wages are attached to jobs rather than to people.[22] Market forces operate fully on those positions feeding people into the internal structure (port of entry jobs), but are secondary in importance to other mechanisms regulating earnings and promo-tions with the internal ladders, such as seniority, custom, and tradition.[23]

Job evaluation is one such mechanism prevalent in sizeable enterprises charac-terized by internal labor markets, unions, structured personnel practices, and significant government regulation.[24] Job evaluation processes have developed with two objectives: (1) to aid in establishing pay rates for jobs that are not closely connected to external markets,[25] and (2) to provide wage structures that address concerns of internal equity and resolve internal disputes.[26]

Job evaluation is a political and social, as well as economic process. Key in the setting of wages is credibility, i.e., the acceptance of the structure by the parties concerned—management and employees. Consensus is the goal,[27] and the pro-cess exhibits the flexibility necessary to promote its emergence.[28] But with the flexibility comes the possibility of subjectivity and bias as factors, weights, and valuation of key jobs are adjusted to achieve "acceptable results." Indeed any job evaluation process is an inherently subjective technique.[29]

The institutionalist views internal labor market personnel practices as ad-dressing internal equity concerns via consensus and is predisposed to believe that these practices reflect societal tradition and custom. The weight of the evidence on women's place in society and the historical valuation of her efforts in the labor market lead the institutionalist to suspect the male-female pay and occupational distributions emerging from these internal labor market structures. Further, the possibility of internal labor market practices as mechanisms for maintaining the historical consensus (the status quo) leads the institutionalist to question em-ployers' motivation (and the market's ability) to eliminate any discrimination that might be embedded in the institutional scheme.[30] Fighting institution-alized discrimination involves upsetting the rules of the game, posing "a threat to the entire rule and equity structure of the internal labor market."[31] To do so would not necessarily increase profits or further the interests of the historically favored. The mechanism by which such changes could occur naturally in a market setting (especially through the actions of individual decision makers) is unclear.

A Verdict?

Reviewing the competing attempts (quantitative and otherwise) to document factors producing the wage gap and the segregated occupational structure, the institutionalist finds it difficult to swallow the argument that the situation is the product of free choice, that the economic system is free of bias, or that the system is moving naturally toward elimination of any existing bias. Rejection of the adequacy of the simple market model is based on empirical evidence that shows that the wage gap is not explained by measured human capital differences or differences in job characteristics,[32] the belief that "free choice" exchange in a market is an incomplete view of economic reality—that choice is constrained and conditioned by cultural institutions and decades of human history,[33] and that labor market structures and practices such as internal labor markets, job evaluation, and personnel systems can reflect and reinforce constraining as well as positive factors affecting the allocation of resources and the distribution of income. While the neoclassicist may conclude that whatever wage the market sets for a job is the best approximation of its "comparable worth," and while the radical knows that exploitation is inherent in capitalism, the institutionalist recognizes both arguments but can accept neither as a complete answer. The institutionalist would agree that the market mechanism promotes efficiency and erodes discriminatory tendencies, but would argue that because of entrenched institutional forces and the power of historical precedence, market forces are dulled and sometimes need a push. Similarly the institutionalist would recognize the need to understand power relations and class distinctions but would question the need to totally reject the efficiencies of the market economy in pursuing other goals. And so I suspect most institutionalists would recognize the equity concerns of the comparable worth debate and likely be sympathetic with the advocate's desire to eliminate bias and discrimination in wage setting within the boundaries set forth by one pay equity advocate:

> Pay equity [comparable worth] does not mean the destruction of an external, market-based, salary-setting scheme that will be replaced by a purely internal one. The goal of pay equity is to eliminate bias and discrimination in wage setting. This bias may operate through market rates, through the way the employer responds to or relies on the market, *through* biased job evaluation systems, or through purely subjective judgments made by employers. The objective of pay equity is not to overturn the market, but merely to eliminate bias, whatever its source. It would be virtually impossible for firms to establish wages with no reliance on the market and pay equity activists have not asked employers to do so.[34]

The Road Ahead

Neoclassical, institutional, and perhaps radical, economists are not all that different in the ideal world they seek. I suspect economists' propensity for efficiency leads them to envision an ideal world as one in which individual choice rules, within the broad boundary of a social framework protecting individuals from one another. Efficiency and equity (economists' other chief concern) would require that individuals be able to choose their life endeavors from a full set of alternatives based on informed perceptions of their abilities and the consequences of their decisions. The neoclassical economist views the "invisible hand" of market forces as the best approach to this ideal; the radical sees market capitalism as "the invisible finger" where only the capitalist wins; while the institutionalist respects the market but believes it is often "all thumbs" in its treatment of human resources. The institutionalist believes the market has its place but must be put in its place by occasional, though conscious, intervention.

Having sympathy with the desire to eliminate bias and discrimination in wage setting the institutionalist turns to a question posed earlier: desiring to move toward pay equity (as defined above) how do we get there while permitting valued institutions to function?

The institutional economist views the comparable worth movement as aimed at situations in which internal labor markets are at work—specific jobs in particular enterprises sheltered from the market and where market forces may need supplementing. To the institutionalist equity is a goal to be addressed along with efficiency. Job evaluation and other processes are recognized as judgmental but established, prevalent mechanisms in internal labor market settings. Institutional economists do not believe implementation of comparable worth should involve economy- or industrywide governmental wage or job evaluation boards or that comparable worth should be seen as a first step in that direction. The accompanying losses in efficiency would negate any equity gains from such intervention. Rather, to the institutionalist, comparable worth involves efforts to insure that whatever mechanism a firm uses to establish wages within the internal labor market is free of bias; that is, whatever mechanism is applied is consistent across jobs irrespective of the sex of the job holders.

The institutional economist recognizes that attainment of bias-free compensation—the comparable worth nirvana—cannot occur immediately, that there are seldom easy answers, and that progress must occur within the established political-economic bounds of the market system. Within the typology of internal and external labor markets, the institutionalist recognizes important differences between wage setting practices in the private and public sectors. In the public sector there is no counterpart to the concept of marginal revenue product that describes an employer's valuation of labor input in the private sector. The output of most public activities is not sold in the marketplace. Employment in the private sector adjusts to where marginal revenue product equals the marginal cost of labor.

Public employment, on the other hand, faces a different set of constraints. Like the private firm, the public agency must be able to recruit, select, and retain a sufficient quantity and quality of labor. But there is less pressure for productivity and for minimization of labor costs. That is one reason selection by predetermined merit has been mandated by law. There is also pressure not to pay too much lest the ire of taxpayers and legislative watchdogs be aroused. The working environment often differs substantially from that of the private sector. There is more isolation from economic pressures and less from political forces. The mix between pay rates and nonwage benefits differs markedly. Without a market-valued output as a constraint, internal equity is more important than external equity. Individual equity is generally not a consideration. Hence, there is a greater possibility of using job evaluation to create an independent and internally consistent wage structure.[35]

Being subject to political pressures and processes of collective bargaining, absent a true market defense, and more subject to review of compensation practices than the private corporation, immediate progress toward elimination of sex bias in the public sector will continue. Already at least twenty-four states are at some stage of reconsideration of their compensation systems.[36] A number of local governments and public agencies have succumbed to collective bargaining pressures or have politically endorsed comparable worth policies. The rub will come when taxpayers and politicians recognize that higher pay for women can only be achieved within constrained public budgets by lowering the pay of men, raising taxes, or reducing services. Then emphasis will undoubtedly shift to getting more women into male dominated jobs, as contrasted to getting higher pay for predominately female jobs.

That, after all, is a much preferred answer in the long run. Sex-neutral selection systems must go hand in hand with sex-neutral evaluation schemes and aggressive female pursuit of higher paid jobs. Any judgmentally chosen or subjectively determined wage setting schemes treating female dominated jobs differently than male dominated ones should be vulnerable to a prima facie Title VII charge of adverse impact. While the courtroom tide may appear to be swinging away from favorable treatment of comparable worth related cases,[37] this merely confirms that there is no base for it in existing federal law.

The courts will continue to pursue, within existing civil rights legislation, cases where the employer intentionally discriminates by not consistently applying its own chosen compensation system. In response to the courts, initiatives at the state and local level, and public pressure, the federal government will eventually review its wage setting practices for bias. As efforts are made in the public sector, employers in the private sector will alter their practices to promote fairness, to protect themselves from costly litigation, and to compete for human resources. Gradual, reasoned implementation through existing institutions will quell any tremendous cost concerns.[38] As individual economic actors take actions consistent with pay equity, the status quo will change and the system will move in a

direction compatible with the comparable worth ideal. The institutional economist, I believe, sees comprehensive, persistent but eclectic action on many
fronts—political, legislative, judicial, collective bargaining, social, and administrative—as removing bias and closing the wage gap.[39]

I suspect this policy prescription is not very satisfying to the conservative
neoclassical economist since it does suggest intervention and if you assume
perfect competition almost any intervention is bad. Similarly, it is probably not
very satisfying to the comparable worth advocate for it sounds very much like
letting the market work, letting social processes work naturally without open
intervention. In reality the prescription goes well beyond this. It endorses a
philosophical commitment to combating bias within the segments of the economy
shielded from the corrective aspects of competition, and advocates that constant
continued pressures simultaneously on several fronts—the courts, the political/le-
gislative process, and at the bargaining table—will further progress toward
eliminating sex-related bias in wage and salary administration.

Summary and Conclusion

The institutional economist is eclectic. He believes in the power of market forces
but argues that institutions and social traditions matter and that economic outcomes will differ with different institutional structures. The institutional approach is interdisciplinary, drawing from law, sociology, psychology, and anthro-
pology as well as economics. The institutionalist recognizes and welcomes the
viewpoints of the neoclassical and the radical economist and evaluates these
paradigms in terms of the institutions and institutional forces seen operating in
the economic system. While lacking any grand analytical framework comparable
to the neoclassical or radical economist, the institutionalist's goal is one the three
viewpoints share—to describe, predict, and prescribe. What emerges from institutional analysis is a "hands-on" view of the economic system; a mediation
between competing groups and methodologies; suspicion and distrust of any
general purpose analytical tool or those who use such; a denial of theoretically
easy answers; and a tendency of sometimes getting so close to the trees that the
arguments advanced are not easily integrated into a consistent statement of the
theoretical forest originally examined.

Relative to comparable worth the institutionalist begins with the generalizations of the neoclassical framework. Recognizing that the labor market is not an
auction market and that this framework is a first cut, the institutional economist
builds upon the foundation by examining the empirical evidence, by exploring
other explanations of any observed phenomena, and by immersing himself in the
real world institutions and processes of wage setting. Doing so, I believe, leads
the institutional economist to be sympathetic with the equity concerns voiced by
comparable worth advocates but leery of those who would sell easy answers or
push the controversy to espouse upheaval of the basic market system. The institu-

tionalist would emerge from the facts (1) committed to the comparable worth ideal within that segment of the economy characterized by the mechanisms of internal labor markets where clear market signals are absent and (2) favorable to a combination of comprehensive, persistent but eclectic actions on the political, legislative, judicial, collective bargaining, social, and administrative fronts moving toward pay equity within the current institutional framework.

Notes

1. Though often necessary, labels are dangerous. An insightful recitation of labels related to labor economics is Clark Kerr's piece, "The Intellectual Role of the Neorealists in Labor Economics," *Industrial Relations* 22,, no. 2 (Spring 1983): 298–318. My use of the term "institutionalist economist" is most closely identified with what he labels "neo-realist."

2. Jerry L. Petr, "Fundamentals of an Institutionalist Perspective on Economic Policy," *Journal of Economic Issues* 18, no. 1 (March 1984): 1.

3. Kerr, *Industrial Relations*, 304.

4. *Comparable Worth: Issue for the 80s*, A Consultation of the U.S. Commission on Civil Rights, 1 (Washington, D.C.: Government Printing Office, June 1984).

5. General Accounting Office, *Comments on Report on Comparable Worth by the United States Commission on Civil Rights* (Washington, D.C.: Government Printing Office, June 1985.

6. This basic foundation may not be the same used by those approaching comparable worth from the viewpoint of social philosophy or administrative practice. For some distinctions between these alternative approaches see Thomas Mahoney, "Approaches to the Definition of Comparable Worth," *Academy of Management Review* 8, no. 1 (1983): 14–21.

7. F. Y. Edgeworth, "Equal Pay to Men and Women for Equal Work," *Economics Journal* 32 (December 1922): 1–39.

8. See Andrea Beller, "Occupational Segregation by Sex: Determinants and Changes," *Journal of Human Resources* 17 (Summer 1982): 371–91.

9. Andrea Beller, "Changes in the Sex Compositions of U.S. Occupations," Paper (March 1984).

10. Donald Treiman and Heidi Hartmann, *Women, Work, and Wages: Equal Pay for Jobs of Equal Value* (Washington, D.C.: National Academy Press, 1981) and Paula England, M. Chessie, and L. McCarmack, "Skill Demands and Earnings in Female and Male Occupations," *Sociology and Social Research* 66, (1982): 147–68.

11. The examples of these arguments are plentiful. See Solomon Polachek, "Occupation Segregation: A Defense of Human Capital Predictions," *Journal of Human Resources* 20 (Summer 1985): 437–39, for an extensive but by no means exhaustive list of articles demonstrating a link between lifetime labor force participation patterns and wages.

12. See Reuben Gronau, "Sex-Related Wage Differentials and Women's Interrupted Labor Careers—The Chicken or the Egg," NBER Working Paper (October 1982); Gordon Green, "Wage Differentials for Job Entrants, By Race and Sex" (Ph.D. diss., George Washington University, 1933); Ellen Greenberger and Laurence Steinberg, "Sex Differences in Early Labor Force Experience: Harbinger of Things to Come," *Social Forces* 62 (1983): 467–86; Richard Levinson, "Sex Discrimination and Employment Practices," *Social Problems* 22 (1975): 533–45; and Daphne Greenwood, "The Economic Significance of Women's Place in Society: A Neo-Institutionalist View," *Journal of Economic Issues* 17, no. 3 (September 1984: 663–80.

13. Such arguments are often extrapolations from Gary Becker, *The Economics of Discrimination* (Chicago: University of Chicago Press, 1957).

14. Francine Blau, *Equal Pay in the Office* (Lexington, Mass.: D. C. Heath, 1977).

15. James P. Smith and Michael Ward, "The Acceleration in Women's Wages" (The Rand Corporation, Paper, 1984).

16. See Thorstein Veblen, *The Theory of the Leisure Class* (Boston: Houghton Mifflin, 1973 [1899]; Veblen, "The Beginnings of Ownership," "The Barbarian Status of Women," and "The Economic Theory of Woman's Dress," in Leon Ardzrooni, ed., *Essays in Our Changing Order* (New York: Augustus M. Kelley, 1964), and Edythe Miller, "Veblen and Women's Lib: A Parallel," *Journal of Economic Issues* 6 (September 1972): 59–79.

17. Paula England, "Socioeconomic Explanations of Job Segregation," in H. Remick, ed., *Comparable Worth and Wage Discrimination: Technical Possibilities and Political Realities* (Philadelphia: Temple University Press, 1984); Rosabeth Kanter, *Men and Women of the Corporation* (New York: Basic Books, 1977); M. Reich, D. Gordon, and R. Edwards, "A Theory of Labor Market Segmentation," *American Economic Review Proceedings* (May 1973): 359–65; and Martin Brown and Peter Philips, "The Evolution of Labor Market Structure: The California Canning Industry," *Industrial and Labor Relations Review* 38, no. 3 (April 1985): 392–407.

18. Quote is from Karl Marx, "Economic and Philosophic Manuscripts of 1844," Robert Tucker, ed., in *The Marx-Engels Reader* (New York: W. W. Norton, 1972). Also see Simone de Beauvoir, *The Second Sex*, ed. H. M. Parshley (New York: A. Knopf, 1953). From de Beauvoir: "Proletarians have not always existed, whereas there have always been women. They are women in virtue of their anatomy and physiology. Throughout history they have always been subordinated to men, and hence their dependency is not the result of a historical event or a social change—it was not something that occurred. . . . They have no past, no history, no religion of their own. . . . They live dispersed among the males, attached through residence, housework, economic conditions, and social standing to certain men—fathers or husbands—more firmly than they are to other women." Other references include G. Nemerowicz, *Children's Perceptions of Gender and Work Roles* (New York: Praeger, 1979); Jean Stockard and Miriam Johnson, *Sex Roles: Inequality and Sex Roles Development* (New York: Prentice Hall, 1980); and England, "Socioeconomic Explanations." For some evidence that women's low returns to job requirements and job tenure occur across all jobs and not just "women's jobs," see Robert Buchele and Mark Aldrich, "How Much Difference Would Comparable Worth Make," *Industrial Relations* (Spring 1985): 222–33.

19. For greater development of these ideas see Ray Marshall and Beth Paulin, "The Employment and Earnings of Women: The Comparable Worth Debate," in *Comparable Worth: Issue for the 80s.*

20. See David Gordon, R. Edwards, and Michael Reich, *Segmented Work, Divided Workers* (New York: Cambridge University Press, 1982).

21. The uninitiated reader is referred to Peter Doeringer and Michael Piore, *Internal Labor Markets and Manpower Analysis* (D. C. Health, 1971). In short, internal labor markets are administrative units in which jobs have elements unique to a specific firm such that the jobs within the structure face limited competition from outside the structure. Relative wages reflect custom and institutionalized rules rather than direct supply and demand considerations. Doeringer and Piore have postulated that as much as 80 percent of the labor force works in internal markets.

22. See the discussion of the "job competition" model in Lester Thurow, *Generating Inequality* (New York: Basic Books, 1975).

23. Describing and analyzing the emergence and operations of these internal structures and workplace rules has been a traditional domain of institutional economists and

industrial relations specialists. See John T. Dunlop, "Industrial Relations and Economics: The Common Frontier of Wage Determination," *Industrial Research Association Proceedings* (December 1984). Dunlop writes: "I do not believe that microeconomic theory is adequate to provide a useful understanding of internal labor markets and their effects of internal and external movements of labor, on internal wage structures for job classifications in enterprises of size, and for on-the-job training. These are vast areas of labor market experience and wage determination that need to be incorporated into a consolidated industrial relations and economic perspective."

24. There appears to be some disagreement in the literature as to how widespread is the practice of job evaluation. Donald Schwab contends that "most firms in the private sector probably do not use job evaluation" but that since surveys of compensation practices tend to oversample large firms "it may be that the majority of private sector employees are covered by a job evaluation plan." D. Schwab, "Using Job Evaluation to Obtain Pay Equity," in *Comparable Worth: Issue for the 80s*. In his article, "Comparable Worth and Realistic Wage Setting" in the same volume, Herbert Northrup says that "job evaluation plans cover only a minority of employees and most systems are informal." See D. Belcher, *Compensation Administration* (Englewood Cliffs, N.J.: Prentice Hall, 1978) for survey evidence of the widespread use of formal job evaluation systems.

25. See David Schwab, "Job Evaluation and Pay Setting: Concepts and Practices" in E. R. Livernash, *Comparable Worth: Issues and Alternatives* (Washington, D.C.: Equal Employment Advisory Council, 1980).

26. L. R. Burgess, *Wage and Salary Administration* (Columbus, Ohio: Charles E. Merrill, 1982), and Marcia Miceli, J. Blackburn, and S. Mangum, "The Comparable Worth Controversy: A Review of Some Recent Legal Developments and Research Issues," Paper (1985).

27. Alvin O. Bellak of Hay Associates in his article "Comparable Worth: A Practitioner's View" (in *Comparable Worth: Issue for the 80s*) says "job evaluation is, at its best, a disciplined objective process for rank ordering jobs on an agreed upon compensable value scale. It works because it essentially satisfies the common interest of, as it were, the governors and the governed" (78). Donald Schwab (*Comparable Worth: Issue for the 80s*) states "job evaluation serves as a loose and flexible set of rules within which management and employees (and their representatives) can work out differences regarding relative pay rates" (88). Institutional economists have long recognized this goal of job evaluation. Sumner Slichter wrote "job evaluation was used by management . . . to establish principles and practices for future wage administration, and partly to stabilize the wage structure and eliminate continuous bargaining over particular rates after unionization" (*The Impact of Collective Bargaining on Management* [Washington, D.C.: Brookings Institution, 1960]): 561.

28. For an introduction to job evaluation procedures see Douglas T. Bartley, *Job Evaluation* (Reading, Mass.: Addison-Wesley, 1981) and Donald J. Treiman, *Job Evaluation: An Analytic Review* (Washington, D.C.: National Academy of Sciences, 1979).

29. Schwab, *Comparable Worth: Issue for the 80s*, 89. Research on job evaluation has suggested (1) the possibility of sex bias—J. A. Grune, "Comparable Worth: Issues and Perspectives," *Industrial Relations Research Association Proceedings* (December 1982) and S. Smith, "Men's Jobs, Women's Jobs and Differential Wage Treatment," *Job Evaluation and EEO: The Emerging Issues* (New York: Industrial Relations Counselors, 1978), though some experimental research does not support the hypothesis—R. Grams and D. Schwab, "Impacts of Sex Composition and Salary Level on Judgments of Content in Job Evaluation," *Proceedings of Midwest Academy of Management*, 1983; (2) that different evaluation techniques yield different job hierarchies—R. J. Snelgar, "The Comparability of Job Evaluation Methods," *Personnel Psychology* 36 (1983): 371–80; and (3) that different evaluators score jobs differently within a single job evaluation system—see

Grams and Schwab, "Impacts of Sex Composition."

30. As aptly summarized by M. Rozen, "In grinding out its consequences the market has no respect for human life. . . . The market will faithfully reflect the distribution of advantage within a society. That is why is is so beloved by those that are well off." Marvin Rozen, "The Market is No Miracle Worker," *Challenge* (September/October 1985): 47–50.

31. Doeringer and Piore, *Internal Labor Markets*, 41.

32. See Mary Corcoran and Greg Duncan, "Work History, Labor Force Attachment, and Earnings Differences Between the Races and Sexes," *Journal of Human Resources* 14 (1979): 1–20; M. Corcoran, G. Duncan, and M. Ponza, "A Longitudinal Analysis of White Women's Wages, *Journal of Human Resources* 18 (Fall 1983): 497–520; John Angle and David Wissman, "Work Experience, Age and Gender Discrimination," *Social Science Quarterly* 64 (March 1983): 1:66–84; M. Hill and J. Morgan, "Dimensions of Occupation," in Greg Duncan and James Morgan, *Five Thousand American Families* (: Institute of Social Research 1979); E. Wright and L. Perone, "Marxist Class Categories and Income Inequality," *American Sociological Review* (February 1977): 32–55; M. Feber and J. Spaeth, "Work Characteristics and the Male-Female Earnings Gap," *American Economic Review Proceedings* (May 1984): ; Paula England, "Failure of Human Capital Theory to Explain Occupational Sex Segregation," *Journal of Human Resources* 17 (1982): 358–70.

33. See Clarence Ayres, *The Theory of Economic Process* (Chapel Hill: University of North Carolina Press, 1944); Wendell Gordon, *Institutional Economics: The Changing System* (Austin: University of Texas, 1980); Marc R. Tool, *The Discretionary Economy: A Normative Theory of Political Economy* (Santa Monica: Goodyear, 1979); and J. Fagg Foster, "Current Structure and Future Prospects of Institutional Economics," *Journal of Economic Issues* 15 (December 1981): 943–47. Foster states: "the allocation of resources and the final distribution of real income are affected by, and even carried on through institutions other than the market and price. And some of those institutions, such as family and government, are far older than the market. . . . Then, since the agreed assignment of economics is to explain the institutional determination of the level and character of real income, economists cannot avoid analyzing all of the cause and effect relationships among whatever institutions exhibit such relationships."

34. Joy Ann Grune, "Pay Equity is a Necessary Remedy for Wage Discrimination," *Comparable Worth: Issue for the 80s*, 169. The sentiment expressed here is supported in the National Academy of Science review of what comparable worth entails: "Acceptance of a comparable worth . . . approach does not require an absolute standard by which the value or worth of jobs all be measured. . . . No such standard exists. . . . Paying jobs according to their worth requires only that whatever characteristics of jobs are regarded as worthy of compensation by an employer should be equally so regarded irrespective of the sex, race, or ethnicity of job incumbents" (Treiman and Hartmann, *Women, Work and Wages*, 70).

35. For a more detailed discussion of differences in wage setting between the public and private sector see Stephen Mangum, "Comparable Worth and Pay Setting in the Public and Private Sector," accepted for publication by the *Journal of Collective Negotiations in the Public Sector*.

36. Bureau of National Affairs, *BNA's Employee Relations Weekly* 3 (April 8, 1985): 419–20.

37. American Nurses' Association v. State of Illinois, 606 F. Supp. 1313 (1985); AFSCME v State of Washington, Appeal from the U.S. District Court for the Western District of Washington (1985).

38. For a recital of dire predictions see George Hildebrand, "The Market System" in E. R. Livernash, *Comparable Worth: Issues and Alternatives* (Washington, D.C.: Equal

Employment Advisory Council, 1982); Peter Germanis, "Comparable Worth Part 1: A Theory with No Facts," Washington, D.C.: Heritage Foundation no. 336 (1984); and Peter Germanis, "Comparable Worth Part 2: The High Cost of Bad Policy," Heritage Foundation no. 337 (1984).

39. Sar A. Levitan and Clifford, M. Johnson, "Comparable Worth: In Praise of Muddling Through," *The Journal/The Institute for Socioeconomic Studies* 10 (Summer 1985): 36–52; and Buchele and Aldrich, "How Much Difference would Comparable Worth Make," *Industrial Relations* (Spring 1985): 222–33.

10

THE POLITICAL ECONOMY OF COMPARABLE WORTH

Heidi I. Hartmann

This chapter will begin with a discussion of what comparable worth is and what it is not and I will continue with a presentation of a standard neoclassical approach to comparable worth, arguing that comparable worth policy is perfectly compatible with some aspects of a neoclassical approach to labor markets. I will then suggest how a feminist political economy perspective broadens our understanding of comparable worth policy. Finally, in discussing some of the criticisms leveled at comparable worth by all parts of the spectrum of economic thought, I will indicate how attention to the specific gender issues of comparable worth policy from a feminist political economic perspective broadens and alters our understanding of the operation of labor markets. Labor markets and work places emerge as arenas of gender struggle as well as class struggle.

The phrase comparable worth is now generally recognized. Public service announcements appear in many newspapers and magazines stressing the importance of comparable worth for women workers. In the last presidential election all the major Democratic candidates supported the concept of comparable worth, and the party platform endorsed it. Comparable worth has now become accepted by a large number of public leaders, at least as a concept that deserves support and exploration. And this despite rather vociferous opposition by the current administration, whose officials dismiss it as "looney tunes," issue reports condemning it, and enter court cases opposing it. This relatively recent, vocal opposition to the concept notwithstanding, I am surprised at how rapidly the concept has gained public acceptance. Seven years ago when I began work on the National Academy

The author is at the National Academy of Sciences and of the National Research Council. The views expressed herein are those of the author and not of the National Academy of Sciences.

of Sciences study on comparable worth,[1] most people with whom I came into contact had never heard of it. Comparable worth has now been implemented by several states in their civil service systems and by private employers as well, although the comparable worth label is not always applied to the reevaluation of jobs and realignment of wages that take place.[2]

What Comparable Worth Is and Is Not

Advocates of comparable worth have developed a consensus view of comparable worth as a particular set of strategies with a particular focus that calls for the examination of the job content of predominantly female and predominantly male jobs, and, when warranted, the realignment of their relative pay rates. Advocates see comparable worth as another facet of equal employment opportunity and as an issue of basic fairness and justice (hence the newer more commonly used term in the women's and labor movements—pay equity). The essential argument is that the wages of jobs held predominately by women (''women's jobs'') are depressed by discrimination; if men held them these same jobs would pay more.

The focus of the comparable worth strategy as it is pursued today is on the employment practices of an individual employer. The typical strategy is developed by employees, generally unionized, who are concerned about the equity of wage rates at their work place. It begins with a study of wage rates and job categories, often—in the public sector—mandated by legislation, in which some type of job evaluation system is used to measure the content of work according to such criteria as skill, effort, and responsibility. The study typically shows that jobs with similar evaluations are paid differently by the employer, with those jobs held predominantly by women paying less than those held predominantly by men. The remedy that is suggested is the realignment of the wage rates of those jobs. The results of the study can then be used to support collective bargaining or litigation (or both).

Most lawsuits thoroughly examine the employment practices of the employer. The mainstay of a case that argues that discrimination has affected the wage rates of an *entire* occupation (as opposed to a discrimination case that argues that *individual* women have been discriminated against in pay in a particular job) is the existence of sex segregation in the firm's employment structure. If there were not an extreme job segregation by sex throughout the labor market such that some jobs are readily identifiable as female jobs and others are readily identifiable as male jobs, the issue of comparable worth could not arise. Hence, any evidence that the employer has knowingly and intentionally maintained the sex segregation of jobs can certainly contribute to a demonstration that the employer is also responsible for their relative wage rates. Newman has often said that comparable worth can be seen as garden variety, sex-based wage discrimination, and once put in the context of discrimination the mode of attacking a comparable worth problem becomes clear. The comparable worth strategy, like other equal employment opportunity strategies, is employer-based, requires investigation and study, and points to an obvious remedy—wage realignment and back pay. It should also be clear from this approach that affirmative action, opening up the sex-segregated job opportunities, is a critical component of redress.

It is also important to note that, like other equal employment opportunity policies, comparable worth is as relevant to jobs in which minorities predominate as it is to those in which women predominate since such jobs may pay less because of the race or ethnicity of the incumbents.[3] To date, however, its application to jobs dominated by minorities has rarely been pursued, perhaps because many more jobs are sex-typed than race-typed, at least when national data are studied.[4]

Comparable worth is also being directly addressed in union negotiations; it has been for years, though without the comparable worth label. Unions have always been concerned with equity and have sometimes assigned a disproportionate share of the wage increase that results from a bargaining effort to particularly low-paying jobs. The comparable worth movement, however, has certainly heightened the awareness of unionized women workers about pay equity issues. Resolutions passed at annual union conventions and, in some cases, accompanying legal strategies, such as within the American Federation of State, County, and Municipal Employees (AFSCME), have brought wage equity bargaining issues to the center of attention.[5] Unfortunately most of the American labor force is not unionized and so this remedy is not available to many women workers.

In contrast to this modest employer-by-employer approach well established in equal employment law as well as in collective bargaining, opponents of comparable worth, particularly in the business press, often raise the spectre of governmentwide regulation of wage rates in all industries and in all firms, with wage tribunals dictating uniform wages across the entire economy. Even when they do not envision such rigid regulation, opponents often state that endless litigation will embroil the courts in determining the value of jobs in work place after work place, clogging the courts and preventing the market from operating. In either case the market is prevented from operating "naturally." Opponents stress that comparable worth advocates want to measure the intrinsic worth of jobs without regard to their current market prices. Rarely do they acknowledge that comparable worth could be seen as a remedy for discrimination that might be embodied in current prices. Equity and efficiency are seen as totally incompatible, and competitive forces demand that efficiency win out. Even comparable worth's base in equity is challenged; rather it is seen as special interest pleading by those women who have traditionally female jobs (and who don't want to bother to enter traditionally male jobs that are better paid) to overturn the results of market forces because they want more money. Comparable worth is portrayed as a totally economically irrational policy that would be exorbitantly expensive and might even bring the economy to a standstill by disrupting the efficient allocation of resources. Or if such total catastrophe were avoided, at least comparable worth would result in hardship for women, because higher prices for their labor would put many women out of work. Hence, at worst it would destroy the economy; at best it would destroy those it purports to help.

Traditional Economic Justifications for Comparable Worth

Implemented as the advocates suggest, comparable worth policy would consist of the gradual cumulation of changes in individual work places over time. It would probably result in a wage structure that would look significantly different from that which we have today, yet the dire predictions of hardship, bankruptcy, and massive unemployment made by the opponents are hardly likely to occur. In some current cases, the cost of change in women's and men's relative wage rates has been on the order of 5 to 10 percent of the total payroll. Actually, this modest increase makes sense. Of a gross wage gap between women and men of 40 percent, perhaps half is not due to discrimination in employment.[6] At most half the gross gap, or 20 percent, could be remedied by comparable worth, then, but even all of that is unlikely because not all employment-based discrimination takes place within a single work place (some results from women and men working for different employers).[7] If the full 20 percent were remedied, women would get a 37.5 percent raise, and, if women were half the work force, the wage bill would go up 12.5 percent, which could be phased in over several years. Hardly revolutionary from an economic point of view.

One can argue not only that implementing comparable worth would not be terrible costly, but also that it makes good economic sense, from an efficiency viewpoint. The comparable worth issue comes about, first of all, because of inequality of opportunity, via the extreme sex segregation of jobs, and then, further, because of a discriminatory wage setting process (which fails to remunerate the same characteristics of jobs as highly when they are found in women's jobs as when they are found in men's jobs). Discrimination—barriers to free movement in the labor market and the resulting incorrect prices—is inefficient. Insofar as discrimination alters the relative wage rates of jobs that are typically held by men and women, men and women are not being utilized in the most efficient ways. Comparable worth can be seen as adjusting market wage rates to remove the bias that results from discrimination. In this sense, then, comparable worth would make the market work better as opposed to totally eliminating the place of the market and administratively determining the relative wages of jobs. Basketball players on national terms may always earn more than secretaries and cleaning personnel earn less. Comparable worth is not likely to change that, but it does seek to eliminate whatever effect sex discrimination has had in determining the relative wages of occupations that have been dominated by women or men.[8] Some reallocation of labor, some shifting of women and men from one occupation to another, and some unemployment may well result from a general realignment of the wage rates of men's and women's jobs. However, this realignment would occur slowly over many years.

Most economists would accept the argument that discrimination results in the less than ideal allocation of human resources and human talent, is therefore inefficient, and should be eliminated. Moreover, it is generally agreed that although the elimination of discrimination would result in some change in the way the market operates (for example, if blacks can play on professional white baseball teams, there might be some decline of professional black teams) these effects are thought to be transitory, small, and of minor cost relative to the benefit to be reaped from the better allocation of resources.

But there is little agreement on the extent of discrimination against women. In particular there is disagreement about whether the lower wages of women's occupations are the result of discriminatory processes or such factor as culture, society, or women's preferences. And there has been little research on the potential effects of discrimination on the relative wages of occupations, as opposed to those of individuals. It is possible that we will find that wage discrimination affects relative occupational pay rates less than comparable worth advocates think it does. It is also possible that we will find more wage discrimination than opponents think exists. If theoretical and empirical research determines that discrimination does affect the relative wage rates of occupations, agreement to seek the realignment of these wage rates within discriminating firms (which presumably would require a degree of interference with the behavior of employers) ought to be forthcoming.

Even if empirical consensus were achieved on the degree of discrimination, however, it appears that little consensus would emerge among economists regarding the implementation of comparable worth. There are four distinct approaches by mainstream economists to the debate over comparable worth. First, there are those who deny there is any discrimination against women in the labor market in any form—therefore comparable worth policy is unnecessary, thoroughly misguided, and harmful. Second, there are those who believe there is a small amount of discrimination in the labor market. Existing remedies, such as equal pay for equal work and equal access, are more than adequate to cope with any problems. Comparable worth is a costly and inappropriate remedy. Third, there are those who believe discrimination is substantial and affects occupational wage rates, but who nevertheless believe comparable worth is the wrong remedy. They argue that changing prices without changing the underlying supply and demand curves (via, for example, education or affirmative action) will lead to misallocation and inefficiency. Higher wages will encourage more women to enter female occupations at the same time they will reduce demand, creating severe unemployment problems for women. In such a market, only the most qualified women will get the jobs—most likely better educated white women. Less well educated minority women will be cut out of the labor market. Fourth, there are those who agree with comparable worth advocates that comparable worth remedies are likely to be reasonably effective for a particular type of labor market problem. These economists generally hold a more institutional view of the labor market, a view that suggests that changing a price is a limited form of interference without significant repercussions (other than raising women's wages). The National Academy of Sciences report on which I worked is generally compatible with this last stance.

Making the Case for the Existence of Discrimination against Occupations

I have found it useful to think of two aspects of discrimination that can affect average occupational wages. The first is that generally recognized by economists—what we might view as market-based discrimination. It comes about because of the tracking and channeling of women into a restricted set of jobs and opportunities, that is, from overcrowding.[9] In the overcrowding model equal access to all jobs would result in a realignment of wage rates. Wages of formerly women's jobs would rise because the supply of women to these jobs would decrease as new opportunities opened to women, while the wage rates of formerly men's jobs would fall because the supply to these jobs would increase as women entered them. According to the overcrowding explanation women, because of exclusion, are in oversupply to those occupations open to them, thus driving down their wage rates. In short, if equal opportunity existed in the labor market the free market would be restored and would raise women's wages, both because the wage rates of women's jobs would increase and because women could earn better wages in the formerly male jobs they entered.

There can be a second source of the discrimination in women's wage rates, however. Some part of the underpayment of women's jobs could be due to what we might call direct wage discrimination, above and beyond that resulting from overcrowding. Imagine that today's women's jobs were done by men and that there were just as many men available to do them as there are now women (the relative supply of men and women just discussed would not be an issue). The suspicion is that the same jobs when done by men would be paid more. Many women have come to believe that their work is undervalued precisely because it is typically women's work. They believe that such features of jobs as caring, nurturing, and being polite and friendly are underpaid, at least when women do them. For example, if men were nurses, it is held, nursing would be paid more, not because there were fewer men available to do it than there are women, but because men doing the job would cause its skills to be recognized in a different way (and perhaps it would also be the case that men would define the job somewhat differently and do it somewhat differently). It is quite likely, given what we know about social and cultural beliefs, that the devaluation of things associated with women is deeply embedded in all our social practices and does indeed affect wage rates. Comparable worth advocates generally believe job evaluation plans can identify the effects of both sources of discrimination.

The Role of Job Evaluation

Job evaluation is a technique that attempts to identify what it is about jobs that is valued. Its appeal for the pay equity issue is obvious. If we know what it is that is valued we can make sure it is valued in the same way in the jobs of women, men, and minorities. Hence, job evaluation plans look at the specific content of jobs: the kinds of skills and effort that are demanded of the worker. Some say these plans measure the "intrinsic worth" of jobs. For example, it is less intellectually demanding to be a ticket taker at a movie theater than it is to sell the tickets and make change, but it might require more assertiveness and more physical ability to keep a customer without a ticket from entering the theater than the cashier must have to make change. Job evaluation plans would rate different features of jobs to arrive at total "job worth" scores.

Job evaluation, developed in the 1930s and 1940s as part of the general trend toward scientific management, was designed to compare and rank jobs throughout large work places. As work places grew larger they grew more complex, and more management was required to coordinate workers and to hire, fire, pay, or promote them. The development of personnel offices, personnel procedures, and job evaluation brought order to haphazard personnel processes. Several major types of job evaluation systems exist, including broad classification schemes like the federal civil service system and more quantitative plans known as "point-factor" plans, most of which are "policy capturing plans." They attempt to model or "capture" the firm's existing pay policy and to bring any outlying jobs into conformity with the firm's general policy.

Pay policies can and do differ among firms. For example, it is widely held that in comparison to some other high-technology firms, at IBM sales capability is compensated well relative to technical expertise. In the steel industry the degree of responsibility in jobs is compensated more relative to other factors than in other industries. Why? Because steel making has many dangerous components and responsibility is important to prevent accidents and death. In general, we can expect that the relative wages of jobs within work places will differ according to the values that the employer has developed (sometimes in conjunction with employees).

Many, perhaps most, job evaluation systems are "installed" by consultants. A job evaluation consultant can come into any work place and, by studying the existing pay structure, determine what the employer implicitly values. A policy-capturing plan developed for the firm can make those values explicit. Typically each job will be described and rated, according to established criteria, on a variety of job factors thought to be related to pay: how many people are supervised? how long does it take to train for the job? how much physical effort is required? The measure of the job factors can then be regressed against the existing wage rates to develop a policy line, around which many of the jobs cluster.[10] Of course, there will be outliers and these are usually brought into alignment with the policy line over time or are exempted. In any case, however, these plans essentially use existing wages to determine the weights (the coefficients in the regression equation) of the factors identified, and, hence, the relationship between the total scores for each job in the plan (the sum of its weighted factor scores) will replicate the relationship between their wage rates. These plans do what they were designed to do: replicate and rationalize the internal wage hierarchy.

Job evaluation consultants also come into firms with ready-made plans that establish the weights of the different factors and thereby determine what is to be valued in jobs. These are sometimes called "a priori" job evaluation systems; of course, even these systems have a relationship to market wages. They are often the result of many applications at many different work places and have evolved, through trial and error, from what has best replicated the market place.

In sum, job evaluation plans work by identifying what it is that is currently valued in jobs via study of their job factors and wage rates, by developing rational bases for those wage rates, and by bringing all wage rates into rational relationship with one another. The plans are then used to determine the wage rates of new jobs created within the firm. The standard job evaluation procedure for deriving weights essentially preserves many aspects of the market relationships between jobs.

But, job evaluation plans do not appear to measure "intrinsic job worth" any more than wages do. Indeed, since they were developed to replicate the market, without any consciousness that the market may discriminate against women and women's jobs, most current plans are not very useful for measuring job worth in a bias-free way; they often include factors that implicitly favor men's jobs over women's, in order to rationalize the higher wages men's jobs usually receive.

The National Academy of Sciences report pointed out several weaknesses of job evaluation plans: (1) the subjective nature of many of the judgments made in rating jobs; (2) the lack of attempt to remove the discriminatory component of wages in the development of factor weights; (3) the tendency of many firms to use several different types of job evaluation plans for different types of work—blue collar, clerical, and management, for example; and (4) the lack of attention to the complexities of measurement and modeling. But the reports concluded that, with proper attention to these problems, these evaluation plans could be used to determine the relative worth of jobs, without bias due to sex.[11] Moreover, several completed studies of wage structures have used relatively "unimproved" job evaluation plans and have nevertheless determined that women's jobs were paid about 20 percent less than men's jobs with the same job evaluation scores. These results occurred for at least two reasons. First, all types of jobs were evaluated with one plan, rather than several. This alone forces a comparison of men's and women's jobs on their content. Second, these studies were usually carried out with the advice of a labor-management committee that was already attuned to comparable worth issues and monitored the consultants' decisions.

When used in a relatively unbiased manner, job evaluation plans can get at what I called "direct" wage discrimination—the undervaluing of the characteristics found in women's jobs *because* they are in *women's* jobs. With uniformly applied job evaluation, characteristics of jobs must be valued the same regardless of what jobs they are found in. The comparable worth strategy, via bias-free job evaluation, is not an attempt to overthrow the market but is simply the elimination of the sex discriminatory component of market wages and consequently, is not necessarily at odds with the operation of labor markets.

It is important to note that comparable worth advocates are not arguing that a single job evaluation plan should be foisted upon all employers. There are no universal criteria for job worth (each job evaluator or employer has so far been free to develop his/her own criteria). But they are arguing that certain standards should be applied to job evaluation plans so that they will not implicitly rationalize discrimination but rather help identify it.

Certainly one could imagine a more radical form of policy than is currently guiding the comparable worth movement. Perhaps wage tribunals, as are common in the United Kingdom and Australia, would be a good idea. Perhaps comparable worth should be tied to other forms of public control over corporate decision making. Perhaps equal wages for everyone should be the goal. These alternatives do not seem likely in the short run in the United States, however, and in my view, the current form of the comparable worth struggle has a good deal of radical potential. What does a radical economic perspective, particularly a feminist one, add to our understanding of comparable worth?

The Perspective of Feminist Political Economy

A political economy perspective on wages recognizes that wages are socially and politically determined by custom, practice, the level of organization of workers and managers, and the results of past struggle—essentially the standard of living that a particular class segment, race or ethnic group, or gender has been able to achieve. Marx recognized that wages for skilled workers would generally be high enough to cover their costs of acquiring those skills, for example, and that immigrant groups could be paid less than native workers because their expected standard of living and their general level of organization was less.

Modern Marxist economists have developed a radical variant of internal labor market analysis and older institutional economics to understand how and why these differentials among workers are perpetuated and maintained in today's labor markets.[12] In this view, supply and demand are not unshakable god-given forces, a law unto themselves, but, rather, simply the accumulation of all of the above factors as well as government policies, domestic and internal competitive pressures, and so on. And in this view the comparable worth strategy can be seen as yet another attempt to influence wages by strengthening the bargaining position of women workers. As such it is as legitimate as any other attempt to influence wages, many of which (including discrimination) have already been incorporated in the wage rates that currently obtain.[13]

In more basic Marxist terms, the struggle for comparable worth can be seen as an attempt to shift more of the costs of reproducing labor to capital. Schematically, one can view the 1970s and 1980s as a period of capitalist speed-up, when, because of deterioration in husbands' wages, the average family had to send a second adult, the wife, into the labor market to maintain its standard of living. Thus capital winds up with 16 hours of labor from the family rather than 8 without significant increase in costs, which amounts to an effective reduction for the capitalist in the costs of reproducing labor power per hour worked. By demanding higher pay for women's jobs, the comparable worth strategy attempts to raise the capitalist's cost of reproducing labor power and to provide the family with more income, to raise its standard of living, and to compensate it for the wife's time now lost from the family and given to the labor market. If men's wages are not reduced as a result of comparable worth strategies, comparable worth has the potential to raise the share of income going to the working class as a whole. For women supporting families alone, without men's wages, the increase in income is of course, crucial to their maintaining a decent standard of living.

Women have historically had a lower standard of living than men.[14] Willingly or not, they *have* worked for less. They are often viewed as secondary wage earners, supported by men, whatever their class level and whatever their need to provide their own support. For this reason it is not sufficient to consider women's situation in the labor market from a class perspective alone. To understand women's position it is necessary to use a perspective that places gender, as well as class, in the center of analysis. From a feminist political economic perspective, the central importance of the comparable worth strategy is that it provides an ideology that convinces women workers that they are worth as much as men. This in turn encourages them to organize and demand higher wages. Comparable worth is a revolutionary strategy in that it has the potential to change the way women see themselves (and perhaps the way others see them as well).

To some extent the progress of the comparable worth issue shows that women workers fundamentally have begun to alter their self-perceptions.[15] Although it has much in common with other equal employment opportunity demands that have been heard for at least twenty years, the comparable worth message is a much more radical one, affects many more women workers, and is more collective in its outlook. A woman who wants access to a male-dominated job conveys the message: "I want a good job like yours." If she wants equal pay in a "male job" she conveys: "I deserve equal pay because I'm doing men's work." But if she demands comparable worth she conveys the message: "Women's work is worth as much as men's. My job is as good as your job," which means "your job is not better than mine."

Comparable worth challenges the belief that women are secondary earners, that men are the only or rightful household heads, that women's primary job is family work. When women demand comparable worth they are demanding wages equal to men's; they are demanding an equal chance with men to be economically independent. Wages that reflect greater value for what women do are crucial to women's ability to be financially independent. That women want economic equality with men is not necessarily to say that women no longer want to live with or marry men. But women argue that men's unique privilege to have a wage large enough to support a family should be eliminated; a family wage should not be a matter of male privilege but should be equally available to all.

Women are increasingly likely to be nonmarried (single, separated, divorced, or widowed) and to be heading their own households. For example, divorced women are now much more likely to maintain households of their own (in 1950, 60 percent of divorced women ages 25–36 did not head their own households; in 1980, 80 percent of them did).[16] In 1960, of all white women 15 and over, 36 percent were never married, separated, divorced, or widowed. By 1982, the percentage had increased to 43 percent. For black women over the same period, nonmarriage increased from 52 percent to 67 percent. Black women can now expect to spent only 22 percent of their lives married, whereas white women will spend 43 percent.[17] Of all households, the "traditional" household with the working husband, nonworking wife, and children at home, accounts for only about 8 percent, and even of all households with children under 18, the traditional type accounts for less than a third. Married women, especially mothers, are more likely than not to be in the labor force, and to be contributing directly to the financial support of their families. This configuration accounts for about 54 percent of those households with children. The remainder, 13 percent, are single-parent female-headed households.

Because family formation and household structures are changing, because women are very likely to have sole responsibility for supporting themselves and/or their children for some part of their lifetimes, and because women's participation in the labor market is increasing, women—through comparable worth and other means—are saying they need and want a "family" wage just as much as men do.[18]

Comparable worth also has the potential to bring about a cultural revaluation of the work women typically do in family and home care. If tasks such as nurturing and caring for people become more valued when done in paid jobs, they may come to be valued more in general, whether done in paid or unpaid work. Moreover, by raising the value of tasks that have been labeled female, comparable worth may result in more men participating in them, both in the labor market and in the home. And, if women have incomes more equal to men's, their bargaining power in relationships with men is likely to be increased, possibly resulting in men's taking on more household tasks.[19] Thus, although some critics have suggested that comparable worth will simply reify the existing sexual division of labor, it seems to have some potential to change it.

Although comparable worth has potential to bring about fundamental change in relations between women and men, it is, of course, not a complete program for change. Even in the limited area of equal opportunity in employment, other strategies, such as affirmative action and equal access, will continue to be needed. And employment is but one avenue, though perhaps the best, for economic self-sufficiency for women, the ultimate requirement for equality of the sexes. A socialist-feminist economic program would necessarily include consideration of such concerns as the provision of child care and care for the elderly, health insurance, and a shorter working day.[20]

Implications for Political Economy

A feminist political economy perspective suggests, then, that the central importance of comparable worth is its potential to alter the economic base of gender relations. Such a perspective also has implications for the practice of political economy. First, it again suggests that the actions of male workers in the work place are as relevant to outcomes for women workers as are the actions of managers.[21] This means that the process of struggle for higher wages for women is likely to directly challenge male co-workers as well as managers. Although management most often assigns workers to jobs, tracks them, and sets their wages, male workers, often as not, have influenced this process to the detriment of their female co-workers, even if only by acquiescence. Some well-known early comparable worth cases were court challenges of collective bargaining agreements that accorded lower wages to women's jobs that had received scores equal to men's jobs by the companies' job evaluation plans. (Significantly, the challenge was brought by the same union that had previously agreed to the wages, perhaps partly out of concern that it could be sued for its former role in acquiescing to the companies' blatant discriminatory policies.[22]) Phillips and Taylor cite research on London garment workers to provide an example of more active participation of men in attempting to keep women's jobs from getting high-skill ratings and high wages that would equal theirs. Male immigrants working in garment manufacturing wanted to preserve their patriarchal privileges over the women in their ethnic group, who also worked in the factories and shops, and so organized to prevent the women's jobs from being rated as highly.[23] From this came the false distinction of "working on the whole garment" versus working on pieces; the analysis suggests the skills involved are not different.

This leads to a second point for consideration by practitioners of political economy. In recent years, history, economics, and sociology have focused on the labor process. Work cultures, particularly cultures of resistance, have been described in many work places, particularly among male workers. The work process of women's jobs, too, needs reexamination. At least partly in response to Braverman's work on management's attempt to deskill jobs,[24] a number of studies showed how many skills, and how much pride in their work, most workers retain, even in seemingly deskilled jobs like those involved in the manufacture of paper cups.[25] Work on women's jobs[26] is now beginning to rectify the imbalance. In the comparable worth context, the emphasis is on getting payment for these formerly unrecognized (or purposely ignored) skills. In a recent case study of how a job evaluation study, motivated by comparable worth, was implemented for Oregon's civil servants, Joan Acker noted that human relations skills appear to be much more highly rated when they are found in service workers' jobs (which are predominately female).[27] If the ability to cajole people, to calm them, to help them is valued in one arena, it ought to be equally valued in another. Just as the shop floor has come to be seen as an arena of struggle for workers' control and dignity, so much the nursing home floor, the retail shop, the food counter, or the office. In particular, in light of male involvement in the definition and labeling of skills, this must be seen as another aspect of jobs over which struggle occurs. Although skill has some objectifiable, measurable elements as its base, its current definitions and labels mark it as the outcome of a political process.

These observations require expanding one's view of the role of gender struggle in the work place, as well as one's understanding of the labor process. In contrast to my earlier opinion, for example, that the primary locus of gender struggle is over who gets which jobs,[28] it is now clear that the very creation and definition of jobs is at issue. The work place is not characterized by a fixed hierarchy of good jobs and bad jobs determined by the requirements of technology or the production process but by a fluid job structure which (1) can be organized in many ways, with different combinations of jobs at different skill levels, and (2) is subject to gender as well as class struggle over the labeling and organization of its various components. As Phillips and Taylor note, the new conception requires rethinking many interpretations in political economy.[29] For example, Braverman suggests that as the clerical occupations were expanded and deskilled, women—with fewer skills—could be hired to fill the new jobs.[30] An alternate explanation suggests that when women were hired to fill the old jobs (because of increased demand for workers and because women with high school educations had the qualifications for them), the job labels and definitions changed more than their actual content. The jobs came to be considered deskilled because women now did them; the skills were relabeled to legitimate the lower wages women could be paid for the same work.

In addition to broadening our understanding of the labor process and of the role of gender struggle in that process, comparable worth also raises general issues for the entire working class, not only gender-based issues for women workers. (Moreover, as noted above, it also makes sense to think of women workers attempting to get raises as part of class struggle as well as of gender struggle.) The comparable worth strategy opens up the process of wage determination for discussion by workers. It asks why workers in various jobs get paid what they do. How much discretion and authority does each job have? How much skill and training is required to do it? Such questions obviously allow workers to compare themselves to others, usually including a number of managers as well.

Some of the opposition, especially from the private sector, probably is based in a reluctance to have these questions raised. Comparable worth cases have arisen most often in the public sector not because that sector is not subject to the competition of the marketplace (as some would have us believe), but because detailed job descriptions and their wage rates, the information needed to make a comparable worth claim, is already available. Thus, I believe comparable worth opens up a new arena for class struggle as well, in that it can challenge the basis of all wage rates, especially managerial differentials. It has the potential to make wage differentials less idiosyncratic, more predictable, and more subject to control.

Criticisms of Comparable Worth

But often comparable worth is not seen in a favorable light by radicals. For example, at a progressive conference on full employment in San Francisco, comparable worth was only begrudgingly endorsed,[31] and in *Storm Clouds over the Horizon*, by Bennett Harrison, Barry Bluestone, and Lucy Gorham, there is a footnote that implies that comparisons between jobs are not possible. Perhaps the notion of comparison is the heart of the problem. Does the comparable worth strategy require that objective, measurable differences between jobs exist, and does it accept the existing hierarchy among white male jobs as the correct and legitimate one? If there is an objective skill-based job hierarchy, does that give workers more or less control over what happens to them in the work place? Will control necessarily be ceded to the technical experts who design and implement job evaluation? (Certainly, on this basis many unions have argued against job evaluation.) I don't believe the answers to these questions are fully known. My own view is that characteristics of jobs are measurable and they can be ranked on the basis of measured differences. But the values placed on the measured characteristics, and hence the resulting ranks, are negotiable. In that sense comparable worth does not require ceding decision making to the technocrats who design and implement job evaluation procedures. But it does suggest that once a system of values and measurement is in place, workers and managers alike are likely to be required to abide by it.

A second criticism heard from both ends of the political spectrum, is that the benefits of comparable worth will accrue most to the best educated, most skilled women (predominately white and middle class), whereas the negative effects will fall on the least educated women (more likely to be minority members). The argument goes that when the wages of women's jobs are raised, demand will fall. More women will be competing for fewer jobs, which only the best qualified will be able to get; they will benefit from the high wages, and everyone else will be unemployed. This argument depends on knowing what the quantitative employment effects will be—will they be large and negative? We don't know. At least one study of implementation in Australia suggests not.[32] The argument also overlooks the fact that gender differences currently exist everywhere along the job hierarchy, not just at the upper, professional end. Low wage women workers earn less than low wage male workers; the wages of those women, too, would be affected by comparable worth strategies. In fact, in some cases it has been low wage minority women in social service jobs that involve personal care (home health aides, aides for the disabled, etc.) who have gotten the largest raises.[33] Some people argue that in the long run those jobs will be lost to minority women because of their higher wages, but that is saying that there will always be surplus workers (unemployment is here to stay); that minority workers are objectively less qualified than white workers; or that employers will discriminate. There are remedies for all these problems. To the extent some of them are real, they simply illustrate the necessity for comparable worth not to be the *only* strategy labor pursues. Affirmative action is critically important, as are full-employment policies and job training programs.

My own view is that on balance the problems with the comparable worth strategy are less important than the benefits. The benefits from the point of view of women are obvious, but benefits can accrue to male workers as well, and to the working class as a whole, in the form of opening up discussion of wages and jobs on the one hand and an overall higher share of income going to workers, on the other.

Conclusion

Women's demand for an equal ability to support themselves and their families is a fundamental challenge to the nature of gender relations today. The economic dependence of women on men is deeply embedded in our social structure. But the norm and reality of lifelong marriage and male support of women is disappearing. Equal earnings for women are both a cause of and a response to that disappearance. Comparable worth, which attempts to revalue what women do, is a fundamental challenge to these older notions of male economic superiority. Comparable worth challenges the cultural devaluations of women and women's work. In doing so it challenges the notion that women should be economically, socially, and culturally dependent on men. I suspect that much of the heat generated in opposition to comparable worth, on both the right and the left, is really a displaced response to this much more fundamental challenge to the status quo. The right vocally defends the free market, and the left assails technocracy—but the problem is really women's economic independence.

Opponents of comparable worth do not come out and say women belong in the home (or at least in low paid jobs). It's difficult for men to give up their power and privilege, but one could certainly argue that a unified workers' movement requires it. Far from seeing gender revolution as a sequel to class revolution, one could see it as a precondition. Comparable worth and other movements for women's equality in the work place give working men a second chance to incorporate women into the labor movement as equals. Many of them are taking that chance. Whatever its relation to class struggle, however, comparable worth is a crucial aspect of gender revolution. That is its central importance. The nature of the opposition indicates, I believe, that comparable worth challenges something more basic than the laws of supply and demand or even class solidarity. It questions the bases of our most intimate lives and says this, too, we must change.

Notes

1. Donald J. Treiman and Heidi I. Hartmann, eds., *Women, Work, and Wages: Equal Pay for Jobs of Equal Value* (Washington, D.C.: National Academy Press, 1981).

2. See Bureau of National Affairs, Inc., *Pay Equity and Comparable Worth*, A BNA Special Report, (Washington, D.C.: Bureau of National Affairs, Inc., 1984) and National Committee on Pay Equity, Comparable Worth Project, and National Women's Political Caucus, *Who's Working for Working Women: A Survey of State and Local Government Pay Equity Activities and Initiatives* (Washington, D.C.: Comparable Worth Project, National Committee on Pay Equity, and National Women's Political Caucus, 1984) for more on recent developments.

3. See Randy Pearl Albelda, *Race and Comparable Worth* (Geneva, N.Y.: Department of Economics, Hobart and William Smith Colleges, April, 1985).

4. Using data on broad occupational categories from the decennial censuses, racial segregation has fallen quite dramatically since World War II, whereas sex segregation has not. The index of segregation, which compares the similarity of two distributions—in this case men and women or blacks and whites—across a set of occupational groups, fell from 43 to 24 for racial segregation among men and from 46 to 41 for sex segregation among whites between 1940 and 1981 (Barbara F. Reskin and Heidi I. Hartmann, eds., *Women's Work, Men's Work: Sex Segregation on the Job*, Report of the Committee on Women's Employment and Related Social Issues, National Research Council [Washington, D.C.: National Academy Press, 1985]).

5. In a bargaining context wage equity or comparable worth can be pursued without elaborate job evaluation studies, simply by identifying some of the worst cases and stressing the reasonableness of the demand, but the studies may have importance beyond their immediate results. If one looks at the wage determination process as essentially a political one where the outcome is largely determined by the political power of various actors, then the supporting studies may be necessary to enhance the political power of women workers within their unions. Supporting studies can legitimate the women's demands, help convince others, and strengthen their own convictions. Likewise, bringing legal cases and involving the courts can be seen as an attempt to enhance the power of the weaker parties in the wage bargain.

6. See Treiman and Hartmann, *Women, Work, and Wages*.

7. It is important to note that, even if eventually enacted within all firms, comparable worth policies would not reach all discrimination in the labor market. Equal access to all occupations and all firms would still be necessary as would equitable promotion policies. There are wage leaders and wage followers in the labor market; firms at the high end of the wage hierarchy and firms at the low end. A computer operator in retailing, for example, is likely to continue to earn less than a computer operator in engineering. Comparable worth within firms is not going to change that, but enforcement of equal access policies can assure that the high-wage firms are equally accessible to women and men, minority members, and majority whites. Likewise comparable worth will not aid women who want

to be plumbers; equal access will. And comparable worth will not help secretaries become managers, but equitable promotion policies will.

8. And if comparable worth is understood as sex-based wage *discrimination*, even arguments that it would be costly or might lead to some unemployment won't hold up against the basic issue of justice and the importance of removing discrimination that is legally prohibited. The same arguments of economic hardship were heard in the South after the passage of the 1964 Civil Rights Act; nevertheless wages of jobs held predominantly by blacks were raised as part of legal remedies that also called for racial integration of jobs. Subsequently, the southern economy expanded.

9. This concept is elaborated by Barbara R. Bergmann, "Occupational Segregation, Wages and Profits When Employers Discriminate by Race or Sex," *Eastern Economic Journal* 1 (April/July, 1974): 103–10.

10. Job evaluation plans, in assigning weights or "prices" to job factors, are conceptually similar to human capital type wage equations, so beloved by labor economists and sociologists, which assign coefficients to attributes of individuals. A difference in the coefficients (derived weights) when the factors are found in women's rather than men's jobs suggests discrimination. Similarly a nonzero sign on the coefficient for a variable such as percentage of females would indicate that sex composition of the job had an effect on its average wage rate, and would also suggest discrimination.

11. See also Donald P. Schwab, "Job Evaluation Research and Research Needs," in Heidi I. Hartmann, ed., *Comparable Worth: New Directions for Research* (Washington, D.C.: National Academy Press, 1985): 37–52.

12. David M. Gordon, Richard Edwards, and Michael Reich, *Segmented Work, Divided Workers: The Historical Transformation of Labor in the United States* (Cambridge, England: Cambridge University Press, 1982).

13. Linda Chavez, formerly staff director of the U.S. Commission on Civil Rights and currently a special assistant in the White House, is a frequent administration spokesperson on comparable worth. In an ironic shift of current government policy, she often states that women who want comparable worth should organize unions—getting a union to bargain for you is adopting a time-honored "market" solution, whereas comparable worth is a noxious "interference with the market."

14. Laura Oren, "The Welfare of Women in Laboring Families: England 1860 to 1950," *Feminist Studies* 2, no. 3 and 4 (1973): 107–25; Robert M. Spalter-Roth, "Measuring Inequalities and Uneven Changes in the Living Standards of Husbands and Wives in Two-Wage Earner Families: 1968–1979" (Paper presented at the Eastern Sociological Association Meetings, March 4–6, 1983).

15. Heidi I. Hartmann and Karen Nussbaum, "The Clerical Workers' Movement in the U.S." Published in Berlin, Germany in *Dollars and Trauma*, a Journal of American Studies, no. 8 (Oct., 1983): 69–79.

16. Suzanne M. Bianchi, and Daphne Spain, *American Women: Three Decades of Change* (Washington, D.C.: U.S. Bureau of the Census, 1983).

17. Thomas J. Espenshade, "Marriage Trends in America: Estimates, Implications, and Underlying Causes," *Population and Development Review* 11, no. 2 (1985): 193–245.

18. Interestingly, women are now using the "family wage" argument just as male workers used it in the nineteenth and early twentieth centuries, to justify a higher wage. Because men had families to support (because women should stay home to take care of children and child-labor should be abolished), they deserved high wages, men argued. Now women are arguing that because they often wind up as sole support of themselves and their children and because their wages are often crucial to the support of families when husbands'/fathers' wages are low, women need family wages, too.

19. Heidi I. Hartmann, "The Family as the Locus of Gender, Class and Political Struggle: The Example of Housework," *Signs* 6 (Spring), 1981): 366–94.

20. This point is elaborated upon by Wendy Sarvasy and Judith Van Allen, "Fighting the Feminization of Poverty: Socialist Feminist Analysis and Strategy," *Review of Radical Political Economics* (Forthcoming).

21. See Heidi I. Hartmann, "Capitalism, Patriarchy, and Job Segregation by Sex," *Signs* 1, no. 2 (Spring, 1976, Supplement): 137–69 and "The Unhappy Marriage of Marxism and Feminism," *Capital and Class* 8 (Summer, 1979): 1–33.

22. For a fuller discussion, see Winn Newman, "Combatting Occupational Segregation: Presentation III," in Martha Blaxall and Barbara Reagan, eds., *Women and the Workplace: The Implications of Occupational Segregation* (Chicago: University of Chicago Press, 1976): 265–72 and Treiman and Hartmann, *Women, Work, and Wages*.

23. Anne Phillips and Barbara Taylor "Sex and Skill: Notes Towards a Feminist Economics," *Feminist Review* 6 (1980): 79–88.

24. Harry Braverman, *Labor and Monopoly Capital* (New York: Monthly Review Press, 1974).

25. Kenneth Kusterer, *Know-how on the Job: The Important Working Knowledge of Unskilled Workers* (Boulder, Co: Westview Press, 1978).

26. For a collection, see Karen Brodkin Sacks and Dorothy Remy, eds., *My Troubles are Going to Have Trouble with Me* (New Brunswick, N.J.: Rutgers University Press, 1984).

27. Joan Acker, "Sex Bias in Job Evaluation: A Comparable Worth Issue" (Paper presented at the Conference on Ingredients for Women's Employment Policy, Albany, New York, April 19–20, 1985).

28. Hartmann, "Capitalism, Patriarchy, and Job Segregation."

29. Phillips and Taylor, "Sex and Skill."

30. Braverman, *Labor and Monopoly Capital*.

31. William Winpisinger, et al., "Growth and Employment," *Socialist Review*, 14–34 (May-August, 1984): 9–39.

32. R. G. Gregory and Vivian Ho, "Equal Pay and Comparable Worth: What Can the U.S. Learn from the Australian Experience?" Preliminary Draft (Australian National University, 1985).

33. Susan Logston, the statewide grievance representative for the union of employees at Connecticut state community colleges, told me that a recent job evaluation study done of the community college system resulted in almost none of the women deans (each of whom thought their jobs would be upgraded tremendously) getting increases, but in substantial increases for many low-paid minority women and men worked as aides.

COMMENTS:

There is Worth to Comparable Worth: A Critique of Raisian, Welch, and Ward

Elaine Sorensen, University of Massachusetts

The three papers on comparable worth form a broad spectrum of views on this subject. Hartmann's paper explains the purpose of a comparable worth strategy and argues for its implementation from a neoclassical and political economy/feminist perspective. Mangum analyzes the issue from an institutionalist point of view and concludes that a comparable worth strategy is a positive goal for companies that already have an internal labor market structure. Raisian, Welch, and Ward, on the other hand, critique comparable worth policies. They argue that the methodology of comparable worth proposals is arbitrary and subjective, and that implementation of comparable worth will do very little for women's earnings relative to men's earnings. The first two papers are theoretical and descriptive treatments of the subject, while the latter is an empirical analysis of comparable worth. This review will focus upon those empirical efforts.

The Methodology of Comparable Worth Proposals

Raisian, Welch, and Ward argue that the methodology of comparable worth proposals is arbitrary and subjective. However, their empirical analysis of comparable worth methodology has several problems. First, they interpret the goal of comparable worth policies differently than many advocates of this issue. They state that the "goal of comparable worth advocates is to have wages in an occupation be determined by a vector of job attributes." Many advocates, on the other hand, argue that a comparable worth strategy is intended to eliminate the systematic undervaluation of women's work that results from extensive occupational segregation in the U.S. labor market.[1]

The systematic undervaluation of female dominated jobs has been measured by many comparable worth studies. These studies tend to find that female dominated jobs are paid less than male dominated jobs for work that is considered comparable by a job evaluation plan. This undervaluation is measured by the following type of equation:

$$w = a_0 + a_1 J + a_2 F + u \tag{1}$$

where: w is the occupational salary for each occupation; J is the job evaluation score for each occupation; F is a dummy variable that equals 1 of the job is female dominated and 0 if it is male dominated; and u is the random error term.

The dependent variable is the occupational salary, which is of the salary levels that an individual could receive if employed in this occupation. The job evaluation score is a number that measures the overall requirements of a job according to the criteria established by the job evaluation plan. Most comparable worth studies use an a priori factor-point plan to evaluate jobs, the most commonly used job evaluation plan in the United States. These plans select a set of factors and weights before the evaluation. The factors are expected to reflect the requirements of the job, and usually fall into four broad categories: skill, effort, responsibility, and working conditions. Weights assigned for each factor indicate their relative importance. A team evaluates jobs in terms of each factor and assigns a level of points commensurate with the amount of the factor required on the job. These factor scores are summed for each job to produce a total point score, or job evaluation score.

A comparable worth policy can eliminate the effect of F from equation (1) by subtracting its estimated coefficient, or a_2, from the earnings of female dominated jobs. This eliminates the negative effect that being employed in a predominately female job has on the earnings of workers in these occupations. Any factor other than the sex composition of the occupation, that may influence occupational earnings of female dominated jobs is unaffected by the implementation of a comparable worth policy. After the policy is implemented, female dominated jobs have the same earnings equation as male dominated jobs.

In contrast, the authors suggest that a comparable worth policy would subtract a_2 as well as any residual difference between the current salary and the predicted salary from the above equation when determining salaries for female dominated jobs. Thus, occupations would be paid according to their job attributes and not according to the predominate sex of the occupation *or any other factor that may influence occupational salaries*.

Raisian, Welch, and Ward's interpretation of comparable worth detracts from the basic point of the policy, which, according to many of its advocates, is to eliminate from occupational earnings the negative effect of being employed in a female dominated job. Furthermore, it is more susceptible than the first interpretation of comparable worth to changes in the functional form of equation (1) and to changes in the weights used to determine the job evaluation score. Thus, the outcomes generated by the authors' interpretation of comparable worth appear more arbitrary than similar outcomes from a more typical advocate's interpretation.

Second, the authors argue that the functional form used in comparable worth proposals is arbitrary and "not based on science or fact." However, one selection rule that could be used to choose among alternative functional terms is that which maximizes the $\bar{R}^2$. This seems like a sensible selection rule since the reason comparable worth proposals estimate equations like the one above is to explain as much of the wage variation as possible with legitimate factors, such as the job evaluation score, and the sex composition of the occupation. To conduct their analysis of comparable worth, Raisian, Welch, and Ward select a log-linear functional form, which is the standard functional form used by economists to estimate earnings equations. This functional form has become the standard because it is based, in part, on human capital theory and because it produces a high $\bar{R}^2$. Thus, the functional form used in comparable worth proposals could be based upon "science" (part theory, part econometrics) and does not have to be arbitrary. Furthermore, the functional terms already in use by comparable worth studies produce considerably high $\bar{R}^2$s. Tinkering with the functional form will only produce slightly higher $\bar{R}^2$, and will not alter the basic result that female dominated jobs are paid less than male dominated jobs that are considered comparable by a job evaluation plan.[2]

Third, they argue that the job evaluation scores, that are assigned to each job are arbitrary and subjective. A job evaluation score represents the sum of different factor scores, each of which have been weighted according to their relative importance. For example, the Hay system has four factors: "know-how, "accountability," problem solving," and "working conditions." Jobs are assigned a factor score in each of these categories, and the sum is the total point score, or job evaluation score. The factor scores reflect the weight that has been assigned to that factor in the evaluation. For example, in the Hay system, the lowest level of "know-how" received 50 points, while the lowest level of "problem solving" received 12 points, indicating that the lowest level of "know-how" is weighted almost five times as much as the lowest level of problem-solving.

Raisian, Welch, and Ward argue that all weighting structures are arbitrary. They attempt to substantiate this claim by examining a set of occupations and factor scores.[3] After weighting these factor scores equally and deriving a total point score, they find that certain pairs of jobs that have equal total point scores are paid substantially different salaries. But they find such earnings disparities exist among female jobs and male jobs, as well as between male and female jobs. Thus, according to the authors, it is difficult to conclude that the earnings disparity is due to occupational segregation. Furthermore, they argue that if different weights were chosen, different jobs would be considered comparable and different pay inequities would be found.

The authors use pair-wise comparisons to substantiate their claim that different weighting schemes produce very different pay inequities between (and among) male and female dominated jobs. As others have pointed out, pair-wise comparisons are not convincing—it is easy to find outliers that refute a general tendency. Even with the limited set of occupations that the authors report, there still is a general tendency for female dominated jobs to be paid less than male dominated jobs for comparable total point scores, whether you weight the factors equally or allow ordinary least squares regression analysis to select the weights.

Furthermore, the weights are not as arbitrary as Raisian, Welch, and Ward suggest. In most cases, an outside job evaluation expert determines the weights. These weights generally reflect considerable research and development by the job evaluation expert, with the principal aim of explaining as much of the wage variation within a firm as possible. Thus, its not surprising that the weights chosen by the consulting firm produce very high $\bar{R}^2$s. Furthermore, it is possible to impose upon comparable worth proposals a nonarbitrary selection rule, which would require that the weights be chosen to maximize the $\bar{R}^2$. This is the rule that the authors later use in their analysis of the effect of a comparable worth policy on female earnings. However, this selection rule would produce weights very similar to the ones already in use.[4]

The fourth problem with the authors' analysis of comparable worth methodology is that they overlook the important role that job evaluation procedures already play in wage determination. They describe this methodology as if comparable worth proposals were the first to compare wages to job evaluation scores. However, this is not the case. For decades firms have been using job evaluation plans as an instrument in wage determination. Comparable worth proposals use the same job evaluation methodology as firms have traditionally used to evaluate jobs. The basic difference between comparable worth studies and the traditional use of job evaluation plans is not the methodology, but the number of jobs that are compared. In the past, firms have tended to limit comparisons of wages and job evaluation scores to jobs that were similar in some way. Comparable worth studies, on the other hand, compare wages and job evaluation scores of all nonmanagerial occupations within a firm. However, the methodology employed by comparable worth proposals is exactly the same as that traditionally employed by firms.

Thus, in their analysis of comparable worth methodology, Raisian, Welch, and Ward first interpret the goal of comparable worth proposals quite differently than most of its advocates, in a way that accentuates its arbitrary features. Next, they claim that the functional form and weighting schemes employed by comparable worth proposals are necessarily arbitrary, and yet simple selection rules exist for both the functional form and the weighting scheme. Current comparable worth studies do not use these selection rules, but others have found that changing the procedures to reflect these rules does not significantly alter the outcomes of comparable worth studies. Lastly, they ignore that comparable worth studies use the same methodology as employers have traditionally used to evaluate jobs—evaluations which already play a role in wage determination.

The Impact of Comparable Worth on Female Earnings

Raisian, Welch, and Ward also attempt to measure the effect of a nationwide comparable worth policy on the male-female earnings gap. They find that such a policy would eliminate only 7 percent of the earnings gap between women and men and increase labor costs by 1.5 percent. Thus, they conclude that a comparable worth policy is less expensive than others may have expected, but it is *not* an effective way of eliminating the national earnings disparity between women and men.

The basic problem is that they do not have national data that is similar to the data used in comparable worth proposals. Comparable worth proposals examine occupational earnings within a firm, but the authors examine individual earnings within an occupation across different firms. Unfortunately, this approach confuses the issues at hand. Now the sex composition of an occupation may affect earnings for two reasons. First, earnings may be negatively affected by the sex composition of an occupation because of occupational segregation as hypothesized in comparable worth proposals. Second, earnings may be negatively affected simply because women earn less than men in the same occupation. This is because as more women are employed in an occupation, the average earnings within an occupation decline, since women earn, on average, less than men in an occupation.

Since women and men receive the same occupational salary within a firm, comparable worth proposals do not address the second influence of intraoccupational earnings differences between women and men. Therefore, to measure the impact of comparable worth proposals the authors must eliminate this additional effect on earnings. They attempt to eliminate this additional effect by adding yet another independent variable into their analysis, called *CON*. Thus, they run the following equation:

$$\ln w = b_0 + b_1 Z + b_2 \%F + b_3 CON + v \qquad (2)$$

where: w is the average earnings of individuals in each occupation; Z is the set of job attributes; $\%F$ is the percentage of women in each occupation; CON is the concentration of women in each occupation; and v is the random error term.

They claim that comparable worth proposals would eliminate the negative effect of *CON* on average individual earnings within an occupation, rather than the effect of $\%F$. Unfortunately, it is not clear that eliminating the negative effect of *CON* actually eliminates the negative effect of occupational segregation on earnings, the stated goal of most comparable worth policies. Eliminating *CON* from the earnings equation, rather than %*F*, means that the negative effect of %*F* on the earnings is maintained. This remaining influence may reflect intraoccupational earnings differences, as the authors suggest, or it may reflect occupational segregation, which would be eliminated under a comparable worth policy. Without further information, the reader cannot tell whether the total effect of occupational segregation on earnings has been eliminated.

Ehrenberg and Smith, on the other hand, reviewed a number of public sector comparable worth studies and found that implementing comparable worth would increase female salaries by an average of 20 percent.[5]Sorensen estimated that implementing comparable worth in the public sector would increase payroll costs by 8 percent and eliminate 46 percent of the male-female earnings gap in these jurisdictions.[6] Even though these findings are based upon public sector data, they call into question results like those reported by Raisian, Welch, and Ward.

Conclusion

Although these authors critique the methodology of comparable worth proposals for being arbitrary and subjective, after a closer examination of their empirical research I find their analysis exaggerates these problems. Furthermore, their estimates of the effect of comparable worth on female earnings and its subsequent cost are based upon a methodology that is not comparable to the methodology used by comparable worth studies and thus misrepresents the impact of implementing comparable worth. Other studies based upon actual comparable worth studies suggest that up to half of the intra-firm earnings gap between women and men could be eliminated under a comparable worth strategy, and such a policy would only increase labor costs by 8 percent.

Notes

1. See Ruth G. Blumrosen, "Wage Discrimination, Job Segregation, and Title VII of the Civil Rights Act of 1964," *University of Michigan Journal of Law Reform* 12, no. 3 (Spring 1979): 399–502; Ronnie J. Steinberg, "A Want of Harmony: Perspectives on Wage Discrimination and Comparable Worth," in Helen Remick, ed., *Comparable Worth and Wage Discrimination: Technical Possibilities and Political Realities* (Philadelphia: Temple University, 1984): 3–27; and Donald Treiman, and Heidi I. Hartmann, eds., *Women, Work, and Wages: Equal Pay for Jobs of Equal Value* (Washington, D.C.: National Academy Press, 1981): 1–12.

2. For different functional forms and their effect, see Ronald G. Ehrenberg and Robert S. Smith, "Comparable Worth in the Public Sector," (Working Paper No. 1471, NBER, September 1984) and Elaine Sorensen, "Implementing Comparable Worth: A Survey of Recent Job Evaluation Studies," *American Economic Review* (May 1986): 364–67.

3. These scores are based on Ann R. Miller, Donald J. Treiman, Pamela S. Cain, and Patricia A. Roos, eds., *Work, Jobs, and Occupations: a Critical Review of the Dictionary of Occupational Titles* (Washington, D.C.: National Academy Press, 1980): Appendix F.

4. See Elaine Sorensen, "Alternative Job Evaluation Procedures: Their Impact on Comparable Worth" (Paper presented at the Eastern Economic Association Meetings, April 1986).

5. "Comparable Worth in the Public Sector."

6. "Implementing Comparable Worth."

Comparable Worth vs. Affirmative Action: Experience from the California Canning Industry

Martin Brown, Howard University

In her paper, "The Political Economy of Comparable Worth," Heidi Hartmann comments that,

> The mainstay of a [comparable worth] case that argues that discrimination has affected the wage rates of an *entire* occupation (as opposed to a discrimination case that argues that *individual* women have been discriminated against in pay in a particular job) is the existence of sex segregation in the firm's employment structure. . . . The remedy that is suggested is the realignment of . . . wage rates. . . .

The implication of these comments is that a comparable worth remedy to correct wage discrimination is likely to have a more profound impact on overall wage equity than more conventional affirmative action remedies which focus not on changing the entire wage structure of an employer but on increasing occupational mobility through the established wage structure on an individual-by-individual basis.

Experience with comparable worth and conventional affirmative action programs in the California canning industry tends to confirm this implication. The California canning industry has historically employed women as about 60 percent of its work force, a far higher proportion than U.S. manufacturing as a whole. Yet, until 1973 women were restricted to a narrowly defined set of jobs with severely limited promotional opportunities. Women have been almost totally excluded from supervisory, maintenance, warehousing, and machine operative jobs and restricted to the "traditional women's work" of produce preparation in processing and canning departments. Restriction of women to these jobs not only restricted promotional opportunities but also crowded women into the lowest paid job category in the canneries. The "woman's" job category historically paid a wage about 15 percent below the lowest "man's " wage and 25 percent below the median man's wage.[1]

The strict gender stratification of employment in the California canneries was not clearly established until the late 1920s. The process by which this stratification was established was complex, but can be briefly summarized as follows:

(1) Women were excluded from jobs that originally required a high degree of hard physical labor, but which, in most cases, no longer do, because of mechanization and automation. Many warehousing jobs fall into this category.

(2) Women were excluded from jobs that were originally the domain of male-

dominated skilled craft labor, but which no longer require specialized training outside the plant. The operation of cooking and can-sealing equipment falls into this category.

(3) Women were excluded from jobs in which they would supervise men, but not vise versa.

(4) Women were restricted to seasonal jobs characterized by low wages, low job security, and few promotional opportunities, and excluded from year-round jobs.

(5) Women were restricted to simple machine-tending jobs which evolved from jobs that originally involved hand labor and excluded from more complex machine operating jobs, even when such jobs evolved from hand-labor jobs that originally employed women. For example, can labeling was originally a hand-labor job exclusively employing women. When can labeling became mechanized, however, women were totally excluded from this occupation.

This strict gender stratification in the California canning industry was reinforced and rationalized by cultural attitudes—the alleged inability of any woman to deal with the "mechanical" nature of even the simplest machinery (women could passively feed produce into a machine, but could not monitor or adjust machinery)—and by legal institutions—regulations of the California Industrial Welfare Code, in effect since the early 1920s, barred women from any job in which she would ever be required to lift in excess of 25 pounds. The contrived nature of these barriers was demonstrated by the experience of World War II when, in the midst of the wartime labor shortage, the California Industrial Welfare Commission granted an "emergency exemption" of its regulations and many women were successfully employed in previously all-male cannery jobs. However, after the war the California cannery industry reverted to its traditional job structure.

It is likely that cannery operators benefited from the traditional gender segmentation which they maintained in the industry's employment structure. The cultural and legal mechanisms which facilitated the restriction of women to the lowest job categories crowded women into that category, reducing their potential bargaining power. The cultural and legal mechanisms which rationalized women's cannery work as fundamentally different from men's also served to isolate women from the bargaining power of the male-dominated cannery union. The resulting 15 percent wage depression for women workers, who made up more than half of the cannery work force, was undoubtedly worth more to cannery employers in wage bill savings than any loss they may have incurred by failing to promote potentially productive women to high level jobs.

The 15 percent wage differential between entry-level male and female jobs is difficult to explain in human capital terms. Detailed job descriptions of these jobs portray such factors as skills, training, and responsibility required for male and female entry-level jobs as identical. If anything, human capital considerations would suggest that wages should have been lower for male entry-level jobs because male cannery worker jobs were given more of an opportunity to invest in firm-specific human capital, resulting in later payoffs in terms of access to promotion opportunities, more job security, less seasonal work, and higher wages.

In response to pressure from Latino and women's caucuses within the California cannery union (affiliated with the Teamsters Union) and various legal actions under the Equal Employment Opportunity Act, some important changes were made in the employment structure of the California canning industry in the 1970s. Beginning in 1973 the collective bargaining contract was revised so that the entry-level job categories for men and women were combined into a single gender-neutral category as far as wages and access to the seniority, promotional, and benefits systems were concerned. We consider this reform to be primarily a comparable worth type remedy because it did not directly or immediately affect the gender distribution of workers across the wage structure, but it did alter that wage structure itself in a significant way. By abolishing the male-female differential for entry-level jobs, this reform immediately provided a modest but permanent benefit to almost all women cannery workers and significantly increased the equity of the overall wage structure in the cannery industry. However, the remaining wage differential in the California cannery industry (of about 60 percent), between the highest paid and entry level production workers, is unusually large for a unionized manufacturing industry.

Various EEO legal actions in the 1970s did not result in further reform of the wage structure itself, but expanded and implemented the affirmative action type reforms in the California canning industry. These remedies involved various programs to increase the proportion of women workers employed in higher level job categories. These affirmative action type programs greatly benefited those individual women who gained access to promotional opportunities, especially because occupational wage differentials in the canning industry remained rather sharp. However, relatively few women actually gained benefits from this remedy compared to the comparable worth remedy. The percentage of women employed in the top three job categories approximately doubled between 1973 and 1978. Still, in 1978 the percentage of women employed in the top two job brackets was only about one-quarter of their percentage representation in the canning industry work force.

Census data on the annual incomes of California cannery workers for 1970 and 1980 confirms the impression that comparable worth type remedies have had a more profound impact on the overall gender distribution of earnings than have affirmative action type remedies. Figure 1A shows the income distribution for California cannery workers, by gender, for 1970 and Figure 1B shows the same information for 1980. The shape of the income distribution for women cannery workers is almost identical for the two years, indicating little impact from the affirmative action type programs. On the other hand, between 1970 and 1980, the overall women's wage distribution has moved up relative to the overall men's

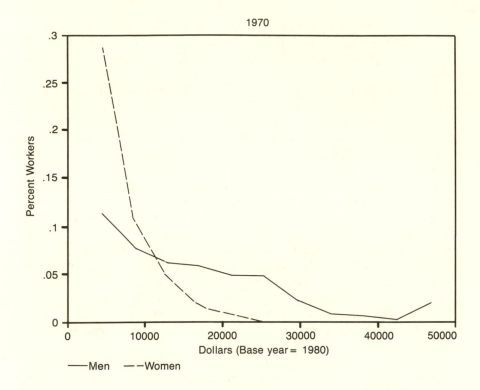

Figure 1A. Annual Incomes of Cannery Workers
Source: U.S. Census Bureau, *California Public Use Sample* (Washington, D.C., 1970).

wage distribution. This is not surprising, given the 1973 abolition of the gender wage differential for entry level jobs. The other notable feature of Figure 1 is that the 1980 income distribution for men shows an increase in the proportion of men at the lower end of the distribution. This may be due to the decision of cannery employers to fill some of the formerly "women's" jobs with men, that is, to more fully integrate entry level jobs now that the employer's advantage of maintaining gender segregation has been eliminated by the comparable worth reform.

As a postscript it is worth noting that the increase in wage equity achieved through the comparable worth type reforms in the California canning industry in the 1970s has been eroded somewhat in the 1980s. Beginning in 1981 the collective bargaining contract allowed employers to pay a "beginners' rate" of $2.00 per hour less for lower category jobs for new workers employed for less than 90 days. Since the lowest level job paid $7.92 in 1984, this $2.00 sub minimum wage represents a substantially larger differential than the historical 15 percent gender differential maintained prior to 1973. In recent years many California canneries

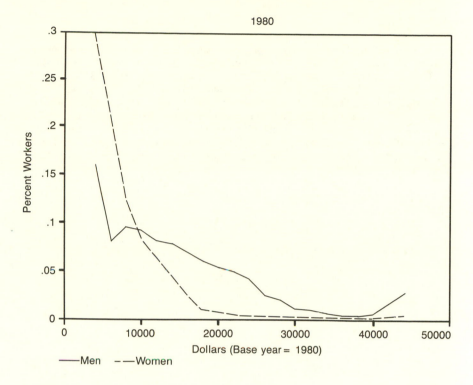

Figure 1B. Annual Incomes of Cannery Workers
Source: U.S. Census Bureau, *California Public Use Sample* (Washington, D.C., 1980).

have relocated in new, more remote areas, so that the ''beginners'' rate may apply to a substantial proportion of the entry-level workers who work in highly seasonal jobs (i.e., of less than 90-days duration). While this development represents a deterioration in overall wage equity in the California canning industry it is less gender specific in its effects than the pre–1973 wage policies.

The experience with comparable worth and affirmative action type policies in the California canning industry does not suggest that the former are necessarily superior to affirmative action policies in achieving wage equity. It does suggest that the effects of a comparable worth type policy are more sweeping and immediate, especially in an industry with declining overall employment opportunities, such as the California canning industry. This study also suggests that comparable worth type policies challenge deeply embedded ideas about gender- (and race-) based wage norms which are perpetuated not only to maintain the cultural status quo within the work force but also because they are profitable. Thus, employers probably will strongly resist the implementation of comparable worth programs and, when possible, find ways to reverse such programs.

Note

1. Documentation for this paragraph and for other data in this paper can be found in Martin Brown and Peter Philips, "The Evolution of Labor Market Structure: The California Canning Industry," *Industrial and Labor Relations Review* 38, no. 3 (April 1985): 392–407; Martin Brown, "A Historical-Economic Analysis of the Wage Structure of the California Fruit and Vegetable Canning Industry." Ph.D. diss., University of California, Berkeley, 1981 (unpublished); California Industry Affirmative Action Trust, "Status Report," 1979–1983, mimeos, unpublished; and Martin Brown and Peter Philips, "The Historical Origin of Job Ladders in the U.S. Canning Industry and Their Effects on the Gender Division of Labour," *Cambridge Journal of Economics* 10, no. 2 (June 1986): 120–45.

INTERNATIONAL DIVISION OF LABOR

PAPERS

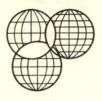

PART IV

11

LONG-RUN DETERMINANTS OF THE INTERNATIONAL DIVISION OF LABOR

Stephen E. Reynolds and Stephen F. Seninger

Introduction

The secularly rising and record trade deficits that have been registered in the U.S. accounts in recent years and allegations of deindustrialization of the U.S. economy have focused public attention on the international division of labor (IDL) and the role of the U.S. in that division. Few, if any, analysts would be likely to deny the role of international trade and competition in determining the position of the U.S. in the IDL. Therefore, the traditional theory of international trade provides one approach to the determinants of the IDL and the U.S. position within the global allocation of labor.

Traditional neoclassical trade theory envisions international trade as a mechanism that permits an extension of the national division of labor into a more specialized division than would be the case within the confines of the domestic market. International trade is viewed as compensating for the at least partial international immobility of factors of production. In the absence of trade the pattern of domestic demand in conjunction with the domestic production possibilities (reflecting resource endowments and technology) would determine the division of labor. Autarky commodity and factor prices would differ markedly

Stephen E. Reynolds is Associate Professor of Economics at the University of Utah. Stephen F. Seninger is a visiting Associate Professor of Policy Sciences and Research Economist at the Thomas M. Bradley Center for Employment, Training and Education Research, University of Maryland, Baltimore County.

among countries—even with identical demand conditions. Domestic divisions of labor would vary systematically across countries so that relatively greater employment would be found in industries whose technologies favored relatively greater use of a nation's relatively abundant resources, with identical demand conditions.

In a nontrading system characterized by perfect factor mobility in response to factor return differentials, factor movements would tend to equalize relative and absolute factor returns. For countries with similar demand conditions and constant returns production conditions the domestic division of labor would be identical. There would be no basis for international trade in differences in autarky commodity prices, nor any basis for differentiation within the IDL.

International trade, too, under conventional assumptions, results in the *ex post* elimination of differences in autarky commodity prices and in the elimination of differences in autarky factor prices—in spite of international factor immobility. Such results are obtained through a pattern of international commodity trade flows which result in each nation being a net exporter of its relatively abundant factors of production. This leads to international differences in the domestic division of labor. A greater share of employment would be found in industries whose technologies favored intensive use of a nation's abundant resources than would be the case with autarky or international factor mobility. This conclusion cannot be stated more strongly because of the indeterminacy of the domestic structure of production. Thus it is expected that the differences among nations in their domestic divisions of labor (associated with differences in factor endowments) will be exacerbated by international trade even as the differences in commodity and factor prices are reduced.

The welfare consequences of a trade-created division of labor are part of the core of traditional trade theory. The effect of trade in lowering (raising) the prices of importable (exportable) commodities shifts production away from (toward) industries producing them, reducing (expanding) employment in those industries. This shift in production along the long-run transformation curve represents a welfare-improving move in the Pareto sense. In the absence of market distortions (deviations from the competitive, mobility, and externality assumptions), free trade is envisioned to lead to static welfare maximization for each nation and for the world as a whole. Contributions to the theory of international trade and welfare such as those by Samuelson, Baldwin, Bhagwati, Ramaswami, Johnson, Cordon, and others can be used to examine various market distortions that require policy intervention. Different policy interventions can be rank ordered according to their impact on welfare.[1]

From the perspective of traditional trade theory "increasing returns" are a source of market distortions which upset a variety of first- and second-order conditions for welfare maximization. In contrast to this view—which relegates the phenomena of increasing returns to a minor role—is one that makes irreversible dynamic scale economies in manufacturing the basis for a process of cumulative causation leading to productivity growth differentials among nations.[2] International differences in labor productivity within manufacturing make for export advantage, a current account surplus and export-led economic expansion. Adjustment in the current account surplus takes place through acceleration (slowing) of income growth in the surplus (deficit) country. Growth of the market leads to an increase in the domestic division of labor and ". . . with an increase in the division of labor, capital and output grow together."[3] The consequence of this growth process is a strengthening of initial differences in manufacturing labor productivities among nations.

This second view emphasizes agglomeration effects at the local and national level derived from dynamic scale economies which are concentrated in manufacturing but endemic throughout that sector. Relative concentration of employment in manufacturing favors more rapid labor productivity growth which leads to a self-reinforcing pattern of production and international trade which favors further concentration of employment in manufacturing. Balanced international trade in manufactures enhances the IDL and accelerates growth of the total market—leading to wide spread welfare gains for all trading partners. Imbalance of manufactures trade may enhance the growth of some countries relative to that of others whose growth may be stunted.[4]

Traditional Trade Theory and the IDL

The core of traditional neoclassical trade theory is general equilibrium theory (with some dynamic extensions). The basis theorems of the theory relate commodity outputs and factor prices to changes in output prices and in factor supplies. Further, they identify which commodities are exported and which are imported. The clearest results of the theory are obtained when:[5]

(1) the number of countries, of factors, and of commodities is in each case equal to two (thus, all commodities are traded).

(2) factors are mobile domestically at no cost among alternative employment but are completely immobile among countries.

(3) commodities move internationally without impediment (including zero transport costs).

(4) both commodity and factor markets clear competitively (agents act as price takers adjusting quantities to market prices).

(5) the same technical knowledge about commodity production is available at no cost to all countries and those production functions exhibit constant returns to scale, diminishing marginal products,, and an absence of externalities.

(6) relative factor endowments among countries are more similar than are the relative factor intensities among industries.

(7) individuals consume (without external effects) as if they were maximizing identical homothetic utility functions

Thus, the traditional model is a long-run model in which prices are flexible, resources are mobile, exchange rates are determined by commodity flows, and money is neutral.[6]

The theory identifies the pattern of trade as a function of either the difference between autarky and post-trade prices or of factor supplies. A country will export the commodities the production of which is relatively intensive in the factor with which the country is relatively well endowed. It will import the commodity the production of which is relatively intensive in the factor which is relatively scarce in that country. Little imagination is required to challenge the empirical relevance of the above assumptions and by implication the empirical relevance of the theory's predictions regarding the pattern of trade.

Since exports are clearly the excess of production over consumption (and imports, the excess of consumption over production) the emphasis on comparative production costs in the theory is obtained by neutralizing (by assumption) the effects of demand on the cross-country (but *not* the aggregate) pattern of commodity production. Even then various departures from the other assumptions are troublesome for the theory and its predictions. Leamer examines these problems succinctly and clearly.[7]

Even within the confines of the above assumptions of the traditional trade model it is difficult to derive conclusions regarding the international division of labor. The general conclusion is that trade will reflect differences in autarky comparative costs which are the consequence of the interaction of differences in national relative factor endowments with differences in relative factor intensities among the production processes for commodities. These assumptions are also sufficient to yield factor price equalization across nations.

In that case Bhagwati has demonstrated that the only conclusion regarding production patterns is that factor proportions in each country will be the same in each industry and that the country more abundant in a particular factor (e.g., skilled labor) will have a production bundle more heavily weighted toward skilled labor.[8] It is possible that the country with abundant skilled labor might produce a commodity less intensive in that factor than some commodity produced in a skilled-labor scare country. Only the overall weighting of factor intensities of production can be predicted in the presence of factor price equalization.

One formulation of traditional trade theory that is particularly promising for examining the IDL is that of Vanek.[9] Under certain assumptions—including factor price equalization across countries—the factor content of a country's trade can be inferred from factor endowment rankings. Leamer[10] defends the assumption of factor price equalization with reference to empirical work of Krueger[11] which implies the similarities of factor prices across countries. Leamer's empirical testing of traditional trade theory predictions with respect to the pattern of trade and the sources of comparative advantage is carried out using the Heckscher-Ohlin-Vanek (HOV) variant of the theory. Leamer's work is both the most recent and the most econometrically sophisticated attempt to empirically validate traditional trade theory. We shall make use of his empirical results.

We note, however, that Krueger rejects empirical factor price equalization.[12] She argues that in its absence the factor proportions theorem should be viewed as a theorem about the international pattern of specialization of production—not of trade—leaving to demand characteristics the determination of whether a commodity that is produced is an export or an import substitute. Impediments to trade in the form of transportation costs or tariffs may prevent factor price equalization. However, Deardorff has demonstrated that trade impediments in combination with trade in intermediate goods (even without factor price equalization) prevent us from concluding that all of the export industries of a capital-abundant nation will use more capital-intensive techniques than will its import competing industries.[13] We cannot even draw similar conclusions regarding the goods that the country produces and those that it does not.

If we are to draw any conclusions regarding the international division of labor from traditional trade theory they must be drawn from the HOV variant. That variant predicts that a country will export the services of its abundant factors and import the services of its scarce factors. Commodities are perceived only as a bundle within which factor services are contained. In a world characterized by large numbers both of commodities and of factors of production a country may be said to be abundant in a factor if its share of the world supply of that factor exceeds its consumption share of world output. The consumption share may be thought of as a weighted average of abundance ratios with weights equal to the world earnings of the factor.[14] We may conclude that abundant factors will be employed disproportionately (in relation to consumption) in export industries.

It is the pattern of world factor endowments among nations that is seen to determine the IDL regardless of whether labor is abundant or scarce in a particular country. Abundant labor may be employed disproportionately in industry because capital too is abundant or in agriculture when land is abundant. Changes in the international division of labor reflect international differences in rates of population growth, savings rates, rates of qualitative improvement of labor, or rates of depletion of industry-specific factors such as mineral deposits.

Leamer's recent empirical examination of the pattern of world trade in the context of the HOV theorem is of interest for what it implies about the IDL.[15] He examines net exports in terms of ten commodity aggregates and eleven factors of production for fifty-eight countries in 1958 and in 1975. One need not agree with the author that his empirical results demonstrate the fundamental correctness of the Heckscher-Ohlin theory of international comparative advantage, i.e., that factor abundance determines the pattern of trade. However, the reader must note the high proportion of the variance in net exports that is accounted for (50 to 90 percent for all but two countries).

Leamer concludes that in 1958 the ". . . uneven distribution of highly-skilled workers in particular and workers in general were the primary causes of trade."[16] In 1975, capital was the most important variable—followed by deposits of oil and natural gas. With respect to U.S. trade, Leamer states:

Abundance of human capital was important in 1958 but not very in 1975. Capital was actually scarce in 1958, though unimportantly so. In 1975 capital abundance was the primary determinant of U.S. trade.[17]

Leamer's references to highly skilled workers and to human capital are with respect to a category of professional and technical workers. Although this is the only variable that might display any technological or knowledge advantage of American workers, it is a broad category which includes physicians, lawyers, and teachers as well as scientists and engineers. The explosion of the educational establishments in less developed countries in the post independence decades between 1958 and 1975 may have reduced in fact and even more in appearance the American abundance of this factor. It may also be that there is a reduced role for skilled labor in production.

Following the OPEC petroleum price increases capital-abundant manufacturing nations found it difficult to reduce purchases of petroleum and thus necessary to increase manufactured exports. This seems to shift from 1958 to 1975 the importance of physical capital as a determinant of world trade. Considering the world economy's short-run adjustment in 1975 to the "first oil shock," we should be cautious in concluding that a permanent shift in the determinants of world trade and the IDL has taken place. We may compare Leamer's conclusions with those of other empirical literature by reference to Deardorff's exhaustive review of it,[18] wherein he concludes that it is clear that U.S. comparative advantage derives from the knowledge possessed by its workers or its firms and that the role of capital has shifted to become positively related to U.S. net exports in recent years.

The focus on factor abundance as the determinant of world trade patterns and the IDL leads us to look to changes in factor abundance to explain the shifts in the U.S. position in world trade and in the production and employment structure of its industries. Some say that what is happening is an "overtaking of the American economy" by the more advanced developing countries. Finger, for example, argues this thesis, emphasizing the infamous relatively low share of GNP allocated to investment in the U.S. for the past two decades.[19] In the 1960s it is alleged the U.S. had the most technologically advanced industries in the world, but this basis for our exports has been eroded by our decision to invest only a small portion of our national product. Undeniably, the share of U.S. GDP devoted to gross domestic investment (GDI)—16 percent in 1982—is the lowest among the industrial nations and close to half that for the East Asian newly industrializing countries (NICs).[20]

The 1982 absolute share for the U.S. is three percentage points below that in 1960, when the U.S. was among the lowest of the industrialized nations in terms of the share of GDP going to GDI, but the shares for the East Asian NICs were still lower than in the U.S. To place this observation in perspective, however, consider the impact of the larger GDP and more slowly growing labor forces of the advanced industrialized countries generally and of the U.S. in particular. World Bank data show that in the U.S. GDI grew at an annual average rate for 1970–1982 of 1.3 percent.[21] This was faster than for other industrialized market economies except France (1.3%), Austria (2%), Canada (3.3%), Japan (3.3%), and Ireland (4.2%). However the East Asian NICs registered much faster average annual growth rates of GDI for the same period: Korea (11%), Hong Kong (13.6%), and Singapore (8.7%).

Developed countries can increase capital availability per worker, even with low rates of gross domestic investment, relative to less developed countries (LDCs) generally and even relative to the East Asian NICs. World Bank calculations indicate that although Korea's share of GDI in GDP in 1980 was 31 percent compared to 18 percent in the U.S. this implied GDI per potential entrant into the labor force of $29,850 in the former compared to $188,990 in the latter.[22] Overtaking of the capital abundance of the U.S. by even middle-income LDCs seems a long way off. Similar calculations for the industrialized nations of Japan, France, and Germany imply GDI per potential new worker to be between two and three times that for the U.S. Nevertheless it is the East Asian NICs—in addition to Japan—that arouse fears of the loss of U.S. competitiveness in international trade in manufactures and the shift in the U.S. position in the IDL that this implies.[23] This fear results from the rapid growth of manufacturing production and export from these countries in the 1960s, 1970s, and 1980s.[24]

The calculations of GDI per potential entrant into the labor force beg the question of the allocation of GDI. Krueger has admonished us to look to the factor abundance within the traded goods sector when there is no factor price equalization.[25] However, the HOV model with factor price equalization yields results that are unaffected by resource absorption in the production of nontradeables.[26] We have already seen in the context of that model that a capital-scarce nation might produce and even export some commodities that were capital intensive.

Some authors argue that first Japan[27] and now the East Asian NICs have brought about a dynamic change in comparative advantage through targeting industries for promotion. Shinohara adds that, "To take the place of traditional trade theory, a new policy concept needs to be developed to deal with the possibility of intertemporal dynamic development." He is, however, flatly wrong in arguing that traditional trade theory "does not take into account the possibility of dynamic change in the comparative advantage or disadvantage of industries over a coming 10- or 20-year period."[28] It does, of course, through the effects of, for example, high savings rates and accumulation (such as in the Japanese and East Asian NIC cases) on the abundance of capital.

The traditional theory does not, however, suggest that comparative advantage will be shifted by targeting industries for promotion, as Japan is alleged to have done, except in the special (and presumably rare) case of an "infant industry." Appropriate policies for promotion of an "infant industry" as well as the conditions necessary to justify policy intervention have been developed by Baldwin,

Johnson, and Cordon[29]—in the context of traditional trade theory where irreversible scale economies external to the firm are associated with the "infant" and where short-run static welfare losses from a subsidy yield social returns in excess of the social rate of return on alternative investments. The pertinence of "learning by doing" activities to the "infant industry" case has been noted.[30] Scott alleges, however, that, "the Japanese appear to have been the first to recognize that advantages could be created through the mobilization of technology, capital, and skilled labor not just to nurture a few infant industries to supply the domestic market but as a way of nurturing the whole industrial sector toward areas of growth and opportunity in the world market."[31]

Hufbauer and Baldwin found significant impacts of scale economies on the pattern of international trade—and by implication on the IDL.[32] Hufbauer has suggested as an alternative to the factor proportions theory a "neo-technology" explanation of trade patterns which would combine scale economies and differences in technological knowledge as well as a product cycle by which knowledge was disseminated. Leamer argues that such an alternative hypothesis was not sufficiently well articulated to be tested as an alternative to the HOV hypothesis.[33] Helpman and Krugman have since expounded much new theory regarding the role of increasing returns and imperfect competition in international trade.[34]

Product Cycles, Endogenous Technology, and Relocation

Alternative approaches to traditional trade theory explanations of the IDL emphasize labor supply conditions as interregional and international determinants of manufacturing location and competitiveness. Endogenous technology—in contrast to orthodox, exogenous specifications—also plays a major conceptual role in alternative approaches. Indeed the interaction between labor supply conditions and endogenous technology results in a "footlooseness" of manufacturing production facilities in contrast to a dependence on nontradeable raw material input requirements. This interaction can best be understood in the context of product life cycles and manufacturing process cycles which provide a useful, analytical perspective on the IDL. As discussed below, the cycles framework represents a significant methodological departure from traditional trade theory.

Labor's preeminent role as a location determinant for manufacturing firms is a key aspect of the IDL and is due to several factors. Since labor cost is a high proportion of total production costs, it is an extremely cost-sensitive factor of production. This is particularly true in terms of unit labor costs which are the basis for markup pricing by imperfectly competitive producers. Labor's position as a highly differentiated factor of production over space accentuates the sensitivity of production costs to wages. This differentiation shows up not only in money wage variations but also in the form of other, socioinstitutional motivating forces. Unionization and worker cohesiveness, surplus labor supplies, and political co-option in recipient NICs are other location determinants which vary internationally. These features in turn condition the terms of exchange between labor and managerial capital as far as controlability, work conditions, and technology utilized in the production process.

Technology is an integral part of labor's role as a location factor. As a partially endogenous choice technology suggests a range of production techniques which confront management within different organizational environments. Assembly plant operations can be highly automated using sophisticated capital equipment and quality control monitoring along with skilled and technical labor inputs. An alternative configuration would entail machinery that basically transfers the product in preassembled form through various manual assembly stages of production, a technique based on unskilled workers.

Moreover, job restructuring reinforces the endogeneity of technology. Management in pursuit of cost savings may redefine and subdivide skilled work tasks into several more simplified and unskilled tasks. This restructuring circumvents the need for skilled and technical labor and shifts the firm's labor force requirements to the unskilled end of the labor input spectrum.

Endogenous technology and job restructuring are especially characteristic of the *cyclical evolution* of a manufacturing firm. Product cycles have been a frequently used approach to changing labor skill requirements over the evolutionary path of the production process.[35] The basic theme of the product life cycle is a three-stage transition from an initial research and development intensive stage of innovation and product design through a second stage of rapidly rising output and sales with technology shifting toward high volume, standardized production. This is followed by a third, mature sales and output regime where rates of market expansion stabilize and there is an increased dependence on economies of scale via standardized production processes and unskilled labor inputs.

Employment levels increase significantly in the second stage of rapid market growth as firms move toward high volume production, a shift that is accompanied by an increased demand for unskilled workers and a reduction in the demand for skilled technicians and which is sustained into the maturity phase as endogenous technological change occurs in the production process itself. Skill-intense, small-batch production centering around worker groups is the norm during the innovation stage, followed by standardized production in the subsequent stages of rapid market expansion, and eventual maturity.

The skill configuration of labor inputs is diluted toward unskilled, low-wage labor by the third stage of the product life cycle. This evolutionary deterioration in the skill composition of labor demand is consistent with a strategy of lowering unit labor costs as competitive pressures and a lack of new markets force management to seek cost savings. Relocation and a spatial decentralization of production facilities to low-wage production areas abroad is one location strategy that is consistent with a growing concern for cost containment.

Relocation of branch assembly plants, which are no longer reliant on proximity to major research centers and highly skilled labor pools facilitates a technical shift toward large volume, standardized assembly. A reduction in agglomerative, locational pulls leads to a footlooseness of plants toward low-wage labor markets and locations. This in turn leads to a spatial division of labor into skilled technical employment in the older, agglomeration regions and low-skilled, nonunion employment at the decentralized assembly plants. The capital movements and spatial redirection in investment accompanying this pattern lead to what some call the spatial rationalization of production,[36] which shows up internationally by the establishment of (a) foreign branch plants and (b) indigenous manufacturing firms in low-wage, newly industrialized economies.

Output and sales levels along with their rates of change are the key barometers of the product cycle. Alternatives to this emphasis on product include a manufacturing process cycle[37] and an innovation cycle.[38] The latter is closely related to the product life cycle although it emphasizes change as originating from the internal organization of production at all stages rather than solely from a research and development and new product stage.[39]

The manufacturing process cycle developed by Suarez-Villa with its six stages is the most detailed cyclical framework.[40] Deskilling and job restructuring alter the skill requirements toward low-skill labor during a fourth phase which is accompanied by a strategy of mass production efficiency and maximization of scale economies. This perspective, unlike the product life cycle, places a heavy emphasis on organizational environments—similar to the innovation cycle—as well as on labor and technological requirements of production. Process innovation characterizes the fourth phase, thereafter tapering off in the last two stages as competitive market pressures constrain resource availability for additional process innovation. During the tail end of the manufacturing process cycle management priorities shift toward labor cost minimization and overall cost containment.

These largely metaphoric and hueristic cycles do serve a useful purpose in tracing a changing labor skill configuration, which is tied directly to endogenous technology via research and development, job restructuring and deskilling, and process innovation—which seeks alternative ways of utilizing labor rather than the design or application of new tools or equipment.

Both the product life and manufacturing process cycles also motivate capital investment—dependent on the simultaneously changing labor requirements and process technology. An industry accelerator effect propels capital investment away from comparatively low levels of research and development outlays on specialized production and testing equipment aimed at craft-type batch production of customized output. A rapid expansion in output to meet a growing market requires large capital investment in productive capacity, which is continued into but not sustained throughout the period of maturity. The qualitative content of capital is contingent on both the changing process technology and shifts in the feasible mix of skilled and unskilled workers. Capital evolves from early forms of highly specialized equipment to larger pieces of automated and mechanized equipment. This reflects a shift toward large batch, assembly line activities that may ultimately progress toward manual assembly mass production based on predominantly unskilled labor, which further dilutes the technological sophistication of capital equipment in terms of machinery designed primarily for transfer activities.

The temporal and spatial characteristics of labor costs and the labor skill configuration are major features of plant relocation and the international mobility of capital investment. From the temporal sequence of production there are few incentives for relocation during the intense research and development and innovation of the initial stage, a condition characteristic of both the product life and manufacturing process cycles. A strong preference of skilled and technical workers toward industry agglomeration points is characteristic during this stage (i.e., bay areas in San Francisco, Boston, and also Sunbelt cities). Agglomeration phenomena are complementary to these locational preferences in terms of well-developed labor pools of skilled, highly trained, and educated workers as well as technical complementarities of auxiliary firms and suppliers. Profits per unit of output yield to higher wages for skilled labor due to agglomerative locational pulls.

During some point within the temporal sequence of production and marketing, higher profits per unit of output are necessary and can be achieved through standardized production based on unskilled, low-wage labor along with a reduction in demand for skilled labor inputs. This production phase during a second stage of mass marketing in the product life cycle provides the conditions for relocation. These conditions are attenuated during the third stage of maturity characterized by stabilization of growth rates in output and sales. A strategy of maintaining high profits per unit of output in combination with a reduced agglomerative pull facilitates spatial decentralization of production in response to the spatial availability of low-skilled, low-wage labor.

Spatial variations in labor cost and availability complement the profit driven, cost minimizing strategy of relocation. International variations in unskilled labor costs interact with differing wage elasticities of demand for skilled versus unskilled workers. Wage elasticities of demand for unskilled workers are comparatively high in contrast to skilled labor via the derived demand for unskilled labor in terms of the ease of factor substitutability, particularly with capital. Capital is easily substituted in mechanized work processes aimed at standardized production, a pattern that may result in increased capital-unskilled labor ratios in branch plant operations. Moreover, these capital inputs are available at competitive prices now that its product and technology are well established since the firm is no longer dependent on specialized venture capital sources. All of this suggests a relatively high wage elasticity of unskilled labor demand which makes the employment of unskilled workers quite sensitive to fluctuations in market demand for output. A lack of "quasi-fixity" for unskilled labor[41] and an absence of fixed employment costs make the link between marginal value product and wage extremely sensitive to changes in market demand.

An employer's relocation criteria of low-wage labor market areas generates an increased footlooseness of assembly plant operations, which offers a spatial dimension to demand elasticities for low-skill labor and, as a result, makes employment more susceptible to product market fluctuations. The supply side of low-wage, unskilled labor markets is usually characterized by labor force groups with low marginal attachments to jobs and to the labor market. Minority workers, women, and youth represent especially viable labor pools for unskilled, secondary jobs within segmented labor markets. High turnover, minimal skill/training requirements, and a lack of career advancement are all characteristic of the secondary job segment. Indeed, the inherent instability of such jobs serves the interest of managerial capitalism in maintaining flexibility in their work force with respect to market fluctuations in demand and price and to spatial shifts in location.[42]

Product and manufacturing cycle approaches to the IDL represent significant divergences from traditional, Heckscher-Ohlin trade theory. The latter assumes an international immobility of production factors, while a cycle approach is predicated on the mobility of capital. A geographic redirection of capital investment away from industrialized economies toward NIC locations implements relocation of production facilities internationally in the cycles framework. Indigenous manufacturing firms in NICs are also dependent on capital mobility in terms of foreign investment as well as knowledge and technology transfers from advanced manufacturing industries. Knowledge and technology transfers are not without cost since trade barriers and transportation costs are explicit characteristics of a cycles approach.

The major point of divergence between a traditional explanation and a cycles explanation of the IDL rests upon (a) the nature of the production function and (b) the relative emphasis on dynamic relations and phenomena. Traditional trade theory à la Heckscher-Ohlin-Vanek postulates identical production functions in all countries (based on a cost-free international diffusion of technology) for each industry. A linear, homogeneous restriction on the production functions with the usual diminishing marginal productivity conditions for each factor leads to a number of well-known and well-behaved results. These are fortified by nonreversibility of factor intensities which allows international variation in factor endowments to be exported vis-à-vis tradeable goods. A full-employment resource condition caps off this predominantly static rendition of traditional trade theory.

Product and manufacturing process cycles rely on malleable, evolving production functions as noted in the shifting skill configuration of labor inputs over the cycle. This changing production function is accompanied by temporal variations in the qualitative and quantitative dimensions of capital inputs. In contrast to traditional trade theory, factor reversibilities can occur throughout the course of the cycles. Indeed the whole notion of endogenous technology reinforces the concept of an evolving production function, an evolution that is the *raison d'etre* for plant relocation abroad, the spatial rationalization of production, and the international division of labor.

Finally the cycles' emphasis on increasing returns to scale dumps linear homogeneity overboard. Indeed, a temporal emphasis on cycles, an evolving production "function," and endogenous technology make for a dynamic framework. The linchpin of the dynamism is increasing returns to scale which create the necessary conditions for the IDL.

Verdoorn Effects and Labor Productivity

Scale economies in foreign-based manufacturing are a critical condition and dynamic for the cost-containment and spatial decentralization strategies in the later stages of the product life and manufacturing process cycles. An increased division and specialization of labor via endogenous technology and separability in production forms the basis for this dynamic. Our formulation, based on Verdoorn's law, emphasizes scale economies operating through output and employment adjustments to changes in export demand. This is in contrast to more traditional and static formulations based on an exogenous technology interacting with price adjustment mechanisms in output and factor markets. Scale economies lead to greater labor productivity which, in turn, enhances the already low-labor-cost advantage of manufacturing plants in NICs. Verdoorn's law provides a useful conceptualization of the various dynamic interactions of scale effects, labor productivity, and foreign cost competitiveness.

The Verdoorn effect or law was originally formulated as a long-term planning tool for estimating future levels of labor productivity in national economies. In his original article Verdoorn analyzed employment and output time series data for a number of countries and discovered a fairly constant, long-term relation between the growth of labor productivity and the volume of industrial production.[43] Verdoorn interpreted this relation in terms of an elasticity of productivity with respect to output with estimated values of approximately .45 based on fourteen European countries during the interwar period, an estimated value that suggested an average increase in labor productivity of 4.5 percent for a 10 percent change in the volume of industrial production.

The potential application of this concept to interregional and international scale economies remained relatively unnoticed until Kaldor's work where the "Verdoorn Law" was initially applied to advanced, industrialized countries and, somewhat later, to the issue of regional growth and development.[44] Verdoorn's law on an interregional level was formulated by Kaldor in terms of an output adjustment mechanism characteristic of interregional trade flows that eventually leads to regional growth rate disparities. Industrial output, based on economies of large-scale production is exported to other regions with exogenous changes in export demand impacting regional production and employment levels. This exogenously generated export demand becomes the motivating force for regional output changes in the industrial sector that, in turn, affect labor productivity. Higher rates of output growth generate, by the Verdoorn law, higher rates of labor productivity growth, a scale economy process at the "macro" level for geographically separate trading units.

Kaldor argued that the Verdoorn law was essentially a dynamic version of scale economies since it is concerned with the rates of change of productivity and output rather than a static relationship relating the level of productivity to the scale of output. Moreover, this dynamic version embeds scale economies as a component of economic growth through their effect on growth rates of labor productivity. This dynamic perspective fits into an international disequilibrium cumulative causation framework since variation in scale economies can perpetuate growth differences, given an initial advantage by some country over others, through the process of increasing returns, which growth itself induces.

A formulation suggested by Dixon and Thirlwall,[45] who derived a condition for equilibrium growth within a trading unit that includes a Verdoorn coefficient along with other export demand and domestic sector parameters, illustrates Kaldor's interpretation of the Verdoorn law. Output growth is motivated by exogenous growth in export demand or,

$$g_t = k(x_t) \tag{1}$$

where g_t is the rate of growth of output in time t and x_t is the rate of growth of exports, while k is the (assumed) constant elasticity of output growth with respect to export growth. Scale economies per Verdoorn effects for a country appear in the growth rate of labor productivity (p_t) which is partly dependent on the growth rate of output itself (sometimes referred to as Verdoorn's law), or,

$$p_t = v(g_t), \text{ or in linear form, } p_t = r_a + vg_t. \tag{2}$$

The constant term, r_a, represents an autonomous rate of productivity growth composed of disembodied progress on the one hand and technical progress embodied in the rate of capital accumulation per worker on the other. Dixon and Thirlwall interpret the Verdoorn coefficient, v, as an induced rate of productivity growth that is also dichotomized into embodied and disembodied rates of technical progress.

The Verdoorn coefficient can take on values between zero and unity $(0 < v < 1)$ with variations in v creating a differential pattern of comparative performance, with some trade units experiencing higher growth rates over time. Industry variation in the determinants of r_a and v combined with international variations in industrial composition can lead to differences in international growth rates. The growth rates are demand induced via the growth of export demand which is exogenous to the industrial sector. This is in contrast to re-source-constrained growth given by exogenously determined growth rates of labor and capital in combination with an exogenously given technical progress over time.

A crucial issue with regard to dynamic scale economies is the level at which they are appropriable. If they are internal to the firm they become the basis for monopolistic competition, product differentiation, intraindustry trade, and per-haps the development of the multinational corporation. If the scale economies are external to the firm they may be consistent with perfect competition. The output of an industry may exhibit increasing returns reflecting the size of that domestic industry, the size of that industry in the world economy, and the size of other industries (either domestically or internationally) providing intermediate inputs and goods. In the case of external economies which arise from economies of scale in the production of intermediate goods, Ethier has pointed out that it is the tradeability of the intermediate goods that determines whether those external effects are felt nationally or internationally.[46]

Helpman and Krugman make a similar point with respect to the dynamic scale economies associated with the process by which firms improve their technol-ogies.[47] They note that such economies resulting from innovations are not likely to be associated with a perfectly competitive organization of an industry but rather with learning curves and concentrations of large firms within industries. In such a case external effects involve the diffusion of knowledge. If innovations spread through physical and social contacts, the spatial dimension of the diffusion process will lead to the external effects being felt nationally (or perhaps only locally) and agglomerative forces will result. If innovations are embodied in the products that are produced (which can be taken apart to see how they work) and if the products are tradeable, the economies will be felt internationally.

In the case of dynamic scale economies history matters in a way in which it does not in comparative static analysis. Traditional comparative static trade theory leads us to expect that cumulative output in an industry will be different in a trading situation than in an autarky situation and will differ further depending on the liberality of the trading situation. Although scale effects of "learning by doing" are irreversible (what is learned is not forgotten because of a subsequent reduction in scale), "The question is not where you are after trade compared with where you were before, but where you are after trade compared to where you *would have been* without trade. . ."[48] or in a different trading situation. In this case comparative static analysis may be useful in exploring the consequences of alternative histories. However, where there are imperfectly competitive markets, and the implied potential for strategic game playing, Helpman and Krug-man caution that there are many possible outcomes which comparative static one-period (e.g., long-run equilibrium) models may not capture. Today's IDL depends on that it was in the past. The future IDL depends on what it is today.

Institutional Factors and Empirical Patterns

While product and manufacturing process cycles along with the dynamics of Verdoorn/Kaldor scale economies are argued to be major determinants of the IDL, there are other institutional factors at work. These additional factors enhance NICs' labor cost advantages in foreign markets for manufactured goods and contribute to determining the global division and allocation of labor.

Assembly abroad by U.S. manufacturing has been an increasing source of U.S. imports within recent years. Tariff items 806 and 807 permit the duty-free entry of U.S. components sent abroad for processing or assembly. U.S. imports under 807, for example, were more than $21 billion in 1983 and included relatively unsophisticated manufactures such as apparel and simple metal products.[49] Also included within these import flows were more advanced electronic products, automobiles and parts, and office machines.

Intrafirm trade characterizes a large proportion of import flows into the U.S. under the 806/807 arrangement. By the late 1960s more than half the value of duty-free components reimported came from U.S.-owned investments abroad. The dollar magnitude of imports from U.S. manufacturing affiliates in developing countries approached $3 billion in 1977. Certain manufactured import goods have been predominantly related-party transactions. Grunwald and Falmm estimate that between half and all imported televisions and from 90 to 100 percent of semiconductors and motor vehicle imports under 806/807 were related-party transactions.[50] This kind of institutional development and corporate response is consistent with U.S. manufacturing firms' realization of the trade advantages from an IDL concentrated on low-wage NIC labor markets.

These factors aimed at encouraging production abroad to maintain U.S. competitiveness in world markets are also consistent with relocation strategies of cost containment on the downside of the product and manufacturing process cycles. As Grunwald and Flamm point out, relocation or subcontracting through assembly production facilities in low-wage NIC economies provide a low-cost production platform for U.S. manufacturing firms.[51] In order to maintain parity or perhaps a competitive edge over indigenous firms U.S. producers abroad also need to have access to capital, marketing, and technology.

Overall, the institutional factors interacting with corporate capitalism's strategies and motives result in a trade-promoting IDL subject to transportation costs. The high value-to-weight ratios of apparel and electronics in many cases reduce trade barriers represented by transport costs and qualify these types of manufacturing activities as prime candidates for an internationalization of labor. Indeed, separability of production into component production, assembly/testing, and packaging adds to an international dispersion of manufacturing that is based on large inputs of unskilled labor.

Import penetration data for NIC exports to the U.S. and other OECD countries indicate a pattern of international competitiveness of NIC manufactures. That penetration has also elicited a protectionist response from developed countries (DCs), a response that has been aimed especially at the East Asian NICs.

Hughes and Krueger find a low correlation between the extensive import controls designed to limit the growth of imports from the East Asian NICs and the increase in developed countries' market penetration by the former.[52] This leads them to conclude that administrative protection is not only costly (with the costs apparently falling primarily on the protectionist) but largely ineffective. Post–1976 increases in protection to some extent reduced the share of imports into the Economic Community in clothing and textiles and footwear and succeeded in slowing growth in the first (but not the last category) to the U.S. The NICs response to protection was to diversify exports geographically and to move into higher quality goods in the protected product groups. DC market penetration by the East Asian NICs continued to grow in the last half of the 1970s but more slowly than in the first half.

> In Hong Kong diversification was largely the result of private initiatives, in Taiwan private initiative was supported by public liberalization measures, and Singapore and Korea made major but very different policy interventions. Singapore raised real wages between 1978 and 1981 by 10 percent a year to push entrepreneurs up-market and drive out marginal low-labor-productivity firms that were unable to make the move. Real wage increases, reflecting productivity gains, were having the same impact in Korea up to the mid 1970s, but then continued to rise rapidly largely because of the excessively capital and technical-skill-intensive orientation of government policy. Whereas diversification in Hong Kong, Singapore, and Taiwan came smoothly, Korea's policy combined with the lack of confidence arising out of political problems and failure to liberalize the economy, resulted in its lagging behind the other Far Eastern exporters in moving up-market within the relatively labor intensive production categories. . . .[53]

In discussing import penetration—the ratio of imports to apparent domestic consumption (domestic output, plus imports, less exports)—of DC markets by LDC manufactured exports, Cline distinguishes between traditional goods and nontraditional ones.[54] The former refers to those goods in which LDC manufactured exports have traditionally been concentrated, e.g., processed foodstuffs, textiles, apparel, footwear, and wood products. Cline further divides, nontraditional goods, following the categories of Lall,[55] into "process" products with relatively standard technology and "engineering" products for which production technology must be adapted to individual markets. Process industries include, for example, paper, chemicals, plastics, and sporting goods. Engineering industries include, for example, machinery, transport equipment, radio, television, and electrical products. The nontraditional products have generally higher capital-labor ratios and higher skill intensities than do traditional products.

Although import penetration grew most rapidly for the U.S. market (from 1.05 to 2.28 percent from 1970 to 1978) and to a nearly equal extent for France, the highest degree of penetration (2.5 percent in 1978) was experienced by Japan—closely followed by West Germany. Cline suggests that the explanation for an observed more rapid growth of U.S. manufactures imports from LDCs (relative to U.S. GDP growth) may lie in the activities of U.S.-based multinational enterprises (MNEs) as a part of their strategies to develop cheap international sources of supply for standardized components or to a greater degree of openness of the U.S. market. However, Cline's data on the incidence of nontariff barriers (NTB) to trade in manufactures—which now seem to be quantitatively more important than tariff barriers—indicate that the U.S. ". . .has the highest coverage (but not necessarily the highest intensity) of NTB protection in manufactures among the seven major industrialized countries."[56] Supporting Cline's first suggestion—are the observations that in 1977 (the year of the last U.S. Commerce Department survey) 13 percent of all U.S. imports came from foreign subsidiaries of U.S.-based MNEs and in 1984 four of Taiwan's top ten exporters were U.S.-based MNEs.[57]

Penetration of LDC manufactures exports into industrial country markets remained low at an aggregate level through the 1970s. Nevertheless there were some individual product categories in particular DC markets that experienced high levels and rapid growth in import penetration—in the U.S. between 1970 and 1978 penetration grew from 3 to 12 percent in apparel and from 1 to 14 percent in footwear.[58] In these cases, as well as in a number of nontraditional LDC export categories, LDC gains in import market share were at the expense of Japan.

The shift toward exports of nontraditional manufactures as opposed to traditional ones was most important for Mexico (with the former rising from 31.6 percent to 54.1 percent between 1970 and 1978) and for Singapore (where the former rose from 34.4 percent to 71.5 percent). Except for Hong Kong, for whom the share of nontraditional manufactures declined, the East Asian NICs all showed substantial increases in the share of nontraditional goods in their exports of manufactures.[59] The East Asian NICs also showed the most rapid growth in their shares of the market for manufactured imports in industrial countries, raising their combined shares from 2.3 percent to 5.9 percent (primarily in the U.S. and Japanese markets which are proximate to them).

These shifts in world manufactures trade are difficult to reconcile with traditional trade theory, but they provide only circumstantial evidence for the role of increasing returns. A comparison of 1965–1978 productivity growth in Japanese and U.S. manufacturing by Norsworthy and Malmquist could be used as evidence against the argument for the importance of Kaldor-Verdoorn effects on labor-productivity growth. These authors conclude that

> greater capital investment and greater processing of materials per worker have led to far greater labor productivity growth in Japan. However, growth in the

efficiency of all productive inputs combined has not been much greater in Japan than in the United States. The major source of the difference stems from the higher rates of growth in the capital and materials inputs used in conjunction with the Japanese labor force.[60]

Labor productivity grew between 1965–1973 at an annual rate of 2.5 percent for U.S. and 11.08 percent for Japan. For 1973–1978 it grew at 1.83 percent per year for the U.S. and 5.42 percent for Japan. Annual rates of manufacturing output growth in the same periods were 3.76 percent and 1.08 percent for the U.S. and 12.46 and 2.85 percent for Japan. Annual rates of labor force growth in manufacturing were similar for the two countries in the earlier period, while in the second period the rates were −0.75 percent for the U.S. and −2.57 percent for Japan. In the two periods, the annual rates of growth of capital in manufacturing were 16.54 percent and 2.05 percent for Japan and 3.65 percent and 1.95 percent for the U.S. The authors note that in the earlier period Japanese productivity actually fell at an annual rate of about 4 percent.

Norsworthy and Malmquist's neoclassical approach posits that an increase in the capital-labor ratio leads to an increase in output per worker and a decline in the output-capital ratio. Kaldor's approach suggests that growth in income (market size) leads to an increase in output per worker which leads to an increase (through accumulation) in capital per worker, with the output-capital ratio remaining constant. Interpretation of the Norsworthy and Malmquist results and their implications for the role of increasing returns depends upon whether a 4 percent annual decline in capital productivity is considered to be large or small in the face of a 16.52 percent annual increase in the stock of capital and 1.37 percent annual increase in labor. Since neither energy consumption nor materials consumption kept up with capital accumulation, we view the decline as small— consistent with Kaldor.

Conclusions and Policy Implications

Traditional trade theory might predict perfectly the international patterns of trade in some year and, as we have seen, shed some light on the IDL in spite of the indeterminacy of industry-specific production. Nevertheless it is poorly designed to identify the change in the IDL over time if dynamic economies of scale differ substantially among industries and diffuse so as to lead to national, rather than international, external effects and to imperfect competition. We believe that evidence supports the increasing returns view rather than the constant returns, traditional trade model. Formal empirical testing of these alternatives will be the topic of a subsequent paper. Some of the policy implications of increasing returns for changes in the IDL are explored below.

The implications of a major role for increasing returns in determining the IDL for trade and development policies differ among DCs, NICs, and other LDCs.

The DCs will attempt to maintain the economic viability of their domestic manufacturing industries against foreign manufacturing imports. They will also make long-run, allocative adjustments of the work force within impacted industry sectors. Policy strategies aimed toward these goals for developed economies are likely to focus on protectionist trade policies, industrial policies for promotion of domestic manufacturing industries, and—as discussed above—institutional arrangements aimed at enhancing domestic industry's access to low cost production platforms abroad.

Policy strategies for NICs are likely to focus on ways to realize and perpetuate labor cost advantages as a source of competitiveness in world markets for manufactured goods while permitting wages to rise. Objectives for such policy strategies include (a) growth and development with some alleviation of internal distributional inequalities, (b) development and national ownership of particular industries, and (c) a degree of national economic independence. The policy strategies that might accompany these goals include sector-specific policies of subsidizing either inputs (particularly labor) or production in manufacturing, subsidizing exports of manufactures, imposing tariffs on manufactured imports, and in general seeking a growing share of international markets in order to realize dynamic scale economy-labor productivity effects.

Other LDCs are likely to attempt to follow the NICs integration of their economies into the world economic order. However, a protectionist response on the part of DCs may leave them little choice but to retreat into autarky. Protectionist trade legislation before the U.S. Congress (with severe anticipated effects on exports of manufactures—especially textiles—not only from the NICs but also from poorer LDCs) has elicited warnings of retaliation against U.S. exports from China and South Korea and from the Association of Southeast Asian Nations (ASEAN), which is collectively one of the largest trading partners of the U.S.[61]

Only dynamic scale economies might justify (on conventional welfare theory grounds) policy intervention in manufacturing industries in either DCs or LDCs. Where the scale economies are internal and static, appropriate policy is to gain access to them through integration of the domestic economy into the international one. Even where there are substantial "learning-by-doing" effects associated with scale of output (which may be a common phenomenon for LDCs as they enter manufacturing) Behrman notes that so long as they are internal to the firm no intervention is warranted.[62] He argues, less convincingly, that external benefits from such a process are likely to apply only to the DCs and then only when they are on the technological frontier. The existence of external scale benefits may warrant subsidy to the process that produces them but only if the benefits exceed the opportunity costs on the subsidy.[63] In the context of examining the effects of exports of oil on manufacturing production Van Wijnbergen has noted that it is well known that a posited temporary increase in natural resource exports raises the relative price of nontradeables and shifts resources into that sector, away from production of other tradeables (including manufactures).[64] Where there are learning-by-doing effects specific to the production of the other tradeables (manufactures) he concludes that an increase above the otherwise optimal subsidy to production of manufactures (or else the accumulation of foreign assets) is warranted. By a less than perfect analogy we might wonder whether a nation relatively abundant in natural resources would be justified on welfare grounds in providing a larger subsidy to production of manufactures (in order to capture the external dynamic scale economy-labor productivity effects associated with growth in manufactures production) than a nation scarce in natural resources and thus free of the tendency for labor to be diverted away from manufacturing.

Krugman has presented a model of technological competition featuring interdependence of the returns to research and development expenditures in two international trade partners-competitors.[65] The crux of the model is that protectionism by one nation reduces the breadth of the market for and the expected returns to research and development in the other nation. Therefore the optimal amount of these activities there falls, as well. This increases the relative likelihood of technological breakthrough in the first country, which then receives the rents associated with innovation. Protection of the domestic market becomes the foundation for export success. The existence of the consumption losses associated with protection reduces the likelihood of a net gain to the nation, however, and a direct subsidy to research and development would have a higher expected return in terms of national welfare. The generalized theory of market distortions is clear on the appropriateness of intervening where the distortion arises and on the ambiguity of the welfare consequences where multiple distortions exist and some are altered.[66]

The first best policy intervention—in an otherwise distortion-free world—in the case of the dynamic external (but internal to the nation) scale economies of the Kaldor-Verdoorn type would be subsidy to the activity generating them. That could be to research and development, to research and development employment, to production of manufactures (or only some manufactures), or to employment in their production. Restriction on imports, however, imposes consumption costs with no general conclusion possible for the welfare consequences. To argue the importance of dynamic scale economies-labor productivity effects in determining the pattern of productivity growth, international trade, and the IDL is *not* to make a case for protectionism.

The traditional paradigm—in the absence of monopoly power in international trade—supports the wisdom of a policy of unilateral free trade. The increasing returns paradigm gives weight to the importance of multilateral balance in manufactures trade. The information requirements for identifying which activities and which industries to promote are substantial. Protectionism necessarily narrows the prospective market and reduces the scope for the division of labor and the gains therefrom. The free trade argument becomes an argument for multilateral free trade and market sharing as the route to jointly expanded manufactures trade and the attendant shared productivity growth. With respect to national policy toward the IDL, we agree with Weber that "Our discussion strongly supports the free trade doctrine in its very essence, namely in its assertion that protectionist policy is fruitless as a rule and that all countries have a common economic interest in the abolition of tariff barriers."[67]

Notes

1. Jagdish H. Bhagwati, "The Generalized Theory of Distortions and Welfare," in Jagdish N. Bhagwati, Ronald W. Jones, Robert A. Mundell, Jaroslav Vanek, eds., *Trade, Balance of Payments, and Growth: Papers in International Economics in Honor of Charles P. Kindleberger* (North-Holland Publishing Co., 1971: 69–90.

2. Irreversible dynamic scale economies contrast with reversible static scale economies in terms of the standard representation of an industry production function by an isoquant map. In the case of static scale economies, proportional movements out an expansion path for the industry result in more than proportionate increases in output, and more than proportionate contraction in output when backed down the expansion path. In the case of irreversible dynamic scale economies, movement out the expansion path shifts the whole isoquant map toward the origin. The more rapid is movement out the expansion path, the more rapid is the shifting of the isoquant map. Furthermore, in the event that the industry subsequently is backed down the expansion path there is *no* reversing of the previous shifts in the isoquant map. Output growth leads to new knowledge which raises factor productivity. More rapid growth of output leads to more rapid growth of knowledge and to more rapid growth of factor productivity. Subsequent decline in output does not lead to a loss of knowledge or to decline in productivity—although it may lead to less (or to no) growth in productivity.

3. Nicholas Kaldor, *Economics without Equilibrium* (Armonk, New York: M. E. Sharpe, 1985): 67.

4. Ibid.

5. Edward E. Leamer, *Sources of International Comparative Advantage: Theory and Evidence* (Cambridge, Mass.: MIT Press, 1984).

6. See Sven W. Arndt, "Comment on Flacco, Laney, Thursby and Willett: Exchange Rates and Trade Policy," *Contemporary Policy Issues* 1 (January 1984): 10–22.

7. Leamer, *Sources of International Comparative Advantage*.

8. Jagdish H. Bhagwati, "The Heckscher-Ohlin Theorem in the Multi-Commodity Case," *Journal of Political Economy* 80 (September-October 1972): 1052–1055.

9. Jaroslav Vanek, "The Factor Proportions Theory: The N-Factor Case," *Kyklos* 21 (October 1968): 749–56.

10. Leamer, *Sources of International Comparative Advantage*.

11. Anne O. Krueger, "Factor Endowments and *per Capita* Income Differences Among Countries," *Economic Journal* 78 (September 1968): 641–59.

12. Anne O. Krueger, *Growth, Distortions, and Patterns of Trade among Many Countries* (Princeton Studies in International Finance No. 40, Princeton, New Jersey: International Finance Section, Department of Economics, Princeton University, 1977).

13. Alan V. Deardorff, "Weak Links in the Chain of Comparative Advantage," *Journal of International Economics* 9, (May 1979): 197–209.

14. Leamer, *Sources of International Comparative Advantage*.

15. Ibid.

16. Ibid., 200.

17. Ibid.

18. Alan V. Deardorff, "Testing Trade Theories and Predicting Trade Flows," in

R. W. Jones and P. B. Kenen, eds., *Handbook of International Economics* (Amsterdam: North-Holland, 1982).

19. Michael J. Finger, "Trade and the Structure of American Industry," *The Annals of the American Academy of Political and Social Science* 460 (1982).

20. World Bank, *World Development Report 1984* (New York: Oxford University Press, 1984), 227.

21. Ibid., 225.

22. Ibid., 87.

23. Bruce R. Scott and George C. Lodge, eds., *U.S. Competitiveness in the World Economy* (Boston: Harvard Business School Press, 1985).

24. William R. Cline, *Exports of Manufactures from Developing Countries* (Washington, D.C.: Brookings Institution, 1984).

25. Krueger, *Growth, Distortions, and Patterns of Trade.*

26. Leamer, *Sources of International Comparative Advantage.*

27. Miyohei Shinohara, *Industrial Growth, Trade and Dynamic Patterns in the Japanese Economy* (Tokyo: University of Tokyo Press, 1982), and Bruce R. Scott, "National Strategies: Key to International Competition," in Scott and Lodge, *U.S. Competitiveness in the World Economy*: 71–143.

28. Shinohara, *Industrial Growth*, 24.

29. Robert E. Baldwin, "The Case Against Infant-Industry Protection," *Journal of Political Economy* (May–June 1969): 295–305; Harry G. Johnson, "Optimal Trade Intervention in the Presence of Domestic Distortions," in R. E. Baldwin, et al., *Trade, Growth and the Balance of Payments: Essays in Honor of Gottfried Haberler* (Chicago: Rand McNally, 1965): 3–34; and W. M. Corden, *Trade Policy and Economic Welfare* (Oxford: Clarendon Press, 1974).

30. Baldwin, "The Case Against Infant Industry Protection".

31. Scott, "National Strategies," 95.

32. G. D. Hufbauer, "The Impact of National Characteristics and Technology on the Commodity Composition of Trade in Manufactured Goods," in R. Vernon, ed., *The Technology Factor in International Trade* (New York: Columbia University Press, 1970): 152–231; and Robert E. Baldwin, "Determinants of the Commodity Structure of U.S. Trade," *American Economic Review* 61 (March 1971): 126–46.

33. Leamer, *Sources of International Comparative Advantage.*

34. Elhanan Helpman and Paul R. Krugman, *Market Structure and Foreign Trade: Increasing Returns, Imperfect Competition and the International Economy* (Cambridge, Mass.: MIT Press, 1985).

35. John Rees, "Regional Industrial Shifts in the U.S. and the Internal Generation of Manufacturing in Growth Centers of the Southwest," in W. C. Wheaton, ed., *Interregional Movements and Regional Growth* (Washington, D.C.: The Urban Institute, 1979); and Stephen Seninger, "Employment Cycles and Process Innovation in Regional Structural Change," *Journal of Regional Science* 25 (1985): 259–72.

36. Doreen Massey, "Industrial Restructuring as Class Restructuring: Production Decentralization and Local Uniqueness," *Regional Studies* 17 (1983): 73–89.

37. Luis Suarez-Villa, "Industrial Export Enclaves and Manufacturing Change," *Papers and Proceedings of Regional Science Association* 54 (1984): 89–112, and "Industrialization in the Developing World, Process Cycles and the New Global Division of Labor, *Canadian Journal of Regional Science* 8 (1985): 1–44.

38. Edward Malecki, "Product Cycles and Regional Economic Change," *Technology Forecasting and Social Change* 19 (1981): 291–306, and "Technology and Regional Development: A Survey," *International Regional Science Review* 8 (1983): 89–126.

39. In the innovation cycle approach, process innovation and innovative activity occur

during a phase II that is accompanied by product improvement as well as extension of the product mix. Learning curve mechanisms aimed toward expansion of production and decreased costs lead to a third stage of large-scale, standardized production. Labor costs become a particularly important part of the cost reduction strategy which is realized by spatial relocation and decentralization policies (Malecki, "Product Cycles").

40. Suarez-Villa, "Industrial Export Enclaves."

41. Walter Oi, "Labor as a Quasi-Fixed Factor," *Journal of Political Economy* 70 (1962): 538–45, and "The Fixed Employment Costs of Specialized Labor," in J. Triplett, ed., *The Measurement of Labor Costs* (Chicago: University of Chicago Press, 1983): 63–122.

42. Most of the employment, technological, location, and capital implications of the product life cycle have been investigated in one form or another. A neoclassical, competitive industry framework developed by Nelson and Norman (Richard Nelson and Victor Norman, "Technological Change and Factor Mix over the Product Cycle," *Journal of Development Economics* 4 [1977]: 2–24) focuses on the mix of skilled and unskilled labor in relation to a vintage model of capital. Location and spatial implications are explored by Clark (Gordon Clark, "The Employment Relation and Spatial Division of Labor: A Hypothesis," *Annals of the Association of American Geographers* 71 [1981]: 412–24) and Storper and Walter (Michael Storper and Richard Walter, "The Spatial Division of Labor: Labor and the Location of Industry," in L. Sawyers and W. K. Tabb, *Sunbelt/Snowbelt: Urban Development and Regional Restructuring* [New York: Oxford University Press, 1984]) who trace the relocation of production facilities and spatial division of labor in the context of a changing process technology with industry growth. Other, less formalized models, such as Rees ("Regional Industrial Shifts") investigate the interregional relocation of manufacturing in the context of technology-intensive industries and a product cycle framework which are empirically applied to the Southwest using shift-share techniques. Malecki ("Technology and Regional Development") provides a comprehensive survey.

43. P. J. Verdoorn, "Factors that Determine the Growth of Labor Productivity" (translation by A. P. Thirlwall) *L'Industria* (1949): 1–13.

44. Nicholas Kaldor, *Causes of the Slow Rate of Growth of the United Kingdom: An Inaugural Address* (Cambridge: University Press, 1966) and "The Case for Regional Policies," *Scottish Journal of Political Economy* 17 (November 1970): 337–48.

45. R. J. Dixon and A. P. Thirlwall, "A Model of Regional Growth-Rate Differences on Kaldorian Lines," *Oxford Economic Papers* 27 (July 1975): 201–14.

46. Wilfred J. Ethier, "Internationally Decreasing Costs and World Trade," *Journal of International Economics* 9 (1979): 1–24.

47. *Market Structure and Foreign Trade.*

48. Ibid., 39.

49. Joseph Grunwald and Kenneth Flamm, *The Global Factory: Foreign Assembly in International Trade* (Washington, D.C.: Brookings Institution, 1985).

50. Ibid.

51. Ibid.

52. Helen Hughes and Anne O. Krueger, "Effects of Protection in Developed Countries on Developing Countries' Exports of Manufactures," in Robert E. Baldwin and Anne O. Krueger, eds., *The Structure and Evolution of Recent U.S. Trade Policy* (Chicago: University of Chicago Press, 1984): 384–418.

53. Ibid., 412. Recent slowing of its labor productivity growth and its rising unit, manufacturing labor costs (relative to other East Asian NICs, Japan, and the U.S.) suggest that Singapore has pushed too fast. ("New Miracle Needed," *The Economist* [31 August 1985]: 67).

54. Cline, *Exports of Manufactures.*

55. Sanjaya Lall, "The International Allocation of Research Activity by U.S. Multinationals," *Oxford Bulletin of Economics and Statistics* 41 (November 1979): 313–31.

56. Cline, *Exports of Manufactures*, 58.

57. *The Economist* (31 August 1985): 67.

58. Cline, *Exports of Manufacturers*.

59. Ibid.

60. J. R. Norsworthy and David H. Malmquist, "Recent Productivity Growth in Japanese and U.S. Manufacturing," in William J. Baumol and Kenneth McLennan, eds., *Productivity Growth and U.S. Competitiveness* (New York: Oxford University Press, 1985): 67.

61. *Far Eastern Economic Review* (5 September 1985): p. 53; (28 November 1985): p. 54.

62. Jere R. Behrman, "Developing-Country Perspective on Industrial Policy," in F. Gerard Adams and Lawrence R. Klein, eds., *Industrial Policies for Growth and Competitiveness: An International Perspective* (Lexington, Mass.: D. C. Heath and Co., 1983): 153–85.

63. Corden, *Trade Policy*.

64. Sweder van Wijnbergen, "The 'Dutch Disease': A Disease After All?" *The Economic Journal* 94 (March 1984): 41–55.

65. Paul Krugman, "New Theories of Trade Among Industrial Countries," *American Economic Review* 73 (May 1983): 343–47.

66. Bhagwati, "Generalized Theory."

67. Alfred Weber, "Location Theory and Trade Policy" (translation by Wolfgang F. Stolper) *International Economic Papers* 8 (1958): 133–46.

12

THE INTERNATIONAL DIVISION OF LABOR

Ray Marshall

Introduction

The value of a theoretical construct for understanding the international division of labor depends heavily on the uses to be made of that construct or conceptual framework. These uses are a more certain test than an appeal to facts, because the same facts can support different theories. A common test of particular general economic theories (like the Marxist or neoclassical) is how compatible a particular or partial theory is with that paradigm's general principles. This kind of partial-general congruence test is valid, but its acceptability depends on the extent to which the general body of thought provides a valid understanding of basic causal forces.

Those who are mainly interested in policy matters in the dynamic real world ordinarily are very skeptical of the utility of general paradigms for policy purposes. We therefore tend to be eclectic. We can see limitations as well as strength in most of the major paradigms. Eclectics also tend to be more tentative than those who adhere to strong, dogmatic positions. Dogmatists often defend their conceptual systems as being more "rigorous," but it is hard to avoid the conclusion that, in policy matters at least, those who adhere to strong systems would rather be rigorously wrong than vaguely correct.

Another major difference between the eclectics and those with strong, dogmatic, abstract intellectual constructs involves the degree of abstraction of a particular kind relative to the more multidimensional activities that eclectics see in the real world. For example, the neoclassicals are likely to force causal relationships into individual motive systems because that is the only kind of behavior their theoretical constructs can explain unambiguously. Similarly, Marxists are likely to assign primacy to class struggle motives because that is most compatible with the Marxist dialectical paradigms. In my view both of these systems assign too little weight to other motives (national pride or humiliation; such group identifications as nationalism, tribalism, or race; dignity; or altruistic values) that have been strong forces in human affairs.

Most of these general paradigms also seem to lack a sense of long-run strategies to achieve less than teleological objectives. For example, there is little that static neoclassical trade theory can do to explain unambiguously the kind of dynamic comparative advantage theory used by the Japanese as the basis for their very successful post–World War II economic policies. Of course, neoclassicals can modify their theory to explain any phenomenon. This flexibility, and the validity of much of their basic theoretical system, gives neoclassical theory strong intellectual appear—especially for those who do not seem overly bothered by tautologies, circularities, and highly restrictive assumptions about human motives. For policy purposes, however, a theoretical system that explains everything explains nothing and therefore is not very useful.

Similarly, most policy analysts very clearly see the relationships between theoretical constructs and policy recommendations—although we recognize full well that some policy matters can only be explained by political bargaining or strategic factors and not by any "rational" economic thought. We also recognize that such political decisions considered "irrational" in neoclassical economic terms can be very "rational" in political terms. Moreover, we are impressed with the importance of conflicting interests and therefore recognize—with the best of the welfare economists and neoclassicals—that there can be no unambiguous, uniquely determined welfare function or "national interest" apart from the resolution of differences by the exercise of political power within the framework of viable institutions and rules.

The basic assumption of this paper is that the international division of labor is determined by power interactions between nation states and by interest groups interacting within and between nation states. While these interest group relationships can become relatively stable at any particular time, there are dynamic forces tending to change these relationships within and between states.

This paper considers some factors that seem to have been important determinants of the international division of labor between 1945 and 1985. The first section outlines the nature and importance of the international economy in the postwar period. This is followed by discussions of the reasons for the decline in competitiveness of the American economy relative to the Japanese and some industrializing countries. The main factors discussed include the obsolescence of the authoritarian American management system geared mainly to the mass production of goods by relatively unskilled workers; declining productivity growth; the slowdown in technological innovation; high capital costs; the targeted industrial policies of other countries; and, most important, the obsolescence of incoherent and passive economic policies in an internationalized information era where other countries pursue more active policies and where the international economic institutions and policies geared to the conditions of the immediate postwar period are both obsolete and in disarray.

Internationalization

Internationalization of the American economy and the globalization of markets have altered the context within which the international division of labor must be understood. Internationalization has changed the effectiveness of traditional macroeconomic policies, transformed labor market institutions and industrial relations systems, and subjected enterprise management practices to the requirements of international competition. International markets, in turn, have been major determinants of the international division of labor.

Internationalization of the American and other national economies has accelerated markedly since World War II, especially during the 1970s. International transactions accounted for 9 percent of U.S. gross national product in 1950 and about 25 percent in 1980. In 1982 over half of all profits for American corporations came from overseas, and U.S. exports accounted for a third of all U.S. cropland (in fact, more U.S. than Japanese land was used to feed the Japanese), a fourth of farm income, and an eighth of all jobs: indeed, in 1977 about 70 percent of all goods manufactured in the United States competed with imports.[1] Similarly, an estimated 15–20 percent of the growth in the U.S. work force during the 1970s probably came from immigrants (legal and illegal) and refugees.

These aggregate statistics actually understate the extent to which the American economy has been integrated into the world economy. Trade has been particularly important in the manufacturing sector. Exports increased from 9 percent of U.S. manufacturing production in 1960 to 19 percent in 1980; during the same period, imports increased from 5 percent of domestic production to about 23 percent. A New York Stock Exchange study found that imports increased as a proportion of domestic production in 28 out of 40 industries between 1972 and 1982.[2] These industries accounted for roughly 70 percent of total U.S. production in 1977.

The internationalization of national economies was accelerated by a number of forces, especially the general conviction in the U.S. and Western Europe that an open and expanding trading system would stimulate the growth of world economies. This conviction derived from the belief that virulent protectionism had contributed significantly to both the Great Depression and World World II. To avoid a recurrence of these disasters, the U.S. jointed with other countries to form institutions and develop rules and policies to facilitate international trade and finance; these included the General Agreements on Trade and Tariffs (GATT), the international Monetary Fund and the International Bank for Reconstruction and Development (World Bank), the Organization for Economic Cooperation and Development (OECD), and aid programs for the reconstruction of Europe and Japan.

The dominant role of the United States in the international economy made it possible for American interests to prevail, and most American and European economic interests favored a relatively free, open, and expanding global economy. The United States had over half of the world's industrial output in 1950; our economy was actually strengthened during World War II while our major competitors were devastated by the war, and we emerged with a backlog of technology, much of it developed for military purposes, that provided the basis for unprecedented growth in productivity and total output. The dollar became the currency of international commerce, and English became the language of international transactions. The theory of the trading process was comparative advantage—that the welfare of the whole world was enlarged through a competitive free trade, open market system where each "country" concentrated on producing those things for which it had the greatest advantage or the least disadvantage. It was recognized that trade could not be free for developing countries with "infant industries" and exceptions were acknowledged for national security reasons, but free trade was the norm.

Advances in information, communication, and transportation, which integrated world product, commodity, and capital markets and greatly increased the international mobility of labor, also strengthened the international trading system.

Demise of the Bretton Woods Institution

The Bretton Woods international economic system facilitated the growth of the international economy until the early 1970s, when events began to erode its basic institutions. Bretton Woods was founded on three basic principles: free trade, fixed exchange rates, and autonomy of domestic economic policy. In addition to the overwhelming economic strength of the United States, this system was reinforced by the fact that most countries closely regulated their financial markets, while capital and trade flows were relatively small, and change was slow enough to facilitate relatively easy adjustments in domestic markets.

The Bretton Woods system started unraveling in 1971 when the U.S. suspended the convertibility of dollars to gold, and in 1973, when the fixed exchange rate system was abandoned in favor of floating exchange rates. The theory behind floating exchange rates was that free trade and capital movements would prevent persistent over- or undervaluation of currencies and automatically balance international trade flows. An overvalued currency would penalize exports and an undervalued currency would contribute to inflation by raising the cost of imports. It therefore was assumed that the problems for countries with misaligned currencies were sufficiently serious to encourage them to adopt economic policies to produce realignment. Floating exchange rates would therefore free countries to pursue independent domestic economic policies.

Unfortunately, floating exchange rates have not had this happy outcome. Speculators play a much larger role in an internationalized global economy with floating exchange rates. There are, moreover, much larger supplies of money than needed for goods and services transactions, and stop-and-go national economic policies have created considerable uncertainty. There have been particularly wide fluctuations in currency values.

Another major force undermining the Bretton Woods system was the massive increase in international trade and capital flows, which overwhelmed a system based on the assumption that trade would be mainly in goods and of secondary importance to domestic economic activity, and where adjustments would take place slowly. Indeed, international transactions increased much faster than the growth of national economies. Between 1960 and 1980, in real terms, exports grew at an annual rate of 6.7 percent, while gross domestic product (GDP) grew at only 4.4 percent. The ratio of world trade to GDP was 12.2 percent in 1960 and 21.8 percent in 1980. Increased internationalization was not restricted to a few countries—the process was pervasive.[3]

There were equally dramatic increases in foreign investment. By 1982, U.S. investments abroad were $834.2 billion, and foreign assets in the U.S. reached $665.2 billion. International financial flows were accelerated by the progressive liberalization of financial markets during the 1970s and 1980s. Most direct investment is by multinational corporations, whose investments doubled during the 1970s. In the industrialized countries portfolio investment almost doubled again between 1975 and 1981, and it grew by two-and-one-half times over the same period in the developing countries. In the latter, portfolio investment rose from only 5 percent of capital flows in 1961–63 to 32 percent in 1981. On a global basis, capital flows increased almost tenfold between 1975 and 1981.

Another example of increased international interdependence is the growth of the Eurodollar market—which represents dollars held and traded abroad, primarily in Europe. This market originated in the late 1950s and subsequently grew by leaps and bounds, reaching over $1 trillion in 1983. The Eurodollar market attracts massive sums through competitive interest rates. The huge international capital market is very volatile because it is largely uncontrolled by public entities.

There also has been a huge increase in debt, especially of the United States and the non-oil developing countries. The total debt of the latter countries rose from about 22 percent of their GDP in 1973 to 35 percent in 1983. In 1985 developing country (LDC) debt was over $800 billion. The U.S. financed its huge trade and budget deficits during the 1981–87 period with massive inflows of capital from abroad. In 1982, U.S.-owned assets abroad exceeded the assets owned by foreigners in the U.S. by about $150 billion. Annual earnings on these net foreign investments of about $30 billion allowed the U.S. to run sizeable merchandise trade deficits. By by 1985 the U.S. investment position, built up over sixty-five years, was wiped out.

Labor markets have not been as internationalized as financial, commodity, and manufactured product markets, but they too have become more integrated by improvements in transportation and communication. Although economists traditionally have assumed labor to be an immobile factor of production, workers always have migrated in response to income and employment opportunities. Some consider the postwar economic "miracles" in Europe, especially in Germany, to be due in some significant measure to the labor market flexibility made possible by the importation of "guest workers" from eastern and southern Europe. During 1965–85 there were large-scale international movements of workers, some legal, some illegal. Indeed, some estimate the contribution of immigrants to American labor force growth as at least 20 percent during the 1970s. Worldwide, there were an estimated 20 million migrant workers in the late 1970s, 12 million of whom were form the developing countries. These migrants were heavily concentrated in certain regions: North American, 6 million; the Middle East, 3 million; and Western Europe, 5 million.

Migrant worker remittances to their home countries have been an important source of foreign exchange for some countries. Between 1970 and 1980 these remittances increased at an annual rate of about 26.5 percent. Worker remittances to the LDC countries were only $3 billion in 1970, but had reached $24 billion by 1980. By 1982 the remittance receipts by the middle-income oil-importing countries accounted for an estimated 34 percent of their current account deficits.

The chief integrating entities in the international economy were multinational companies, whose activities were greatly strengthened by information and transportation technologies, the deregulation of markets, and shrinking barriers to the movement of capital and goods. Transnational corporations have attained international dominance because they face no effective countervailing organization. They have evolved ". . .into large transnational entities, not limited by constraints of domestic market size or costs of inputs, but, on the contrary, availing themselves of the most advantageous conditions in labor, capital, and goods markets."[4]

The emergence of international corporations, joint ventures, and consortia complicates the concept of international competitiveness among nations. Indeed, production sharing between countries in a given product like automobiles often makes it very difficult to identify an American product—its components will be produced in a number of different countries.

Assessments by the Commerce Department make it clear that a distinction exists between ownership of a "U.S. corporation" and the geographical location of its operations. Before internationalization, a corporation's ownership and production took place in a single country. During the 1970s and 1980s, however, this pattern changed and corporations became really *transnational*. International companies not only locate marketing and sales activities overseas, but production and, to a lesser extent, research and development as well. These arrangements are carried out by a host of contractual forms including wholly- or partially-owned subsidiaries, joint ventures, licensing agreements, production contracts, and other types of international agreements, rather than to improve the welfare of its workers or residents of the country in which the organization's ownership is located.

These developments have caused national industries to become largely obsolete for analytical purposes. These changes also require modification in some statistical categories formerly used to analyze international transactions; for example, data on exports and imports now must include the foreign content of U.S. exports and the U.S. content of foreign imports. The full implications of these changes are not yet well understood, in part because the existing data sources are obsolete.

Consequences of Internationalization

The internationalization of markets has a number of important implications. On the positive side, international economic integration has promoted greater efficiency in the use of the world's physical and financial resources; expanded managerial skills, knowledge, and technology in the developing countries and allowed higher standards of living for many of the world's people.

But internationalization brings with it many problems. In many countries the benefits of industrialization and international trade are not equitably shared, and income distributions in the U.S. and in many third-world countries are becoming more unequal. Moreover, internationalization brings with it a loss of national control over economic policies and domestic economies. In addition, the nature of the economy has changed to such an extent that international economic rules that appeared to be effective in the 1950s and 1960s are no longer applicable to the 1980s.

Perhaps the most important aspect of international economic interdependence is the extent to which it changes the nature of domestic policy making. As the experiences of the United States in the late 1970s and France in the early 1980s demonstrate, traditional national Keynesian demand stimulus policies have been weakened by international leakages: stimulus at a time when most major economies are depressed tends to limit domestic economic expansion by accelerating foreign imports. This was a particularly serious problem for the United States in the recovery from the 1981–82 recession, when foreign imports offset a large part of the increased demand. Imports were especially important for American capital goods markets during the 1981–84 business cycle, when 95 percent of the increased demand for U.S. capital goods during the recovery was met by imports.

Global interdependence also produces serious "boomerang" effects from national policies. For example, the 1981 U.S. tax cut and the ensuing recession created huge budget deficits, greatly increasing the federal demand for money. The fact that the federal government's borrowing requirements at a time of monetary constraint offset most of net private domestic savings put strong upward pressure on real interest rates. High real interest rates attracted foreign capital, which, as noted, greatly increased net foreign debt. These policies have negative effects on other countries, which, in an independent world, boomerang back to the U.S. For example, high U.S. real interest rates caused serious trouble for European countries, which were forced to tolerate higher interest rates and unemployment levels because lower interest rates would have accelerated the flight of their capital to the United States. U.S. policies boomeranged back to this country because rising unemployment diminished European demand for American exports.

Thus, major economic problems are created by economic integration and interdependence in a world where most policy instruments are still mainly national and internationally uncoordinated. Because of its size and the importance of the dollar as a reserve currency, U.S. economic policies have had a particularly strong impact on the rest of the world.

International Trade

Internationalization also necessitates a reconsideration of the theoretical underpinnings, institutions, and practices of the international trading system. The principle of comparative advantage, upon which free-trade policies are based, rests on a number of assumptions which must be reexamined in the light of postwar international economic experience. Static classical trade theory assumed comparative advantage to be based on (a) natural endowments and (b) product competition between private profit-maximizing companies. Other assumptions included competitive markets, so that no resources were involuntarily unemployed; instantaneous adjustments; and gradual change. Under these conditions, it is easy to show that all countries gain by an open trading system in which each country specializes in those things for which it has the greatest advantage or the least disadvantage.

As with the theory of freely fluctuating exchange rates, however, reality has been very different. Perfect competition does not govern national domestic markets, so countries do experience unemployment. Similarly, governments and transnational oligopolistic enterprises and cartels are heavily involved in international markets. Almost all governments except that of the United States have active trade policies to support national economic objectives. Following the Japanese practice, many countries have adopted the theory of dynamic comparative advantage, meaning that they adopt strategies to create comparative advantage and improve industry mix rather than simply having comparative advantage revealed by markets. Moreover, in modern markets, trade is very likely to be based on a combination of absolute factor costs and the economic strategies of multinational corporations and governments, as well as comparative advantage. Economic activity is based on national and enterprise strategies, not just on the interplay of short-run market forces and profit maximizing. Free trade usually is justified in the United States on the basis of maximizing short-run profits and consumer satisfaction; Japan and the "little Japans" are more interested in strengthening national power, productive capacity, and market share than in short-run profit maximizing. Moreover, change is not gradual in the internationalized information world and trade is not just in goods—whole factories and technologies are exported. The consequence of these changes for the United States and other high-wage industrialized countries is that jobs can be lost and wages and working conditions can be reduced by international competition. An open trading system can cause some countries to gain at the expense of others. However, market forces within the framework of enforceable rules can cause an open international trading system to benefit people in most countries.

Economic interdependence causes domestic economic policies to affect others, even when the policies are taken by nations not as large as the United States. For example, after World War II a number of countries adopted export-driven industrial policies designed to develop key industries, usually in competition with U.S. firms. These industrial policies ordinarily involved a number of instruments designed to make domestic firms become more competitive in international markets. The policy instruments most commonly used included protection of domestic markets from outside competition until domestic firms could build greater capacity than could be sold in their domestic markets; various subsidy arrangements, especially subsidized capital costs; exchange controls; and restriction of foreign investments in domestic markets. Because of the overwhelming economic superiority of the U.S. in the postwar period, other countries' targeted industrial policies had very little early impact on the American economy. In time, however, the growth of other countries relative to that of the U.S. caused many Americans to become much more concerned about the negative impact of these policies on the competitiveness of American companies.

Industrial policies are not limited to the developed countries like Japan and western Europe—Mexico, Korea, Brazil, Taiwan, and other developing (or newly industrialized) countries also have export-driven industrial policies which help them either to penetrate American markets or to compete with American products in other foreign markets. The indirect effects of some of these policies can be very important. For example, if countries like Mexico develop capital-intensive export industries, they may create very few jobs in their domestic economies, displace labor, widen income differentials, and stimulate emigration, especially to the United States.

The immigration problem is a particularly serious labor market problem for the United States. If its borders remain relatively open in a world where other industrialized countries have virtually closed theirs, greater global population pressures will focus on the United States through legal and illegal immigration or through intensified trade competition with those countries. Some idea of the magnitude of this problem is suggested by the fact that at least 700 million jobs—more than presently exist in all of the industrialized market economies—will have to be created in the developing countries just to keep joblessness from increasing above the 1985 level of 40–50 percent. In a highly interdependent global economy, the third-world's unemployment problems become the problems of all nations.

Multinational Corporations

Multinational corporations (MNCs), which owe their power to the control of scarce and mobile capital and technology in a job-short world and to their information monopolies, have emerged as the principal economic organizations in the global economy. The information revolution strengthened the MNCs' global activities. Within countries, labor organizations traditionally have been able to maintain their standards by expanding with the market, thereby taking labor out of competition by a combination of legislation and collective bargaining. However, the growth of truly international collective bargaining-type labor organizations has many obstacles, including nationalism, high levels of worldwide unemployment, diverse national laws and customs, and differences in the power and motives of national labor movements.[5] Similarly, despite several attempts by the Organization for Economic Cooperation and Development, the United Nations, and the International Labor Organization, no international entity has been able to fashion effective, enforceable codes of conduct for MNCs.

What are the implications of MNCs for the international division of labor? The neoclassical paradigm views the activities of international corporations as essentially benign. These enterprises improve the conditions of countries in which they operate by distributing resources more rationally in response to markets and the pursuit of profits—shifting resources from areas where they are relatively plentiful to areas where they are scarce, thereby increasing competition, improving efficiency, creating jobs, raising wages, and improving the distribution of income.[6]

Unfortunately, as in most of its applications to labor matters, experience and empirical tests have found the neoclassical model inadequate. Indeed, as Hymer and Kindleberger (1976) have pointed out,[7] international activities of multinational corporations are logically incompatible with the neoclassical assumptions of competitive markets. If markets were competitive, international companies would not be able to compete with local firms; if markets are not competitive, the MNCs' effects are not necessarily benign. Raymond Vernon extended our understanding of market imperfections with his "product cycle" analysis.[8] In Vernon's view, companies were motivated to invest overseas, after first exporting to those markets, in order to realize continuing rents on the MNCs' technology and management practices before they were generally adopted in foreign markets. Richard Caves extended the analysis of imperfect markets by developing the idea of sector-specific capital, which permits cross-investment in industries where corporations are in different countries while profits are differentiated between sectors in each country.[9] Further supporting the conclusion that multinationals require market imperfections is the finding of a high correlation between multinational investments and concentration ratios in both the receiving and sending countries.[10]

The findings that international corporations frequently do not transfer much new capital from the outside but rely heavily on local capital sources cast further doubt on neoclassical conclusions about the beneficial effects of MNCs.[11] Moreover, multinationals frequently form alliances with domestic political interests in the foreign countries to monopolize and distort local markets and engage in capital-intensive or other production practices more appropriate to the MNCs' home countries than to the foreign markets in which they invest. These forms of production are likely to displace people from labor intensive agriculture or manufacturing, increasing joblessness and polarizing income distributions. Thus, according to Theodore Moran:

> In the extreme, foreign companies might capture the commanding heights of the host economy, soak up indigenous sources of capital as they drive local firms out of business, create a small labor elite for themselves while transferring the bulk of the workers into the ranks of the unemployed, and siphon off oligopoly profits for repatriation to corporate headquarters. This would hardly be favorable for the rate of growth or the structure of the development process.[12]

Do the failures of the neoclassical paradigm therefore favor the Marxist and *dependencia* theories?[13] In the Marxist analysis the multinational uses its economic power to strengthen capitalist control over and extract surplus value from the workers in foreign countries. A number of efforts have been made to test the relationship between MNC investment and economic welfare in particular countries, but these generally have produced inconclusive or ambiguous results. In an apparent refutation of the *dependencia* conclusion, Reuber found a positive correlation between the stock of foreign investment and GNP per capita in the third world.[14] However, Dolan and Tomlin found a negative relationship between growth and foreign investment stocks but a positive relationship between foreign investment flows and growth rates.[15] The positive relationship with flows and negative relation to stocks suggests the possibility that the impact of MNCs on host countries has changed through time—at first retarding and then promoting growth.

Besides their restrictive assumptions, a major problem for both the neoclassical and the Marxist paradigms is the static, deterministic nature of their analysis. Reality is more complicated. In fact, as in other transactions, a dynamic bargaining model appears to be much more appropriate. Such a model would stress the importance of the power relationships between the principal actors—e.g., MNC managers, governments, or other interests. The relative bargaining power between governments and corporations will depend on such matters as the advantages to the MNC of operating in a particular country relative to the risks involved, as well as the alternatives available to governments. Research within the framework of the bilateral monopoly model suggests that the lower limit to the bargain could be what is necessary to induce the MNC to locate in a country and prevent it from withdrawing later: the upper limit might be the price at which the country would prefer to do without the MNCs' investment.[16]

A more dynamic approach to the bargaining model is provided by Raymond Vernon's "obsolescing bargaining" concept.[17] According to this view, a government might have to offer an MNC a large initial inducement to overcome the risk and uncertainty of locating in that country. However, once the MNC is in the country, a government's bargaining power might increase, depending on such matters as the ease of nationalizing or otherwise controlling the company and the government's ability to generate competition with the MNC. The obsolescing bargaining concept therefore predicts that the host country is likely to gain more favorable conditions from the MNC through time. However, much depends on the country's bargaining skills, tactics, and strategies, as well as the power relations between the MNC and the government. On the other side, corporations can strengthen their power relative to governments by bargaining skills and manipulating the political processes with in a country.

What about the sharing of the gains within a country once the MNC locates there? Marxist-*dependencia* writers have tended to emphasize the dominant influence of the MNC, and the neoclassicals are likely to emphasize the primacy of market forces and the political weaknesses of the MNCs. Again, reality is more complex. There is little evidence of an unambiguous tendency for MNC managements to form ideological alliances with local entrepreneurs. Indeed, MNC alliances with local interests appear to be very diverse.[18] Far from being able to dominate those governments in every case, "the data suggest that multinational corporations do not do well in head-to-head public confrontations with local authorities."[19]

There is also considerable diversity in the ability of workers to protect themselves from foreign MNCs. In fact, in some cases the state acts as a protector of its citizens who work for MNCs, but the workers tend to lose this protection if the state nationalizes the MNC's property.[20] In general, worker protection in third world countries depends on their political power and the nature of the industrializing elites.[21] However, it is unlikely that most workers will be able to improve their conditions very much through nonpolitical organizations in developing countries, though skilled workers can achieve collective bargaining in craft-oriented unions that represent a small part of the work force. Industrialization improved the workers' bargaining power in the developed countries until rapid internationalization during the 1970s.[22]

Are American Companies Losing Their Competitiveness?

The evidence suggests that the American economy does in fact have serious competitiveness problems. There is no one index of trouble, but several taken together are very troubling:

• The U.S. merchandise trade balance, which had been positive every year from 1893 to 1970, became negative in 1971; except for 1973 and 1975, this balance has been negative ever since. A good part of this negative merchandise trade balance has been because of energy price problems, but there also has been a decline in the nonenergy merchandise trade balance. In addition, the large appreciation of the dollar after 1981 has contributed to a rapidly widening trade deficit, which hit $170 billion in 1986.

Detailed studies by Data Resources, Inc. in 1984 and 1985 confirm the decline in the competitiveness of American industry.[23] The DRI studies show that the U.S. faces massive disadvantages in labor costs, productivity, capital costs, and other key factors compared with Japan and other industrial countries, not just in steel and autos but in practically every industry. The most concrete manifestation of the problem was the growing U.S. trade deficit.

Moreover, it is not true, as the critics argue, that America's competitive advantage in high-tech exports offset its disadvantage in basic manufacturing. Bruce Scott has shown that "the United States was not shifting its comparative advantage toward high-technology areas" between 1965 and 1980, "but was building on advantages it had had for years."

> Much the same holds true for West Germany and France. Neither of these countries has significantly improved its high tech market share. . . .
>
> The Japanese pattern reveals striking differences. The magnitude of changes between 1965 and 1980 indicates much faster and farther-reaching adjustment, with Japan gaining a share in high-technology areas and losing it in low-technology sectors.
>
> The Japanese have shown that it is possible to upgrade a national industrial portfolio; it appears to be the only major industrial power to have done so.[24]

In general, the U.S. had favorable trade balances in high-tech industries during the 1970s and unfavorable balances in non-high-tech areas. Since 1981, the U.S. balance has deteriorated.

• A second major sign of declining competitiveness for the American economy is its declining share of world GNP. The U.S. share declined from 26 percent in 1960 to 22.5 percent in 1980.

• The U.S. share of world exports has declined from 14.5 percent in 1965 to 10.3 percent in 1983 (Table 12.2). However, these overall data conceal important industrial differences. The U.S. share of the value of the world's manufactured goods exported declined from 26 percent in 1960 to 18 percent in 1980.

It makes some difference, however, whether trade figures are measured in constant or current dollars. The 1984 study for the New York Stock Exchange suggests that in constant price and volume terms, our proportion of the world's exports remained virtually unchanged between 1962 (14.8 percent) and 1980

Table 12.1

GNP Shares	1960 (%)	1980 (%)
European community	26	22.5
Japan	5	9
Other developed countries	10	10
Developing countries	11	15
Communist countries	22	22

Source: U.S. Department of Commerce, International Trade Administration, *U.S. Competitiveness in the International Economy* (October 1981).

(14.7 percent).[25] (However, the U.S. share had declined to 12.3 percent by 1982.) What this means, of course, is that despite substantial depreciation of the dollar between 1977 and 1980, the U.S. was unable to regain its relative share of the value of manufactured trade. This also means that the U.S. had to give up greater exports in order to secure the same imports; consequently, American producers experienced lower profits and lower real wages. The data also show that the U.S. share of high-tech exports declined between 1962 and 1980.[26] Moreover, between 1965 and 1980 the U.S. held market share in aircraft and parts, and gained shares only in office, computing, and accounting machines and agricultural chemicals. The data show, in addition, that Japan developed much faster than the U.S. in most high-tech areas. The data show, in addition, that Japan developed much faster than the U.S. in most high-tech areas. The U.S. regained its share of some traditional areas as the dollar depreciated in the late 1970s, but not in the high-tech areas, where price competition is less important than in older industries, and quality and dependability of supplies are more important. Japanese economic policy and management systems appears to give them significant competitive advantages in these nonprice areas.

Some analysts argue that these market share statistics are no cause for alarm because it was natural that the United States would lose its relative position as other countries developed in the postwar period. There is some truth in this argument, of course, but a careful reading of the evidence suggests that government policies, not natural forces, helped foreign producers gain at the expense of American firms. Moreover, the prevailing view among some economists that there is nothing to worry about is based on a static view of the economy, which sees no strategic importance in what is done this year relative to the future. According to analysts at the Berkeley Roundtable on the International Economy, declining market shares could signify

a loss of the capacity to compete in future products and future markets, not just the industrial catch up of our partners. In semiconductors, for example, Japanese

Table 12.2

Shares of World Trade

	1960	1965	1970	1975	1980	1982	1983
United States	16	14.5	13.7	12.2	10.7	11.0	10.3
EEC	34	34.3	36.1	33.9	32.4	30.7	31.4
Japan	3	4.5	6.1	6.3	6.3	7.2	7.6
Other developed countries	14	15.1	15.8	13.5	12.3	13.0	13.7
Developing countries	22	19.4	17.2	23.7	28.4	26.4	24.6
(Of which OPEC)	(6)	(5.4)	(5.3)	(12.8)	(14.4)	(10.8)	(8.8)
Communist countries	11	12.2	11.1	10.3	9.8	11.6	12.3

Sources: Council of Economic Advisors, *Economic Report of the President*, February 1984, 338; 1960 figures, U.S. Department of Commerce, International Trade Administration, *U.S. Competitiveness in the International Economy* (October 1981).

world market share has been built on an expansion of sales in the United States and Europe, while imports as a share of the Japanese national market have remained constant. The declining U.S. world market share suggests a growing Japanese competitive strength. Indeed, Japanese market positions are providing the base for further capital and R&D investment with Japanese investment running at 45 percent of gross sales. In sum, our national shift into technology intensive sectors is not as secure as it may at first seem.[27]

• One of the most important indicators of an ability to compete is technological change, where there are some troubling developments. A number of studies have concluded

that America's technology advantage in a number of advanced technology industries has seriously eroded in ways likely to cause competitive problems in world markets. For example, ten years ago, America's technology position in microelectronics was unchallenged. Now, in a range of critical areas, the Japanese have gained or are verging on leadership. Unless current trends are reversed, the advantage the U.S. currently holds will erode further.[28]

Indeed, a 1985 Commerce Department study concluded that the Japanese had attained a significant research and development lead over the United States in what many scientists believe will be the next generation of high-speed electronics technology.[29] Japan's lead is in new nonsilicon electronics that can lead to computers, telecommunications switches, and signal processing chips capable of data calculations many times faster than current technologies. The Commerce

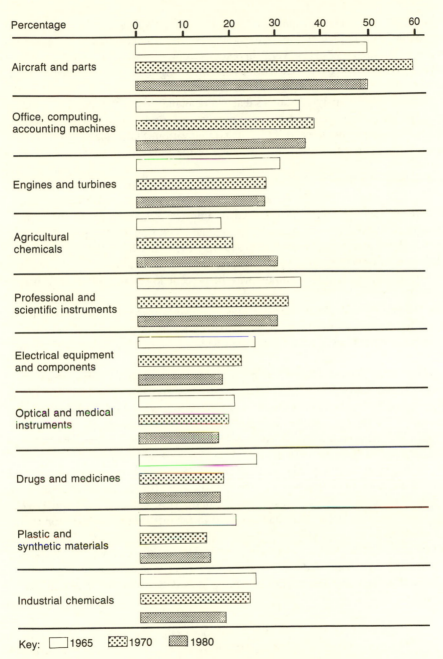

Key: ☐ 1965   ▨ 1970   ▧ 1980

Figure 12.1. U.S. Share of World High-Technology Exports
Source: Bruce Scott and George Lodge, eds., *U.S. Competitiveness in the World Economy* (Boston, Mass.: Harvard University Press, 1985), 29.

Department study pointed out that Japan had been "aggressive in acquiring, improving, and implementing. . .technologies whose conceptual aspects were developed in the U.S." However, "in optoelectronics in particular, the Japanese have made major, original contributions and their original creative contributions in this field are expected to increase in the future."

Static economic analysis assumes that where an industry is "strategic," it will be supported by buyers who demand its output. The trouble with that assumption is that there can be no demand if there is no innovation. Static analysis therefore assumes, in turn, an unrealistic knowledge of the innovation.

• A most important indicator of declining competitiveness is declining real wages. Real wages are important, of course, because really being competitive implies the ability to maintain or improve real income. In this connection, real average weekly earnings in manufacturing (gross pay, in constant dollars) rose steadily between 1949 and 1973, but have fluctuated since 1973, and in 1984 were still below their 1973 levels.[30] Real take-home pay for the average nonagricultural worker was 14 percent lower in 1985 than it was in 1973.

• Despite these declines in real wages, however, during the early 1980s the pretax returns on manufacturing assets also declined to the point that the average manufacturing company would have been better off investing in bonds (Figure 12.2).

These data suggest, overall, that the U.S. has reason to worry about its competitive position. It is true, as the optimists contend, that much of our competitiveness problem is due to the disruptions following the Reagan administration's 1981 tax cuts, which, together with the Federal Reserve's monetarist policies, put the economy into a deep recession. However, the U.S. also has other problems that predate the 1981 tax cuts. The U.S. had substantially higher labor and capital costs than any other country; in 1985, no country's manufacturing wages were more than 75 percent of those of the U.S. (thanks to the overvalued dollar). The net real after-tax cost of capital in the U.S. between 1974 and 1984 was over 5 percent in the U.S. and almost 0 in Japan.[31] Some analysts contend that realigning exchange rates will restore our competitive position. There are, however, serious problems with that argument. For one thing, it will not be easy to overcome the structural deficits resulting from our misguided economic policies. As the Berkeley Roundtable suggests, it will be difficult to regain lost markets:

> In many industries, market share itself, once gained confers cost advantages with respect to distribution and production. Accordingly, it may take U.S. firms considerable time to lose sales when the dollar rises, but once lost, a market position is difficult and expensive to rebuilt. In short, in many markets the U.S. may be in the process of ceding first-mover advantages to others.[32]

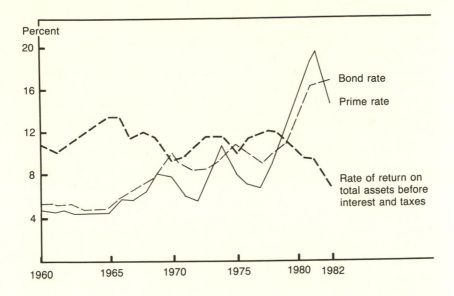

Figure 12.2. Rate of Return on Total Assets in Manufacturing Corporate Bond Rate and Prime Rate, 1960–82
Source: Bruce Scott and George Lodge, eds., *U.S. Competitiveness in the World Economy* (Boston, Mass.: Harvard University Press, 1985), 31.

Many optimists, basing their reasoning on static economic analysis that pays very little attention to the synergistic relationship between industries, argue that a loss of competitiveness in manufacturing is of no consequence because our disadvantages in manufacturing will be offset by advantages in other areas, especially services. There are several problems with this line of reasoning. First, the trade in services is not likely to be large enough to compensate for the manufacturing trade deficits. Second, the symbiotic relations between manufacturing and services is such that high value-added services are likely to be related to high value-added manufacturing. Third, the static argument that the composition of industry or trade is unimportant because automatic market forces will yield the best possible outcome for the nation's welfare is at variance with how the world actually works.

The Decline in Productivity Growth

One of the most disturbing factors involved in the declining competitiveness of American industry is the slowdown in productivity growth that started during the 1960s and worsened markedly during the 1970s. Productivity growth recovered somewhat following the 1981–82 recession, but the previous growth levels had not been achieved by 1985, at the peak of the recovery from the recession, and

U.S. productivity growth performance remains far below that of our principal competitors, especially the Japanese. Productivity growth affects real wages, economic growth, inflation, and unemployment, all of which are significantly more serious problems for the United States than they were in the 1960s.

The decline in productivity growth experienced by all industrial countries in the 1960s, but especially after the first oil price shock in 1973-74, is one of our most serious economic problems. While the average level of productivity is still higher in the United States than in other countries, between 1950 and 1980 the rate of growth in the U.S. was lower than in any country (see Table 12.3). The fastest rate of growth has been in Japan, whose productivity is about two-thirds to three-fourths of the U.S., but the average levels are higher in Canada, France, and Germany. At present trends, these countries could overtake the United States by the end of the 1980s and the Japanese could overtake us by the end of the century. Indeed, these countries already have higher productivity than the U.S. in some manufacturing industries.

Manufacturing Productivity

Because of its significance in international trade, manufacturing productivity growth is very important for international competitiveness. As can be seen from Table 12.4 and Figure 12.3, manufacturing productivity gains were lower in the United States than in other major industrial countries both before and after 1973. However, the slowdown between 1973 and 1983 was pervasive, although it was greatest relatively for Germany and Japan, which had the highest rates of productivity growth between 1950 and 1983.

Table 12.5 shows the combined influence of the rising value of the dollar on hourly pay (wages plus fringes) differentials in manufacturing. In 1981, Germany had virtually closed the gap with the U.S., and Sweden's level was 8 percent higher than the U.S. by 1984, however, the expensive dollar had increased this gap, despite relatively low wage increases in the U.S. for 1984, no country's hourly compensation levels were more than 75 percent of the U.S. average, and Japan's was only 56 percent of the U.S. Compensation levels in Taiwan, Mexico, South Korea, and Brazil were less than 15 percent of that of the U.S. The decline in the value of the dollar after 1985 caused wages to be about equalized between the U.S. and Japan, but for European wages to again be higher than those in the U.S. However, wages remained much lower in Korea and other third world countries whose currencies have not appreciated relative to the dollar. Clearly, therefore, developing countries, wage rates made the United States noncompetitive in industries where other things (technology and management) could be standardized.

The experts disagree about whether or not U.S. productivity improvements after 1979 imply a significant reversal of the decline. According to those who believe the upturn signifies an end to our productivity problems, productivity

Table 12.3

**Trends in International Productivity
(Average Annual Change in Gross Domestic Product Per Employed Person)**

Country/period	1950–65	1965–73	1973–80	1950–80
United States	2.4	1.6	0.1	1.6
Canada	2.7	2.4	0.0	2.0
Japan	7.2	8.2	3.0	6.5
France	4.8	4.6	2.7	4.2
Germany	5.6	4.3	2.8	4.6
United Kingdom	2.2	3.2	1.6	2.2
Italy	5.6	5.8	1.8	4.8
Netherlands	3.3	4.6	1.8	3.3
Belgium	3.2	4.3	2.4	3.3

Source: U.S. Department of Labor, Bureau of Labor Statistics, Office of Productivity and Technology.

Table 12.4

Manufacturing Productivity, U.S. and Other Major Industrial Countries, 1950–83

	Output per employee hour in manufacturing (average annual percent change)			Change 1950–73 to 1973–83
	1950–83	1950–73	1973–83	
United States	2.5	2.8	1.8	−1.0
Canada	3.5	4.3	1.8	−2.5
France	5.4	5.8	4.6	−1.2
Germany	5.6	6.5	3.7	−2.8
Japan	9.0	10.0	6.8	−3.2
United Kingdom	3.0	3.3	2.4	−0.9

Source: U.S. Department of Labor, Bureau of Labor Statistics, *Trends in Manufacturing: A Chartbook*, (April 1985, Bulletin 2219).

growth will resume and perhaps reach even greater levels because most of the basic causes of the earlier slowdown (the oil price shocks, inflation, the addition of 20 million new workers to the work force, government regulations, and low research and development expenditures) are over and have left the economy leaner and stronger than before.

Index, 1950 = 100   Ratio scale

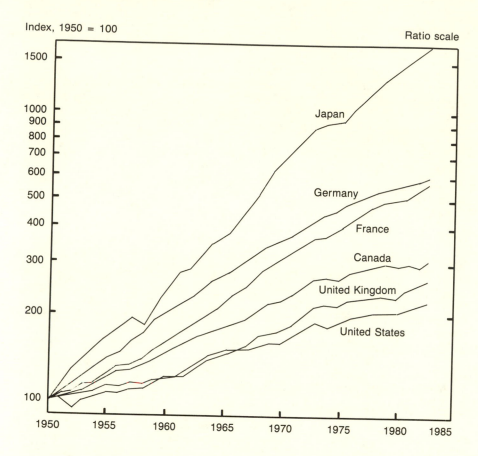

Figure 12.3. Output per Employee Hour in Manufacturing
Selected Countries, 1950–83
Source: Bureau of Labor Statistics

Those of us who are skeptical of this view argue that as of late 1986 there was
no evidence of a significant turnaround in the trend. Indeed, there appear to have
been only modest improvements from the very low productivity growth levels of
the 1970s. Moreover, while other countries had not completed their recoveries
from the 1981–82 recessions, their productivity growth rates were substantially
higher than ours. Bureau of Labor Statistics data on trend rates of of gross
domestic product per employed person reveal the following growth rates:

1948–65	2.6%
1965–73	2.1
1973–79	0.6
1979–83	1.0

Table 12.5

Manufacturing Productivity[1] and Labor Costs in 10 Countries: Average Annual Rates of Change, 1973–84[2]

Country	Output per hour			Hourly compensation		
	1973–84	1983	1984	1973–84	1983	1984
United States	2.0	4.3	3.5	8.8	3.4	3.6
Canada	1.7	6.4	4.0	11.0	6.8	1.6
Japan	7.3	5.1	9.5	8.1	3.4	3.2
Denmark	3.6	3.0	4.1	11.0	4.3	5.9
France	4.6	4.3	5.0	15.1	12.2	8.9
Germany	3.3	4.7	4.7	7.6	4.1	3.6
Italy	3.7	2.4	6.3	19.3	16.7	10.4
Norway	2.3	5.9	1.7	11.3	11.4	6.8
Sweden	2.9	8.4	6.8	11.6	9.0	10.8R
United Kingdom	2.3	6.7	3.9	15.9	7.2	7.9

	Unit labor costs in national currency			Unit labor costs in U.S. dollars		
	1973–84	1983	1984	1973–84	1983	1984
United States	6.7	−0.8	0.1	6.7	−0.8	0.1
Canada	9.2	.3	−2.3	6.3	.5	−7.0
Japan	.8	−1.7	−5.8	3.1	3.1	−5.7
Denmark	7.2	1.3	1.7	2.5	−7.6	−10.1
France	10.0	7.6	3.7	4.5	− 7.1	−9.5
Germany	4.1	− .5	−1.0	4.4	−5.4	−11.2
Italy	15.0	14.0	3.9	4.8	1.6	−10.1
Norway	8.8	5.2	5.0	5.9	−7.0	−6.1
Sweden	8.4R	.6	3.8R	2.7R	−17.6	−3.7R
United Kingdom	13.4	.5	3.8	9.2	−12.9	−8.4

R = Revised.

[1]Although the productivity measure relates output to the hours of persons employed in manufacturing, it does not measure the specific contributions of labor as a single factor of production. Rather, it reflects the joint effects of many influences, including new technology, capital investment, capacity utilization, energy use, and managerial skills, as well as the skills and efforts of the work force.

[2]Rates of change computed from the least squares trend of the logarithms of the index numbers.
Source: Data supplied by the U.S. Bureau of Labor Statistics, Wash., D.C., 1986.

Overall, productivity increased by only 1.6 percent in 1984 and did not increase at all in 1985. Business productivity increased by only 2.1 percent in 1984 and .3 percent in 1985. Manufacturing productivity for 1985 was a disappointing 2.6 percent.

Average annual productivity growth rates (not cyclically adjusted) for various countries were:

	1973–79	1974–83
Japan	2.9%	2.9%
W. Germany	2.9	1.8
U.K.	1.2	1.6
U.S.	0.3	−0.9

Thus, relative to both the past and to other countries, U.S. performance after 1979 hardly suggests an end to productivity problems. Moreover, since it is not at all clear how much energy prices, demographic shifts, and other factors contributed to the slowdown, it is far too early to conclude, as some have, that "the long-awaited boon in productivity growth is here."[33]

Management and Industrial Relations Systems

Because of its importance to productivity, many experts attribute superior performance in Japan and other countries primarily to superior management. Athos and Pascale, for example, argue that "a major reason for the superiority of the Japanese is their managerial skills."[34] Managers themselves consider management deficiencies to be the basic cause of the productivity slowdown in the United States in recent years. A 1982 survey of 236 top-level executives in the United States concluded that "Management ineffectiveness is by far the single greatest cause of declining productivity in the United States."[35]

The American System

One of the most influential studies of corporations was made during the depression by Adolf Berle and Gardiner Means, who argued that "the separation of ownership from control (of large public corporations) produces a condition where the interests of owner and of ultimate manager may, and often do, diverge and where many of the checks which formerly operated to limit the use of power disappear."[36] Many critics during the depression, as well as the 1970s and 1980s, believed a major problem for American corporate managers was their preoccupation with their personal welfare, unchecked by stockholders, who are so dispersed or uninterested that they pay very little attention to corporate affairs, being interested mainly in stock prices or short-run dividends.

In an influential article published in 1980,[37] Robert Hayes and William Abernathy of the Harvard Business School attributed the "marked deterioration of competitive vigor" and the "growing unease about the overall economic well-being" of American business "not to general economic conditions alone," but to "the failure of American managers to keep their companies technologically competitive over the long run." Hayes and Abernathy therefore attribute managerial failure mainly to various aspects of the

American management system, especially:

(1) The reliance on "principles which prize analytical detachment and methodological elegance over insight, based on experience, into the subtleties and complexities of strategic decisions. As a result, maximum short-term financial returns have become the overriding criteria for many companies."

(2) American managers are increasingly financial and legal experts with limited technical training and little "intimate hands-on knowledge of the companies' technologies, customers and suppliers."

(3) The short-run profit-maximizing orientation also will lead managers to pursue unproductive and debilitating conglomerate mergers. These managers divert resources from more productive undertakings, shift managerial attention away from core technologies and markets; ". . .the great bulk of this merger activity appears to have been absolutely wasted in terms of generating economic benefits for stockholders."

Others, including many business leaders themselves, have made similar criticisms of American management. Robert Reich, former director of policy planning at the Federal Trade Commission, strongly criticized American managers for concentrating too much on accountants, lawyers, and financial experts (the "pie slicers") and not enough on engineers and inventors (the "pie enlargers").[38] In a similar vein, Seymour Melman, Columbia University industrial engineering professor, questions whether American managers as a group are "interested in and capable of restoring competence in production" required for national industrial renewal. "A generation of managers has been trained by our business schools to make money, not goods. Gripped by a dogma called 'management science,' the schools have played an important institutional role in the erosion of the competence for production."[39]

American managers became a source of national pride and international envy during and after World War II. In fact, in 1968 the French journalist Servan-Schrieber in *The American Challenge* argued that U.S. management methods were so superior to the European that the Americans were in the process of taking over the European economy. However, according to Melman:

> As managers' competence in making goods becomes increasingly rare, and ploys for making money dominate, industrial decay spreads. Top managers in central offices leave entire communities and regions economically stranded. Imported goods replace American goods. Jobs in producing occupations are severely reduced, hardly affected by the trickle of work in high-tech industries. . . .[40]

Reginald Jones, former chairman of General Electric, believes too many corporate managers let their companies get "fat and sloppy" in the boom years of the 1950s and 1960s and therefore failed to meet foreign competition in the 1970s. There were many other reasons for their economic decline (world economic turmoil, government regulation), but according to Jones, "the evidence is that our foreign competitors are moving quickly to adopt the new technologies that will dominate the factories and offices of tomorrow.''[41]

Jones concluded:

> . . . there is a legitimate complaint against the tyranny of Wall Street, with its myopic concentration on quarterly results. . . . There has been a fundamental change in the ownership of American industry—a great decline in the investor and an increase in the trader, who was also under great pressure for results.[42]

The Japanese Management System

As noted, many experts believe Japan's main advantage over the United States to be its management system. The traditional contrasts between the American management system and the Japanese management system are as follows:

• The Japanese system is characterized by lifetime employment, where regular workers are hired until age fifty-five, whereas American workers have limited job security and are less likely to retain their jobs during recessions. The lifetime employment system has the disadvantage of high levels of concealed unemployment during recession, but has the advantages of (a) giving workers and employers long-term relationships; (b) making employers more willing to provide better training; and (c) causing workers to identify more with the company and to be more willing to be rotated into a variety of jobs. Lifetime employment therefore contributes greatly to flexibility in labor use. It causes Japanese management to view regular workers as fixed costs and therefore to see to expand output and market share, especially during slack business periods, rather than the American practice of attempting to maximize short-term profits by holding prices up and laying off workers. Lifetime employment reflects the longer time perspective of Japanese managers, who give heavy emphasis to the development of the latest technology.

• The Japanese seniority and bonus compensation system compensates workers more for education and seniority or age than for the specific job they do. In fact, regular Japanese workers view their work as careers rather than jobs. American wage systems are likely to compensate the job while Japanese systems compensate the worker. A large part of the Japanese worker's wage is likely to be in the form of a semiannual bonus; this creates a much more flexible compensation system since during economic downturns it is much easier not to pay a bonus than to try to cut wages. Wage increases are negotiated each spring and are likely to reflect economic conditions. Moreover, the spread between the salaries of top managers and workers in likely to be much smaller than in the United States, providing greater unity between workers and managers.

• The main structure of collective bargaining in Japan is the enterprise, reflecting strong company identification and lifetime employment. Unions are mainly concerned with the level of wages and not the structure. Most American employers seek to avoid unions, while major Japanese employers apparently consider unions to be an integral part of the system in core enterprises. This attitude in part explains the less adversial labor-management relationship in Japan since the turbulent 1950s.

• In Japan there is a heavy emphasis on communications and consensus management, which is a hard thing for Westerners to understand. It is an amalgam of control from the top, but consensus-building in order to be sure the group thoroughly understands the decision. A typical Japanese view is "I am led by my superior to make a decision, rather than making it myself."[43] The Japanese view is "I am led by my superior to make a decision, rather than making it myself." This clearly is a different concept from the Western idea of participatory democracy.

The Japanese have a strong sense of group consciousness that has deep cultural and historical roots. Cooperation has been necessary to survival in Japan. Group consciousness also is deeply embedded in Confucian thought. American thought emphasizes individual satisfaction whereas the Japanese see individual satisfaction as deriving from the group and not from individuals, so some mechanism is required to be sure individuals understand their responsibilities.

The American system, by contrast, stresses hierarchical decision-making processes, fragmentation of work, and individual responsibility. It is deeply embedded in Western religion, Anglo-American law and custom, and in the American "scientific management" system, which was developed to fit early mass production manufacturing that used primarily unskilled labor. There are those who believe the Japanese system is better suited to coordinating work in a modern global information setting, where workers have considerable discretion, and where quality is critically important. The American system attempts to control quality and work performance through management oversight, detailed work standards and specifications, and individual wage payment systems based on the job. Proponents of the Japanese system argue that group responsibility, coupled with strong identification with the company, generalized training, and heavy emphasis on quality control through preventing defects by means of good engineering and worker participation systems give Japanese companies a decided advantage.

Because of these differences in management practices it is not surprising that a U.S. Chamber of Commerce Study found that only 9 percent of American workers thought they would benefit from increased productivity, and only 23 percent thought they were working at full capacity, whereas 93 percent of Japanese workers believed they would benefit from improvements in their firms' productivity and profitability.[44]

William Ouchi,[45] summarizes the differences between American and Japanese management organizations as follows:

Japanese organization	*American organization*
Lifetime employment	Short-term employment
Slow evaluation and promotion	Rapid evaluation and promotion
Nonspecialized career paths	Specialized career paths
Implicit control mechanisms	Explicit control mechanisms
Collective responsibility	Individual responsibility
Holistic concern for workers	Segmented concern for workers

Another comparison[46] of Japanese and American managerial characteristics is:

	Japanese (Orchestra conductor)	American (Military commander)
1. Basic role	Organize environment	Decision making
2. Characteristic	General manager	Specialist
3. Expected ability	Organize team efforts	Individual creativity
4. Communication	Free form	Hierarchy
5. Key in management	Human relations	Functional
6. Administration	Consensus	Objective
7. Authority	Centralized	Decentralized

Are These Contrasts Valid?

The contrasts often made between Japanese and American management systems do have some basis in reality, but both are clearly stereotypes and based on myths, which mask considerable diversity. One of the myths is that the Japanese system is deeply rooted in Japanese culture and cannot be transferred to other places. Actually the system is compatible with Japanese culture, but many aspects of it—especially lifetime employment, harmonious labor-management relations, and enterprise unionism—were developed during the 1950s after a period of considerable labor-management conflict in the immediate postwar period. Japanese public officials, in close cooperation with business and labor leaders, developed an export-driven industrial policy which emphasized quality production at low cost, in order to overcome Japan's economic problems and the early (before the 1960s) image of "made in Japan" as a mark of inferiority.

It is also a myth that the Japanese "miracle" is due to the Japanese management system. Indeed, it is curious how many "one-factor" explanations there are for the so-called "Japanese miracle." However, the evidence shows the Japanese management system to be part of and closely related to larger systems, all of which go together to explain Japanese economic performance. It would be difficult—if not impossible—to single out any one part of a system or subsystem as *the* explanation. Because they are much better organized than we are, the concept of "systems within coordinated systems" is more obvious in Japan than it is in the United States. Other factors in the overall Japanese system include:

• There is a great deal of national homogeneity and cohesion caused by history and the absolute necessity to be competitive in international markets. Japanese managers give much more attention to the national interest in their corporate strategies and are much more likely than their American counterparts to have a close working relationship with the government, as well as with their unions. The virtual absence of the adversary relationships that characterize American labor-management and public-private negotiations facilitates consensus-building, worker participation, and better government regulatory and economic policy. Japanese health, safety, and environmental regulations, for example, are as stringent as those of the U.S. and cost more relative to GNP, but they are more effective because they are based on consensus cooperation and not litigation. The homogeneity of the Japanese population also means that they do not have to spend as much energy trying to build harmony as is necessary in the United States.

• Japanese workers in large export-oriented companies apparently are better educated and trained than their American counterparts. Over 90 percent of Japanese high-school-age youths are graduated from high school and 40 percent of these go to college. Regular Japanese workers undergo extensive training on the job, including math and technical subjects. Japanese high school students typically take six years of science and math, one year of calculus, and six years of English, and Japan, with half the population of the U.S., educates twice as many engineers. In the early 1980s in the United States, half of all high school graduates took no 11th or 12th grade math or science, only 16 percent took one year of chemistry, 9 percent one year of physics, and 7 percent one year of calculus; at the same time, 25 million Americans could not read or write; 72 million Americans—including 47 percent of black 17-year-olds and 56 percent of all Hispanics—were functionally illiterate.[47]

• The Japanese management system also has worked within the framework of a relatively well-coordinated comprehensive, export-driven industrial policy based on close public-private cooperation. That policy was made possible by a permissive international market, especially during the Korean War and the 1950s and 1960s. The ingredients of that policy included the maintenance of low interest rates; a credit system that reduced risks to the enterprise and made it possible for companies to have relatively high debt-equity ratios, relieving management of the need to rely on stock markets and facilitating long-range decisions; high savings and investment ratios; trade policy to encourage exports and limit competitive imports until Japanese industry was ready to compete; production sharing, whereby low-wage work was sent to the third world while high-wage work was kept in Japan; and heavy emphasis on technology.

By contrast, the U.S. has followed uncoordinated trade and economic policy; has promoted policies leading to high interest rates; has had very limited control over immigration, given lower priority to human resource development, and developed no strategy other than the brute force of very imperfect markets to shift people out of declining industries; has done little through either tax or other policies to develop cooperative regulatory processes, discourage unproductive conglomerate mergers or encourage long-run technological viability, or to increase savings and productive investments; and has done relatively little to develop a coherent trade policy that reconciles the legitimate concerns of workers and producers with those of consumers based on the realities of the modern world. The only consistency in American economic policy is its lack of coherence and continuity and the ideological faith that the market will take care of things.

• The Japanese management system (JMS) is likely to be misinterpreted if one concentrates on the relatively small 15 to 20 percent of the work force that has security. As Table 12.6 shows, many American workers actually have greater job tenure than the Japanese.

In Japan job security is greater for relatively young workers, especially males, but older American workers have greater job tenure than older Japanese workers.

This raises another important qualification about the management system in Japan, namely that it permits job security for between 15 and 20 percent of the workers concentrated in about a third of the economy heavily devoted to exports. This system conceals inefficiencies in the rest of the economy and is made possible by less secure "shock absorbers," many of which would not be either legal or feasible in the U.S. These include a subcontracting system where workers have lower wages and much less security; a secondary labor force made up of older workers, women, minorities, and the less-educated; production sharing; and the bonus system, which, as noted, provides wage flexibility.

It also should be noted that the Japanese economy is less productive than the American economy (because average productivity in Japan is only about two-thirds to three-fourths that of the United States), even though some core export industries are more productive, though generally less profitable than their American counterparts. It is also clear that the Japanese, with limited resources, have done an excellent job with public and private management systems in managing their resources for maximum economic growth, productivity, and international competitiveness.

Finally, the Japanese system faces strains that probably will make it less competitive in the future. Those who would rush to emulate the Japanese should recall that there have been many other "models" in the world which no longer look very promising: the British, the Dutch, the Swedish, the German, the American, and even, for some, the Yugoslavs and the Soviets. The problems that will confront the Japanese system include growing worldwide competition, especially from the third world; the aging of the Japanese population, which will place great strain on the "lifetime" employment system; the need to invent (rather than import and adapt) technology; the changing composition of industry, especially the growth of services, where productivity growth is harder to maintain; and

Table 12.6

Job Tenure in the U.S. and Japan

Age	% with same companies for 20 or more years		
	U.S.	Japan all	male
25–39	1	7	11
40–44	7	22	31
45–49	17	23	32
50–54	25	17	24
55–59	30	13	18
60–64	33	9	13
65 +	35	11	14

Sources: U.S.: R. E. Hall, "The Importance of Lifetime Jobs in the U.S. Economy," *American Economic Review* (September 1982); Japan: Kogi Taira, "Economic Growth, Labor Productivity, and Employment Adjustment in Japan," paper presented to the 1982 annual meetings of the Industrial Relations Research Association.

changing tastes of the Japanese, who have been willing in the past to sacrifice quality of life for economic growth, but who probably will be more reluctant to do so in the future.

Conclusion

Any understanding of the complex, dynamic constellation of forces affecting the international division of labor must be eclectic. Static neoclassical or Marxist paradigms have some utility, but are inadequate, especially as foundations for economic policy. In third world and industrialized market economy countries, international market forces as well as the nature of domestic economies and public policies will determine the shift of economic power between countries. Internationalization was accelerated by the institutions put in place immediately after World War II. Based largely on the overwhelming power of the United States, these institutions assumed "free trade" based mainly on static orthodox trade theory. However, the emergence of Western Europe, Japan, and the newly industrialized countries and the greater volume of economic transactions have eroded the viability of these institutions. The major shifts in economic power in the 1970s and 1980s were from Europe and the United States to Japan and the Pacific rim countries. The main causes of these shifts have been higher wages and capital costs in the United States, as well as the development of very competitive export-driven industrial policies and production systems, especially in Japan. The Japanese management system is especially competitive relative to the older authoritarian American management systems in oligopolistic enterprises. However, the lack of coordinated, coherent U.S. economic policy is at least as responsible for foreign penetration of American markets as management systems. Clearly, however, the fact that the U.S. is a high-wage country means that multinational countries will tend to shift jobs out of the U.S. unless there are other advantages—technology, skilled workers, supportive economic policies, superior management, proximity to markets—that compensate for wage differences. If wages between the U.S. and other countries become more equal, as they have been as a result of the devaluation of the dollar after 1985, poor management systems and passive economic policies will cause a continued erosion of the U.S. industrial base and national economic power.

In discussing global matters we often speak as if countries gain or lose from international transactions; however, it is the different economic interests within countries that benefit or lose from these transactions. The clear gainers are multinational corporations, which, especially those operating from the United States, are losing their national identities. However, the power of multinationals is neither static nor absolute. The main losers from international transactions have been (a) relatively high-wage American workers, whose wages are being driven to lower international levels and (b) American companies that are unable either to compete in international markets or to shift to foreign operations. Consumers have gained if their real incomes have not been reduced more by their losses as producers than they have gained through lower-priced, higher-quality imports. Is is a mistake to assume, however, that competition forces all foreign producers' lower costs to be passed on to consumers—domestic importers and foreign producers share cost differentials through higher profit margins since foreign and domestic products tend to sell at the same prices in national markets.

It is not clear how much most third world workers gain from international transactions. Many clearly do not benefit very much and in many third world countries income distributions are widening. There is, moreover, considerable displacement of third world workers by capital-intensive production techniques more appropriate to first world conditions. These developments contribute to high levels of joblessness as well as economic and political instability.

The United States has done better in maintaining job growth, but Europe has maintained higher real wage growth and income support for displaced workers. However, a major problem of the welfare states of Europe is how to prevent international competition from eroding their traditional high-income support levels—which means that they too must pay more attention to flexibility and productivity. Japan appears to have done a much better job of maintaining real wage growth and low levels of unemployment through highly productive management systems and better coordinated economic policies. However, it is doubtful that Japan can sustain rates of growth in the 1980s and 1990s comparable to those of the 1960s and 1970s.

It also is highly unlikely that the international economic systems will grow as much in the future as they did in the postwar period. Indeed, it will take considerable effort to prevent the international system from stagnating or degenerating. The main threats to the system are:

1. The decline of U.S. economic hegemony, which means there is no single entity whose interests will maintain economic order. A confederation of nations is required to reestablish the international system, but that appears unlikely at least for the rest of this decade. Moreover, the only IMEC country that could provide the leadership for such a confederation is the United States, whose economic policies have unilaterally destabilized the international system and whose laissez-faire "free trade" ideology prevents American leaders from establishing the economic governance mechanisms required to strengthen a relatively open and expanding trading system.

2. The industrialized countries are too preoccupied with their own problems to realize that a broader view of their own self-interest requires much greater attention to the economic health of the developing countries. High external debts will block the development of the third world countries for at least the rest of this decade.

3. In the absence of strong, steady growth and predictable economic policies in the U.S., there is a danger of stagnation at high levels of unemployment in the U.S. and other countries, exacerbated by degenerating protectionism that will deny all countries the positive benefits of an expanding and open international trading system.

4. There is considerable policy confusion in most major European countries as well as the United States. This policy confusion results from the lack of consensus on economic policies to replace the Keynesian system that served these countries very well until the late 1960s, but was unable to deal with the problems of internationalization and structural change.[48]

As a result of the trends outlined in this paper there is a tendency for manufacturing and mining to shift to Japan and the newly industrializing and developing countries and for service, financial, and information work to shift to the United States and Western Europe. This does not mean, of course, that the U.S. and Western Europe will have no manufacturing and that other areas will not have financial service, and other workers—it is a matter of marginal shifts and relative composition. The United States and Western Europe will not retain high value-added service activities without high value-added manufacturing. There is a tendency, for example, for economies to lose their advantages in technological innovation when they lose competitiveness in the commodities. Innovation is likely to be by enterprises experiencing growing market share, not by those who are losing it. Unless the United States and other advanced industrial countries maintain technological and organizational advantages, competition is likely to be mainly on the basis of labor costs (assuming financial markets to be internationalized). High-wage countries will therefore experience declining real wages unless technology, higher quality human resources, or better management systems give them productivity advantages. Moreover, since most advances in technology must be embodied in products workers are not likely to learn advanced technologies without sophisticated manufacturing capacities. This means, in turn, that countries (or geographical areas) wishing to maintain real wage advantages must have sophisticated manufacturing capability in order to sustain technology and must emphasize productivity, quality, flexibility, and human resource development. The U.S. currently has a significant technological lead, but it is not clear that it has world-class human resource development or management systems. This implies a continued decline in competitiveness and real wages.

The eclectic or institutional approach provides several advantages in understanding these trends in the international division of labor. The first is to provide a more flexible conceptual framework to let the empirical evidence lead to conclusions rather than forcing those conclusions into more restrictive deductive theoretical systems. Second, the eclectic approach is better able to deal with dynamic events, which have multiple causation and therefore do not lead to necessarily predetermined outcomes. The relationship are more organic, synergistic, and cumulative than mechanical, as implied by both the Marxist and neoclassical paradigms. Finally, the eclectic approach facilitates the development of enterprise, organizational, and public strategies to shape economic development and outcomes by relying on combinations of market forces and policy intervention to cause long-run results—as the Japanese have done. It would be very difficult for either the Marxists or the neoclassicals to explain unambiguously either the loss of competitiveness of the American economy or the emergence of the Japanese and East Asian economies as satisfactorily as can be done with an institutionalist or eclectic approach. Japanese national strategies have been important reasons for their economic success and the absence of a coherent national strategy has been responsible for the failure of the United States to make the most effective use of its resources. The importance of strategy means that enterprises and countries can choose their futures through policy intervention more than implied by either the Marxist or the neoclassical approaches.

Notes

1. New York Stock Exchange, *U.S. International Competitiveness: Perception and Reality* (New York: NYSE, 1984).
2. Ibid.
3. International Monetary Fund, "The Realities of Economic Independence," *Finance and Development* (March 1984): 28–32.
4. Ibid., 30.
5. See Lloyd Ulman, "Multinational Unionism: Incentives, Barriers and Alternatives," *Industrial Relations* 2 (1975): 1–31.
6. See Michael Todero, *Economic Development in the Third World* (New York: Longman, 1981) and Arthur McCormack, *Multinational Investment: Boon or Burden for the Developing Countries?* (New York: W. R. Grace & Co., 1980).
7. Stephen Hymer and Charles Kindleberger, *The International Operation of National Firms* (Cambridge, Mass.: MIT Press, 1976).

8. Raymond Vernon, "International Investment and International Trade in the Product Cycle," *Quarterly Journal of Economics* (May 1966): 190–207.

9. Richard Caves, *Multinational Enterprises and Economic Analysis* (Cambridge, Mass.: Harvard University Press, 1982).

10. F. Fishwick, *Multinational Companies and Economic Concentration in Europe* (Paris: Institute for Research and Information on Multinationals, 1981); T. A. Pugel, *International Market Linkages and U.S. Manufacturing: Prices, Profits and Patterns* (Cambridge, Mass.: Ballinger, 1978); and J. M. Connor, *The Market Power of Multinationals: A Quantitative Analysis of U.S. Corporations in Brazil and Mexico* (New York: Praeger, 1977).

11. S. Lall and P. Streeten, *Foreign Investment, Transnationals and Developing Countries* (London: Macmillan, 1977).

12. Theodore Moran, "Multinational Corporations and the Developing Countries: An Analytical Overview," in T. H. Moran, ed., *Multinational Corporations: The Political Economy of Foreign Direct Investment* (Lexington, Mass.: D. C. Heath, 1985): 4.

13. For this perspective see Fernando H. Cardoso and Enzo Faletto, *Dependencia and Development in Latin America* (Berkeley: University of California Press, 1979); Ernest Mandel, *Marxist Economic Theory* (New York: Monthly Review Press, 1968); and Thomas J. Biersteher, *Distortion or Development: Contending Perspectives on the Multinational Corporations* (Cambridge, Mass.: MIT Press, 1978).

14. D. L. Reuber, *Private Foreign Investment in Development* (Oxford: Clarendon Press, 1973).

15. Michael B. Dolan and Brian Tomlin, "First World-Third World Linkages: External Relations and Economic Development," *International Organization* (Winter 1980): 41–63.

16. Edith Penrose, "Profit Sharing Between Producing Countries and Oil Companies in the Middle East," *Economic Journal* (June 1959): 238–54; and Charles P. Kindleberger, *Economic Development*, 2d ed. (New York: McGraw Hill, 1965).

17. Vernon, *Multinational Spread*.

18. Jorge I. Dominguez, "Business Nationalism: Latin American National Business Attitudes and Behavior Towards Multinational Enterprises," in *Economic Issues and Political Conflict: U.S. Latin American Relations* (London: Butterworth, 1982); and Stephen J. Kobrin, "Foreign Enterprises and Forced Divestment in LDCs," *International Organization* (Winter 1980): 65–88; and Peter Evans, *Dependent Development: The Alliance of Multinational, State and Local Capital in Brazil* (Princeton: Princeton University Press, 1979).

19. Moran, "Multinational Corporations," 15.

20. Richard Sklar, *Corporate Power in an African State: The Political Impact of Multinational Mining Companies in Zambia* (Berkeley: University of California Press, 1975).

21. Clark Kerr, John Dunlop, F. Harbison, and Charles Meyers, *Industrialism and Industrial Man* (Cambridge, Mass.: Harvard University Press, 1960).

22. Ray Marshall, *Labor in the South* (Cambridge, Mass.: Harvard University Press, 1967).

23. Otto Eckstein, et al., *The DRI Report on U.S. Manufacturing Industries* (Data Resources, Inc., McGraw-Hill, 1984); J. Steven Landefeld and K. H. Young, "The Trade Deficit and the Value of the Dollar," *Business Economics* (October 1985): 11–17; and Roger Brinner, "The United States as an International Competitor" (Testimony before the Joint Economic Committee of the U.S. Congress, March 12, 1985).

24. Bruce Scott, "National Strategies for Stronger U.S. Competition," *Harvard Business Review* (March-April 1984): 77–91.

25. New York Stock Exchange, *U.S. International Competitiveness*, 12.

26. See Figure 12.1; Bruce Scott and George Lodge, *U.S. Competitiveness in the World Economy* (Boston, Mass.: Harvard Business School Press, 1985), 28; and President's Commission on Industrial Competitiveness, *Global Competition: The New Reality* (Washington, D.C.: GPO, 1984), vol. 3, 13.

27. Steven Cohen, David Teece, Laura Tyson, and John Zysman, "Competitiveness" (Working Paper for the President's Commission on Industrial Competitiveness, November 8, 1984), 17.

28. Ibid., 19.

29. U.S. Department of Commerce, *Japanese Technology Evaluation Program Report on Opto- and Microelectronics* (Washington, D.C.: GPO, 1985).

30. U.S. Bureau of Labor Statistics, *Employment and Earnings*, various years.

31. Brinner, "The United States as Competitor."

32. Cohen et al., "Competitiveness," 32.

33. Karen Anderson, "The Elusive Productivity Boom," *New York Times* (April 8, 1984): sec.3,1.

34. A. G. Athos and R. T. Pascale, *The Art of Japanese Management* (New York: Simon and Schuster, 1981), 21.

35. Arnold Judson, "The Awkward Truth About Productivity," *Harvard Business Review* (September–October 1982): 93–97.

36. Adolf Berle and Gardiner Means, *The Modern Corporation and Private Property*, (New York: Macmillan, 1933), 6.

37. Robert Hayes and William Abernathy, "Managing Our Way to Economic Decline," *Harvard Business Review* (July–August 1980): 67–77.

38. Robert Reich, "Pie Slicers vs. Pie Enlargers," *Washington Monthly* (September 1980).

39. Seymour Melman, "Managers' Debacle," *New York Times* (November 4, 1983): A–27.

40. Ibid.

41. See Peter Behr, "American Management," pt. 1, *Washington Post* (January 17, 1982).

42. Peter Behr, "American Management: Serving Only the Present," *Washington Post* (January 20, 1982).

43. Ken Ohmae, "Japanese Companies Are Run from the Top, *Wall Street Journal* (April 26, 1982).

44. Public Agenda Foundation, *Putting the Work Ethic to Work* (New York: Public Agenda Foundation, 1983).

45. See William Ouchi, *Theory Z* (New York: Avon Books, 1981).

46. Taken from testimony of Yawata Keiske before the Joint Economic Committee, U.S. Congress, June 22, 1981.

47. Adult Performance Level Project, College of Education, University of Texas-Austin, 1983.

48. For an elaboration of this theme see Ray Marshall, *Unheard Voices: Labor and Economic Policy in a Competitive World* (New York: Basic Books, 1987).

PART IV

13

GLOBAL TRANSFORMATION OR DECAY?

ALTERNATIVE PERSPECTIVES ON RECENT CHANGES IN THE WORLD ECONOMY

David M. Gordon

Automate, emigrate, or evaporate.
> —*New York Times* on international competition, March 4, 1982

To many observers and activists, recent transformations in the global economy have seemed increasingly threatening to the job security, working conditions, and livelihoods of workers in the advanced economies. The power of labor has seemed to wither as multinational corporations sweep irresistibly around the globe.

Widespread analytic preoccupation with tendencies toward a New International Division of Labor (NIDL) and the Globalization of Production (GOP) have reinforced these trepidations. For many, these twin tendencies manifest such deep structural transformations that group or government efforts to swim against the currents appear to have become increasingly futile.

The roots of these concerns are obvious. Controlling for the business cycle, unemployment has been rising steadily in advanced capitalist countries since the

The author, who is on the faculty of the New School for Social Research in New York City, is grateful to Lyuba Zarsky for excellent research assistance. He would also like to thank seminar and conference participants at the New School for Social Research, the University of Massachusetts at Amherst, and Cornell University, as well as Bennett Harrison, Alain Lipietz, and Samuel Bowles for helpful reactions to earlier formulations of some of these arguments. The gross excesses in the chapter remain the author's responsibility.

early 1970s. Workers in many traditional industries, such as auto and steel, have suffered devastating employment losses. Employees in scores of sectors have confronted increasingly insistent corporate demands for concessions on wages, benefits, and working conditions and have faced more and more frequent warnings about plant shutdowns and capital relocation. Intensifying international competition appears to be casting its shadow more and more broadly across the economic landscape, chilling the spirit of growing numbers of organized and unorganized workers alike.[1]

Some of these concerns are clearly warranted, since there have been some striking changes in the dynamics of the world economy over the past fifteen years. But many of these concerns about an NIDL and the GOP may also be misplaced, stemming from a transposition of trend and long cycle, confusing the effects of continuing stagnation in the world capitalist economy with the auguries of an emerging transformation of the global capitalist order. It is not always easy to discriminate between the decay of an older order and the inauguration of a new.

One important source of this possible conflation of stagnation and transformation, I suspect, lies at the heart of the subject of this volume—in the analytic foundations of alternative views of labor economics.[2] Since so many of the phenomena associated with the New International Division of Labor and the Globalization of Production affect labor and appear to reflect changes in the political economy of production and labor markets, our perceptions of these trends have been shaped inexorably by the inherited wisdom of the principal prevailing traditions of labor economics. Insofar as those traditions may be inadequate, so may be our understandings of recent changes in the global economy.

I argue that recent perceptions about the NIDL and the GOP have indeed been distorted and that we can substantially improve our understanding of recent changes in the global economy. I think in particular that we can profit analytically from application of the emergent framework for studying social structures of accumulation (SSAs).[3] Viewed from that perspective, I believe, recent changes in the global economy are best understood not as a symptom of structural transformation but rather as a consequence of the erosion of the social structure of accumulation which conditioned international capitalist prosperity during the 1950s and 1960s.

This argument leads directly to the somewhat unconventional corollary that we have not recently witnessed the emergence of a fundamentally new international division of labor or an acceleration of the globalization of production. One cannot preclude the possibility of such transformations in the future, of course, but it is equally true, I think, that the inception or inevitability of such structural changes is not yet confirmed.

I organize this argument into five sections. I first review the prevailing perceptions of trends toward an NIDL and the GOP and the main apparent analytic responses to those trends by representatives of the three views of labor economics. I then present some synthetic historical evidence on the character and relative importance of recent changes in the global economy which grounds my skepticism about the adequacy of much of the conventional wisdom. A third section then develops an alternative view of these recent trends through application of the SSA perspective, sketching a brief synthetic macro institutional account of the structure and erosion of the global political economy in the postwar period. The final major section reviews some first tentative steps toward formal modeling and empirical testing of the differences between prevailing perceptions and the analysis I develop in this paper. A final concluding section briefly reviews the implications of this analysis.

Prevailing Perceptions of a
Changing Global Economy

Distinguishing among secular, crisis, and transformational trends in the global economy would be difficult enough. Our task is further complicated by a difference between two somewhat divergent hypotheses about structural transformations. I shall refer to these as the NIDL and the GOP hypotheses respectively.

The NIDL perspective places particular stress on a new division of labor between the North and the South, between the advanced and the developing countries.[4] In a critical review of this perspective, Dieter Ernst has usefully summarized its internal logic:

> According to the NIDL theory, a new capitalist world economy has emerged, its main feature being a massive migration of capital from major OECD countries to low-cost production sites in the Third World. The main purpose of establishing such a new international division of labour is to exploit reserve supplies of labour on a world scale. This type of an internationalization of capital requires the existence of world markets for labour and production sites, and of one global industrial reserve army of labour.[5]

The GOP perspective places much less emphasis on the movement of production from the North to the South and much more weight on the centralization and concentration of capital through two related developments: first, the spreading importance of decentralized production sites in both the advanced and the developing countries; and second, the increasingly centralized control and coordination by transnational corporations (TNC) of these decentralized production units. These two trends have combined, according to the GOP, to foster both increasing international interdependence and enhanced TNC leverage over national governments and domestic unions.[6]

There is already a rich literature on the importance of one or another of these two tendencies, although the two hypotheses are not always distinguished with appropriate precision. While there are no obvious formal and comprehensive treatments of these hypotheses from any of the three views of labor economics, representatives from each of the three traditions have tended selectively to emphasize one or another critical dimension of the changes highlighted by the NIDL/GOP perspective.

The Neoclassical Approach

Neoclassical labor economists appear to have responded with equanimity to recent changes in the global economy. Insofar as it appears to many that competitive pressures have intensified since the early 1970s, neoclassical economists have in general applauded the effects of that development. The more that labor market imperfections erode, other things being equal, the more likely it becomes that increasingly rigorous cost minimization is guiding the geographic allocation of resources internationally and the circulation of commodities among production sites around the globe.[7]

Analytically, this appears to reinforce the general neoclassical inclination to view the international division of labor as both technically determined and productively efficient. Recent changes in the pattern of resource allocation are therefore likely to be viewed as desirable movements toward an appropriate global specialization based on factor costs and resource endowments. The razor's edge of comparative advantage has reasserted itself. William Branson's useful review essay stresses this aspect of recent developments:

> In the ten years or so after World War II, the United States had a false boom in exports of goods that are relatively labor intensive in production. But after the mid–1950s comparative advantage reasserted itself with the growth of industrial capacity in Europe and Japan. The United States trade pattern moved back to a base in comparative advantage. . . . In the 1970s, growth in industrial capacity in the LDCs seems to be generally along lines of their comparative advantage. This is strengthening the pattern of United States trade in a world of increasing specialization and interdependence.[8]

Robert Lawrence agrees in his assessment of underlying trends for the U.S. economy:

> The United States has been developing a growing comparative advantage in high-technology and resource-intensive products, while its comparative advantage in labor-intensive and capital-intensive products manufactured with standardized technologies has been eroding. There is, therefore, a correspondence between the U.S. industries experiencing slow economic growth because of sluggish domestic use and those experiencing declining comparative advantage.[9]

The policy implications of this analytic emphasis follow naturally. As ever, economic actors should try to avoid interfering with the market signals guiding resource allocation. If it is true, as the neoclassical account would appear to stress, that a relatively efficient pattern of international specialization is asserting itself, then we should resist the natural political temptation to stem those tides. This inclination appears to guide a strong neoclassical counteroffensive against recent proposals for some kind of "industrial policy" initiatives to cushion the blows and counter the impact of recent NIDL/GOP tendencies.[10] Charles Schultze has recently stressed this traditional neoclassical policy concern with particular vigor:

> In general, when government extends its control over the allocation of resources, monopoly and oligopoly interests are protected, prices are driven up, natural industrial change is impeded, and the consumer suffers. . . . As a way of choosing what private goods to produce, you can't beat the market. The right criterion for making such choices is fundamentally that of the market anyway: to produce those goods and services that people want to buy, at a price that brings in a reasonable profit.[11]

For those who worry about the economic consequences for workers of these market shifts, neoclassical economists are typically reassuring. Robert Lawrence projects, for example, that "Given reasonable economic expansion and international price competitiveness, structural change should now be relatively easy to accommodate in the remainder of the 1980s."[12]

The Institutionalist Approach

Fueled by their continuing interest in concrete economic behavior, institutionalists have provided us with some of our richest and most acute recent accounts of the changing global economy.[13] Although it is often difficult, virtually by methodological definition, to generalize about the institutionalist literature, recent accounts appear to have stressed two central aspects of the changing global economy. These two concerns reflect continuing institutionalist focus on the interplay of unions and large firms in the coordination of production.

Some, particularly Piore and Sabel,[14] have stressed the production dimensions of recent changes in the topography of comparative advantage. Inferring a "second industrial divide," they have argued that the character and recent acceleration of automation have undermined traditional "mass production" methods and have heightened the relative cost advantages of new, technologically advanced "small-batch" modes of organizing production. This shift has tended to reward those economies in which it has been easiest for entrepreneurs either to wriggle free of the institutional web of traditional production relations or to start from scratch on the foundations of a new complex of more flexible institutions. Piore and Sabel conclude: ". . .the spread of flexible specialization suggests that the way out of the crisis requires a shift of technological paradigm and a new system of regulation. If recovery proceeds by this path, then the 1970s and 80s will be seen in retrospect as a turning point in the history of mechanization. . . ."[15]

Institutionalist narratives have also stressed the special importance of shifts toward more flexible and technically advanced methods of administrative coordination, permitting much more efficient centralized coordination—whether in the advanced or the developing countries—of decentralized production sites. This tendency has both strengthened the relative leverage of firms that are best equipped for centralized coordination, the TNCs, and has reinforced the relative attractiveness of smaller, decentralized production sites. Bluestone and Harrison conclude:

> Centralization is the aspect of modern capitalist development that gave rise to the process of conglomeration. But centralization has also undermined the economic stability of communities across the country indirectly, through its tendency to increase the degree of absentee control of a community's economic base. All of these shifts of facilities or transfers of ownership during the 1960s and, with greater intensity and at a more rapid pace in the 1970s, have radically altered what some have called the 'geography of industrial organization.'[16]

These two aspects of the GOP combine to outline the potential shape of a new era. Piore and Sabel write that:

> . . . it is conceivable that flexible specialization and mass production could be combined in a unified *international* economy. In this system, the old mass-production industries might migrate to the underdeveloped world, leaving behind in the industrialized world the high-tech industries and the traditional dispersed conglomerations in machine tools, garments, footwear, textile, and the like—all revitalized through the fusion of traditional skills and high technology.[17]

The Marxist Approach

Many Marxists have been surprisingly slow in responding to recent changes in the global economy. This probably stems to some degree from a dissonance between (a) the apparent advantages that Third World economies have appeared to gain in recent years (through the NIDL/GOP) and (b) the traditional presuppositions about imperialist exploitation which dominated earlier generations of Marxian analysis. In the traditional view, to choose Mandel's formulation, "the law of value inexorably compels the backward countries with a low level of labour productivity to specialize on the world market in a manner disadvantageous to themselves."[18] If it has been true in recent years that many newly industrializing countries have been overcoming and indeed transforming these traditional terms of disadvantage, what of the traditional inexorability? As Alain Lipietz has sharply observed in reviewing the reactions of many traditional Marxists, "Two stopped watches clock the movement of history. The South is stagnating? The 'dependency' watch gives the exact time. A 'new industrialization' is emerging? It's time for a 'take-off.' The 'newly industrializing countries' are entering a crisis? Well, dependency theory has always argued. . . .''[19]

Some Marxists have nonetheless responded directly to recent developments.[20] Three main characteristics seem to be reflected in these recent responses.

1. Many Marxists appear to have subscribed unequivocally to the NIDL/GOP hypotheses. One reads frequently of a "world-wide reorganisation of capitalist production[21] and of its direct links to the evolution of the recent international crisis of capital.[22]

2. Among those highlighting the possibility of a movement toward an NIDL/GOP, Marxists in particular have emphasized the critical importance of low wages and surplus labor in the periphery as a source of capital relocation. Frank explains: "Costs of production are reduced by moving industry to the Third World, particularly labor-intensive industries. . . . From the point of view of the world capitalist economy this is a transfer of part of industrial production from high- to low-cost areas.''[23]

3. Like neoclassical economists, some Marxists have tended to emphasize the intensification of competition on a world scale and the increasingly rigorous determination of production sites by the cost-minimizing calculus of capitalist firms. Froebel concludes: "The extra profits promised by a world-wide reorganization of capitalist production in accordance with these new conditions for individual firms, and the universalisation of this reorganisation through the mechanism of competition, are sufficient to explain the *possibility and reality of such a reorganisation in a qualitative sense.*''[24]

These inclinations lead to a strong policy emphasis on the futility of government interventions in an era of accelerating capital mobility and spreading capitalist integration of the world market.[25] In the advanced countries, "Keynesian and neo-Keynesian economic and social policies demonstrably do not work any longer. . . .''[26] In the Third World, similarly, "one government after another is falling over itself to offer favorable conditions to international capital. . . . In fact, the whole state apparatus has to be adapted to the Third World role in the new international division of labor.''[27] The power of capital reasserts itself once again!

A Skeptical View of the Evidence for the NIDL/GOP Hypotheses

There can be little question that some important recent changes have taken place in the global economy or that workers in advanced countries have been experiencing wrenching dislocation. But there is good reason, it turns out, to be cautious about the conclusions that much of the literature has been drawing from these trends. The NIDL/GOP hypotheses refer to the union of several generalizations about recent tendencies in the global economy. I have tried to organize relevant empirical evidence on the most important of these generalizations. Given my concern to distinguish among trend, cycle, and transformation, I have tried wherever possible to array data over as long a historical period as possible. Where data have permitted, I have compared trends over the last several long swings of the world capitalist economy and have compiled observations for the postwar period which measure changes from one business cycle peak to another.[28] Since I do not have the space here to review the wealth of available data on all relevant aspects of the NIDL/GOP hypotheses, I shall merely highlight some of the most important conclusions from continuing work-in-progress.

The Globalization of Production?

It seems incontrovertible that there has recently been rapid growth of industrial production in many developing countries, particularly in those typically designated as "newly industrializing countries" (NICs):[29]

• Between 1966 and 1984, for example, the developing countries—including the NICs—increased their share of total world industrial production from 12.2 percent to 13.9 percent (see Table 13.1).

• Between 1966 and 1984, similarly, the NICs increased their share of world manufacturing production from 5.7 percent to roughly 8.5 percent (Tables 13.1 and 13.3).

It is much less obvious, however, that this trend augurs the transformations that the NIDL or the GOP imply. In order to put them in some kind of perspective, it seems necessary to consider the evolution of production shares over the broad sweep of long swings in the world capitalist economy.

Table 13.1 presents a synthetic tabulation of shares of world industrial production among relevant economic groupings since the middle of the nineteenth century, choosing reference dates to correspond as closely as possible to the peaks and troughs of the three long swings for the past 155 years. How large are the recent swings in global industrial production within a long-term historical perspective?

The NICs' share of total industrial production increased by 3.7 percentage points from 1966 to 1984—a period of 13 years. We can see that this shift in production shares is smaller than many major historic shifts and is larger than some. The United Kingdom suffered a loss of 6 percentage points over the roughly 15 years from 1886–1900 to 1913, for example, but lost only 1.4 percentage points from 1966 to 1979. The NICs' 1966–79 increase was roughly comparable to the EEC's loss in production share from 1966 to 1979, to pick another example, but far smaller than the gains by the United Kingdom from 1840 to 1870, the United States from 1913 to 1926–29, or the Soviet Union from 1951–1966.

The long-swing framework allows us to organize these data more usefully.

Table 13.1

The Global Distribution of Industrial Production

Country or grouping	1870	1896–1900	1913	1926–1929	1938	1948	1966	1973	1979	1984
United Kingdom	32%	20	14	9	10.2	6.7	4.8	3.8	3.4	3.0
Eur. Econ. Community	—	—	—	—	27.5	15.4	18.8	17.2	15.5	14.1
France	10	7	7	7	7.7	5.4	5.3	5.0	4.8	4.4
Germany	13	17	14	12	12.3	4.6	8.1	7.4	6.4	5.8
Rest of EEC	—	—	—	—	7.5	5.3	5.4	4.8	4.3	3.9
United States	23	30	36	42	28.1	44.4	35.2	29.5	28.3	28.4
Japan	—	1	1	3	5.7	1.6	5.3	7.8	7.4	8.2
Other advanced econs.	15	17	20	19	10.9	9.4	7.1	8.2	7.3	7.3
Centrally pl. econs.	—	—	—	—	7.2	8.4	16.7	19.5	23.5	25.4
USSR	4	5	4	4	4.9	6.3	11.1	12.4	14.2	14.7
Other CPEs	—	—	—	—	2.3	2.2	5.6	7.1	9.3	10.7
Less developed econs.	3	3	4	3	10.4	14.0	12.2	14.0	14.6	13.9
European NICs					2.9	1.9	2.1	2.8	3.0	2.9
Latin America					2.2	4.3	4.1	6.7	6.7	6.3
L. America NICs					1.3	2.9	3.2	3.6	4.2	4.3
Other Asia					2.7	2.5	3.1	2.8	3.1	2.9
Other Asia NICs					0.2	0.1	0.4	0.7	1.3	1.3
Other LDCs					2.5	5.3	2.9	1.7	1.7	1.8

Sources: For 1870 to 1926–29, Walt W. Rostow, *The World Economy: History and Prospect* (Austin, Texas: University of Texas Press, 1978), Table II-2; for 1936 to present, Branson, "Trends," Table 3.9; and United Nations, *Yearbook of Industrial Statistics* (New York: United Nations, various years).

Based entirely on the data in Table 13.1, Table 13.2 provides a summary of these shifts in the distribution of industrial production, identifying those groups of countries whose production shares respectively expanded, declined, and were essentially unaffected during the onset of the three respective stages of accumulation. It appears, that major shifts in the global distribution of industrial production have taken place from the peak of one long swing to the peak of the next—during the periods which Gordon, Edwards, and Reich have identified respectively as the phases of "exploration" and "consolidation" of a given SSA.[30] Once these gains have been achieved, it appears that the production shares of these emergent clusters of industrial powers stabilize or decline slightly during the contraction period of that same long swing.

More specifically, during the constitution of the first stage of accumulation, from 1820 to 1870, the production shares of the United Kingdom and the United

Table 13.2

Stages of Accumulation and the Global Distribution of Production

Stage	Country grouping	Dates	Shares (%)	Dates	Shares (%)
I.	U.K. & U.S.	1820–70	28–55	1870–1900	55–50
	Other advanced		72–38		38–41
	Rest of world		--- 7		7- 9
II.	U.K. & France	1870–1913	61–40	1913–1938	21–17
	U.S. & Germany		36–50		50–45
	Rest of world		22–29		29–38
III.	U.K. & U.S.	1913–66	50–40	1966–1984	40–31
	EEC & other DME		40–26		26–21
	Japan & CPEs		6–22		22–34
	LDCs		4–12		12–14

Source: Based on data in Table 13.1.

States expanded from 28 percent to 55 percent. During the comparable period of the second stage, the combined share of Germany and the United States grew from 36 percent to 50 percent. During the exploration and consolidation of the third stage, the shares of Japan, the centrally planned economies (CPEs), and the LDCs rose from 9 percent to 34 percent. In these three cases, the expanding group's share of global industrial production increased by an average relative increase in shares of 0.4 percentage points per year—a rate of expansion roughly three times the comparable rate of expansion for the NICs from 1966 to 1984.

Table 13.3 reorganizes the data from Table 13.1, distinguishing among (a) the developed market economies (DMEs) whose shares began to decline before or after 1966; (b) Japan and the CPEs, the two sets of mature industrial powers whose shares continued to grow after 1966; and (c) the less-developed economies (LDCs). Table 13.3 suggests two striking conclusions. First, the periods of consolidation and expansion during the first two stages of accumulation represented a simple shuffling of shares among the DMEs, with their combined share holding strong at 89 percent as late as 1926–29. Second, the dramatic decline in the DMEs' share during the postwar period cannot be attributed to an expansion in the relative importance of the LDCs, since the latter's share was no higher in 1984 than it had been in 1948. If anything, indeed, the LDCs have simply recouped the losses in production shares which they suffered from 1948 to 1966. The single most dramatic development of the past thirty-five years is the continuing (relative) expansion of Japan and the centrally planned economies, not the LDCs.

Is it not possible, nonetheless, that this recoupment is taking place at an accelerating rate, portending continually more dramatic shifts to the LDCs or the NICs in the future?

Table 13.3

The Composition of Global Production

Year(s)	DMEs (excl. Japan)	Japan & CPEs	LDCs
1870	93%	4%	3%
1896–1900	91	6	3
1913	91	5	4
1926–29	89	7	3
1938	76.7	12.9	10.4
1948	76.0	10.0	14.0
1966	65.8	22.0	12.2
1973	58.7	27.3	14.0
1979	54.5	30.9	14.6
1984	52.8	33.6	13.9

Source: Based on numbers and sources from Table 13.1.

Table 13.4

Developing Countries' Share of Manufacturing Value-Added

Year	Total LDCs Share	Total LDCs ann. %Δ	NICs Share	NICs ann. %Δ	Other LDCs Share	Other LDCs ann. %Δ
1938	10.1%		4.4		6.0	
1948	14.0	+3.5	4.9	+1.1	9.1	+5.2
1966	12.2	−0.7	5.9	+1.1	6.3	−1.7
1973	14.0	+2.1	7.1	+2.9	6.9	+1.4
1979	14.6	+0.7	8.5	+3.3	6.1	−1.9
1984	13.9	−1.0	8.4	−0.2	5.5	−2.0

Δ = "change"

Tables 13.4 and 13.5 organize the data from Table 13.1 to help evaluate this possibility. We see in Table 13.4, on the one hand, that the non-NIC LDC share of industrial production fell dramatically from 1948 to 1966 and has remained relatively constant since then. We see, on the other hand, that the NIC share of industrial production has indeed expanded fairly steadily during most of the postwar period—although that increase in relative shares appears to have come to an abrupt halt during the 1979–84 cycle.

Table 13.5 presents data on the rates of growth of the indices of industrial production underlying these data on production shares. It shows clearly that LDC industrial production grew rapidly from 1948 to 1966 then at a slightly more rapid

Table 13.5

Growth in Volume of Developing Countries' Industrial Production

Periods	Total LDCs ave. ann. %Δ	NICs ave. ann. %Δ
1948–66	9.4%	14.4%
1966–73	10.7	13.0
1973–79	4.5	7.8
1979–84	0.9	1.8

Sources: Based on data and underlying sources for Table 13.1
Δ = "change"

rate to 1973, and at successively declining rates for the 1973–79 and 1979–84 cycles. The figures for the NICs are consistent with this pattern. The rates of growth of the volume of production from 1948 to 1966 were the most rapid of the postwar period, while the rates of growth in 1966–73, 1973–79, and 1979–84 were both slower and successively declining in comparison to the first phase of long-swing expansion.

None of these tables is decisive, but the combined historical data seem to warrant three provisional conclusions about the NIDL and the GOP presuppositions:

1. The recent shifts of industrial production toward the LDCs and the NICs are not particularly large by relevant historical standards.

2. These recent shifts are not nearly as large as the gains made by the LDCs during the depression and World War II and have served largely to recoup the losses in the LDC share which those countries experienced between the late 1940s and the mid–1960s.

3. It is not at all clear, perhaps most strikingly, that there is an accelerating relative shift of industrial production toward the NICs since the early 1970s. According to the data on shares in Table 13.4, the most recent business cycle is inconsistent with that impression. The underlying data in Table 13.5 suggest, moreover, that the growth in the actual volume of NIC industrial production actually slowed after 1966 but merely at a slower rate than the slowdown in DME industrial production, permitting NIC shares to rise. If and when the advanced world begins to recover from the current crisis, is it obvious that the NICs' shares of global production will continue to rise?

In short, it is not yet possible to distinguish the NIDL/GOP hypothesis from one that links the recent increases in NICs' shares of global industrial production to the effects of the recent crisis on advanced countries' growth rather than to the onset of a new structure of global production. One final figure underscores the need for such care of interpretation: Between 1973 and 1984, when concern in the advanced countries' about the GOP began to intensify, the NICs' share of global industrial production increased from 7.1 percent to 8.5 percent. Viewed against the backdrop of the global history of capitalism, a total shift in share of 1.3 percentage points during a period of stagnation and economic instability does not seem large enough to warrant conclusions of fundamental transformation. There has been much ado, this suggests, about a relatively inconclusive trend.

North/South Recomposition of Industrial Production? Some popular versions of the NIDL, as well as mainstream neoclassical commentary, imply that there has been a global shift in the composition of industrial production, with an increasingly specialized division of labor between the North and the South. This would seem to imply, somewhat more specifically, that the composition of industrial production in the LDCs has moved in opposite directions from that in the DMEs, that industrial production and employment have shifted within the LDCs toward greater representation of those industries in which it has gained comparative advantage, and that it has consequently shifted (proportionately) toward other industries in the DMEs.[31]

This hypothesis is not confirmed by the data. We can look at both aggregate and disaggregated data on the composition of industrial production within the LDCs and the DMEs.[32] In the aggregate, the heavy-industry share in DME manufacturing value-added rose from 62 percent in 1960 to 67.2 percent while the LDC heavy-industry share rose from 32.7 percent in 1960 to 56.6 percent in 1978; the latter is rapidly approaching the former, leading to convergence in the industrial structures of the two groups. At the disaggregated level, we can look at thirty-one 3-digit manufacturing industries for the developed and developing economies between 1963 and 1978. Of those thirty-one industries, there were thirteen in which there were no significant changes (of 0.2 percentage points or more in their respective shares of total manufacturing value-added) between 1963 and 1978. Of the remaining eighteen 3-digit industries, there were fifteen in which the share of total value-added moved in the same direction in the LDCs and DMEs and only three in which the respective industry shares moved in the opposite direction.[33]

Import Competition and "De-Industrialization"? Some proponents of the NIDL and GOP appear to attribute a large share of stagnant or declining manufacturing employment in the DMEs to increasingly intense import competition from the NICs. This analysis has surely prompted many of the more fervent demands for protectionist legislation in the DMEs.

There are obviously many potential reasons for shifts in relative manufacturing output and employment: differential rates of productivity growth, different elasticities of final output demand with respect to varying rates of growth in aggregate consumption or to changes in the income distribution, or differential susceptibility to import competition. Disentangling these potential effects requires analysis of the relationship among the several constituent sources of variations in the growth of manufacturing output and employment.

Among many studies for the United States, three recent studies provide some especially useful information; I have not yet seen comparable exercises for other advanced countries.

Lawrence uses input-output tables to decompose the sources of relative growth in manufacturing employment in 3-digit U.S. industries between 1972 and 1980. Overall, he found that the stagnation of domestic activity in the United States accounted for a *decline* in manufacturing employment of 1.5 percent while changes in foreign trade effects actually accounted for an *increase* in manufacturing employment of 2.1 percent.[34]

Grossman looks more closely at the several 3-digit industries in the United States which everyone agrees (and the data suggest) have faced the stiffest competition from production sites in low-wage locations abroad. He estimates that even in these industries total employment was only 10.9 percent lower in 1979 than it would have been if there had not been intensified price competition from foreign supplies. Even in those industries most vulnerable to competition from the NICs, in other words, import price competition had a relatively minor effect on total employment.[35]

Bluestone, Harrison, and Gorham pursue an even more focused decomposition of changes in U.S. manufacturing employment.[36] One can distinguish, among the industries they study, between those that suffered large employment declines and those that enjoyed employment increases between 1973 and 1980, excluding those that experienced changes of less than 25,000 in employment and those for which interaction effects dominate discrete partial effects and for which their decomposition model "cannot provide an adequate explanation of employment change. . . ."[37] There was a total difference between these two groups of 887.4 thousand in employment change. Of this, 559.1 thousand was due to differences in the growth of final demand. Only about 20 percent was attributable to a rising import share of final sales. Another 29 percent was accounted for by a rising ratio of final sales to domestic value added, an effect which the authors attribute at least partly to the "possible impact of *component* imports in these industries. . . ."[38] While this is a possible explanation of this effect, it is equally plausible that the rising ratio of crude materials prices to output prices between 1973 and 1980 could have accounted statistically for all of this difference, leaving nothing left over for the effects of the "shift of American corporate production activity out of the country [or] the sourcing of foreign components for assembly into American products."[39] Therefore remaining somewhat agnostic about the sources of this change in the sales/value-added ratio, we would be left with one-fifth of the difference in employment prospects due to import competition, a significant but not predominating effect.

These studies do not prove anything by themselves, but they do seem to point to a common conclusion: The stagnation of manufacturing employment in at least the United States appears to be due much more to the slower growth of final

Table 13.6

Employees per Establishment, U.S. Manufacturing

Year	Employees per establ.
1899	22.0
1914	24.6
1921	33.7
1929	40.5
1937	51.4
1951	47.7
1967	45.6
1972	42.1
1977	41.6
1984	39.0

Sources: Historical Statistics of the United States (Washington, D.C.: GPO, 1976), Series P-1,5; Statistical Abstract of the United States (Washington, D.C.: GPO, 1986), Table 1334. See note 42 for adjustments.

demand than to the intensification of price competition from abroad or to an increase in imports' shares of domestic final consumption.

Industrial Decentralization? Some GOP proponents stress an accelerating decentralization of industrial production, with a spreading tendency toward more geographically dispersed, multinationally more diffuse, and/or smaller-scale sites of production.[40] We have already reviewed available evidence on the international redistribution of production. What about trends toward smaller-scale sites of production?

I am limited once again to data only for the United States. As Harry Jerome argued in his classic study of Mechanization in Industry, the reversal of the historic increase in plant size took seed in the 1920s.[41] Aggregate data on employees per establishment, presented in Table 13.6, confirm his early arguments, with peak establishment size being reached in 1937.[42] Since then, there is an obvious but slight downward trend in establishment size in manufacturing, from an average of 47.7 production-workers per establishment in 1951 to an estimated 39.0 in 1984. The data are inconsistent with the hypothesis of an accelerating rate of decrease in average size since 1972. The same conclusions pertain for the entire private sector: The percent of all employment in establishments with under twenty employees has remained essentially constant during the recent period of "reorganization," barely increasing from 26.9 percent in 1976 to 27.6 percent in 1983.[43] At least for the United States, the trend to smaller sites highlighted by GOP observers does not seem to reflect major recent changes in employment organization but rather a long-standing movement away from the huge establish-

ments built up during the period of what Gordon, Edwards, and Reich characterize as the "homogenization of Labor."[44]

Establishment size is only part of the GOP hypothesis, of course, since it also
highlights the increasing decentralization of production, particularly in manufacturing. But one needs to be careful in formulating and interpreting this trend.
Viewed on a global scale, it is certainly true that more and more products are
"world products," with components manufactured multinationally and assem-
bled in one country only at the final assembly stages. But this trend has mixed and
ambiguous implications which we shall explore in a subsequent section. Beyond
that, the evidence in support of some parts of this hypothesis is not particularly
clear-cut. The percentage of production workers in U.S. manufacturing employed in multiunit companies increased slightly during the early postwar years
but has remained essentially constant, at roughly 70 percent, since the mid-
1960s. The growth of manufacturing capacity in the Third World, as Jenkins also
stresses,[46] has in fact become increasingly concentrated, rather than decentralized, with a rising share of LDC production held by a relatively small number of
countries. Even in the United States, where there has been an obvious longer-
term movement of industrial employment away from the "Rustbelt" of its traditional concentration, the recent experience of states such as Massachusetts suggests that the process of geographic deconcentration has reflected as much a
process of industrial recomposition, with dramatic declines in industries such as
steel, as it has a process of inexorable movement away from the Northeast to the
rest of the country.

TNC Domination? We encounter, finally, the impression that large transnational corporations have gained increasing control over the world economy and
have substantially enhanced their relative economic power over individual national economies.

Large TNCs are certainly larger and have acquired significant economic
leverage. The top 200 global industrial corporations accounted for 17.7 percent
of total (nonsocialist) world GDP in 1960, for example, while that share increased
to 28.6 percent in 1980.[47] But the powerful are just as capable of competition
among themselves as are the small-fry. Almost all of the increase in TNCs'
relative economic importance reflects the increased importance of TNCs outside
the United States. Large corporations (in the top 200) from Germany, France,
Japan, the U.K., Italy, and the Netherlands increased their share of global GDP
from 4.3 percent in 1960 to 11.7 percent in 1980, while U.S. TNCs (in the global
top 200) increased their share from 12.8 percent to 14.3 percent. The battles
among these groupings of national giants appear to be fiercer than ever. Wladimir
Andreff concludes that "International centralization has recreated competition
on a wider scale, with huge amounts of capital opposing each other in the
developed countries and in the NICs."[48]

The final test is the bottom line: Have TNCs, with their access to higher profit rates in the Third World and their increasing power within the global economy, managed somehow to immunize themselves from the crisis of the global economy since the mid–1960s? Relying on a data set for 373 leading TNCs compiled by Andreff,[49] we find that average U.S. TNC profit rates were 8.1 percent during the prosperous years from 1963–66, 6.7 percent during the 1967–73 business cycle, and 7.0 percent during the 1974–79 cycle. For non-U.S. MNCs, the corresponding averages were 3.7, 3.3, and 3.0 percent respectively. While TNCs have witnessed slightly less deterioration, on average, than non-TNCs in their respective countries, their increasing power has not been sufficient to protect their profitability from the gathering storm.

The Recomposition of World Trade?

Some versions of the NIDL/GOP analysis emphasize apparent shifts in the growth and distribution of world trade. When I read or hear such discussions, I sometimes get the image of commodities literally buzzing around the globe at ever-increasing rates, produced anywhere and destined for everywhere. Are there data that can help illuminate the nature and relative importance of recent changes in world trade patterns?

Table 13.7 presents a continuous series on rates of growth in the real volume of international trade over the past three long swings. The data suggest the critical importance of the long swing in shaping trade growth. The expansion of international trade was most rapid during periods of long-swing expansion in the stages of British and U.S. hegemony—long swings I and III respectively. Trade growth was more sluggish during the period of expansion in the intermediate stage of interimperialist rivalry from 1900 to 1913 and then actually declined in the interwar years through 1938.

Has movement toward an NIDL moderated the expected (long-swing) slowdown in trade growth during the 1970s? We can test for this possible effect by comparing trade growth in long-swing contractions with trade growth in precedent long-swing expansions. If we compute the relative decline in rates of trade growth from their peaks in phases A or B to those in phase C, as the second and third columns show, the relative slowdowns in swings I and III were quite comparable. If anything, the slowdown in trade growth from IIIB to IIIC was more pronounced than the comparable slowdown from IB to IC from 1860–70 to 1870–1900.[50]

These data measure trade in all goods and services, while the NIDL/GOP hypotheses refer primarily to trade in manufactured goods. The right-hand columns of Table 13.7 provide data on manufactures trade growth from 1948. (Comparably disaggregated data for manufacturing trade are apparently not available for earlier decades.) The proportionate slowdowns are almost exactly equal to those for the total (real) volume of trade.

There is one further test about the behavior of trade growth during the 1970s:

Table 13.7

Growth in Real Volume of World Trade

Stage of long swing	Years	Ave. ann. % change	Ratios C:A	Ratios C:B	Ave. ann. % change, mfg. trade	Ratios C:A	Ratios C:B
I A	1840–1860	4.8%					
B	1860–1870	5.5					
C	1870–1900	3.2	0.67	0.58			
II A	1900–1913	3.8					
B	1913–1929	0.7					
C	1929–1938	–1.1	—	—			
	1938–1948	0.0					
III A	1948–1966	6.6			7.8		
B	1966–1973	9.2			10.0		
C	1973–1984	3.2	0.48	0.35	3.7	0.47	0.37

Sources: Rostow, *The World Economy*, table II-5; *United Nations Statistical Yearbook* (New York: United Nations, 1972, 1984).

Table 13.8

Growth in Global Production and Trade

	Years	(1) Growth in ind. prod.	(2) Growth in global trade	(3) Ratio of (2) to (1)
I A	1840–1860	3.5%	4.8%	1.37
B	1860–1870	2.9	5.5	1.90
C	1870–1900	3.7	3.2	0.86
II A	1900–1913	4.2	3.8	
B	1913–1929	2.7	0.7	
C	1929–1938	2.0	−1.1	
	1938–1948	4.1	0.0	
III A	1948–1966	9.0	6.6	0.73
B	1966–1973	6.7	9.2	1.37
C	1973–1984	3.1	3.2	1.03

movement toward an NIDL and the GOP might have resulted in a more moderate slowdown of international trade than one would have expected on the basis of the stagnation of global production. Table 13.8 provides data to assess this possibility, adding figures on the rate of growth of global industrial production to the data on trade growth presented in Table 13.7. Column (3) compares the relative slowdowns in production and trade for phases IB-IC and IIIB-IIIC. In both long swings, the ratio of trade growth to production growth rose from the A to B phases and then fell dramatically from the B to C periods. It would be difficult to argue definitively, on the basis of these data, that the pace of trade growth in 1973–84 was somehow better protected against underlying declines in industrial production than had been true in the earlier phase of crisis from 1870 to 1900; the ratios of trade to production growth rates in columns (3) were 0.86 in 1870–1900 and 1.03 in 1973–84, a scant difference in trade adjustment.

By both kinds of comparisons, then, trade growth appears to be a function of the structure and timing of successive long swings in the global capitalist economy. It would be difficult to argue, on the basis of these data, that these historic patterns of trade growth had yet been affected by trends toward an NIDL or the GOP since the early 1970s.

Increasing Trade Dependence? The DMEs have obviously become more dependent on international trade. Among the OECD countries, for example, exports as a percentage of GDP increased from 11.8 percent in 1951 to 18.6 percent in 1979.[51] As with shifts in the location of industrial production, however, the meaning of this trend must be interpreted carefully. Trade as a percentage of GDP in the advanced countries rose dramatically from 1840 to 1913 but then plummeted during the 1920s and 1930s. It did not regain its levels of 1913 until about 1970. From this historical vantage point, the increases after World War II do not solely reflect a secular increase in trade dependence but at least partly reflect a continuing restoration of trade dependence after its regression from 1913 through World War II.

Trade dependence has continued to rise since the early 1970s, however. Will this trend continue? Historical experience suggests the strong impact of rising protectionism during or immediately after long-swing contractions. Data on recent trends also suggest a deceleration in the rate of rising trade dependence after 1973 compared to the growth in 1948–66 and 1966–73. The media are currently saturated with indicators of spreading protectionist impulses.

We need to be cautious, in short, about the significance of recent increases in trade dependence among the DMEs. Trade as a percentage of GDP in 1913 was double its level in 1870. Trade dependence in 1979, comparably, was double its level in 1951. The rise from 1966 to 1979 does not guarantee a continuing increase in the 1980s and 1990s, nor does it protect against a regression comparable to the 1920s and 1930s. We shall return to this issue in discussing the evolution of the postwar SSA.

The Globalization of Trade Shares? The NIDL perspective in particular would appear to suggest a shift in export shares away from the DMEs toward the LDCs as a result of the rising export prominence of the NICs. Table 13.9, which presents historical data on the distribution of country and regional shares of international trade over the last several long swings, shows that the two most important shifts in the distribution of trade shares between the DMEs and the LDCs occurred long before the apparent advent of the NIDL. As the aggregated summary in Table 13.10 indicates, LDC trade shares increased from 26 percent to 32 percent from 1938 to 1950 and then declined from 32 percent in 1950 to 19 percent in 1966. The movement in LDC shares since 1973 has been governed entirely by movements in the share of the Middle Eastern countries; the nonoil exporting LDC trade shares moved from 16.5 percent in 1966 to 15.8 in 1973 and 15.9 in 1984.

Judging from these data, it appears that the recent gains in the export shares of the less-developed NICs have scarcely begun to recoup their relative losses in the earlier postwar years. As Table 13.9 shows, for example, the Latin American and Asian NICs accounted for 7.8 percent of total world exports in 1950; their share dropped to only 3.7 percent in 1966, and had climbed back up to 6.3 percent in 1983. The NIDL emphasizes the more recent gains, but a longer historical perspective raises some interesting questions about their relative importance.

Shifts in Trade Flows? The NIDL hypothesis also stresses the likelihood of important shifts in the direction of international trade flows. Have more and more of DME imports been coming from LDCs and from NICs in particular?

Table 13.9

Geographic Distribution of World Trade Shares

	1840	1870	1901–1905	1913	1928	1937[a]	1938	1950	1966	1973	1979	1983
U.K.	28	31	20	21	21	21	13	10.0	7.8	5.3	5.5	5.7
Ger-Fr/EEC	19	20	19	19	15	13	20	15.4	27.1	30.0	28.1	30.4
U.S.	7	8	11	11	14	12	10	16.7	15.0	12.2	10.8	9.3
Japan	—	—	1	1	3	4	4	1.4	4.5	6.4	6.3	8.7
Other adv.	23	19	25	23	19	19	18	17.9	16.3	16.4	14.5	15.9
CPEs	—	—	—	—	—	—	8	6.1	9.7	10.1	9.3	10.1
USSR	5	5	4	6	4	4	1	3.0	4.2	3.7	3.9	4.2
Other	—	—	—	—	—	—	7	3.1	7.4	6.4	5.4	5.9
Latin Am.	8	6	7	8	9	8	7	12.4	6.5	6.0	5.2	5.4
NICs	—	—	—	—	—	—	3	5.0	2.2	2.0	1.9	2.9
Asia	3	4	6	7	10	12	11	11.7	5.7	5.2	6.1	8.2
NICs	—	—	—	—	—	—	—	2.8	1.5	2.1	2.3	3.4
Other LDC	2	3	2	4	5	7	6	6.0	4.3	4.4	4.5	2.3
Middle East	—	—	—	—	—	—	2	1.4	2.9	4.2	8.7	4.6
Rest of world	5	4	4	4	—	—	—	—	—	—	—	—

Sources: For 1840–1937, Rostow, *The World Economy;* and for 1938–83, United Nations, *Statistical Yearbook,* various years.
[a] 1937 and 1938 are included separately here in order to indicate the break between the two series.

Table 13.10

The Composition of International Trade Shares

Year(s)	Advanced Europe & U.S.	Japan, USSR, & Sov. Bloc	LDCs	NICs
1840	77%	5	18	
1870	78	5	17	
1901–1905	75	5	19	
1913	74	7	19	
1928	69	7	24	
1937	65	8	27	
1938	62	12	26	
1950	60	7.5	31.5	7.8
1966	66.2	14.4	19.4	3.7
1973	63.9	17.5	19.8	4.1
1979	58.9	15.6	24.5	4.2
1983	61.3	15.9	19.3	6.3

Source: Based on Table 13.9.

Has there been a significant shift in the direction of trade of manufactured goods on a global scale? Table 13.11 provides a first glimpse of historical trends in the directionality of foreign trade between the advanced and the developing economies.

Part A of the table presents at least partial evidence confirming the NIDL emphasis on rising (relative) imports from the LDCs to the DMEs. In 1973, for example, 61 percent of international trade involved industrial countries' trading with themselves; by 1983, that figure had dropped to 47 percent, suggesting a move toward greater trade involvement with the LDCs.

But three problems immediately arise with that observation. First, the change from 1973 to 1983 only partly reverses a much more significant change during the earlier postwar years. In 1953–55, 40 percent of international trade involved trade within the group of DMEs; by 1983, after the large increase to 62 percent in 1966, the DMEs trade with themselves had fallen back down to 47 percent, still significantly above its share at the beginning of the postwar period.

Second, this part of the table confuses movements in trade of primary and manufactured products and remains sensitive to the relatively sharper fluctuations in primary product prices. Part B abstracts from these problems by focusing on the directionality of trade in manufactured goods. It shows that there was a massive increase in DME mutual trade involvement from 1935 to 1970 and relatively modest decline afterward. The most important figures, from the perspective of the NIDL hypothesis, are probably those in the column on total exports accounted for by DME exports to other DMEs. In 1935, that percentage

Table 13.11

The Directionality of World Trade

A. Composition of Total World Trade (%)

Year(s)	Total	Industrial countries			Nonindustrial countries		
		Within	Outside	Total	Within	Outside	Total
1876–80	100	50	23	73	4	23	27
1913	100	49	23	72	5	23	28
1928	100	46	23	69	8	23	31
1935	100	26	32	57	12	30	43
1953–55	100	40	25	65	10	25	35
1966	100	62	18	80	4	16	20
1973	100	61	18	79	6	15	21
1979	100	56	19	74	7	19	26
1983	100	47	20	67	9	23	32

B. Composition of Manufacturing Trade

	Exports				Imports			
	AICs		LDCs		AICs		LDCs	
Year	within	outside	within	outside	within	outside	within	outside
1935	29.5%	56.8	9.1	4.5	30.4	4.3	8.7	56.5
1970	74.3	20.3	2.0	3.4	71.9	6.5	2.0	19.6
1979	67.1	22.3	3.9	6.6	NA	NA	NA	NA
1983	64.1	22.6	4.6	8.8	NA	NA	NA	NA

Source: Simon Kuznets, "Quantitative Aspects of the Economic Development of Nations," *Economic Development and Cultural Change*, July 1967; Alice H. Amsden, "Profit Effects, Learning Effects, and the Directionality of Trade," unpublished paper, 1983; and United Nations, *Yearbook of International Trade Statistics* (New York, United Nations, 1981, 1984).

was only 29.5 percent. It leaped to 74.3 percent in 1970. By 1983 it had declined to 64.1 percent. Once again, that recent shift seems relatively insubstantial if viewed in its proper historical context.

Third, the data in Table 13.11 do not distinguish between the NICs and other LDCs. Table 13.12 provides that breakdown for the postwar period.[52] Two conclusions seem most striking: (1) DMEs imported a smaller proportion of their total imports from nonoil exporting LDCs in 1983 than they had in 1959 and (2) even though the relative proportion of DME imports from the NICs had increased since 1966, it does not yet appear to have regained the level achieved in 1959.

In every case, according to these data, a long-swing pattern seems prominent in trends for the directionality of trade; recent trends fit within that pattern.

Table 13.12

Composition of Advanced Countries' Imports from Developing Countries

Year	Total imports	All LDCs	Oil-ex.	% of DME Imports from LDCs Nonoil	NICs	Other
1959	100%	22.0	4.0	17.9	8.1	9.9
1966	100	21.8	6.1	15.8	5.4	10.4
1973	100	21.4	8.3	12.8	6.8	6.0
1979	100	29.7	14.5	15.2	8.5	6.7
1981	100	31.1	16.5	15.6	8.2	7.4

Source: Same as Table 13.11
Note: NICs and Other columns sum to Nonoil.

Multi-Nationalization of Commodity Production? Some GOP proponents also emphasize that intrafirm "trade" of partially finished commodities, through out-sourcing and direct intrafirm multinational transfers, has increased in recent years. Recent studies of the automobile, electronic, and aircraft industries provide dramatic case evidence of these trends.[53]

It is probably impossible to assess the relative magnitudes of this trend on any kind of aggregative basis. It has undoubtedly played an important role in at least some industries, but it is not at all clear that the quantities involved are either accelerating or irreversible. The most pertinent time series I've found suggests a very modest increase in recent years: In 1966, intrafirm trade of majority-owned foreign affiliates of U.S. TNCs equalled 19 percent of total U.S. imports. By 1977, that ratio had barely increased, rising to only 22 percent. In 1966, correspondingly, the percent of U.S. manufacturing imports accounted for by trade between parent companies and majority-owned affiliates abroad was 41 percent, while in 1977 it was 40 percent.[54] Among U.S. imports governed by tariff provisions controlling for parts-assembly abroad, similarly, the proportion of total import value represented by value-added abroad equalled 51.7 percent in 1966 and 50.6 percent in 1979, suggesting no increase in the proportion of value-added in those designated products which accrues in overseas production sites.[55]

There is some recent evidence, further, that at least some of the pioneering industries have been pulling back from such trade. Growing problems of traffic control and rising air freight costs have apparently blocked rapid diffusion of intrafirm commodity trade.[56]

Mostly because of problems of quantification, I remain doubtful about this dimension of the NIDL/GOP hypothesis. If the trend is crucial, in any case, I suspect that its sources and implications have been misperceived. I will return to this aspect of recent international trends.

A Shift in Investment Flows?

Some who articulate the NIDL/GOP hypotheses often imply that investment is flowing away from the advanced countries in search of more lucrative overseas opportunities, leading to an accelerating leakage of fixed capital investment from the developed economies. This general impression turns out, however, to be substantially misleading. Because MacEwan has elsewhere provided a useful and relatively detailed review of the available evidence,[57] I shall merely summarize here the main conclusions that he and I have both reached in our reviews of the data.

• The rate of growth of real direct foreign investment has slowed, not accelerated, in the advanced countries. (The common impression to the contrary is largely due, as MacEwan notes, "because the data are usually presented . . . without adjustment for inflation."[58]

• The share of direct foreign investment going to the LDCs has not increased—remaining more or less constant—since the late 1960s.

• Rather than increasing their acquisitions of foreign affiliates, the net rate of acquisition of affiliates by U.S. TNCs (and apparently by other countries' TNCs) has slowed substantially since the early 1970s.

• At least for U.S.-based firms, foreign direct investment has become increasingly selective, concentrating in just a few industries and beginning to ignore many of the traditional manufacturing industries in which overseas investment spread in the 1950s and 1960s. In particular, as MacEwan emphasizes, the share of overseas investment in the financial and trade services has increased dramatically since the early 1970s. Even in the East Asian NICs, site of a large proportion of the vaunted "export promotion zones," less than half of direct foreign investment by U.S.-based firms in 1980 was in manufacturing.

By any of these measures it is difficult to sustain the conclusion that investment capital is racing away from the advanced economies, draining off our shores at an accelerating pace.

Crisis in the Postwar Global Economy

If we are not yet experiencing a fundamental transformation in the global economy, how do we explain recent appearances? I shall frame a very schematic account of recent tendencies in the world economy, outlining the institutional foundations of the postwar social structure of accumulation (SSA) and its erosion since the mid-1960s. I shall then summarize the principal differences between this account and a number of other prevailing approaches before turning to a partial formalization and some preliminary tests of those differences in analytic expectations.[59]

The postwar boom was itself premised, at least for the purposes of this discussion, on three crucial institutional features of the global economy:

1. Both domestic growth in the advanced countries and their relative access to international trade were based on a tightly structured and carefully negotiated relationship between productivity growth and wage growth.

2. State policy during the expansion period, itself grounded in the security provided by the Bretton Woods system and the central role of the U.S. dollar, encouraged trade growth among the advanced countries, leading to an increase in the share of international trade taking place among advanced countries from 40 percent in 1953–55 to 61 percent in 1973 (see Part B of Table 13.11).

3. The combined effect of these first two trends contributed, other things equal, to a close relationship between movements in advanced countries' relative unit labor costs and changes in their relative shares of world markets and trade growth.

Beginning in the mid–1960s, for a variety of reasons which Bowles, Weisskopf, and I outline in some detail in *Beyond the Waste Land*, the foundations of this postwar system began to erode. Increasingly from the late 1960s and early 1970s, a sequence of interconnected global tendencies became more and more pronounced.

• Corporate profits on fixed direct investment fell in most of the advanced countries,[60] leading to increasing uncertainty and hesitation about real productive investment and an increasing tendency toward "paper investment" or what is otherwise called "increases in financial assets."

• Because of movement toward flexible exchange rates after the collapse of the Bretton Woods system in 1971, there was an increasing synchronization of business cycles among the advanced countries after 1971, leading to increasingly volatile fluctuations of economic activity.[61]

• Exchange rate fluctuations themselves became increasingly volatile, further reinforcing uncertainty about global conditions and expectations.[62]

• This prompted governments to pay more and more attention to money-market intervention in order to insulate their economies from exchange rate fluctuations. These interventions, in turn, led to increasing volatility and international variance over time in short-term interest rates.

• This led to further preoccupation with paper investment and to increasingly rapid movement of short-term financial capital across international borders.

This set of interrelated and mutually reinforcing tendencies obviously affected the investment horizons and global behavior of multinational capital. I think that three effects of this spreading global instability have been most important and have informed widespread perceptions of underlying international transformation.

First, stagnation has spread everywhere and affected everyone's conditions and expectations. It is worth reiterating the earlier reports that perceptions of deindustrialization, at least in the United States, have resulted almost entirely from slower growth in final demand—and yet give rise to impressions of import competition.

Second and consequently, multinational corporations have sought increasing protection from falling profits and spreading instability by searching for production enclaves where rates of profit on current investment could somehow be "protected" by special privileges and by higher rates of exploitation.

Third, and probably most important in shaping recent perceptions, TNCs have sought stable and insulated political and institutional protection against the increasing volatility of international trade and the collapse of dollar-based "free-market" expansion of international trade growth. "Over the past ten years," a 1984 United Nations survey concluded, "flexible exchange rates generated an erratic pattern in relative prices and made basic signals of resource allocation very noisy."[63] In this respect, I would argue that the central features of the emergence of the NICs lie not in their low wages or their technical adaptations, since wages are low almost everywhere in the LDCs and new technologies could be applied anywhere.[64] Rather, what seems especially striking about the NICs is the increasingly political and institutional determinations of production and trading relationships. TNCs negotiate with each other and host countries for joint production agreements, licensing, and joint research and development contracts. They search among potential investment sites for institutional harbors promising the safest havens against an increasingly turbulent world economy.

This is a highly schematic account whose generalizations can only be adequately substantiated through much more detailed and quantitatively rigorous analysis than I have yet been able to pursue or than space in this volume permits. I limit myself to a brief and purely exemplary review of some of the kinds of empirical trends that are at least consistent with and tend to support this institutional/historical account:[65]

• Foreign direct investment has become increasingly selective. The percentage of U.S. overseas fixed investment stocks accounted for by just six Latin American and Asian NICs—comparable data for Taiwan are not available—increased by one quarter between 1971 and 1978.[66] Of the stock of total direct investments received by LDCs, similarly, the share received by tax havens and the NICs increased from 50.6 percent in 1967 to 70 percent in 1978, while the share of other non-OPEC LDCs fell from 21.7 percent to 13 percent over the same period.[67] By the end of the 1970s, nearly half of all manufacturing exports by majority-owned affiliates of U.S.-based TNCs to the United States emanated from only four countries: Brazil, Mexico, Singapore, and Hong Kong. Of total employment in Export Promotion Zones in 1978, similarly, 72 percent was located in just six countries: the Republic of Korea, Singapore, Malaysia, the Philippines, Mexico, and Brazil.[68]

• TNCs' investment and production for export in LDCs is now concentrated in highly specialized and institutionally particular economic sites. TNC affiliates in these protected offshore sites enjoy a modern form of colonial trading privileges. Lipsey and Weiss report, for example, that U.S. exports to LDCs are a positive function of the number of U.S.-owned affiliates located in foreign

countries, suggesting mutual trading agreements and reciprocal supply arrangements.[69] In corollary fashion, other advanced countries' exports to LDCs are a
negative function of the presence of U.S.-owned affiliates in those countries,
indicating that foreign competitors are at least partly screened out of access to
those countries by the presence of U.S.-owned affiliates. Affiliates of firms from
a single dominant home country, further, now account for more than 50 percent of
all affiliates located in 73 of 124 developing countries, while that same position of
single-country dominance characterizes only 6 of 25 DMEs.[70] This leads to the
apparent corollary that NIC economic fortunes bear a relatively direct positive
relationship to the degree of TNC involvement in and trading relationships with
them.[71]

This impression is further supported by the trend[72] that U.S.-owned affiliates
abroad are increasingly likely to direct their exports to the United States primarily
or even exclusively if located in the Asian NICs: the ratio of exports to total sales
of U.S. majority-owned foreign affiliates in Asian NICs had increased from 23.1
percent in 1966 to 61.9 percent in 1977, for example, and roughly half of this
increase was accounted for by the rise in the share of exports to the U.S. (out of
total sales) over the same period.[73] In Latin American countries, by contrast,
more than 90 percent of the sales of U.S. manufacturing affiliates in 1977 were
still directed to local markets, and that percentage had scarcely changed since the
mid–1960s.[74]

The net result, apparently, is a significant shift in international trading patterns
away from a trans-Atlantic to a trans-Pacific pattern of trading specialization.[75]

• In 1970, for example, 28.2 of European DMEs' exports went to the United
States, but that portion fell to 20.9 percent in 1983. In 1970, similarly, 30.4
percent of U.S. exports traveled to European DMEs but only 25.2 percent in
1983. The same reduction of trans-Atlantic flows affected the rest of the Americas: In 1970, 29.6 percent of Latin American exports traveled to the European
DMEs; that share had dropped to 18.4 percent in 1983.

• In 1970, by contrast, 23.9 percent of U.S. imports had come from Japan and
other Asian countries; by 1983, that trans-Pacific share had increased to 33.8
percent.

• Out of total world trade, more aggregatively, trans-Atlantic trade fell from
13.1 percent in 1970 to 8.7 percent in 1983 while Pacific Basin trade increased
from 10.2 percent in 1970 to 14.2 percent in 1983.[76]

Contrasting Perspectives

This account, however schematic, helps clarify some important differences with
other prevailing perspectives on recent changes in the global economy. Two major
differences of analytic emphasis seem most important.

First, I would argue that we have *not* witnessed movement toward an increasingly "open" international economy, with productive capital literally buzzing

around the globe, but that we have moved rapidly toward an increasingly "closed" economy for productive investment, with production and investment decisions increasingly dependent upon a range of institutional policies and activities and a pattern of differentiation and specialization among the countries in the LDCs. The international economy, by the standards of traditional neoclassical and Marxian models of competition, has witnessed *declining* rather than *increasing* mobility of productive capital. Production and investment decisions are relatively less, not more, influenced by pure market signals about short-term cost and price fluctuations.

Second, and correspondingly, the role of the state has grown dramatically since the early 1970s; state policies have become increasingly decisive on the international front. Governments have become more and more involved in active management of monetary policy in order to condition exchange rate fluctuations and short-term capital flows. They have become actually and potentially decisive in bargaining about production and investment agreements. And, small consolation through it may be, in an era of spreading monetarist conservatism, everyone including transnational corporations has become increasingly dependent upon coordinated state intervention for restructuring and resolution of the underlying dynamics of crisis.

Toward Some More Formal Hypothesis Tests

This section suggests some small steps toward a more formal analysis, which may help distinguish more precisely than the preceding institutional accounts and one-dimensional empirical tabulations between the alternative perspectives on recent changes in the global economy.

These steps draw on the concluding remarks of the preceding analysis. I argued there that one important contrast involves differing perspectives on trends toward "open-ness" and "closed-ness" in the world economy. Many conventional renditions of the NIDL/GOP hypotheses suggest a more competitive and open global economy since the early 1970s. My account suggests the opposite—a difference that can be pursued along several important analytic dimensions. I shall refer to the two competing perspectives as the NIDL/GOP and the SSA-Decay hypotheses respectively.

Capital Mobility

One important difference involves the degree of capital mobility in the global economy. The NIDL/GOP perspectives would suggest an increasingly unrestrained and rapid mobility of capital since the early- to mid–1970s, a pace of circulation that Bluestone and Harrison call the "hypermobility of capital."[77] The analysis sketched above would appear to suggest a diminishing mobility of capital since the mid–1970s—as corporations have placed increasing emphasis on investment and production in havens from the swirling trade winds.

By conventional expectations about market competition, we ought to be able to test these divergent views of capital mobility by tracing the degree of variability in profit rates among countries. Other things equal, increasing capital mobility and its corollary international competition should result in a reduction in the variance of profit rates among national economies—the classic tendency toward an equalization of profit rates. By contrast, again holding other factors constant, decreased capital mobility should result in a modulated tendency toward equalization of profit rates and even, perhaps, in a widening variability of profitability among countries.

Data are difficult to develop for these purposes, and I have not conducted separate primary research on profit rate variations. There are nonetheless some basic data, constructed in consistent fashion, for net rates of return in manufacturing from 1952 through 1983 among seven advanced countries, including Canada, France, Germany, Italy, Japan, the United Kingdom, and the United States.[78] I have calculated the coefficient of variation of manufacturing profitability among these seven countries and plotted the resulting index in Figure 13.1.

What do the numbers tell us? We would expect a rising coefficient of variation during the period of movement toward the peak of the postwar long swing, particularly as U.S. economic power helped provide some rents accruing to U.S. corporate advantage and as relatively protectionist policies bore economic fruit in Japan. We would then expect relatively diminishing coefficients of variation from the mid-sixties into the early seventies as increasing international competition began to threaten U.S. corporate profits and pull it toward the mean of the other advanced countries. The index plotted in Figure 13.1 confirms these expectations.

But what about the subsequent period? If the NIDL/GOP hypotheses are correct, we should expect a continuing narrowing of profit rates, as a result of increasing international competition, through the early 1980s. But we find, in fact, the opposite, with a sharp increase in the coefficient of variation of manufacturing profit rates from 1977 through 1982.[79] This trend would appear to be relatively more consistent with the SSA-decay perspective.

The Determinants of Investment

In work-in-progress aimed at applying the SSA perspective toward a Marxian investment function, Bowles, Weisskopf, and I have stressed (a) the importance of the "expected rate of return" as a determinant of investment and (b), from an open economy perspective, the role of variations in the opportunity cost of foreign investment as one important determinant of the attractiveness of domestic fixed investment. The higher the relative rate of return on foreign direct investment, the lower we would expect the rate of net domestic investment.

This analysis, which appears to find strong support in our ongoing economet-

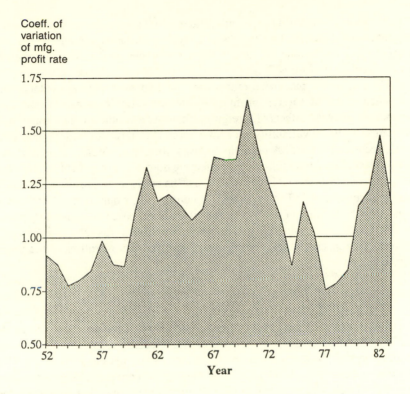

Figure 13.1. Profit Competition?
The Coefficient of Variation of Manufacturing Profitability in Seven Advanced Countries.
Source: See Note 78.

ric analysis, lends itself quite naturally to tests of alternative views of recent trends in the global economy. If the NIDL/GOP hypotheses are correct, one ought to find econometrically that the relative effect of foreign investment opportunities on domestic fixed investment would have increased since the early 1970s, other things equal, as a result of qualitatively more attractive investment opportunities abroad, a trend toward "capital hypermobility," and a general tendency toward a relatively more international market. If my alternative SSA-decay account were more apt, then one ought to find that the relative effect of foreign investment opportunities on domestic fixed investment would have dampened, other things equal, as a result of the increasing volatility of international markets and the increasingly uncertain and/or indeterminate meaning of the opportunity costs of foreign investment.

In our joint econometric explorations and in my own extensions of that work, we tentatively conclude that the SSA-decay hypothesis is supported while the NIDL/GOP expectations are not.[80] We test for changes in the international environment in two ways.

First, relying on piecewise regression, we find fairly strong evidence of a dampened effect of foreign profitability on domestic investment after 1973. Second, we filter the effects of foreign profitability on domestic investment by an index measuring the variability over time in the U.S. terms of trade; other things equal, according to the SSA-decay hypothesis, foreign profit rates should become less and less pertinent in the calculus affecting domestic investment, in the words quoted earlier from the UN supplement, as "basic signals of resource allocation [become] very noisy." The hypothesis is confirmed by our econometric estimations: as the variability of the U.S. terms of trade increased after the early 1970s, the effect of foreign profitability on domestic investment was substantially diminished. (This adjustment also significantly improved the overall fit of the investment equation.)

The Determinants of Trade Shares

A similar test of diverging expectations could also be developed through econometric exploration of the determinants of single-country shares of total foreign trade, at least for the advanced countries in the postwar period. If the NIDL/GOP perspective has merit, one ought to find that the influence of changes in relative unit labor costs on movements in own-country trade shares had increased since the early 1970s. If the SSA-decay perspective has greater merit, correspondingly, one ought to find that the association between relative unit labor costs and trade shares began to attenuate after the early 1970s.

This test is somewhat more difficult to pursue in part because of less well-established expectations about other determinants of trade shares and also because the best consistent series on relative unit labor costs extends backward only to 1960. The econometric results are therefore very provisional, but they once again appear to provide support for the SSA approach. I have regressed the rate of change of the U.S. share of OECD exports on the rate of change of an index of U.S. manufacturing unit labor costs relative to those of the major U.S. competitors and an index of the variability of U.S. exchange rates over time.[81] Other things equal, U.S. export shares should increase when relative U.S. real unit labor costs decline, while this effect should be dampened with relatively increasing variation over time in relative exchange rates. In order to test for differences in expectations of the NIDL/GOP and SSA-Decay hypotheses, I have used a piecewise regression to test for changes in the slope of the coefficient on relative real unit labor costs for the first period of changes in the Bretton Woods system, from 1971 to 1973, and again for the subsequent period of intensifying international competition, from one perspective, and increasingly volatile trade relations, from the other. If the accelerating capital mobility perspective were correct, one would expect, if anything, an enhanced coefficient of changes in relative unit labor costs on changes in export share as a result of the increasingly assertive force of market pressures. If the alternative view were more appropriate, one would expect to find diminished or even perverse influences of movements in relative real unit labor costs on changes in export shares. Based on these tests, it appears that the period beginning in the 1970s witnessed a loosening connection between movements over time in relative unit labor costs and in the U.S. share of foreign trade. In a variety of alternative specifications, the basic coefficient on changing relative unit labor costs is negative and significant while the piecewise coefficient for 1974–82 is consistently of the opposite sign and statistically significant as well. For the years from 1962 through 1970, U.S. export shares behaved as anticipated by the emphasis of the SSA analysis of the structure of trading relationships in the period of postwar expansion. After 1973, during a period of decay of those relationships, that pattern of behavior dissolved.

Conclusion

I have reviewed prevailing presuppositions of rapid movement toward a New International Division of Labor and the Globalization of Production. I have suggested both that a number of empirical indicators of recent developments, viewed in historical context, do not support these presuppositions and that an alternative institutional account of the postwar global economy suggests a substantially different set of expectations about recent changes. Some very preliminary, relatively more formal, quantitative explorations of these different expectations appears to provide provisional support for my alternative view.

But why the fuss? Some who have seen or heard early versions of this analysis have wondered if I wasn't splitting hairs, emphasizing differences beyond any reasonable proportions. (One friend remarked that he had "never seen so much weight placed on a second derivative, on a change in a rate of change, in my scholarly life.")

I think that these differences in expectations matter, in the end, for political reasons. The NIDL/GOP perspectives have helped foster, in my view, a spreading political fatalism in the advanced countries. If we struggle to extend the frontiers of subsistence and security at home, one gathers, we shall stare balefully at capital's behind, strutting across the continents and seas, leaving us to amuse ourselves with our realized dreams of progress and the reality of our diminishing comparative advantage.

I disagree with these political inferences. The breakdown in the postwar system has reflected an erosion of socially determined institutional relationships. TNC responses since the early 1970s reflect their own political and institutional efforts to erect some shelters against the winds of spreading economic instability. The TNCs are neither all-powerful nor fully equipped to shape a new world economy by themselves. They require workers and they require consumers. Workers and consumers helped shape the structure of the postwar system, and we are once again in a position to bargain over institutional transformation. The global economy is up for grabs, not locked into some new and immutable order. The opportunity for enhanced popular power remains ripe.

Notes

1. For recent comparative data on growth rates and unemployment in selected advanced countries, see *Economic Report of the President* (Washington, D.C.: GPO, 1986): Tables B-110 and B-109 respectively. For a useful review of the character and impact of capital flight in the U.S., see Barry Bluestone and Bennett Harrison, *The Deindustrialization of America: Plant Closing, Community Abandonment, and the Dismantling of Basic Industry* (New York: Basic Books, 1982).

2. I share this volume's premise that there are three distinct (although obviously overlapping) views of labor economics—neoclassical, institutionalist, and Marxist—and shall presuppose the usefulness of that premise in this paper. See David M. Gordon, *Theories of Poverty and Underemployment* (Lexington, Mass.: D. C. Heath, 1972) chaps. 1-2, for a partial review of the recent revival of this traditional trichotomy.

3. The concept of the social structure of accumulation and its potential implications for theoretical and historical analysis are most fully developed in Samuel Bowles, David M. Gordon, and Thomas E. Weisskopf, "Power and Profits: The Social Structure of Accumulation and the Profitability of the Postwar U.S. Economy," *Review of Radical Political Economics* (Spring-Summer 1986): 133-67; David M. Gordon, "Stages of Accumulation and Long Economic Cycles," in T. Hopkins and I. Wallerstein, eds., *Processes of the World-System* (Beverly Hills, Calif.: Sage Publications, 1980); David M. Gordon, Richard Edwards, and Michael Reich, *Segmented Work, Divided Workers: The Historical Transformation of Labor in the United States* (New York: Cambridge University Press, 1982); and Samuel Bowles, David M. Gordon, and Thomas E. Weisskopf, *Beyond the Waste Land: A Democratic Alternative to Economic Decline* (New York: Anchor Press/Doubleday, 1983). Complementary French conceptions of *modes de régulation* and *modes d'accumulation* are presented in Michel Aglietta, *A Theory of Capitalist Regulation: The U.S. Experience* (London: New Left Books, 1979) and Alain Lipietz, "Behind the Crisis: The Exhaustion of a Regime of Accumulation. A 'regulation school' perspective on some French empirical works," *Review of Radical Political Economics* (Summer-Spring 1986): 13-32.

4. The NIDL hypothesis is probably best represented by Folker Froebel, Jurgen Heinrich, and Otto Kreye, *The New International Division of Labor* (New York: Cambridge University Press, 1980).

5. Dieter Ernst, *Restructuring World Industry in a Period of Crisis—The Role of Innovation: An Analysis of Recent Developments in the Semi-conductor Industry* (Vienna: UNIDO, 1981), 287.

6. Although the literature does not stress this distinction between the NIDL and the GOP perspectives, the latter is probably best represented by Ernst, *Restructuring World Industry*; Bluestone and Harrison, *Decentralization of America*; Alain Lipietz, "De la Nouvelle Division Internationale du Travail á la Crise du Fordisme Périphérique" Working Paper No. 8225, CEPREMAP, November 1982); Michael J. Piore and Charles F. Sabel, *The Second Industrial Divide: Possibilities for Prosperity* (New York: Basic Books, 1984); and Bennett Harrison, "Cold Bath or Restructuring?" *Science and Society*, Forthcoming. I am grateful to Bennett Harrison for help in clarifying the differ-

ence between these emphases in the GOP perspective and the sharper North/South focus of the NIDL orientation.

7. Since the formalism of neoclassical economics often leads to neglect of immediate institutional tendencies, there does not appear to be a vast neoclassical literature on the NIDL and GOP. Perhaps the most representative response from a largely neoclassical perspective is the excellent book by Robert Lawrence, *Can America Compete?* (Washington, D.C.: The Brookings Institution, 1984).

8. William H. Branson, "Trends in United States International Trade and Investment since World War II," in Martin Feldstein, ed., *The American Economy in Transition* (Chicago: University of Chicago Press, 1980), 236.

9. Lawrence, *Can America Compete?*, 75.

10. For a direct statement of the implications for trade policy itself, see Robert Z. Lawrence and Robert E. Litan, *Saving Free Trade: A Pragmatic Approach* (Washington, D.C.: The Brookings Institution, 1986).

11. Charles Schultze, "Interview on Industrial Policy," *Harper's* (May 1985): 47.

12. Lawrence, *Can America Compete?*, 83. Less neglectful of workers' interests than many, Lawrence and Litan, *Saving Free Trade*, chaps. 4–5, also stress the need for effective trade adjustment assistance in the United States to cushion the transitional blows for workers.

13. Because of the relative theoretical indeterminacy of the institutionalist perspective, one is never entirely certain about membership in this camp. For the purposes of this discussion, I am prepared to consider the recent treatments by Bluestone and Harrison, *The Deindustrialization of America*, and Piore and Sabel, *The Second Industrial Divide* as largely institutionalist for a variety of reasons, some of which are treated here and some of which are sketched in the following section. There is a further interesting trend toward an integration between the microinstitutionalist dimensions of this work and a broader macroinstitutional framework, closely associated with the French "régulation" school, and an explicit macroeconomic analysis which builds upon largely post-Keynesian foundations. For these tendencies, see Michael J. Piore, ed., *Unemployment and Inflation: Institutionalist and Structuralist Views* (White Plains, N.Y.: M. E. Sharpe, 1979), and "The Theory of Macro-Economic Regulation and the Current Economic Crisis in the United States" (Working Paper in Economics No. 285, MIT, July 1981).

14. Piore and Sabel, *The Second Industrial Divide*, chaps 6–7.

15. Ibid., 252.

16. Bluestone and Harrison, *The Deindustrialization of America*, 160.

17. Piore and Sabel, *The Second Industrial Divide*, 179; italics in original.

18. Ernest Mandel, *Late Capitalism* (London: New Left Books, 1975), 74.

19. Lipietz, "De la Nouvelle Division," 2; translated from the French.

20. I have found the survey article by Rhys Jenkins, "Divisions over the International Division of Labor," *Capital & Class* (Spring 1984): 28–57, especially useful. See also the recent discussion by John Willoughby, *Capitalist Imperialism, Crisis and the State* (New York: Harwood Academic Publishers, 1986), especially 49–50.

21. Folker Froebel, "The Current Development of the World Economy" (United Nations University, 1980 Working Paper), 16.

22. Harrison, "Cold Bath or Restructuring," provides one useful account of the linkages between these observations and traditional theoretical concern within the Marxian tradition for intercapitalist competition.

23. Andre Gunder Frank, *Crisis: In the World Economy* (New York: Holmes and Meier, 1980), 319, 320.

24. Froebel, "Current Development," 27; italics in original.

25. This argument has perhaps been advanced most directly by Hugo Radice, "The National Economy: A Keynesian Myth?" *Capital & Class* (Spring 1984): 111–40.

26. Frank, *Crisis*, 314.

27. Ibid., 320.

28. I do not assume axiomatically that there have been long swings in the world capitalist economy since the 1790s but merely seek to allow for the possibility that trends and transformations in the global economy have been conditioned by such alternating periods of expansion and stagnation; see Gordon, Edwards, and Reich, *Segmented Work*, chap. 2; and David M. Gordon, Thomas E. Weisskopf, and Samuel Bowles, "Long Swings and the Nonreproductive Cycle," *American Economic Review* (May 1983): 151–57, for evidence on long swings in the global and U.S. economy. For dating of business cycle peaks in the postwar economy, where relevant, I have relied on Center for International Business Cycle Research, "Dating National Business Cycles in the Postwar Period" (Mimeograph, 1982). If possible, I have organized data to correspond to four successive periods demarcated by business-cycle peaks in the postwar U.S. economy: 1948–66, 1966–73, 1973–79, and 1979–84. (See Bowles, Gordon, and Weisskopf, *Beyond the Waste Land*, chap. 2, for a justification of these specific periods for the United States, the most important actor in the global economy in the postwar period.) The most recent business cycle had not yet completely peaked in 1984, by at least some measures, but 1984 was the most recent year for which comparable data were available at the time of final revision of this paper; it comes after a sufficiently long period of expansion, from 1982 through 1984, that it should not distort the peak-to-peak comparisons very much, if at all.

29. I follow Branson, "Trends," among others, in classifying the following countries as NICs for this empirical exercise: Ireland, Spain, Portugal, Greece, and Yugoslavia in Europe; Argentina, Brazil, and Mexico in Latin America; and the "Gang of Four" in Asia—Singapore, Taiwan, Hong Kong, and the Republic of Korea. (Branson actually excludes Ireland.) This creates a slight inconsistency in some of the series that follow, for which I shall try to correct where possible: Ireland, Spain, Portugal, and Greece are included in many conventional tabulations among advanced industrial countries rather than among LDCs, but they are also classified as NICs for the purposes of testing the NIDL/GOP hypotheses.

30. Gordon, Edwards, and Reich, *Segmented Work*.

31. It is important to note that this implication does not necessarily flow from the GOP hypothesis. Indeed, the GOP perspective might argue the opposite: that increasing decentralization of production has produced a convergence in the composition of industrial production between North and South.

32. See, among others, United Nations Industrial Development Organization, *Survey* (Vienna: UNIDO, 1982), tables 5, 7.

33. These calculations are based on data in UNIDO, *Survey*, table 7.

34. Lawrence, *Can America Compete?* It is important to note that these data, covering the period up to 1980, do not take into account the subsequent period in which the rising value of the dollar substantially eroded the U.S. trade deficit—an exchange rate effect which cannot itself be ascribed in some simple sense to underlying "structural" shifts in the global economy.

35. Gene M. Grossman, "The Employment and Wage Effects of Import Competition in the United States," (Working Paper No. 132, National Bureau of Economic Research, March–April 1982).

36. Barry Bluestone, Bennett Harrision, and Lucy Gorham, "Storm Clouds on the Horizon: Labor Market Crisis and Industrial Policy" (Working Paper, Economic Education Project, 1984).

37. Ibid., 29.

38. Ibid., 17; italics in original.

39. Crude materials prices, the available measure closest to the prices of intermediate

and raw materials supplied to the U.S. manufacturing sector and therefore not included in value-added, increased relative to output prices by 13 percent. This would have accounted for a difference in employment change between these two groups of more than 400 thousand, a difference greater than that which is attributable to the change in their respective ratios of value-added to final shipments.

40. See, for example, Doreen Massey, *Spatial Divisions of Labor: Social Structures and the Geography of Production* (London: MacMillan, 1984) and Philip Cooke and A. Rosa Pires, "Production Decentralization in Three European Countries," in *Environmental Planning* (April 1985).

41. Harry Jerome, *Mechanization in Industry* (New York: National Bureau of Economic Research, 1934).

42. The standard source for the data on average establishment size is the *U.S. Census of Manufactures*. There are two problems with the published data for the years for 1977 and 1982, the two most recent available manufacturing censuses. First, there was a change in recording procedures for small establishments in 1977 which appears to have resulted in a large one-time increase in the total number of establishments recorded; regression forecast analysis of the data for the postwar period suggests that the total number of establishments in 1977 would have been roughly 330,000, instead of 360,000, if traditional procedures had been sustained. Second, while 1967, 1972, and 1977 were all years slightly prior to their respective business-cycle peaks, 1982 was at the trough of a major recession, with manufacturing employment undoubtedly dampened by temporary layoffs. The data in Table 13.6 adjust for these problems in two respects. First, 1984 is substituted for 1982, the actual year of the most recent census, in order to provide a comparison with 1967, 1972, and 1977 at a more or less comparable point in the business cycle. Second, the total number of manufacturing establishments in 1977 and 1984 consistent with the pre–1977 administrative reporting procedures was projected by straight-line forecasts from a regression trend established for the 1951–72 period (with an R^2 of 0.88), providing a more consistent basis for historical comparison in the postwar period. (On reporting procedures, see U.S. Bureau of the Census, *U.S. Census of Manufactures, 1977* [Washington, D.C.: GPO, 1979] Technical Introduction).

43. *Statistical Abstract*, Table 881.

44. Gordon, Edwards, and Reich, *Segmented Work*.

45. *Statistical Abstract*, Table 1334.

46. Jenkins, "Divisions."

47. Frederick F. Clairmonte and John H. Cavanagh, "Transnational Corporations and Global Markets: Changing Power Relations," Paper, Institute for Policy Studies (Washington, D.C., 1982).

48. Wladimir Andreff, "The Internationalization of Capital and the Re-ordering of World Capitalism," *Capital & Class* (Spring 1984): 77.

49. Ibid., table 3.

50. These comparisons have been elided for long swing II because of the incomparable collapse of trade and the arbitrariness of ratios involving the negative figure for 1913–29 and 1929–38.

51. Based on Organization for Economic Cooperation and Development, *National Accounts* (Paris: OECD, 1969, 1982).

52. I have not yet been able to find consistent data at this disaggregated level for years prior to 1959.

53. See United Nations Centre on Transnational Corporations, *Salient Features and Trends in Foreign Direct Investment* and *Survey on Transnational Corporations: 1983* (New York: United Nations, 1983) for useful summaries of this evidence.

54. United Nations Centre on Transnational Corporations, *Transnational Corpora-*

tions and International Trade: Selected Issues (New York: United Nations, 1985), table IV.2.

55. Data provided to the author from unpublished U.S. Tariff Commission tabulations.

56. See Ernst, *Restructuring World Industry*, for considerable discussion of these problems.

57. Arthur MacEwan, "Slackers, Bankers, Marketers: Multinational Firms and the Pattern of U.S. Direct Foreign Investment" (Working paper, May 1982).

58. Ibid., 15.

59. The analysis in this section is very close to and relies heavily on recent discussion by Arthur MacEwan ("Slackers"; "Interdependence and Instability: Do the Levels of Output in the Advanced Capitalist Countries Increasingly Move Up and Down Together?" *Review of Radical Political Economics* [Summer & Fall 1984]; "Unstable Empire: U.S. Business in the International Economy" [paper, April 1985]), for whose insights and continuing attention to the global dimensions of the current crisis I am especially indebted. The arguments here also depend heavily on my joint work with Bowles and Weisskopf, especially Bowles, Gordon, and Weisskopf, *Beyond the Waste Land*, 1983, although the three of us would all admit that the international dimensions of our analysis have not yet been sufficiently developed.

60. See both Philip Armstrong, Andrew Glyn, and John Harrison, *Capitalism since World War II: The Making and Breakup of the Great Boom* (London: Fontana Paperbacks, 1984) and Thomas E. Weisskopf, "Worker Security and Capitalist Prosperity: An International Comparative Analysis" (Paper, March 1985).

61. See MacEwan, "Interdependence and Instability."

62. These exchange rate fluctuations are not simply the product of increasing variability in the inflation rate. For data on the U.S. exchange rate adjusted for relative movements in the wholesale price index, see Branson, "Trends," table 3.18.

63. United Nations, *World Economic Survey 1984: Supplement* (New York: United Nations, 1985, 11.

64. Hamilton notes (Clive Hamilton, "Capitalist Industrialization in the Four Little Tigers of East Asia," in P. Limqueco and B. McFarlane, eds., *Neo-Marxist Theories of Development* [London: Croom Helm, 1983], 173), indeed, that wages in the Asian NICs are substantially higher than those in any other economies in the region, with the single exception of Japan.

65. As with much of the earlier analysis, I have been limited primarily to an investigation of the behavior of U.S.-based firms.

66. Based on data in UN Centre on Transnational Corporations, *Survey*, Annex Table II.13.

67. Andreff, "Internationalization," Table 4.

68. See Ibid., 160, 155.

69. Robert E. Lipsey and Merle Yahr Weiss, "Foreign Production and Exports in Manufacturing Industries," *Review of Economics and Statistics* (November 1981): 488–94.

70. UN Centre on Transnational Corporations, *Survey*, 37.

71. See Andreff, "Internationalization," for further discussion on this point.

72. Reported in Lipsey, "Recent Trends in U.S. Trade and Investment," National Bureau of Economic Research (Working Paper No. 1009, October 1982), and MacEwan, "Slackers."

73. UN Centre on Transnational Corporations, *Transnational Corporations*, Table I.2.

74. Ibid., and MacEwan, "Slackers," 50.

75. All of the comparisons below are based on data in United Nations *Yearbook of International Trade Statistics* (New York: United Nations, 1984).

76. For these purposes, "trans-Atlantic trade" is defined as exports in both directions between the European DMEs and the U.S., Canada, and Latin America. "Pacific Basin trade" is defined as trade between Japan and other Asian developing countries and trade between those two Asian groupings and the Americas grouping of the U.S., Canada, and Latin America.

77. Bluestone and Harrison, *Deindustrialization*.

78. The data on profitability are expressed as the net before-tax rate of profit on the net fixed capital stock for manufacturing and are drawn from Philip Armstrong and Andrew Glyn, "Accumulation, Profits, State Spending: Data for Advanced Capitalist Countries, 1952-83" (Unpublished tables, Oxford Institute of Economics and Statistics, August 1986), Table 15.

79. I have not been able to update these data beyond 1983, so I cannot speculate about whether the downturn from 1982 to 1983 reflects the beginning of a more sustained reversal of the 1977-82 trend.

80. See David M. Gordon, Thomas E. Weisskopf, and Samuel Bowles, "A Conflict Model of Investment: The Determinants of U.S. Capital Accumulation in a Global Context" (Paper, New School for Social Research, October 1986).

81. Data on exports are from OECD, *National Accounts*, 1984, while data on relative unit labor costs and exchange rates come from U.S. Bureau of Labor Statistics, "Data on Productivity and Labor Cost Trends," (Office of Productivity and Technology data tables, 1986).

PART IV

COMMENTS:

Robert Goldfarb, George Washington University

The Reynolds-Seninger study is the most "neoclassical" of the papers on the international division of labor. It provides an interesting illustration of the way in which a well-accepted starting point in traditional neoclassical theory can be modified to produce a model with quite different features and implications. The ability to append such modifications to a neoclassical framework is an indication of the analytical richness of that starting point.

The paper compares a very traditional version of neoclassical trade theory to the authors' own alternative, which stresses product cycles, what they call endogenous technology, and nonconstant returns to scale. The following list shows some of the important differences between the two frameworks. The fact that their alternative can be categorized as a set of discrete—but important—divergences or changes of assumptions away from the traditional neoclassical model is consistent with the neoclassical framework being its intellectual starting point. I doubt that the authors would argue with this description of the intellectual "ancestry" of their work.

Neoclassical	*Reynolds-Seninger alternative*
A. Inputs immobile across national borders	Some inputs can flow across borders, and capital does
B. Production functions exhibit constant returns to scale	Production functions may exhibit increasing returns to scale (scale economies); moreover, these scale economies may be dynamic
C. Technology does not differ across countries (perfect mobility of technology)	Technology need not be identical across countries (and capital flows may be a source of technology transfers or diffusion)

| D. Patterns of technology change over time are not specified; they are not endogenous to the theory | The product cycle imposes a specified pattern of technology change in some countries |

It seems that the authors' purpose in formulating their alternative analytical framework is to provide a better explanation of the international division of labor (IDL), with special emphasis on explaining changes in its pattern. Indeed, the ability of each alternative to explain existing and emerging patterns seems a very important basis for choosing between the two frameworks.

As a labor economist rather than a trade theorist, I found the version of the paper presented at the conference interesting, highly useful, informative, and provocative. It was provocative in that it raised a number of questions and issues—some of them beyond the scope of the paper—which seemed to merit attention.

One issue concerned the "power" of each of the differences listed below, *considered individually* to modify the implications of the neoclassical trade model. The version of the paper presented at the conference did not provide this kind of analysis. As one example, the suggested analysis involves asking "suppose we took neoclassical assumption A, B, and D from the list, but substituted alternative assumption C for neoclassical assumption C; how would that alter the implications of the neoclassical theory about the international division of labor (IDL)?" Only by this kind of "incremental" varying of assumptions can one discover which of the several differences in the two frameworks account for crucial differences in results.[1] It may be that (say) only alternative assumption (A) combined with alternative assumption (C) are responsible for the distinctive differences in implications of the two frameworks. It deepens our understanding of the power of alternative frameworks to understand how robust the traditional neoclassical theory is to changes in assumptions, and which alternative assumptions are responsible for large changes in results.

While the first question focused on more intensive analysis of alternative assumptions, the second question inquires about the possibility of a somewhat expanded emphasis in the alternative model. The version of the paper given at the conference put heavy stress in the alternative framework on the importance of scale economies, but paid very little attention to possible differences in input costs in explaining changing IDL patterns. My question is whether some added attention to input costs changes might add some explanatory power to the alternative model.

To develop this point, note that there are several possible sources of differences among countries in their ability to utilize resources. Scale economies focus on the physical productivity of inputs, but another potentially important source of differences can be in the cost of each input, even holding physical productivity of inputs constant. If we are interested in knowing how the pattern of production and

trade is changing among countries, this will be affected by changing input productivity and by changing input costs. Changes in the costs of using inputs in a
particular country can be brought on by internal migration, changes in tax laws,
changes in minimum wage laws, changes in the local environment in developing
countries affecting the price of capital, and so forth. The discussion in the paper
of the alternative framework does not pay attention to these kinds of cost influences, but they might turn out to be important in explaining actual changes in the
IDL.

The authors might respond by pointing out that factor price changes are the
essence of the "other" model, the neoclassical one. However, to this stranger to
trade theory, the discussion of the neoclassical model in the paper seems to stress
measures of factor abundance, not the cost of factor use. But changes in minimum
wage laws or other elements cited above can change factor costs without altering
simple measures of factor abundance. Thus, the question is whether sizeable
gains in explaining actual patterns of IDL change can be achieved by adding a
focus on elements affecting factor costs to their alternative framework.

A third issue suggested by the paper, although it is clearly beyond its scope,
concerns implications of factor mobility. Factor mobility—in particular, capital
mobility—plays an important role in the author's alternative framework. But
recent discussions of immigration policy in the U.S. have stressed the existence
of sizable international labor mobility. The fact that both factors can and do flow
leads to the following line of argument. The neoclassical model suggests that
commodity trade can bring about factor price equalization even with complete
factor immobility. Now suppose, quite realistically, that barriers to commodity
trade are imposed, so factor prices are not equalized by trade. These differences
in factor prices across borders create incentives for factor movements. Suppose
further, also realistically, that neither capital nor labor is completely immobile.
The interesting issue this seems to raise is, given factors that are not completely
immobile, and differences in factor prices which create incentives for factor
movements, what can be said about which factors *actually* move? One way to
discuss this issue is to consider the position of a U.S. employer who observes
large labor cost differences between the U.S. and country X. If the U.S. employer
wanted to take advantage of those differences, would he send capital to country X
to employ labor there, or would he try to import country X labor to the U.S.? One
striking difference between the two choices seems to be that the employer has it in
his power to order his capital to be sent to country X, but, in the absence of a
"guest worker" law, he does *not* have it in his power to order labor from country
X to be sent to the U.S. Even with a "guest worker" law, importing country X
labor will not usually result in obtaining that labor at the country X price; the
"guest worker" law is likely to impose a minimum wage above country X's
wage. This argument suggests it may be more attractive to send capital, but this
will not always hold. In farming, for example, the productive land may be in the
U.S., not in country X. There are also organizational and management costs to

setting up a workplace in country X which can be largely avoided by bringing country X labor here. The question of which factors move under what conditions seems worth pursuing.

A fourth question concerns the authors' use of Verdoorn's Law. My feeling is that Verdoorn's Law is not essential to establishing the authors' arguments; that is, the alternative framework does not logically depend on or require Verdoorn's Law. Since Verdoorn is not essential, I would propose its elimination from their framework. The paper's flavor, like most work which starts from neoclassical theory, is basically deductive. Both the neoclassical and the alternative frameworks set forth in the paper start from sets of assumptions, and *deduce* implications. Which framework is more useful would then in principle be decided by confronting the implications of each with "the facts" about IDL and changes in IDL. Whichever framework's implications are closer to these facts would be more useful for understanding the IDL.

Verdoorn's Law introduces a jarring element into this deductive scheme, since it seems to be an empirical finding searching for a theoretical explanation. The authors use this empirical findings, interpreted as evidence of dynamic scale economies, to support and elaborate on one of their underlying assumptions. This is a questionable procedure on two grounds: (1) the central issue about choosing between ("testing") the two frameworks is which has "more correct" implications. Empirical evidence that tries to support assumptions does not provide a substantial test of a theory, since an assumption can conceivably be empirically refutable, yet the theory using that assumption in an artful way may outperform competing theories;[2] (2) even if one does not sympathize with the argument in (1), it is still not perfectly clear what the empirical finding known as Verdoorn's Law really indicates. In my view grand inductive efforts to put definitive interpretations on empirical "laws" deserve to be treated with considerable skepticism. In a recent paper, Bryan Boulier uses a simple economic model to show that Verdoorn-type empirical results depend:

> in a complicated way on characteristics of the production function, factor supply, and output demand and that differences in empirical values...offer little insight into the nature of the underlying economic circumstances that give rise to these differences.[3]

If the authors want to continue using Verdoorn's Law as evidence—and I would argue that they do not need to use it—they should at least confront and answer the Boulier critique.

A fifth issue concerns alternative strategies used by developed nations to meet emerging competition from developing countries. An interesting recent book on the changing location of production activities is *The Global Factory*.[4] This work brings out one particularly interesting factor affecting the location of production. As manufacturing activities in developing countries emerge to compete with manufacturing activities in the U.S., Europe, and Japan, these developed nations each display somewhat different competitive reactions. For example, the authors argue that U.S. firms established affiliates in developing countries to export to the U.S., while European firms "by way of contrast, showed relatively little propensity to serve their home markets through exports from affiliates located in low wage areas."[5] Moreover, European countries tended to make more use of imported low cost labor. This idea of alternative strategies by developed nations to meet emerging competition does not come out in the Reynolds-Seninger paper, yet it does seem to be of some analytical interest, and might conceivably be of some importance in influencing the IDL.

My final comment on the Reynolds-Seninger paper concerns its overall focus. As I understand the paper, the basic implication is that the authors' alternative framework is likely to provide a better basis than the neoclassical framework for understanding the actual pattern of IDL as it has been developing in recent decades. While this claim seems plausible, the version of the paper presented at the conference does not provide the empirical testing (and therefore does not provide the empirical support) for the claim. Since I found the current paper interesting, useful, and thought-provoking, I am looking forward to seeing a sequel in which the implications of the two frameworks are empirically examined.

Notes

1. The assumptions must be varied in groups as well as individually. Besides analyzing neoclassical A, B, and D combined with alternative C, one must also analyze neoclassical A and B combined with alternative C and D, and so forth.

2. For a classic statement of this kind of position, see Milton Friedman, "The Methodology of Positive Economics," in *Essays in Positive Economics*, (Chicago: University of Chicago Press, 1953): 3-43.

3. Bryan Boulier, "What Lies Behind Verdoorn's Law?" *Oxford Economic Papers*, (1984): 165.

4. Joseph Grunwald and Kenneth Flamm, *The Global Factory* (Washington, D.C.: The Brookings Institution, 1985).

5. *Ibid.*, 5.

Garth Mangum, University of Utah

The conceptual format of this conference was to have a neoclassicist, an institutionalist, and a Marxist each address the same labor market problem from the vantagepoint of their own paradigm. The rest of us could then simultaneously test the usefulness of the alternative analytical approaches while profiting from varying insights.

However, for this perhaps most complex of all current economic issues, the departures from the paradigms are more interesting than their applications. Reynolds and Seninger, while staying within the neoclassical framework, reach out constantly to bring into focus institutional complexities. Marshall, while calling his approach "eclectic," fulfills straightforwardly the institutionalist assignment. It is most striking that in what should be the preferred arena for demonstrating the applicability of Marxist analysis, Gordon—as one of our leading Marxists—after a quick summary of the views of others, abandons all pretext and launches a lengthy analysis which of the three alternatives can only be labeled institutionalist. Goldfarb has carefully analyzed the Reynolds-Seninger paper. My comments are on what is not said in the Gordon and Marshall papers.

It is remarkable how little light traditional class-conscious and capitalist-as-colonial-exploiter Marxism can shed on the current international economic scene. The poorest of the poor among nations are not those victimized by capitalist exploiters through a manipulated unfavorable balance of trade. They are either those nations with no economic resources of any kind for anyone to exploit or those burdened by the crude oil monopolies of other less developed nations or the incompetency and despotism of their own postcolonial native rules.

A few multinational firms emanating from developed nations bring their runaway capital to labor surplus nations, with consequent rising incomes in the host underdeveloped country and unemployment and falling real wages in the capitalist country of origin. The Marxist economist has little to offer of Marxist analysis of the international division of labor because current international developments refuse to fit within a Marxist framework.

The institutionalist has an easier task because he doesn't have to force perceived events to fit within any preconceived ideological or analytical framework. He merely observes institutional relationships for explanations of what's happening. Marshall essentially explains why free trade hasn't brought about the neoclassically promised best of all possible worlds and makes a case for pragmatic policy intervention. Gordon devotes his pages to explaining why the new international division of labor and globalization of production—which for some reason he perceives as essentially Marxist arguments—are of little explanatory value on the current scene. Instead, he substitutes the concepts of the "social structure of accumulation" which he never defines or explains but refers the reader to some of his and others' earlier works. However, the few pages of discussion in the section entitled, "Crisis in the Postwar Global Economy" suggest that the term refers to the necessity of synchronizing purchasing power growth with production growth on a worldwide basis. If that is, indeed, the intent of the SSA terminology, it might be the starting point for a useful discussion not provided by either the Marshall or the Gordon papers. Why do less-developed countries (LDCs) as they become newly industrializing countries (NICs) inevitably enter industries that already have worldwide over-capacity? Why have not the industries of the developing countries kept up a pace of investment adequate to make their high-wage processes sufficiently productive to compete with products of low-wage, labor surplus NICs? Why is the U.S. market the target of all of these new competitors? In a world of deprived peoples, why is not the new production absorbed by the have-nots rather than compete for the expenditures of the haves?

The answer is obvious. Only the residents of the wealthy countries have the incomes to purchase what they already have a superfluity of. There is an industrial parade route along which nations move from agriculture to simple labor-intensive industry to basic resource-processing industry to simply assembly to more complex assembly and so on. Each begins by meeting its own markets, in part for import substitution purposes. However, since the country is poor, its consumption capability is limited. To achieve any kind of economy of scale, it is necessary to export. But the hungry world has no purchasing power. Only the developed countries, which are already well-supplied by their own industries, can afford the competing products offered at lower prices.

There is overcapacity in terms of purchasing power but not in terms of need. The long, slow economic development process through which Western Europe and the United States passed had as much to do with developing consumer purchasing power as it did with developing industrial capacity. World economic development is stymied until the same process spreads through the developing world. Paradoxically the developed countries are losing out in the industrial parade because they were so effective in developing consumer-oriented societies that they are limited in what they have left to invest. Effective producers like Japan have such a high savings rate that they cannot adequately consume. The poor nations can neither consume nor invest. The developed nations and the NICs will be at each others' throats until they learn together that creating markets is at least as important as creating production capacity. The social and economic structure of distribution, not of accumulation, is the problem and the challenge.

ABOUT THE EDITORS

Garth L. Mangum is McGraw Professor of Economics and Management, and Director, The Institute for Human Resource Management, University of Utah. Professor Mangum has also served as a labor arbitrator and as an advisor and consultant to various business firms, state and federal agencies, and foreign governments. He is the author of numerous books and articles on labor, industrial relations, and human resources.

Peter Philips is Assistant Professor of Economics, University of Utah. He received his Ph.D. from Stanford University in 1980.